10-93 CN

EXTRAOR

A PRO

JOE FOSS

"Joe Foss is one of those true Americans that come along once in a lifetime. I have found him to be one of the most patriotic, humble, and genuine gentlemen I have ever met!"
—**Roy Rogers**

"An authentic American hero's 'I-did-it-my-way' memoir . . . vivid firsthand accounts of aerial combat in WW II's Pacific theater."
—*Kirkus Reviews*

"My 'old' friend and former AFL Commissioner Joe Foss is a genuine American hero. His book provides an inspiring look into the life and achievements of one of our nation's greatest patriots and fighters for freedom."
—**Jack Kemp**

"Whether dodging bullets in the sky or political arrows on earth, Joe Foss has pushed the envelope during an extraordinarily exciting life. He and Didi have turned out a larger-than-life story about a larger-than-life guy."
—**Barron Hilton,**
Chairman and President, Hilton Hotels Corporation

"Joe Foss—top fighter ace, governor, and Superbowl architect—shaped much of today's America with his bare hands. But that's only half of it. The character of the man is the thing. It comes out of these pages."
—**Vice Admiral James B. Stockdale, USN (Ret.),**
Congressional Medal of Honor recipient,
Highest-ranking POW in Vietnam, Author of *In Love and War*

"Present and future generations now can enjoy *A PROUD AMERICAN,* which provides interesting insight into Joe's fascinating life."
    —**Paul Tagliabue,**
        Commissioner, National Football League

"Joe Foss is one of America's truly authentic heroes. I commend this book to all readers, men and women alike."   —**William R. Bright,** Founder and President,
        Campus Crusade for Christ International

"Joe Foss is a truly great American. This book tells it all."   —**Bob Corbin**, President, National Rifle Association,
        and former Arizona Attorney General

"Every American will want to read this gripping story of one of America's foremost heroes."
    —**General Robert C. Mathis, USAF (Ret.),**
        former Vice-Chief of Staff, United States Air Force

"A wonderful testimony to God's grace in the life of one of my heroes."
    —**Chuck Colson,** Founder and President, Prison Ministries, Inc.

"A fascinating story of a man who spent his life serving others. It's exciting, motivating, inspirational."
    —**Roy E. Weatherby, Jr.,**
        President, Weatherby, Inc.

"*A PROUD AMERICAN* is the inspirational saga of a great life."   —**Senator Larry E. Craig**

"Here in South Dakota we're proud to call Joe Foss a native son. *A PROUD AMERICAN: The Autobiography of Joe Foss* captures the character of this remarkable man, a man of great integrity and boundless energy."   —**Governor George S. Mickelson**

"What John Wayne was to film, Joe Foss tops in real life."
———G. Gordon Liddy

"As America's finest fighter pilot in World War II, a superb governor of South Dakota, and a successful businessman, Joe Foss has become one of America's most admired individuals."
———Richard Nixon

"*A PROUD AMERICAN* is the story of one of the most unique men of our time. Joe Foss has accomplished more in one lifetime than most of us would in ten."
———William L. Armstrong, former U.S. Senator

"Whether it was on the battlefield or in politics, Joe Foss was one of the most unforgettable leaders of his time."
———Don Shula, Head Coach, Miami Dolphins

"Joe Foss truly represents my deep ideal of a living American hero."
———Senator Alan K. Simpson

"Joe Foss's *A PROUD AMERICAN* is a book about values, and I highly recommend it as required reading by every high school student in America."
———General Paul X. Kelley, USMC (Ret.),
Former Commandant of the Marine Corps

"*A PROUD AMERICAN* (is) the fascinating story of an incredible man."
———Alan Shepard, Rear Admiral, USN (Ret.), astronaut

Books by Joe Foss

Top Guns: America's Fighter Aces Tell Their Stories
  (with Matthew Brennan)
A Proud American: The Autobiography of Joe Foss

A PROUD AMERICAN
THE AUTOBIOGRAPHY OF
JOE FOSS

Joe Foss with Donna Wild Foss

POCKET **STAR** BOOKS

New York   London   Toronto   Sydney   Tokyo   Singapore

A Pocket Star Book published by
POCKET BOOKS, a division of Simon & Schuster Inc.
1230 Avenue of the Americas, New York, NY 10020

ISBN: 0-671-75746-6

First Pocket Books paperback printing November 1993

10 9 8 7 6 5 4 3 2 1

POCKET STAR BOOKS and colophon are registered
trademarks of Simon & Schuster Inc.

Cover photo by Neil Leifer, *Time* magazine

Printed in the U.S.A.

DEDICATION

This book is lovingly dedicated to:

Our precious children—
    Coni Foss
    Dean Hall and his wife, Elizabeth
    Cheryl and her husband, Bob King
    Mary Joe and her husband, John Finke, M.D.
    Frank Foss, M.D., and his wife, Pam

. . . and our cherished grandchildren—
    Dona Michelle (Shelly) and her husband,
      Jim Turner
    Misty Ostby
    Nicole Finke
    Kimberly Finke
    Jonathan Foss
    David Foss

. . . and the delight of our hearts, our great-
    grandchildren—
    Krystal Lyn Turner
    Shane Turner
    Shelby Ostby

. . . and love to our stepgrandchildren—
    Michael Dagen
    Keith Dagen
    Brittani Dagen
    Lisa Dagen

WITH GRATITUDE

To my beloved wife for her commitment to working relentlessly and her tenacity in bringing this book to completion—and because she believes in me.

And certainly to the Lord for giving me the opportunity to live a life that now causes me to say many times each day—Thank you, Lord.

WITH GRATITUDE

With love and appreciation to my wonderful husband Joe, who has lived such a unique life and who has been so willing to relate to me the personal events in his life and to answer my many questions. A life such as his could be possible only when orchestrated by a Power greater than our own.

To the many friends throughout South Dakota who saved boxes of clippings, magazines, and pictures and shared them with me.

To my aunt, June Jones, who so tirelessly helped me put together several newspaper-size clipping books.

To good friends who have known Joe for many years and were so helpful in sharing real-life experiences. Some of them are:

Marcella Foss	Hoadley and Ruth Dean
Duke and Kathy Corning	Dona Brown
Charles and Kay Steuerwald	Pete and Oydis Smith
Maxine Isenberg	Bob and Dode Lee
Harry and Faith Tunge	Chuck and Barbara Lien
Justin and Patty Berger	Gordon and Marilyn Edman

To Bob Ellingson for checking the manuscript for accuracy of military references.

To Tom Stoen, who continually nudged my conscience in the early days of my writing, and to his brother, my friend Timothy, for his professional direction.

To my faithful prayer partners who prayed unceasingly:

Sylvia Bjork	Holly DelHousaye
Helen Mann	Marilyn Marco
Bonnie Puntenney	Bonita Norton

Another prayer partner in San Jose, California: Winifred Verbica

Another in Spearfish, South Dakota: Dorothy Johnson

With Gratitude

To Mary Joe and Frank for sharing their true feelings—and to Cheryl for her love and approval.

To Coni and Dean for their early memories and their love for Joe.

To Dr. Bill Bright for his faithfulness, his vision, his wonderful leadership—and his confidence in Joe and me.

To Dr. Vonette Bright for being a role model for me and for her encouragement and friendship.

To Pastor Darryl DelHousaye for his wisdom in shepherding our family and his sage personal advice.

To each of my sisters and their spouses for their encouragement, and for their help in sorting through papers, and in research, cooking, and running the household when I've been sequestered with—the book: Helen and Larry Gieseler, Esther Harsh, Audrey and Bill Wood, and Nan Wild.

To Ellie Martin for her faithfulness, honesty, loyalty, and dependability. For 24 years she has helped me keep our financial and business affairs running smoothly and, through it all, has become a cherished friend.

An angel for me—Judith Markham. Never could I have brought this project to fruition without her expertise, her patience, her gentle temperament, her kindness in listening in times of frustration. She brought it all together—thank you, Judith.

To my wonderful editor, always so ready and willing to encourage me, keep me on track, direct me in the paths I should proceed—defend me, believe in me. Thanks, Paul McCarthy.

Contents

Contents

PART THREE
Full Speed Ahead

There occurs at breathtaking moments in history an exhilarating burst of energy and motivation, of hope and imagination, and a severing of the bonds that normally hold in check the full release of human possibilities. A door is opened and the caged eagle soars.

—John Gardner on Leadership

Joe Foss, in the South Pacific air war, established himself as the American ace of aces. Joe Foss, when he returned to the United States to receive the Congressional Medal of Honor, impressed those who met him as the perfect fighting man, the instinctive and relentless hunter. . . . Tall, handsome, modest, he is the embodiment of the frontiersman of old, the stalker of game, the trailer of human enemies.

—Lowell Thomas
These Men Shall Never Die

A PROUD AMERICAN
THE AUTOBIOGRAPHY OF
JOE FOSS

Prologue

The storm cleared as suddenly as it had struck and the world opened up beneath the clouds. A blue and green kaleidoscope of tropical seas and islands turned slowly beneath the wings of my Grumman F4F Wildcat. Dense green mountain jungle. Breaker-splashed beaches strewn with palm frond umbrellas. A South Pacific paradise.

Beyond the rings of light green water covering the sandy shelves around the Solomon Islands, the scene was not so idyllic. Out there, where aquamarine shaded into dark blue, the Allied navies battled the Imperial Japanese Navy for control of the sea lanes, and there was a lot more at stake than this corner of the world.

I was tired. Today's mission had been another in a long string of frustrating forays. Earlier, one of our daily tropical downpours had cloaked the Japanese warships in an impenetrable veil of tepid rain. Running low on fuel and sunlight, I finally abandoned the hunt and radioed the seven pilots in my flight to turn back. We'd veered off, re-formed, and were now heading southeast, back to Henderson Field on the island of Guadalcanal at the southern end of the Solomon chain.

Seemingly endless missions, flown from an airfield surrounded by the enemy, had taken their toll on all of us. Besides that, I had a rotten case of malaria I couldn't shake. For weeks the fever had come and gone like an evil tide,

A well-chewed cigar became my constant companion and my trademark. But it was never lighted anywhere near an airplane, October 1942.

occasionally taking me out of action completely, restricting me to the mosquito-netted cot in my furnace-hot tent.

Below me now I could see our ships racing for safe havens as the sun sank toward the horizon. From this distance the tiny specks appeared to be cruising in a serene bathtub ocean. This perspective and the noisy drone of my Wildcat's powerful Pratt and Whitney radial engine lulled me into one of those moments between decision and danger, insulating me briefly from the war zone.

Then, gripping the dead cigar between my teeth more tightly, I returned to my habitual surveillance routine, moving my eyes nervously between the earth's surface and the sky around me. When you were upstairs, you had to keep looking.

My flight suit was soaked with sweat and my hair was damp under my close-fitting flight helmet. My mustache and goatee itched with dirt and sweat, but they provided protection from the chafing oxygen mask I needed when we flew above 10,000 feet. I hated the interference of that mask. I hated anything that got in my way. That's why I didn't wear sunglasses. Anything between the naked eye and the sky might hide the enemy, and a scratch or fleck of dust on a lens could look too much like a Zeke at a distance.

Suddenly I spotted a group of Japanese soldiers in the jungle below. They were hanging their rain-soaked uniforms on a makeshift clothesline to catch the last rays of the sun. I gave Captain Greg Loesch the order, and he split off to strafe the naked and vulnerable group, butchering underwear, trousers, and some of the enemy. Several minutes later we sighted a Nip supply truck racing down a slippery, muddy road. It exploded when tracers from my guns ignited the gasoline and ammunition it was carrying.

This ground attack provided only momentary gratification. The Zekes were our real quarry. It was à face-to-face duel I needed, not another wild-goose chase that would lure us away from Henderson Field so the enemy could bombard it. Lately, however, fewer and fewer of the emperor's pilots were challenging our control of the airfield.

Against an evening sky glowing scarlet and orange we began our descent toward the landing strip on Guadalcanal. Coming in low I could see the beach, littered with ruined war machinery and pitted where both the Japanese and Americans had tried to land additional troops. Many of the palms had been felled or beheaded by artillery fire—the only memorial to the hundreds of men who had already died in the fight for possession of this strategic Pacific base.

I throttled back, cutting power, then wound down the hand-cranked landing gear and eased back on the stick to ride the edge of a stall as I touched down. After slowing the plane, I taxied off the strip into the parking area at the edge of the jungle, the world we shared with emerald green tree pythons, giant leeches, and spiders as big as kittens.

I spotted Lieutenant Colonel Sam Jack, our fighter commander, standing on the edge of the strip. Thin and gaunt, like a two-by-four scarecrow, he looked like death warmed over. I shut down the engine. Even from this distance I could see trouble brewing on his face and tension in his arm-crossed stance. I didn't have to guess. I knew why.

As the Operations Officer, it was my duty to organize flight and personnel schedules. For weeks I'd been hiding eight fighter planes in reserve in the jungle instead of sending them out on missions. I knew if the brass found out, I would be about as popular as a hair in a biscuit. Apparently they had.

"Let's eat, Joe," Colonel Jack greeted me. "Even you deserve a last meal. The general wants to see you."

"We're in for it, Colonel," I predicted later as we walked in the dark toward General Mulcahy's tent.

"Well, we know what we think," said the colonel.

Before entering the general's tent, Colonel Jack and I stopped and shook hands, the last gesture of condemned men. An aide ushered us in and left. General Mulcahy told us to sit down, then poured out three glasses of Scotch. Whiskey was rare in these parts, and I savored every drop of it. I could at least die happy.

The general set his own glass down on the desk and started in slow, talking about everything but the matter at hand. When he did finally get to the point, I didn't deny anything.

Yes, I was holding eight planes in reserve, hidden among the palms at the edge of the runway, and I explained why. I didn't believe for a minute that the lull in attacks signified enemy resignation.

"Those Japs are just biding their time, sir," I said. "And those transports lined up on the runway are an open invitation. This isn't LaGuardia Airport." I tried to maintain a tone of deference, but it was difficult. I felt strongly about this. "One of these days, sir, we'll be off flying all over the Pacific and you're really gonna get hit here at home base," I warned.

"With what?" the general demanded. "It's over, Foss! The bulk of their aircraft are gone! I get the intelligence reports, not you!"

"But if the reports are wrong and there are no fighters around to fight back—"

"We need our planes out on the strikes! You can't win a war with your aircraft parked under a palm tree!"

For days I'd spent nearly every waking hour flying or talking to other pilots, and my view of Japanese air strength and strategy differed markedly from the intelligence reports. Those boys sitting around in their top-secret briefings were too far below the clouds to see what was going on. We were the ones sitting behind the .50 caliber guns, facing off against

4

the Nips. We were the ones who'd gotten to know firsthand the personal styles that betrayed how the Japanese airmen were trained and how long they'd flown. We were the ones who could tell how long those Zeros had been in action just by looking at their patches and markings—something the ground boys never saw. We knew the rhythms and personality of the Japanese command—from the receiving end.

Henderson Field had been the fulcrum of the southwest Pacific war effort since its establishment a few months back in August of 1942,[1] and I was convinced that this recent break from concentrated attack was a retrenchment, not a retreat. If the Japanese could take this field, they'd control the air. And if they controlled the air in this area, they were in position to control the Pacific.

You didn't have to be tied into the headquarters in Washington, D.C., to get the message. We were out there. We saw what was happening. But I knew General Mulcahy figured I didn't have the slightest idea what was going on. I was just a dumb air jockey. Besides, a twenty-eight-year-old Marine captain couldn't do much arguing with a brigadier general.

Colonel Jack backed me up as much as he could, but the general just got madder and madder, and redder and redder. He was puffed up like a gobbler in spring heat getting ready for the big jump. The colonel and I sat there getting the short end of the stick and trying to smile about it.

Finally, after three very long hours during which he failed to wring any repentance out of us, General Mulcahy proclaimed, "Tomorrow's your last day, Foss! Do you understand? Consider yourself fired!"

Colonel Jack and I saluted and left. Outside we shook hands

---

[1] Henderson was considered the number-one prize on Guadalcanal. The Japanese had had the field almost completed when the U.S. took it in early August 1942. On August 12 General Vandegrift sent the message: "Airfield Guadalcanal ready for fighters and dive bombers." That same day the first U.S. plane made the first landing on the strip, which a few days later was named Henderson Field after Major Lofton R. Henderson, who led the Marine dive bombers at Midway. (Robert Sherrod, *History of Marine Corps Aviation in World War II*, Washington: Combat Forces Press, 1952, p. 77.)

again and agreed, though it was scant satisfaction, that time would prove us right.

Bad news travels fast, and the few remaining members of our acclaimed "Flying Circus" were waiting for me in my tent—Roger Haberman, Big Bill Freeman, Oscar Bate, Greg Loesch, Boot Furlow, and Frank Presley. Whatever happened would happen to us as a group.

"Well, tomorrow's our last day, boys," I said, splintering the tense silence. "We're headed home."

Some scowled, while others muttered or squirmed in disappointment, despite the fact that we were all exhausted and ready for some R and R.

"But don't celebrate yet," I added. "Tomorrow may be the biggest day of your life. I just have a feeling."

The next morning the boys and I hung out by our Wildcats at the end of the runway, telling stories and killing time, waiting to leave. The other fliers had already headed out on another wild-goose chase.

Despite the cloud ceiling, it was sweltering, and the bombers and transports were lined up in straight, pretty rows, as usual. I flipped the top of my Zippo lighter and turned my cigar between thumb and forefinger until the end glowed red. Then I snapped the lighter shut and strolled over to the Operations dugout, a hole in the side of a bluff surrounded by sandbags and covered by a roof of palm logs and dirt.

"Hey, Joe," said Don Yost, the officer on watch, "would you take my place at this radio while I go to the head?"

"Yes, sir. Glad to," I said.

As I sat there listening to the words coming through the static, I picked up a communication from the radar setup to fighter operations.

"Say, have we got any planes out there around Savo Island?" It was the voice of Navy Lieutenant Madison. "We're picking something up on radar."

"Not that I'm aware," I heard the sergeant on ops duty answer. "There aren't supposed to be any of ours out around Savo at all." That was all I needed to hear. I knew we didn't have any planes out around Savo because I'd been watching the skies all morning.

When Don came back from the trenches, I yelled, "See you later," and raced down the airfield to my men.

"Let's scramble, men!"

Within minutes our eight Wildcats were circling upward against the overcast sky, straining to gain altitude before the enemy arrived on the scene. When we had reached about 12,000 feet, we got a Condition Red call from fighter ops. They'd spotted more bogeys around Savo and were scrambling four more planes from Henderson.

Then I spotted about twelve Zeros far below over Savo Island. We were more than a match for them, especially with our altitude advantage, but there was something peculiar about the way they were flying. Just milling around, doing nip-ups and wingovers, like there wasn't a war within miles. As near as I could figure it, they had to be sucker bait. There had to be some reason they were trying to lure us down there.

Instead of taking the easy kill, something told me to hold back. We kept climbing until we were just below the cloud ceiling at about 18,000 feet, where we circled around, doing the scissors, so that we had eyes and guns pointed in every direction.

Suddenly an opening appeared in the dense white canopy overhead and I circled on up. As I emerged above the cloud stratum, my stomach began churning and my mouth went dry. Instead of flying into blue sky, I was between two thick layers of clouds—along with an armada of Japanese planes.

In a hurried survey I counted roughly eighteen dive bombers, twenty-four of the twin-engined, high-level bombers we called Bettys, and sixty-four Zeros, and many more were flooding in from the northwest. I could hardly believe the size of that force, but I knew they were headed for Henderson.

"Scramble everything!" I shouted into the radio to operations. And for the first time I broke the Marine rule about profanity over the air. "There's a whole shitpot of airplanes up here!"

"Can't you speak English, Marine?" an officer listening from the ground reprimanded instantly.

There was no time for regret. If every fighter on Guadalcanal had been in the air, positioned perfectly to defend the airstrip, they couldn't possibly save the field. Over forty

7

bombers, protected by more Japanese fighter cover than I'd ever seen in one place—perhaps a hundred Zeros—were poised to annihilate Henderson Field and everything on it.

I was used to stiff odds, but that swarm of Japanese locusts shook me to the core. Then, as I nosed over and dropped back down below the clouds, separating myself from the enemy throng, an idea began to take shape. I looked around, checking the position of my men. With courage and luck, maybe we could beat these impossible odds.

At that ominous moment, just before noon on January 25, 1943, I was light-years away from the days when I'd buzzed the fields of our family farm in Sioux Falls, South Dakota, with Roy Lanning's little single-engine Taylorcraft.

PART ONE

Up
in the Air

★ ★ ★

On his fingers Joe ticks off the planes he trained in. The N3N, the O3U, the SNJ. Antiques today, their letters and numbers like forgotten runes to jet jockeys and aspiring astronauts. The F4B4, the Brewster Buffalo, the F4F Wildcat. But from the loins of the ancient Wildcat sprang the Hellcat, then the Bearcat, the Tigercat, the F9F Panther jet of Korean vintage—begin to sound familiar now?—the Cougar, and today the white-hot Tomcat with a Top Gun under its bubble and the fires of Hell up its tail. Whoever writes a history of Navy and Marine aviation had better know how to spell Grumman.

> —David Robinson
> "Joe Foss: The Farm Boy and
> the Cactus Air Force"
> *Marine Corps League*

Chapter 1

Beginnings

☆　☆　☆

I can't remember a time when I didn't want to fly. When I was a kid I would stretch out in the tall meadow grass and watch the birds flying overhead, graceful and silent. *What would it feel like to swirl and dive and soar so freely?* I wondered. *What would it be like up there, no longer earthbound, no longer hemmed in by the geography of hills and streams, fences and highways.*

Because I grew up on a farm, I've been asked if my first attempt at flight was a jump out of the hayloft with an umbrella. That's one trick I never tried, but if we'd had an umbrella, I'm sure I would have.

My mother used to tell folks that I almost got my first taste of flying when I was four years old and managed to climb to the top of our thirty-foot windmill. Actually I made my first leap into the air when I was seven.

My first-grade buddies and I were playing follow-the-leader on our way home from school, and my turn as leader came just about the time we reached an old bridge that spanned a narrow creek.

"Follow me, guys," I instructed, as I led them in a column to the center of the bridge. "Down there," I said, pointing to a sandbar in the center of the stream.

"Oh, no, I'm not gonna jump that far!" declared one of my friends.

My brother Cliff (left) and I, all dressed up for a picture-taking session. I've been told I was 3 years old in this picture.

"This isn't high," I insisted. "It'll be just like flying." With that, I leaped off the bridge into the air.

That was my first lesson in aerodynamics and the effect of gravity. My head banged painfully against my knee, causing one of my teeth to pierce the side of my mouth, and I broke my right collarbone. I won the game, though. Nobody else dared follow my flight plan.

That little sortie didn't dampen my enthusiasm for flight, and I still longingly watched the giant hawks, their wings spread and fixed, riding the thermal currents as the warm air rose skyward from the sun-heated Dakota grasslands. Circling patiently, following their instinctive pattern of surveillance, their sharp eyes endlessly searched for the telltale movement of an unsuspecting chicken, pheasant, gopher, or rabbit. I was awed by their incredible ability to fly so effortlessly.

But birds weren't the only airborne attraction. Almost every day in good weather an open-cockpit Lockheed Vega flew over our farm on its regular airmail route between Sioux Falls and Minneapolis. That old mail plane flew pretty low, and I'd stop whatever I was doing to watch it fly by, waving wildly at the pilot. Sometimes he'd see me and wave back.

Plowing fields and slopping hogs seemed awfully dull to me after watching those open-cockpit biplanes fly over our farm. "Someday I'm gonna get off this old horse-drawn cultivator and get up there and fly with those boys," I'd say.

Beginnings

My father could do anything. I believed that when I was a kid, and fifty-nine years after his death, I still regard him as the most fascinating person I've ever known and the greatest influence in my life.

Pop was born in 1885, shortly after his parents immigrated from Bergen, Norway, to a farm outside Jasper, Minnesota. He was christened Olouse Foss, but eventually changed his name to Frank because he disliked the nickname "Oley" which people insisted on giving him. Few called him Frank, though. His fancy dress and innate showmanship soon earned him the moniker "Foxy." With his Norwegian good looks and his stalky body honed to solid muscle, Foxy Foss made a striking figure.

A born storyteller and charismatic persuader, his schemes and dreams, his vocations and avocations seemed endless. With his brother Martin, he boxed and wrestled in exhibitions at county fairs. For a while he traveled with the Ringling Brothers circus band, and he even toured the country with his own carnival business. Pop loved all kinds of machinery, especially automobiles, and he started one of the first car dealerships in the Jasper, Minnesota, area. He also worked as an engineer for the Great Northern Railway Company, and he ran a bowling alley with his friend Lou McKean.

I loved to hear Pop talk about his younger days and his many adventures. He'd been everywhere and done everything worth doing. His spirit of adventure made me believe there was a whole lot out there in the world worth trying, and that discovery later gave me the determination to try everything that came along in life. Like my father, I've had several careers. And, like him, I believe there are only two speeds in life, full speed and no speed. I've tackled five distinctly different careers at full speed and have survived several "no speed" situations.

Pop was Norwegian on both sides and, like most of his countrymen, he was a Lutheran. My mother, Mary Lacey Foss, who was five years younger, was Scotch-Irish Catholic. The two could not have been more opposite, both in heritage and in personality. Pop was gregarious and loved an audience. He'd sing and spin yarns at the drop of a hat. My mother was dead serious. She had absolutely no sense of humor. I can't remember her ever telling a funny story, or even cracking a smile when someone else told one.

In many ways my mother was ahead of her time, a true suffragette. She hated housework, and cleaning and cooking came far down on her list of druthers. She preferred to be in the barn milking cows or out in the field, where she could plow a mean furrow behind a team of horses and stack hay with the best of them. Small, short, and wiry, Mary Lacey Foss did almost anything a man could do.

Mother's favorite garb was a housedress carelessly tossed over a pair of Pop's old wool trousers. In cold weather she layered a man's suit coat over a heavy sweater, turned up the collar, and wrapped a scarf around her neck, pulled on men's work boots, and donned one of Pop's many hats. Around the farm she always looked like she'd just stepped out of a rag bag. Today she'd probably be considered fashionable. When she went to town she simply changed to a better-quality print dress and a wide-brimmed hat. If the flowers were blooming, she'd stick one in her hatband. I guess she was what folks call a certifiable "character."

When Mother was a little girl, her parents, Margaret and Gregory Lacey, pulled up stakes in Scottsville, New York, and traveled west to South Dakota in a covered wagon. Her father was a Yale graduate and a surgeon, and he left a successful medical practice in New York when he moved west, hoping to cure the asthmatic condition that plagued him. The Laceys homesteaded 640 acres outside of Sioux Falls, but life in South Dakota was not easy for the physically frail. Within a year Gregory Lacey was dead, leaving his wife and four children: Gregg, Frank, Levi, and Mary.

Foxy Foss met Mary Lacey in 1914 when he was working for the Great Northern Railway Company as an engineer. When Mother inherited 160 acres of the Lacey homestead, six miles east of Sioux Falls, she encouraged my father to quit the railroad and take up farming. Mother always felt the only real life was on the land.

Our farm was small as South Dakota farms go, and our house was a four-room outfit made of rough-sawn timber. It was in that house, in one of the two tiny bedrooms, that I was born on April 17, 1915. I still go back to South Dakota every summer, and through the years I've frequently returned to visit the old homestead, which stands within a hundred feet of the house my brother, Cliff, built for his family. No one has lived in the old place since 1962, and most of the furniture is gone, but when I stand there I hear the faint echoes of bygone years and the songs we used to sing. I can point to the spot in the small living room where the big isinglass-window heater used to stand and where Pop would sit and play his fiddle while we all sang "Bringing in the Sheaves" or "Rock of Ages" or some other great old hymn.

Our family consisted of my parents, my younger brother, Cliff, my little sister, Mary Flora, and me. On a typical day we climbed out from under our warm quilts and hurried into the kitchen to stand by the cookstove and jump into our clothes. At that time the kitchen stove was the only heat in the house, except for holidays when my father built a fire in the round isinglass-window heater in the living room. My father and mother would already be out in the barn doing the morning milking and feeding the livestock. Cliff usually hurried to join them, and Mary Flora tagged along. Because Mary Flora was six years younger, and very shy and quiet, she was always "little sister."

Unlike Cliff, who did the daily farm work enthusiastically, I avoided chores whenever possible. Given half an excuse, I was off into the countryside in search of adventure.

When I couldn't escape, my favorite chore was bringing the cows in from pasture because that gave me time for dreaming and exploring. Often I would be late getting back, and Mother would come out of the barn and help me herd the cows in for milking. "What took you so long, Joe?" she'd ask, never really expecting an answer.

I roamed every inch of the valleys and hills surrounding our farm. The closest water was a creek, about half a mile away if I cut across the hills. Its clear waters harbored crayfish and other darting, aquatic creatures. I investigated every bird's nest, badger den, and skunk hole for miles. In those days you could wander wide and free; besides, my uncles owned the property surrounding our farm, and all our neighbors knew us. As long as I didn't knock down fences, spook

15

livestock, or leave any gates open, the world was mine to walk, burrow, and climb.

Nothing revealed the differences between my folks more graphically than voting day. Mother was a dyed-in-the-wool Democrat and Pop was a diehard Republican. A day or so before every election, local or national, a desperate calm descended on our household, and the tension in the atmosphere grew even thicker as election day dawned.

I particularly recall one rainy November Tuesday when Pop hitched up one of our two buggy horses, Sorrel or Fan, so he and Mother could travel the two miles to the country schoolhouse and vote. Cliff and I begged to go along. We loved riding in the buggy, even when it rained. As we started down the road, the two of us boys huddled together under an old buffalo robe in the center of the back seat to avoid the mud that the spoked wheels caught and threw up in a steady stream. Meanwhile, in the front seat, my parents poised themselves silently at opposite ends of the bench, stoically suffering the shower of muck and mud rather than sit close on their way to cast their opposing votes.

At the schoolhouse they descended silently from opposite sides of the buggy and joined the folks gathered about into two partisan groups. When my parents finally voted, they were in and out of the booth so fast it was obvious they were voting a straight ticket. They did their patriotic duty and canceled each other out.

Mother carried a grudge longer than Pop, usually until the outcome of the election was known. Election results were telegraphed from the state capital at Pierre or from Washington, D.C., and posted on a big bulletin board in front of the Sioux Falls newspaper, the *Argus-Leader*. Normally this took several days. In close elections it would take even longer for Mother to reestablish diplomatic relationships with Dad.

She cared deeply about politics, and one of the high points of her life was meeting Franklin Delano Roosevelt when I was awarded the Congressional Medal of Honor. One of the lowest was my public appearance with President Herbert Hoover, whom she referred to as "that old thumper."

We were a patriotic family. Whenever a politician spoke

in our area, Pop took us to hear him. On holidays my father put up flags all around the outside of the house and even decorated our car with little American flags. On the Fourth of July he always ordered fireworks and invited folks from all over to stop in and celebrate our nation's birthday. Between my mother and father, it's little wonder I inherited such red, white, and blue blood.

Considering their political passion, it is somewhat surprising that neither of my parents ever got involved in politics, but in those days most farmers limited their political activities to voting. They took the attitude that government's main duty was to keep everybody, including itself, from interfering with the peaceful lives of ordinary citizens.

This attitude was reflected in an incident that occurred during a Fourth of July celebration and picnic we went to at McKinnan Park in Sioux Falls when I was about fifteen years old. After a speech by United States Senator Peter Norbeck, my father said to a group of his friends, "I think I'll take Joe up and say hello to the senator." The men were all farmers like my father, and one of them protested that a man in overalls should not approach a senator in a suit, even though Foxy Foss was wearing a white shirt and tie under his overalls, as he usually did when he went to town.

"Well, I'm in the uniform of my profession," replied my father, "and if the senator doesn't respect it, he's the wrong guy for the job."

So he took me up to meet the senator. After talking briefly with the man, Dad joined another friend, a Sioux Falls lawyer, to discuss the merits of the senator's speech and the day's activities. At one point my father turned to me and said, "Don't ever get involved in politics, son, because all you'll end up with is an old car and a shiny blue serge suit—if you're honest."

Years later when I became governor of South Dakota, I often thought of those words and wished my father were around to see it.

One fall morning when I was about four years old, I left the kitchen where my mother, wearing Lee overalls and a faded plaid shirt, was canning pheasant. I was looking for

The Foss family homestead in South Dakota, where I was born in the tiny northwest corner bedroom. In the center is the windmill where I first ventured to lofty heights at age four. This picture was taken about 1940.

adventure. Outside, I squinted into the bright sun and looked around. With no radio or television and the nearest neighbor a half mile away, I was used to making my own entertainment.

The stand of box elder was always promising, full of small animals and birds, as were the pine trees, apple trees, and berry bushes my father had planted. The massive two-story barn was good for hours of exploration and make-believe, and the chicken house located over the concrete potato cellar occasionally held some interest. That day, however, something else caught my imagination.

As flies and other biting insects zeroed in on me, and sweat beaded my forehead, a sudden light breeze stirred the hot Indian summer air, and I heard a clicking sound I'd never noticed before. I soon traced it to the tall windmill, used to pump water, that stood between the house and the barn. I shaded my eyes, looked up, and in an instant was racing across the dusty yard.

The rungs of the ladder leading to the top of the tower were far apart. I had to struggle each step of the way on my short legs, but the tug of the unknown kept me going. I could feel myself leaving the heat and insects behind as I entered the realm of birds and breezes. Finally, thirty feet above the ground, I surveyed my new world.

What a thrilling experience to look out across the countryside from my vantage point on the narrow platform at the base of the windmill wheel. I could see the neighbors' houses, far away across the rolling hills, and the livestock in their pastures. A plume of dust rose in the distance. It was my father discing a field behind our team of workhorses. Sparrows fluttered near me, so close I could almost touch them.

I settled back on the platform, savoring my bird's-eye view. In fact, I could see more than anyone would have guessed, for I was blessed with extraordinary vision. An ophthalmologist would later discover that I had 20/10 vision, which meant I was able to see at twenty feet what most people saw at ten.

As I sat on my perch, enjoying the wonderful world I'd discovered, the wind picked up and the windmill creaked in response. The slowly revolving blades accelerated with each gust of wind, and I studied the landscape through the spinning blades.

"Joe! It's time for dinner!" I could hardly hear my mother call, and I didn't want to answer her. I didn't want to return to earth, and I didn't want to reveal my secret place.

I could see her far below, watching for me to come scampering from the trees or the barn. I also noticed that the dust plume had disappeared from the field, and I saw my father driving back to the house.

"Joe!" she shouted again, more insistently. "Where are you?"

Finally I answered. "Up here."

When she saw where I was, her response was predictable. "You come down from there this minute!"

I refused. No matter how much my mother coaxed, I wouldn't budge from my high perch. She finally had to have Dad climb up and get me. And once I was on the ground, I was told in no uncertain terms that there was to be no repeat performance of my aerial act.

Eventually this incident turned into a favored family story, repeated through the years and growing into folklore. But the windmill remained my special place, my private sanctuary, for as long as I lived on the farm When I learned to read, it became my reading chair. When I took up the saxophone, it was my practice studio. I was so comfortable off the ground that I even turned my inclination into a business while I was still a young boy, charging farmers fifty cents for cleaning and greasing their windmills.

Little did I know that someday I would find a home high in the air behind another kind of spinning blade.

Chapter 2

Learning
the Rules

I've been on African safaris, stalked the Arctic polar bear, and hunted the North American continent with outstanding marksmen like Robert Stack, Phil Harris, Jimmy Doolittle, Curtis LeMay, Barron Hilton, Chuck Yeager, Bob Peterson, Charlton Heston, Gary Swanson, Roy Rogers, Robert Taylor, Governor John Connolly, Roy Weatherby, Rudy Etchen, Bob Allen, and Wally Schirra, to name just a few. I've seen some great shooting through the years, including the 1973 One Shot Antelope Hunt in Lander, Wyoming, when my wife, Didi, collected her antelope with a single shot at more than six hundred yards. But the best shot I ever saw was when my dad dropped a coyote on the run from a third of a mile away. The coyote had just killed one of our calves, which were our livelihood, and was trotting along the far end of our property. I don't know how far above and in front of that coyote Pop had to aim to hit him, but he sighted the varmint in from our yard and placed his shot just right with his favorite gun, a 45-70 Springfield, a breech-loading military gun introduced in 1873.

Coyotes team up in packs when they go after calves. They run the animals down and use their sharp, tearing teeth to rip the jugular vein in the neck or tear at the tendons just above the hooves in an attempt to cripple the animal before they kill it. They go for the tender parts first, and that includes everything in the belly. Then they leave the rest and return

With Charlton Heston at an NRA Annual Members Banquet, April 1989, St. Louis, Missouri, in our formal duds—a time I always wear my Congressional Medal of Honor. (Photo by Donna Wild Foss)

On a Liberty Mutual Insurance Company Dove Shoot, September 1990, enjoying the company of Phil Harris (left) and son Dean Hall (center). (Photo by Donna Wild Foss)

to the carcass when they get hungry again and can't find a fresh kill.

Finding those mutilated calves was always an emotional moment for me because I'd helped raise them from birth, weaned them, played with them. My father felt the loss in more practical ways. Losing calves to a pack of coyotes was a hard-felt blow to our family economy. One less animal to take to market could mean postponing the purchase of some new farm equipment or going into another cold winter with less store-bought provisions.

Early in life I also learned about the ever-present threat of smaller predators. Foxes, skunks, hawks, and weasels were the worst. Coyotes normally kept their distance from the farmhouse because they had learned to associate the smell of man with big trouble. Foxes and skunks were bolder—or dumber. They'd come right up to the farm buildings at night and raid chicken coops or go after baby pigs. They would strike like lightning and be gone before anyone knew what was happening.

You couldn't blame them, of course. The wild animals had the land first, and then came man, the biggest predator of all. He arrived on the scene and started clearing the land, building houses, fences, and roads. With the encroachment of civilization on their natural habitat, the animals either had to forage a smaller area or cross the intruder's boundaries. Survival was their natural instinct, and when man arrived and started raising cattle and sheep and hogs and poultry, the predators discovered a whole new menu of tasty entrees! Predators were not all bad either. They kept down the population of rabbits, ground squirrels, prairie dogs, and other rodents and helped eliminate the unfit and diseased.

City slickers who have never lived on a farm tend to misunderstand the age-old battle between farmers and predators. The predator is to the farmer what the shoplifter or house burglar is to the urbanite. When thieves break in and steal from the owner of a house or a business, the loss can be great. When a predator kills a farmer's animals, it destroys part of his livelihood.

This issue of predator control has caused a running feud among various interest groups for years. Farmers and ranchers, environment preservationists, hunters, and the government all view the issue differently, but some of these groups are beginning to work together to find acceptable solutions. For example, the U.S. government recently approved a coyote control method in which only the criminal coyotes are eliminated. Sheep wear collars that release a fast-action lethal ingredient into any animal that bites into the sheep's neck.

But back on our South Dakota farm when I was a boy, the shotgun or rifle was our only deterrent.

* * *

A Proud American

When I was six years old, my father gave me a Daisy BB gun. It was delivered with a detailed and patient lecture on the responsibilities and privileges of gun ownership and a short course in gun safety. I was warned, as all children should be, under threat of corporal punishment, never to point a gun at anything I wasn't prepared to destroy. "Guns are not toys," my father said sternly.

He also taught me the ethics of the hunter: Never waste; never kill in cruelty; and never abuse the herd's future by overharvesting. In those days we lived close to the land, and we knew it was a mutual support system. The land supported us, and we protected the land from being misused and ravaged.

With my Daisy BB gun I learned to handle a firearm safely, which included not shooting at any target where I might damage or destroy property. If I did, I was paid back tenfold with Dad's wooden paddle. I learned this lesson well, and in a year, when I was seven, Pop bought me a Remington .22 rifle.

Boy, was I proud of that rifle. Pop used to load Cliff and me into the buggy and take us out into the hayfields to hunt prairie chickens for dinner. After he'd bagged enough birds, he'd give me a shooting lesson with my new Remington. Cliff was only four or five then, so he had to stay in the buggy.

With ownership of a rifle came certain duties—duties I was thrilled to assume. I was to provide pheasant and rabbit for the dinner table, which was like bringing home money. A pheasant brought from the field meant one more chicken to sell at the market rather than having to eat it for our daily provisions. Similarly, fishing in the Splitrock or Sioux rivers, four or five miles away, was an economic activity, not a sport. Back then I never heard of anybody hunting or fishing for the sport of it; people hunted and fished to put food on the table. Fortunately our land was blessed with an abundance of rabbits and game birds.

I was also given the jobs of protecting the ducks, geese, and chickens from foxes and skunks and of keeping the gopher population under control. In fact, it was hunting gophers that developed my marksmanship.

Gophers are little critters that burrow holes into the sod to make underground homes for themselves. About all they're good for is digging holes, eating farmers' grain, and having lots of little gophers. When they were around, before you knew it, you had whole underground gopher towns, evidenced by the pockmarked surface of holes and mounds of excavated dirt. These gopher works presented a serious threat to farm animals. I saw more than one cow or horse have to be destroyed after breaking a leg in a gopher hole. It was always a pathetic scene, with the animal bellowing hoarsely, laying on its side, its pain-crazed eyes pleading for help. Once I had my Remington, it did not take me long to volunteer for the job of gopher control.

"Okay, Son, you can go in my place," Pop agreed. He offered me a bounty of five cents per gopher and sent me on my first safari.

Let me tell you, I really felt important as I set out for a field where I knew the small animals were busily constructing their pesky villages. There I was, only seven, and Pop was letting me go gopher hunting all by myself.

I bagged about twenty of the little cave-diggers from a distance of twenty to thirty feet, then started home, my chest puffed out a mile. I was so pleased with my success that I started dreaming of bigger and better quarry. Walking home along the country road that ran beside our farm, I soon spotted a likely target.

Crews from the power company had passed through a few days earlier planting power poles in the ground and stringing electrical wire from insulators on the side of every pole. Those crockery-white insulators gleaming in the sunlight were only about as big as a man's fist, but I was sure I could hit one with my new Remington.

Now Pop had told me over and over again never to shoot at signs and other property that didn't belong to me, but I just had to find out if I could hit one of those little insulators.

I looked around. There was nobody in sight. *Who will ever know?* I said to myself. So I picked one about forty feet away and took careful aim, remembering everything my father had taught me about sharpshooting. I estimated how far above the insulator I should aim to allow for the drop of the bullet as it traveled. Checked and corrected for the wind. Took a deep breath. Let it out. Drew another, released half of it, held it, and stood motionless. Keeping both eyes open but concentrating on the aligned bead of my gunsight, I gently squeezed the trigger until the hammer on the rifle dropped.

Bull's-eye! The insulator shattered into a thousand pieces.

Boy, was I surprised! I hadn't meant to destroy the thing, just put a little hole through it.

Then something else happened that I hadn't anticipated. Without the support of the insulator, the electric wire drooped low, almost to the ground. Guilty fear surged through me, tempered only by my distance from the house and a hope that the crew from the power company would fix the line before my father noticed the damage.

I took one more guilty look at the dramatic results of my disobedience and hurried on home.

When I got to the house, Pop was waiting for me. In his hand was his old collapsible brass telescope.

"What did you shoot today, Son?" he asked.

"Gophers, Pop!" I said proudly, holding out my bulging game bag. "Lots of them!"

After a brief pause, he said, "And what else did you shoot?"

Then I knew I was sunk. He'd been watching me through his telescope!

I broke down, sobbing and confessing, thinking for sure I was going to be marched out behind the barn.

Instead, he said, "That insulator was someone else's property, Son, and we don't shoot other people's property, do we?"

"No, sir."

Pop reached out his hand. "Give me the gun, Joe," he said quietly. My father rarely raised his voice, and never when disciplining us. "We'll just put the gun away for a year and see if you're ready to use it then."

I watched dismally as he locked my rifle away in his gun cabinet.

A whole year! I was heartbroken. That rifle meant everything to me, and to a seven-year-old boy, a year seemed like forever.

Later, when I was alone in the house, I tried to pry the latch off the cabinet to get at the gun. I never completed the job because I realized that if I took the gun out, I'd *never* see it again! But the tentative scratches of my disobedience remained on the cabinet, which I still have in my home to this day.

When you get clipped behind the ear you never like it. Yet it was that kind of calm but uncompromising discipline from my father that taught me the consequences of not thinking before I acted. I learned another major lesson in this area when I was a freshman in high school. This time it involved an automobile rather than a gun.

Since Pop's early days as an auto dealer, cars had remained an important part of his life. He loved transport machines of all kinds, and over the years he owned several vehicles. Our first family car was a secondhand, four-door, Model T touring car that Pop bought in 1919 when I was four years old. Next came a dark blue, beautifully crafted 1923 Cadillac touring car that purred like a kitten. Cadillacs were no less expensive or luxurious in those days, but Pop was able to buy the car for only a hundred dollars from his close friend Iver Wangsness, who owned a local garage. The local bootlegger had traded the Cadillac in on a new car and Iver gave Pop first chance at it.

The bootlegger, who ran liquor from Chicago to Sioux Falls, always drove the fastest cars capable of carrying the heaviest load of merchandise, and he traded them as soon as they were the least bit worn or outmoded. His business was too profitable for him to worry about how much he got for the used cars.

Because of its history, this car came with a few options Pop didn't bargain for, including a smoke generator that would spew clouds of oily fumes and a tack spreader that would scatter sharp-pointed roofing nails out of the rear of the car if the authorities were in close pursuit.

I loved all of Pop's cars, but my pride and joy was a flashy, robin's-egg blue Whippet convertible with red striping that I bought when I was fifteen with money I had earned from trapping. Pop allowed me to drive Cliff and Mary Flora and a couple neighbor kids to school in Sioux Falls—but nowhere else, because I was inexperienced at driving on the highway.

"Now, Joe, you drive straight to and from school unless

27

you're instructed otherwise," were Pop's no-nonsense instructions. The "otherwise" referred to specifically designated side trips to such places as Ross Lumber Company or the IXL grocery.

This was no problem until one noon hour on a sunny spring day when a couple of my buddies, Duane Tuttle and Duke Corning, asked me to drive them across town to Cathedral High School to see some girls they knew. At first I said, "No way!" But they kept coaxing, and I finally gave in, thinking, *Pop'll never find out.*

We cruised down Ninth Street, joking, laughing, and singing. We were having such a high old time that I wasn't as alert as I should have been, and when I rolled into the intersection at Eighth Street and Spring Avenue, a car seemed to come out of nowhere from my right. We collided, my car connecting with the other car's left rear bumper. In those days they built cars like tanks, so the only damage was that the bumpers fell off both cars.

The driver came out of the other car like a gorilla wanting me for lunch. "Why don't you watch where you're going, young man! You could kill somebody!"

I started to apologize, and he said, "What's your name, young man?"

"Foss, sir. Joe Foss."

"What's your telephone number, Foss?"

"One-one-F-J-two," I said and nervously did my best to assure the man that I'd pay for his bumper. "Just send me the bill, sir."

We didn't have driver's licenses in those days, but the man did have a business card. He handed it to me, and I gulped. It read: *Brewster, Esquire, Attorney at Law.* The word *attorney* was enough to turn me into one scared rabbit.

I loaded my bumper into the rumble seat, and we drove back to Washington High—without seeing the girls at Cathedral and without all the joking, laughing, and singing.

Afternoon classes were torture. I didn't know whether I wanted them to last forever or hurry up and end. I couldn't concentrate on anything. Brewster had said he would send me the bill, but I wondered if he would also call my father.

I drove home with a ball of dread in my stomach. When I

turned into our driveway, Pop was standing in the front yard talking to my mother's brother, Uncle Frank. I pulled to a stop where I usually parked the car, and Pop called over to me, "Joe! Put the car in the north shed."

"What?" I said. We never put our cars in the north shed.

"Put the car in the north shed and bring me the keys."

When I returned with the car keys, he said quietly, "I understand you were out joyriding this afternoon and got in a little bit of trouble."

"No, sir, I wasn't joyriding."

"Do you remember what your instructions were?"

"Yes, sir," I said. "To go right straight to school and right straight back unless instructed otherwise."

Pop sighed. "Well, Joe, you didn't do that. So we'll leave the car parked until school starts next fall and then we'll see if you've learned anything."

That was in March, and for the rest of the school year I had to walk six miles to school and six miles back. My father drove Cliff and Mary Flora and the others to school, but I walked. Over summer vacation my recreation was limited to whatever was within walking distance, and I missed out on many baseball and football games organized by my friends. It was a hard-learned lesson that would stay with me and help shape the strong sense of responsibility I've carried all my life.

"You have to live by the rules," Pop always said. He believed that "doing the right thing" had nothing to do with social pressure, either positive or negative. It was just something you did because it was right.

And when it came to the rules, Pop believed "Once is enough." He said it once or asked it once, and he expected you to listen and obey. His teaching method was like glue. It stuck.

Chapter 3

Where Hawks Soar

On May 20, 1927, Charles A. Lindbergh left Roosevelt Field in New York to begin a nonstop solo flight across the Atlantic in his single-engine plane, *The Spirit of St. Louis*. Thirty-three hours later he landed in Paris, France, and the historic news flew around the world.

My father loved flying almost as much as I did, so Pop and I devoured every newspaper and magazine article about the flight. Years later I would learn, from Lindbergh himself, that much of what we read had been concocted by an overly enthusiastic press. Even many of the photos printed in the world's newspapers were composites of posed models with Lindbergh's face pasted on to add the drama that real life failed to provide. But at the time my twelve-year-old mind eagerly absorbed every tidbit as fact.

President Calvin Coolidge ordered a naval flagship to bring Lindbergh and his plane back to the United States. Wherever he went, the handsome young flier was welcomed by crowds and celebrated by parades. He even stayed in the White House when he was received in Washington, D.C.

Shortly after returning to the United States, Lindbergh began a nationwide tour in his plane to promote enthusiasm and support for commercial aviation. When we learned that he was going to fly into Sioux Falls, Pop and I were like beavers after fresh timber. The whole family dressed up in our finest outfits, and Pop loaded us all into the car and drove us to Renner Field, five miles north of town, to see the new American hero and his airplane. Renner Field was little more than a hay patch, but it offered much more room for the crowd and the cars than did the Sioux Falls airport.

The crowd went wild as soon as the silvery speck appeared on the horizon. It came closer and closer, finally setting down at the far end of the field. When the plane taxied to a stop, the crowd mobbed it. A tall, thin figure climbed out and everyone roared and cheered and whistled and applauded, while a band played patriotic and military music. I tried to get as close as possible to the platform draped with red, white, and blue bunting and surrounded by hundreds of American flags.

Moments later an official party escorted Lindbergh up onto the platform, and the noise was enough to drown out the explosions in a dynamite factory. I broke through the edge of the crowd and climbed up to the platform, eager to shake hands with my hero. I was only a few feet away from Lindbergh when several men in military uniform grabbed me and threw me off the platform.

I was too excited to be disappointed. In fact, I was so excited that I hardly heard a word Lindbergh said as he greeted the crowd and told about his historic flight. Instead of listening, I elbowed my way back through the crowd to get over to Lindbergh's plane, which now stood majestically alone, totally ignored by the people crowded around the platform. That silver airship was the most beautiful thing I'd ever seen. I dreamed of climbing inside and flying it away.

All the way home I chattered excitedly. "I'm going to be bigger than Lindbergh someday," I vowed to my father, more determined than ever to become a flier. Little did I know that someday I would not only get to shake my hero's hand, but would count him a good friend as well.

Despite my eagerness to be airborne, it was several years before I had a chance to make my first flight. In fact, it happened shortly after Pop took my car away from me, which showed how generous he could be even while being stern. That spring of 1931 I walked in from my six-mile trek home from school one afternoon and was greeted with the remarkable news that Pop and I would be taking a ride in an airplane that very night.

By the time we arrived at the makeshift airstrip next to Covel Lake, the sun was setting and kerosene-soaked burlap bags in steel drums were being lit to provide landing lights. A crowd had gathered to buy tickets; many had come just to watch the plane take off and land. The tickets cost $1.50 each, a considerable extravagance at that time. The crowd's excitement, the dancing flames, and the smell of gasoline and oil had an intoxicating effect on me.

"There it comes!" someone shouted, and the crowd came alive with loud cheers and applause.

At first all I could make out were the red and green running lights. Then I caught an occasional glimpse of shining silvery sides. As the plane descended to the edge of the field, I caught the throaty roar of its engines. Dust swirled when the landing gear touched the ground. Moments later, the plane taxied up to the crowd.

The Ford Tri-Motor was a big plane by Sioux Falls standards, certainly the biggest I'd ever seen. Its silvery corrugated metal sides gleamed in the flickering lights, and I was awed by its size and sleek lines.

The pilot was Clyde Ice. He had soloed back in the spring of 1919 in an old Jenny-type standard biplane powered by an OX-5 engine and now owned an airline called Wamblee Ohanka, a Sioux Indian name meaning "swift eagle." His entire fleet consisted of that single, all-metal Ford Tri-Motor, which was the sixth Ford Tri-Motor ever made, at a cost of $50,000. (Clyde went on to become South Dakota's most famous civilian pilot, logging over 43,000 hours without ever hurting a soul. Years later we became close friends, and Clyde was still flying when he was in his nineties. He died in July 1992 at age one hundred and three.)

The plane rolled to a stop and passengers peered out of the windows lining the side of the fuselage. Pop and I watched and waited while the plane made several more trips. Finally, it was our turn.

We climbed into the plane through a door at the rear. Wicker chairs lined the sides of the cabin—seven on the door side and eight on the other—and each seat had its own tiny window. We settled into our seats, and one of the crew members showed us how to buckle the lap belts. Someone closed the door, and Clyde revved the engines to an ear-splitting roar. The plane began vibrating. I looked out the window, and the lights began to move. Then I realized that it wasn't the lights that were moving—it was the plane!

We taxied to the edge of the grass runway, stopped for a moment, and then the engines roared to an even louder pitch. I thought we were going to shake to pieces.

Suddenly the plane began rolling across the field, gaining speed. I was pressed back into my seat. Outside my window, the ground sped past in a blur and then began to drop away.

We were in the air! What a feeling! What a view!

As the plane circled higher and higher in the night sky over the city of Sioux Falls, I strained to take it all in. Familiar buildings and streets and landmarks seemed so different—like I was looking at them for the first time. I wanted to etch every moment in my mind so I would never forget the experience.

After we landed, Pop and I stayed around and watched a few more takeoffs and landings before heading home. All the way back to the farm we talked about flying. Now I *knew* I had to become a pilot. Every fiber in my body wanted to get behind those controls and fly off into the night.

That same year the Marine Corps stunt exhibition team performed at the Sioux Skyways airport. Four Marine aviators flew F4B4s, called "eggbeaters." They were open-cockpit biplanes with two .30 caliber machine guns that shot, synchronized, through the prop. When I saw that team fly and do aerobatics, I got "Marine" on the brain. Later I would take my own fighter training in F4B4s, and I would get to know all four of those pilots when they were colonels.

My next flight was two years later, in the summer of 1933, when my cousin Ardeen and I heard about a barnstormer, a flier by the name of Billeter from Dell Rapids, South Dakota, who gave passenger rides and would stay up till you asked him to land. If you didn't ask before he was ready to come down, the ride would be free.

Billeter flew an open-cockpit biplane called a Great Lakes.

He had that thing strung together with baling wire and fancied himself a daredevil. In fact, his aerobatics almost always led to very short flights, as terrified passengers screamed for the twisting, turning, upside-down convulsions to end.

I grinned at Billeter as he strapped Ardeen and me into the rear seat, and he smiled back—like he was looking forward to putting the fear of God into us. Once we were in the air and he began his maneuvers, we gripped the sides of the plane until our knuckles turned white, but our screams of laughter never turned to pleas for him to stop. Billeter began to worry about losing a fare and his tactics grew even more extreme. Still we laughed and whooped as sharper turns and faster dives threw us about in the back of the plane. I loved it.

Finally the frustrated pilot landed, shook our hands, and returned our money. I was disappointed that the flight had ended so soon.

Each time I flew the thrill was greater than ever, and I became even more bent on becoming a flier. But circumstances I could never have foreseen made it three more years before I could take serious action to become a pilot.

Within a matter of minutes one dark, rainy March night in 1933, about a month before my eighteenth birthday, my entire life changed.

It was spring plowing time, and Pop was helping my uncle, Frank Lacey, my mother's brother. The Lacey relatives often helped each other when it came time to plant and harvest. Plowing, planting, and harvesting did not wait for convenience. They had to be done on schedule, no matter what the circumstances or the weather.

I had agreed to meet my father at Uncle Frank's after school. The two of them had been working since before daybreak, and evening was approaching when I took over the controls of the tractor and continued plowing while Pop and Uncle Frank went back to the house for supper.

Our part of the country had suffered a drought for several years, but that month we'd had intermittent rain. It had been cloudy all that day, and as darkness settled, a fine mist began to fall. I turned on the headlights of the tractor and kept plowing. Sometime after eleven the wind picked up, and within minutes it was pouring rain. Mud had begun to gum the lugs of the tractor wheels, when I looked up and saw my father running across the field toward me.

"Unhitch that plow and get the tractor back to Frank's," he shouted over the noise of the motor and the howling wind. "You can't work in this mud."

"Okay, Pop!" I yelled back, and slid off the metal seat to unhitch the plow.

"I'll head on home, Son. See you when you get there." He then turned and ran back across the dark, muddy field to the side road where his car was parked.

After disconnecting the plow, I climbed onto the tractor and aimed the lumbering two-cylinder John Deere toward Uncle Frank's barn about a quarter mile away. Minutes later the storm really shook loose. Rain streamed down and blasts of wind whipped water into my face. I pulled my hunting cap low to shield my eyes.

The rear lugs found a hold in the muddy ground, but the front wheels kept slipping, making it difficult to steer. The intervals between lightning and thunder got shorter and shorter. Realizing the strikes were getting closer, I concentrated on driving. I didn't want to be stuck out in the open in the height of the storm.

Once I reached the gravel road, the drive back to Uncle Frank's took less than fifteen minutes. By the time I got there I was as wet as if I'd jumped in the creek, but I didn't go into the house to dry off. I just wanted to get home. So I parked the tractor in the barnyard and ran for my car, grateful to be out of the rain at last.

It was after midnight as I made my way slowly down highway 16. The driving rain was blinding and road conditions were uncertain. I had just topped a slight rise and started down the other side when I spotted a car stopped several hundred yards ahead on the right. Beyond it a downed power line was shooting sparks like fireworks. The flashing light illuminated the shape of a rooster in the rear window of the car, and I recognized the familiar Texaco insignia. It was my father's car.

Why had he stopped? I wondered. Maybe he was waiting

for me, to make sure I got safely around the downed line. As I drew closer, however, I saw that the driver's door was open. Then I saw a body on the pavement beside the car.

I slammed on the brakes, jumped out of the car, and ran, yelling, "Pop! Pop!" I started to bend down to reach for him when out of the corner of my eye I caught sight of something that made me stop.

The slashing wind had toppled a billboard, which had then severed the power line. One end of the slumping wires had caught under the right fender of my father's car. A pole away, the other end danced freely, like a demented snake, spitting out flashes of fire.

In the midst of the hellish scene, my father lay utterly still.

Stunned, frightened, I stood in the downpour staring at my father, afraid to touch him. The only thing I knew about electricity was that it was lethal, and there was my father, facedown on the wet pavement. Even blinded by wind, rain, and fear, I could see he wasn't breathing.

I knew he was dead.

I've had sixty years to try to piece together the events of that night, and I'm pretty certain I know what happened.

Dad must have seen the break in the power line when he came over the rise. It was flashing like an arc-welder. But in the dark and the rain he wouldn't have spotted the low-hanging wire on one side, spooled down over the road where it crossed under the power line.

He slowed cautiously and steered to the right in case another car came up behind him in the treacherous weather. Certainly he knew I'd be along shortly. He probably never saw the wire that caught under the front fender and neutralized the Buick's ignition system, bringing the rolling car to a halt.

Dad always carried a flashlight in the back seat. He must have turned around and grabbed it, thinking the car had developed mechanical trouble. Unaware that his car was charged with high voltage and that he was protected only by the insulation of the rubber tires, he swiveled to the left, placed one foot on the running board, and stepped down, completing the electrical circuit. He was probably dead before he hit the ground.

As I stood there crying, agonizing over what to do, a car drove up behind me, and the driver got out to help. Neither of us knew if the electrical charge would jump from the car and fry us if we touched my father, but we took the chance. Somehow we managed to pull his body away from the car without getting electrocuted ourselves.

Artificial respiration was the only resuscitation procedure I knew, and I began working my father's arms. I kept at it for a long time, but he never showed one spark of life.

I had been around death almost every day on the farm, and yet I never once thought about anyone in my family dying—especially not Pop. He was always there, as sure and certain as the rising sun every morning. Then, in an instant, he was gone.

I had lost the one person I could always lean on, the one person who was always there when I needed him. I had lost my best friend.

Chapter 4

Finding a Way

✬   ✬   ✬

Word of my father's death spread quickly, and relatives and neighbors converged on the farm, offering comfort and help and making all kinds of promises.

"Don't worry, Joe. We'll see that you get help on the farm," they said. "We'll see that you get to college."

None of the promises made that night were ever kept, but I was never bitter about it. People say things at a time of tragedy that are well meant but soon forgotten. Besides, those folks all had enough problems of their own. The Great Depression was strangling the economy, and the drought that had begun in the late 1920s had turned South Dakota into part of the Great Dust Bowl. Frequent dust storms blew away precious topsoil and left sand drifted as high as the fenceposts. Sometimes we had to plow the sand away from the fences so the livestock wouldn't just walk over the top and out to freedom.

My mother was not the sort who would ever expect anyone to take her husband's place. She was a proud, self-sufficient woman. Nevertheless, she missed Pop terribly and buried her grief in her work. After my father died, she always said she was married to the farm.

Thus, at eighteen I began my first career, full-time farming, out of necessity. I was the oldest, and it was my duty to take over Pop's responsibilities. He had taught me to plow a straight furrow, to plant and harvest on time, and to rotate crops. He had done such a good job of instructing me that in some ways it seemed like he was still there, looking over my shoulder.

Keeping up with schoolwork had never been a cinch for me, and the task became harder now as my share of the farm work increased. Time to walk the hills and woods was gone, and I missed the solitude and the hours I'd always spent close to nature. I did my best to fill the considerable void left by my father's death, but my senior year of high school was a tough year, and I became certain of one thing. As soon as possible I wanted to get out of farming.

In the fall of 1934, with my mother's encouragement, I enrolled at Augustana, a Lutheran college in Sioux Falls. To earn money for tuition and books I began working at John Morrell and Company, a meat-packing plant, where I started at forty-three cents an hour and eventually got raised to forty-six. Whenever I could I also worked from midnight to seven at Roy Tollefson's filling station—Tolley's—selling gas and oil, greasing trucks, and changing tires for twenty-five cents an hour. My boyhood friend, Duke Corning, who would later become my business partner, also worked there.

Unfortunately, these part-time jobs, though necessary for my economic survival, interfered with my studies. Before the year was over I'd failed half my subjects and flunked out. When the dean, Dr. Oscar Hofstead, called me in, he said, "Joe, I think you'd better stick to farming next year. You don't have time to go to college."

I took his advice. For the next year I stuck to farming and any other jobs I could get. Besides the service station and the packing plant, I also earned four dollars an hour for playing my E-flat baritone saxophone in the Sioux Falls Municipal Band.[1] I even worked as a janitor at the Presbyterian church, but I lost that job when my friend Ray Sturgeon dropped in one Saturday afternoon while I was on duty and a ladies'

---

[1] I also played in three volunteer bands at various times: the El Riad Shrine Band, the Sioux Falls Elks Band, and the Little Stone Church Band. But once I went off to war, I never played the sax again.

group caught him playing the "Beer Barrel Polka" on the church organ.

Another way I tried to make some extra dough was in the prize-fighting ring. I was a husky 160-pounder, and I had always been a fighter. As a kid, if somebody called me a "farmer" in a less-than-reverent tone, I'd challenge him to a fight. I never stepped back from a good fistfight, and I won a few rounds as an amateur. All of which led me to try for the Golden Gloves Tournament in Sioux Falls.

I was the lightest fighter in my class, and my first bout was with a guy named Mel Anderson from Lake Preston, South Dakota. Before the fight, my boxing coach, Dr. Horton, said, "This guy is big and green. Take him out in the first round."

Well, I did two things wrong. My first mistake was getting in the ring with Anderson. The second one was hitting him and making him mad. He came after me and knocked me down eleven times before the fight was over.

That event also marked my first encounter with the press. There was some controversy as to whether I had been knocked over the top of the ropes or between them. All I could remember was that I landed in the front-row press section, right on top of an old typewriter.

The next day the *Des Moines Register* carried a closeup picture of me, down on all fours with my nose breathing in my right ear. The caption read, "The face of a fallen fighter." Anderson had broken my nose with his first punch. After that I decided I'd better do something else to make a living.

That winter, 1935–36, was the worst I'd ever seen. Temperatures dropped to more than forty below several nights in a row. Heavy snowfall stranded cattle in the fields, and many starved to death. Roads were closed for weeks at a time. Cliff and Mother and I all went to work for the Highway Department that winter, shoveling snow off the highways for a dollar a day.

Everyone assumed that I would inherit the farm and work the land my father had loved. But that year after I had helped my mother make the last of the farm mortgage payments with my outside earnings, I fastened on another option.

By now Cliff had finished high school, and it became apparent that he and my mother could run the farm together, which was just fine with me. If farming was in Cliff's blood, flying was in mine, and I was itching to get on with my plans to become a pilot.

"I'll give you this thing lock, stock, and barrel," I told Cliff. "The mortgage is paid off, and you want to be a farmer and I want to go on and get an education." The deal suited both of us to a tee, and neither of us ever regretted the decision.

In 1936 I turned twenty-one. That was also the year I took up smoking cigars. When I was a boy, Pop had offered me a hundred dollars if I would wait until I was twenty-one before I started smoking. I had promised and I kept my word, even though my father was gone and there was no hundred-dollar reward.

One Friday night during the summer of that year my buddies and I were hanging out in downtown Sioux Falls, scouting around for low-cost entertainment. Somehow we ended up listening to a cocky young guy who was leaning against a lamppost and bragging about what a great pilot he was. He claimed he'd flown eight hours. *Eight hours,* I thought, *only eight hours!* That did it. If that blowhard could fly, so could I.

First thing the next morning I went out to Sioux Skyways, the Sioux Falls airport, and asked how much it would cost to learn to fly. Sixty-four dollars, I was told. That was exactly the amount I made in a month working at Tolley's filling station, which meant I would have to live that month on the additional forty-eight dollars I made playing in the band.

The next day I returned to Sioux Skyways with sixty-four dollars and paid my flight instruction fee. They turned me over to an instructor named Roy Lanning and his Taylorcraft, a high-wing, enclosed-cockpit plane with a single engine that strained to develop a measly forty horsepower.

A few lessons and several days later, I climbed into the Taylorcraft for my first solo flight.

I started the engine and let it idle until it warmed up. Then I eased up on the brakes and pushed the throttle forward a little. The plane began to roll, and I taxied to the end of the runway. In front of me stretched the long, narrow strip of grass from which I would finally launch my lifelong ambition.

I released the brakes and moved the throttle all the way

forward. The Taylorcraft's engine roared as it picked up rpms and I rolled down the runway, gathering speed. The ground whizzed by. I moved the wheel forward and felt the tail lift. Then, ever so slightly, I eased back on the controls and the plane lifted off the ground and began to climb.

How I wished Pop were there to see me.

I was finally soaring with the hawks!

Flying was not an inexpensive sport, even in the 1930s. It cost six dollars an hour just to rent a plane. Given this fact and the time involved, the only way I was going to get the kind of flight time I needed was to join the military. I had broached the subject once, when I was seventeen, but my mother wouldn't hear of it. She valued education highly. I think she always regretted that she had been taken out of school after the third grade, as many girls were in those days because people didn't think education was necessary for women. Her father had been an educated man, and she was determined that I would graduate from college. She'd lectured me long and hard about it, as only my mother could.

So with Mother and Cliff now running the farm, I went to enroll again at Augustana College for the 1937 fall term. Because of my poor record there, however, the dean of students would not admit me, so I went down the road to Sioux Falls College.

While I was on my way to register, I spotted my friend Ray Sturgeon, whose ecclesiastical polka had gotten me fired from my church janitor job. He was mowing the grass in front of the college.

"Where you going, Joe?" he asked.

"To register at the college."

"You got a job?"

"No."

"Come on. I can get you one here."

Ray introduced me to the chief of maintenance at the school, who took one look at me and said, "You look big enough to work. We'll get you signed up here, and then you can run the mower." This set Ray free to paint a ceiling in a classroom, and when I checked on him later he was moving so slow I figured he must think he was painting the Sistine Chapel.

Still faced with finding a place to live and lining up more work to supplement my part-time job with the college maintenance department, I located an inexpensive situation, sharing Mrs. Berdahl's attic with two old friends from high school, Herbie Creighton and Duane Tuttle. To earn my meals, I washed pots and pans in a local restaurant.

Besides working on my business major and trying to earn enough money to pay for my education, I played football, made the track team, and went out for boxing. Making ends meet financially was tough, but as Pop used to say, "If you're willing to work hard and keep smiling, you'll always have a job." Well, nothing much ever happened that was bad enough to keep me from smiling, so I figured I would work my way through college with no trouble.

When I wasn't working or going to school, I was spending as much time as I could afford in the air. And when I wasn't flying, I was talking about flying. At Tolley's, Duke Corning, Pudge Erickson, Duane and Dale Tuttle, and I sat around the grease pit sucking up soft drinks and dissecting every newspaper story and every rumor coming out of the cauldron bubbling in Europe, where a guy with a little square mustache and hair hanging over his eyes was flexing his military muscles.

Wars and rumor of war were in the papers nearly every day. The Japanese had invaded China. German and Italian Fascists were fighting Russian Socialists and Communists in a bitter Spanish civil war. And in Great Britain, politicians were maneuvering to avoid the nationalistic resentments and conflicts threatening to unfurl around the world. We followed all this with a sort of worried fascination.

Since we all loved flying, our bull sessions usually funneled down to the importance of flight strategy and tactics. By the end of World War I, some military strategists had begun to realize the significance of aviation in warfare, but many powerful critics of air power still thought of fighter aircraft as a novelty of questionable military value. Air power was useful in transporting the manpower and mechanisms of war, they said, but not particularly useful in combat.

One notable exception was my childhood hero, Charles Lindbergh. Because Lindbergh had traveled extensively after setting his historic record, he had seen firsthand other nations' efforts to build air forces. He believed in a strong American air force and warned publicly that the U.S. was unprepared for a contest with the most combat-ready air power in the world, the German Luftwaffe. He opposed involvement in what was increasingly viewed as an inevitable European war for other reasons as well, emerging as the leading isolationist in America.

Polls indicated that nine out of ten Americans agreed with Lindbergh's opinion that the U.S. would not benefit from entanglement with Old World quarrels. Of the remaining ten percent, many favored Germany and its ally Italy over England—not surprising, since German and Italian immigrants made up a large percentage of the U.S. populace. Furthermore, resentment against England was not uncommon among Americans of other nationalities, and they thought Britain's attempt to drag the U.S. into a purely European intrigue was an effort to save its own crumbling colonial empire.

Although our country was divided about whether we should enter the fray, I figured I should prepare for the worst. It was time to bring up the matter of enlistment again.

One night when I was out at the farm for dinner, I looked up from the piece of pheasant I was slicing and said, trying to sound nonchalant, "Well, I think I'll join the Army Air Corps next year."

I might as well have dropped a bomb. Cliff and Mary Flora stopped chewing, and Mother laid down her knife and fork like a gauntlet and pronounced, "There's no way you're going to do that! I've wanted you to have a college degree all your life, and now you want to goof it up to run off and fly airplanes!"

I was old enough not to need her permission to enlist, but she made such a big deal about it that I decided to stay in school. However, I did join the Army National Guard. Besides the military factor, I joined for two very practical reasons. First, I liked the uniform—the heavy wool shirts and pants and the boondoggler shoes. I wore them to school every day, until the Army ordered me not to wear my uniform except on official business. Second, I liked the pay. It wasn't very good, but in those days a dollar was as big as a wagon wheel to me.

After a year at Sioux Falls College, where I passed my classes with almost a B average, I transferred to the University of South Dakota in Vermillion, about sixty miles from Sioux Falls. I earned room and board by waiting tables and washing dishes at the Sigma Alpha Epsilon fraternity house, and my pocket money came from a fifty-cents-an-hour job sweeping the floor and cutting meat at a butcher shop owned by Louie Lass and Charley Stark.

I had transferred to the university because they had a government flying course, and I spent most weekends training with the 147th Field Artillery of the National Guard. I loved this introduction to military life, the drilling and the discipline. I also made friends with a number of classmates who shared my love for flying, and we banded together and got the university to establish a Civil Aeronautics Administration course. We all believed there was going to be a war and we wanted to be prepared. The seventy-two-hour ground school was located on campus, and we did our flight training thirty-five miles away near Sioux City, Iowa, at Rickenbacker Field, named after the famous World War I American air ace, Captain Eddie Rickenbacker, a name I would reckon with again in the future.

In the fall of my junior year my roommate, Rollin Fred Smith, left to join the Marine Corps. Soon he was writing to regale me with tales of the Corps, and when he came home on leave and I saw him in his full dress Marine blues, I knew it was the Corps for me!

In February of my senior year, with five dollars in my pocket, I hitchhiked three hundred miles to Minneapolis, Minnesota, to enlist. One of my buddies, Ralph Gunvordahl, went with me, and of the twenty-eight guys who requested pilot training that weekend, Ralph and I were the only two accepted. (Ralph later became one of the famous Flying Tigers in the Burma campaign in the Pacific.)

I qualified to begin E-base training, short for elimination

based training, a merciless course designed to do just what the name implied—eliminate those who didn't measure up. My orders were to report to the Wold-Chamberlain Reserve Base in Minneapolis as soon as I graduated.

I never regretted the years spent earning my business degree. Later I would learn that if you don't understand basic economics in this world, you're a dead duck. My teachers were solid men and women who gave me good advice for daily living that I have used often as I've traveled down the trail of life.

Nevertheless, I yearned to get out and fly full-time.

I've still got the letter I wrote to my mother in April 1940 in which I said: "I'm just having one hell of a time keeping up with my work. They give me enough to last for months. I only got to fly twice this last week. . . . This fine weather makes me want to go out hunting gophers or something far from studying but I think I can stand it another two months."

In June I graduated from the University of South Dakota School of Business Administration and immediately reported for duty at Wold-Chamberlain Field in Minneapolis.

Chapter 5
Flight Training

Hitler's Third Reich was rolling steadily across Europe. One April afternoon in 1940, not long before I graduated from college, I was lying on a sofa in the Sigma Alpha Epsilon house, smoking a cigar and listening to the radio, when a news flash interrupted Glenn Miller's "Moonlight Serenade." A foreign correspondent described the German dive bombers that were spearheading Hitler's onslaught.

On May 10, Britain's Prime Minister, Neville Chamberlain, stepped down and Winston Churchill took his place. On June 10, Italy declared war on Britain and France. By the end of June, when I reported for E-base training in Minneapolis, victims of Hitler's aggression included Poland, Norway, Denmark, Belgium, Holland, Luxembourg, and France.

By now, although still not declaring itself, the United States had moved from neutrality to a state of preparation by expanding its armed forces, building defense plants, and giving aid to the European Allies. The sense of urgency was tangible, and the military began gearing up at top speed.

Anxious for capable pilots, the Army and the Navy cooperated to sift quickly through the applicants, identifying those with the greatest natural aptitudes. This was where the E-base training system came in: It provided a minimum of preparation and a maximum of examination to determine whether or not a prospective pilot should go on to flight

47

school. The concentrated course took only five weeks; less, if you failed to pass any one of the many tests along the way.

They put us through classroom studies in navigation, Morse code, and meteorology, along with a total of twelve hours of flying instruction. That's all. What it meant was that we got some ground training and a chance to solo. If a guy fumbled at any point, he washed out. That was the end of the time and the money they were going to waste on him. They wanted to get rid of those who couldn't handle it before we got to the really tough course—combat. After all, we weren't doing this just to circle the beet patch. It was a one-way street out of there and into action.

In my class there were twelve hopefuls, two other Marines under naval command like myself, and nine with the Navy. About two hundred personnel—support crew, mechanics, chute packers, and such—staffed the E-base facility, making Wold-Chamberlain like a small base. The instructor in charge of our class was Captain Avery Kier. He was an extraordinary teacher and the sharpest dressed Marine I ever knew. Though we called him "Captain Kier, rhymes with fear," and joked that if we made a mistake in front of him, it was "Kier today and gone tomorrow," the man profoundly impressed me. He was courteous, direct, neatly dressed, witty, and quick on the draw. I determined to pattern my own direction and style after him.

During the five intensive weeks that I spent at Wold-Chamberlain, I never mentioned that I had already logged over a hundred hours of civilian flight time. I'd heard that instructors didn't like guys who thought they knew more than everybody else, so I decided not to volunteer anything about my experience.

Nine of us graduated and were given orders to report to the naval air station at Pensacola, Florida. After a month's furlough, which I spent at home helping Mother and Cliff with the farm work and saying good-bye to friends and family, I headed down the road for Pensacola. Literally. I hitchhiked.

Three days later, on a hot August day, my heart pounding with excitement, I walked onto the base in Florida. I was twenty-five years old.

* * *

Flight Training

Pensacola Naval Air Station provided a cram course in basic flying. Mornings were dedicated to the rehabilitation program, a merciless physical conditioning led by Gene Tunney, the world heavyweight boxing champion who had earned his title by defeating Jack Dempsey. Tunney personally led us in calisthenics, football scrimmages, and boxing tournaments. Afternoons and evenings we studied and practiced flight principles and techniques. Once again I kept mum about my previous flight experience. Nobody likes a know-it-all.

Saturday nights were our nights to howl. That's when they let us off the base—until midnight—and we spent most of the time checking out the local bars. Sunday was our day off. I thrived during those six months at Pensacola, and I got through the program without any pilot errors or other difficulties, which is probably a miracle since I was a wild sucker. I'd just as soon fight as eat if some bird gave me a hard time. (In those days I was always ready to do physical battle. I still love conflict and controversy, but today my battles are verbal—although I have been accused of taking an opposing view just to create a good fight if I can find somebody to argue with me.)

In January 1941, after completing primary, instrument, and formation training at Pensacola, I was transferred to the Opa-Locka Naval Air Station in the Miami area for fighter training. Riding a growing wave of confidence, I began advanced preparation for aerial combat in a small, single-seater biplane called the F4B4 (F for fighter, B for Boeing, and 4 for the model).

My specialized education in combat flying began with aerobatic instruction, which meant practicing the twisting and dramatic gyrations of a midair contortionist. This familiarized us with the radical maneuvers essential in life-or-death engagements with an enemy; it was also intended to make us feel comfortable in the aircraft regardless of the position of the plane or the violence of the maneuver.

I loved it. It didn't matter whether I was upside down or going straight up or straight down. I just looked around and adjusted to my position. It was demanding and dangerous sport, and I excelled at it in a way I never had in anything else.

49

I had found my home, and it was in the sky.

When we completed the aerobatic phase of our instruction, they uncrated the ammunition and we began gunnery training. From the air we practiced shooting at targets fixed to the ground, floating in the Everglades, and towed behind planes in the air.

This was where my hunting and shooting experience served me well. Basic training and standard military target practice did not automatically produce expert sharpshooters, especially in crisis situations (and they still don't). Men who had had little or no experience with firearms found moving targets a frustrating challenge. They'd aim where the target was before it moved, whereas those of us who had done field shooting knew the importance of proper lead on a moving target. There were exceptions to the rule, of course—city boys who excelled in combat and farm kids who didn't.

While I was at Pensacola my name was drawn as one of the 1,056 fliers to take part in the Thousand Aviator Study. The purpose of this study was to examine the effects of flying on the individual pilot, to pick up on any conditions that might shorten the career of the aviator, and to determine methods of maintaining the health and safety of the pilot. This involved extensive testing, similar to that which astronaut candidates now undergo. Originally the Navy intended to follow up the Pensacola study subjects only through their flight training years. Following World War II, however, they realized that this large, homogenous group of healthy young men could serve as a remarkable resource and data base from which to study the natural aging process. Thus, I have taken part in follow-up studies and periodic testing throughout my life, and Dr. Robert Mitchell faithfully followed me through this program from the inception until his retirement in 1991.

On March 15, 1941, after seven months of training, I received my commission as a Marine second lieutenant, and on March 29 I was awarded my wings, the proud symbol of a qualified naval aviator. This should have been the happiest moment of my life, but along with my wings I was handed disappointing news. Instead of being shipped out to a base in the U.S. or the Pacific, I was being assigned to flight school as a flight instructor for a primary squadron.

I was devastated. I had my heart set on action. I wanted to get into combat. Instead, my career as a fighter pilot appeared to be over before it started. Age was the problem. I was almost twenty-six, several years older than most of my colleagues, and the military wanted young bucks as fighter pilots—the twenty-one-year-olds. The age thing was a lot of bull. I thought so then, and I still do. Mental attitude was the important thing. They'd headed me off at the gap, as far as I was concerned.

I've always been uncomfortable with emotional displays and have never been one to wear my feelings on my sleeve, so I didn't let on to anyone how I felt. I just returned to my quarters and packed my duffel in silence, while all around me my younger classmates talked excitedly about their assignments to fighter groups. Heading out for Sauffley Field at Pensacola, I determined to be the best possible instructor until I could somehow join a fighting outfit.

A primary squadron was actually a beginner's flying class, and we had to crank our students out as fast as we could. It wasn't unusual for me to spend up to six hours a day in the air. That meant four hour-and-a-half flights with four different students in the yellow Navy biplane called the N3N. It was a grueling marathon of snap rolls, falling leaves, loops, and spins, and it rang your gong pretty good. I always threw in a few extras for my students—slow rolls and whatever else they could take—even an oddball outside loop.

I knew I was a good instructor, but I could not always make good pilots out of the recruits. Some guys didn't have the savvy to think like a pilot. In their minds, they were still earthbound. You had to be able to think in three dimensions, and you either had it or you didn't. Usually I could spot the guys who didn't before they endangered their own lives and the lives of others.

Sitting in the cockpit with an untested pilot in the seat behind you can be a harrowing experience. On many occasions I had to take over the controls to save both our lives when some green young flier made a serious blunder. The long hours in the air, the strain of having to be constantly alert with the inexperienced fliers, added to the administrative duties of a second lieutenant, meant I was really pushing it at times. And when you do that, you're bound to make mistakes. One morning that nearly bought me the farm.

I was testing a young pilot's ability to perform aerobatic maneuvers on command. I would call out the order, and Seaman First Class Leaman would respond as quickly as possible. I should have had my hands on the dual controls, but I was tired, so I relaxed for a few minutes, letting my arms dangle comfortably along the outside of the open cockpit.

At an altitude of only four hundred feet I called out, "Cut throttle!" expecting my student to look for an emergency landing spot. For some harebrained reason he panicked and did a snap roll, a maneuver that would turn the plane upside down almost instantly while flying straight ahead with the throttle on. The roll went awry, however, and the machine convulsed out of control, spinning toward the ground.

I immediately tried to reach for the controls, but the centrifugal force of the spin held my arms back like lead weights. If my hands had been near the controls in the first place, I would have had no difficulty pulling the plane out of the spin. Now there was nothing I could do fast enough to help. Down we went, end over appetite. I did finally get on the controls, but too late to recover. In the seconds before we crashed, I figured my life was over.

We plowed into "V" field—a practice landing field—nose-first, totaling the aircraft. But somehow we both managed to stumble, shaken but undamaged, away from the pile of warped and useless metal and shredded cloth. I was covered with gunmetal blue bruises and it hurt to move for weeks, but I was in the air teaching again after lunch. I took the responsibility for the accident, and Leaman went on to win the Navy Cross.

Other instructors and students did die during training, some in accidents that appeared less lethal than our dramatic nose-dive. I even saw men perish in planes that never left the ground, when they ran off the end of the runway and nosed over.

In some ways, the nine months I spent as an instructor at Pensacola were the longest months of my life. In other ways, those months of experience were invaluable. Only later would

I learn to appreciate what many educators know—that an instructor learns much more than he is ever able to teach.

The world situation was going nowhere fast. Japan had now entered the fray, aligning itself with Germany and Italy. In September 1940 the Land of the Rising Sun marched into French Indochina. That same month the U.S. instituted the Selective Service Act and began building its armed forces. Meanwhile, because of the seriousness of the discussions between Japanese diplomats and the U.S. State Department and to ward off further Japanese aggression, the United States moved its Pacific Fleet (gathered from our seaports in San Diego, San Francisco, and Seattle) to Pearl Harbor on Oahu in the Hawaiian islands.

Then came December 7, 1941.

It was a Sunday, and I had the day off. One of the advantages of being stationed at Pensacola was the fine hunting and fishing in the Florida Everglades and the surrounding ocean. Whenever I could arrange a few hours off duty I'd grab a fishing pole or my Model 12 Winchester 20 gauge shotgun and head for either the beach or the swamps. Later I'd contribute my catch to the officers' mess or trade it to a local restaurant for a meal and a beer. That morning another Marine and two Navy pilots and I went out north of Pensacola hunting doves. By midmorning we had our limit and were headed back to camp, as I had to go on duty at noon as Officer of the Day at Sauffley. On the way, we pulled off at a little roadside diner to trade our birds for a meal.

As soon as we stepped into the place, we knew something was wrong. The atmosphere seemed thick with fear and excitement, and the customers were gathered around a radio, listening intently. We must have looked puzzled, because someone said to us, "Haven't you heard?"

"Heard what?"

"The Japanese have bombed Pearl Harbor. The bases are all on alert." They knew we were military. The civilians in the area could always spot us by the sunburned space between helmet and goggles that made us look like we had wings tattooed on our foreheads.

We dropped our birds on a table near the door and dashed

to the pickup. There was no radio in the truck, so we couldn't get any further news, but we broke every speed limit getting back to Sauffley Field. I parked the truck outside my quarters and ran in to put on my uniform. Within minutes, a call came through for me from the commanding officer, Captain A. C. Reed.

Out of breath from running, I picked up the phone in the Officer of the Day headquarters. "Yes, sir," I said.

"Foss?"

"Yes, sir."

"You're in charge. Double the guard! Get the men back on base. Get them from the bars. Get them from wherever you can get 'em." He sounded as though the Japanese would be landing at any minute.

All I could say was, "Yes, sir," and I thought about our training planes, lined up on the field like sitting ducks.

Since it was Sunday, most of the men were off duty, so my first order of business was a frantic search for enough Marines to guard the base. A few had heard the news and came running. I sent them out to look for more. When these reported in, I sent them out to search for others—like a giant relay. I had barely finished getting enough men to double the lookout when Captain Reed called again, ordering me to triple the guard.

Across the sprawling base I positioned men to watch over the airplanes and other strategic points. Hundreds of planes were parked together, row after row. A saboteur could plant a bomb on any one of the inner trainers, and the explosion and burning fuel would take care of the rest like falling dominoes.

Grabbing six Thompson submachine guns, I set out to arm the sentries. Knowing what I did about firearms, I worried nearly as much about inexperienced and trigger-happy Americans carrying rapid-fire weapons as I did about the "yellow peril." I tried to give the Thompsons to men who had at least fired one before. Most claimed they had checked out on the Thompson at the gun range, but from the way some of those guys fumbled around, it didn't look like they had ever had one in their hands. There wasn't much I could do except warn them to make sure they knew who they were shooting at before they pulled the trigger.

After the guards were in place, I started making periodic checks on them, along with riding herd on the airplanes. Many of the guard posts were inaccessible by truck, so I had to resort to the bicycle kept on base for that very purpose. The bicycle was particularly useful for riding through the columns of planes to look for signs of sabotage. Unfortunately, I had never ridden one before. I'd been riding a horse since shortly after I learned to walk, but there wasn't much call for a bicycle on the farm.

With a Colt .45 on my hip, I wobbled off in the general direction of the first sentry.

By now it was sunset, and the tension level on base could only be described as nuts. Everyone was certain the enemy was going to be coming over the fence any minute.

By the time I arrived at the first guard post I was feeling a little more confident on the two-wheeler, but I still had to concentrate to keep my balance as I crossed the sand-based gravel road.

The skittish sentinel heard me grinding through the loose gravel and shouted, "Halt!" pulling the Thompson into firing position.

I backpedaled hard. The tires slipped on the loose gravel, and I went down on my backside, tangled in the bicycle chain, my pants torn, my hand bleeding, and my blood boiling.

"I'm halted, sailor. Don't shoot!" I yelled.

The guy was just scared and doing his duty, but I had a powerful urge to bend that bicycle over his head.

When the dust settled some hours later, we learned that on Sunday morning at 7:55 A.M. Hawaiian time—12:55 eastern standard time in Florida—360 Japanese airplanes, under the command of Admiral Yamamoto, had attacked Pearl Harbor, catching the entire U.S. military off guard. We had lost eighteen ships at the naval base, over 170 army aircraft at Hickam Field and other nearby military installations, and suffered 3,851 casualties.

America was at war.

Chapter 6
In It at Last

December seventh passed, and with it American isolationism. Congress voted to declare war on Japan the following day, and men lined up at enlistment centers around the country. Before the week was over, Germany and Italy had declared war on the United States, and we replied in kind.

I was really frustrated. We were at war, and I was far from the action. By now I was instructing more advanced students in aerial aerobatics, but that was cold comfort when I wanted to be facing off against the enemy in the skies. It was like a case of poison ivy. Scratching where it itched only made it worse.

After I made a plea for a transfer to a fighter squadron and was turned down because of my age, I decided it was time to take another tack. My only hope as far as I could see was to get tapped for a special assignment. So I began volunteering for every special duty that came along, hoping that if I landed on another command, the commanding officer would be more sympathetic to my desires than Major George Omar, who was in command of Marines at Sauffley.

One of the first volunteer requests I found tacked to the cork bulletin board at base headquarters was an appeal for thirteen pilots willing to train with gliders. The military wanted to use this method to carry troops behind enemy lines in Europe. I signed up and was accepted. Only twelve fliers were actually needed, however, and I was assigned as the thirteenth. I would be the alternate in case one of the twelve failed the training or had to drop out.

All twelve stayed in the program, and once more I was left feeling frustrated and over-the-hill. (Actually I must have had a friend in even higher places than the Marine brass, because most of those glider pilots were killed at Normandy.)

Again I haunted the bulletin board, volunteering for everything that came up. Finally it paid off. On January 1, 1942, I was relieved of my duty as a flight instructor and sent to photography school at the main station at Pensacola, a few miles from Sauffley. For the next four months I studied speed graphics, movie camera operation, developing, and printing. It was then I learned a lesson that has proved useful all my life: Find out the rules before you play the game.

When I volunteered for this stint, I was unaware of the Marine policy that an officer who entered a training program had to score in the top ten percent of the class or receive an "unsat fitness report." If he failed to beat the curve, an officer's career would come to an abrupt standstill.

I was in the soup. School had never come easy for me, and this photography stuff was one tough row to hoe. I had to work sixteen hours a day because many of the enlisted men I was up against had been professional photographers before the war. As a result, I developed an acute aversion to the camera that has lasted my entire life, even when I was producing one of television's most popular sports programs.

Alarming stories from the Pacific only added to my difficulties. The Japanese were waging war throughout the South Pacific, expanding eastward and prevailing against our forces. Rumors and speculations flew around the base, providing a further reminder that I was nowhere near a fighter assignment.

Despite the difficulty of the photography course and the distraction of the war, I made the grade. I was promoted to the rank of first lieutenant and ordered to a billet with VMD-1, the Marine Corps' first photo reconnaissance squad of World War II, based on North Island off San Diego.

San Diego sounded good to me. It was a move that might lead me closer to a fighting role, and my good friend Hap Hanson from Pensacola was in the reconnaissance squadron.

Also, my girlfriend from Sioux Falls, June Shakstad, was now living out in California, working as a dietitian at the Scripps Metabolic Medical Center at La Jolla.

I had met June when I was a sophomore in college. I'd been one of several Washington High School alumni who had been asked by Arthur Thompson, the band director, to play with the high school band in a special concert at the new school's dedication. When I walked into the first rehearsal and saw this sweet little blonde with her lips curled over the mouthpiece of a tenor sax, I vowed I'd get to meet her. I did, and we dated steadily after that.

June had graduated from Iowa State University in 1940 with a degree in nutrition. Her training made it relatively easy for her to find work, and she had gotten a job in the San Diego area because she suspected I might end up there, as most Marines did.

Though I was pleased to be close to June, I almost immediately began scheming to get out of the photo unit. I enjoyed the people I worked with, but I hated the meager flying time allotted to the group. VMD-1 had only three planes—SNJ "Texas Trainers," the plane the services used for instrument training. We had been promised several B24s, converted to reconnaissance planes, but they were nowhere in sight. Also scheduled for delivery was the Grumman F4F-7, a reconnaissance modification of the famous Wildcat fighter. I called it the "gunless wonder" because all it was armed with was cameras. *Oh, boy!* I thought. *All I need is to have the enemy catch me flying around in one of these with cameras and no guns!*

Not only that, it was a flying gas tank, with its hollow wings fitted with rubber gas tanks for extra mileage. If you parked the airplane and forgot to shut the valve off between the two wing tanks, the fuel would drain over onto the lower side and you'd find the dang thing tipped over, one wing up, like a wounded bird.

To add to my frustration at not being able to fly regularly, the Advanced Carrier Training Group (ACTG) was stationed just across the airfield from us on North Island. This became a constant source of irritation as I looked out of the barracks and watched Navy fliers training on F4F Grumman Wildcats—with guns. I would have given an arm and a leg to fly one of those babies.

When I arrived at North Island I told Colonel Al Cooley, head of Air Group Headquarters, that I wanted to be in a fighter squadron.

"You're too damned ancient, Foss!" he said. "Don't you realize you're twenty-seven years old?" I really needed to hear that.

Since I was the most junior officer in the unit, my executive duties were minimal. I had no real days off, but I did occasionally have time to see June in the evenings. I also had time to work on a transfer.

My excellent flight training and status as "junior bird man" paid off. Lieutenant Colonel Ed Pollack, our squadron CO, chose me as his personal copilot when he flew on military business. I'd take the back seat of the SNJ, ride with the colonel to his destination, drop him off, then fly the trainer back home. Colonel Pollock and I gradually became good friends, and he was sympathetic to my desire to fly. This duty gave me the edge I needed to keep up my flying skills, and with that assurance, I set my sights on proving I could fly with the young fighter pilots.

Deciding that the reconnaissance group would be better equipped to survive in a combat zone if they had some knowledge of fighter tactics, I volunteered to attend the ACTG at the naval training facility and then teach the photo squad what I'd learned. My request was approved, provided I obtained Colonel Al Cooley's permission. I then volunteered to pick up our group's mail at wing headquarters each day so I could get better acquainted with Colonel Cooley and his executive officer, Lieutenant Colonel Tom Ennis.

When I felt I had them warmed up enough to broach the subject, I explained how I felt and asked for a set of orders to go to ACTG.

"We could give you orders to go over there," Colonel Cooley consented, "if you can get in. The story is that they're loaded with their own Navy people and don't want any Marines."

"Could I have permission to go over and just talk to them?"

"Sure, go on over," said the colonel. "I don't think it'll do you much good though."

"And if they'll take me, I can get a set of orders?"

"Sure," said Colonel Cooley.

As soon as I was out the door, I drove over to ACTG and started asking questions. I learned that Navy Commander Jessie Young was the one who had the power to admit me to the course, so my next stop was his office at the top of a flight of wooden stairs.

Commander Young was sitting behind his desk concentrating on some papers. Eventually he looked up at me, standing at attention, and demanded gruffly, "What do you want?"

"Sir, I would like to get into your fighter training program, sir."

He looked me up and down. "You're a Marine."

"Yes, sir."

"No chance. ACTG is a Navy outfit and you're a Marine. And we've had nothing but trouble with Marines so far. We don't need Marines. We're too busy training our own people. Besides, you're too old."

"But, sir, I taught Navy men how to fly at Pensacola."

"No, Foss. I said no and I mean it!"

Nearly pleading, I said, "I've just got to get this training, sir."

"You've got to get nothing but out of here," he growled.

I got out. But on the way I kept racking my brain, thinking, *There has to be a way. There has to be something I can do around this dumb place.*

At the bottom of the stairway outside the commander's office I passed a group of officers who were complaining about funeral detail, probably the most hated duty on base.

With the advent of war, all the armed forces had gone into high gear. Fighter training was dangerous at the best of times. In wartime, when the pressure was on to produce competent pilots as quickly as possible, operational accidents were almost a daily occurrence.

We were pushing, pushing, pushing. The sky was a mass of airplanes, even at night, and we couldn't stop everything just because someone spun in and was killed. If you're going to win a war you have to go full speed ahead in every position. Nothing stops you.

Officers on funeral duty had to inform the family of the pilot's death, accompany them to the funeral, and muster a group of men from the company to attend the funeral. The emotional toll was enormous, especially for young soldiers trying to keep up their own courage.

For the rest of the day and most of the night I plotted and schemed. When I returned to Commander Young's office the next day, he barely had time to acknowledge me before I was begging.

"I'll do anything if you'll let me in the program, sir. I'll sweep the hangars. I'll empty the trash. I'll do absolutely anything."

The commander looked like he was ready to strangle me, leaning forward with anger burning in his eyes. But before he could get in a word, I added the kicker, "I'll even take the funeral detail."

Suddenly his expression changed. This was a new twist, and it struck a responsive chord.

"Well, I can't say you're not motivated, Foss," he said. "All right. I'll take you on. But you'll have to be better than all the rest, and there better not be any monkey business or you'll be out—and fast. Now go see Lieutenant Ed Pawka."

Lieutenant Ed Pawka was in charge of one section of the naval training program, and he knew more about aerial combat than anyone I'd ever known. He was an outstanding pilot, and I tried to mimic him. This set my goal pretty high, but he was a good instructor. He'd fly one fighter and demonstrate what he wanted, and I'd be in another fighter, following him through every stage.

Flying the F4F Wildcat was quite a jump from the trainers I'd been flying, or even the Grumman Duck I'd flown in the photo recon group, which was like trying to fly a churn. The Wildcat was the most advanced fighter flown by American pilots at that time and would prove to be one of the toughest fighters ever built. Armed with six .50 caliber machine guns, the Wildcat throbbed with power and handled like a fast and graceful hawk on a strike.

An important part of our training was learning to land and take off from the deck of an aircraft carrier. They simulated this as closely as possible with a wooden mockup of a carrier deck laid out on the runway, complete with cables and markings. Before long I'd mastered the techniques of carrier takeoffs and landings and moved on to sharpen my aerobatic and gunnery skills under Pawka's able instruction.

I was particularly good at "shooting the rag"—a target towed behind a plane.

The rag consisted of a wire frame covered with adhesive material. It was approximately the length of an airplane and about thirty-six inches wide, and the cable used to tow it behind the plane was about three hundred feet long. Each gunner used ammunition with tips dipped in colored paint— red, blue, black, and yellow—and each had his own color.

The tow plane would fly along at about ten thousand feet, towing the rag behind it, and we'd come in a flight of four going in the same direction as the tow plane only 1,500 to 2,500 feet higher and out forward. Then we'd peel off one at a time, climbing 180 degrees in opposite directions, roll over and make a steep dive, coming right straight down—this was called high deflection shooting or an overhead run. The idea was to go by the target (the enemy) from above like greased lightning. Some guys made too flat a run, and if you did this with a bomber you'd get shot in the puss. Coming straight down at any target, you made a very small target yourself and a hard one to hit.

The guy who got the job of flying the tow plane had to have a lot of nerve. It scared some men to death. The fighters had to fly almost straight at the tow plane to shoot the rag, and if they came in at the wrong angle, their guns could cross the body of the tow plane. If they accidentally touched the trigger, the pilot could be a goner, and we heard it had happened a few times when some clown jumped the gun.

My style was to head straight at the target until the very last minute, when I either had to turn or collide. Then I'd pour on the lead just before I swerved away, using the same trigger-finger action I'd used back home to target a pheasant.

As the training progressed, I became less than enthusiastic about returning to the reconnaissance group to share my knowledge of fighter tactics. When I'd gotten Colonel Cooley's orders for my transfer, I'd said, "I'll be back in thirty days or so." Now that I'd had a taste of the real thing, I didn't want to go back. I just wanted to get into the fray.

When I wasn't flying, I was carrying out the funeral detail, as I'd agreed. It was the worst job I ever got into in my life. I've never handled sickness and death particularly well anyway, and here I was having to deal personally with the deaths of fellow fliers, as many as three at one time. Yet I never lost my zeal or wavered in my determination to fly and fight.

Because of the accelerated push to get pilots ready and into the Pacific arena, all ACTG personnel were restricted to the base. This made it impossible for me to see June, even though she was only a few miles away. An occasional phone call was my only contact with her. Finally this got so frustrating that I decided to do something about it. I set everything up by phone, and one afternoon, just a few days before the end of the training course, my buddy Hap Hanson and I left North Island as if we were on official funeral business. We drove into La Jolla, and June and I got married. My mother flew in for the wedding, and Hap was the best man. The wedding was in a small church, and the guests were few. A number of June's friends came, but everyone I knew was on duty.

Technically Hap and I were AWOL, so we had to rush back to the base soon after the ceremony. Of course word of mouth soon spread the news. When my superior officers found out about it, they called me on the carpet for leaving the base, but their chastisement was mostly a formality.

Thanks to Ed Pawka and a lucky combination of natural talent, experience, and desire, I finished ACTG training with the highest gunnery score in my class—actually I think it was about the highest ever recorded coming out of ACTG. I started ACTG on June 3, 1942, and finished on July 19, 1942, and during that time I flew a total of 156.4 hours. Unfortunately, I didn't seem to be any closer to a fighting assignment.

I returned to VMD-1 and found the photo unit's status basically unchanged; they still didn't have the promised aircraft. So I couldn't even train the photo recon pilots in fighter tactics. Once again I began picking up the mail and asking daily for a transfer.

On July 31, two weeks after graduating from ACTG, I walked into Colonel Parmly's office and asked my usual question.

"Anything open up today?"

The colonel didn't answer at first, and I stood at attention while he finished signing some paperwork at his huge desk. I was just getting around to wondering what bad news lurked behind his knowing smile when he looked up.

"You ready to go to war, Foss?"

"Sure! Why? I mean, yes, sir. What changed your mind, sir?"

"Well, we need an executive officer in a fighter squadron out at Camp Kearney."

I was speechless, something he hadn't seen before.

Then Colonel Parmly grinned and said, "Well, don't just stand there, Foss. Go get packed. I'll have your orders typed and waiting for you."

That very day I checked out, and the next day I reported for duty as the executive officer of VMF-121 at Camp Kearney outside San Diego.

VMF-121 had forty Marine pilots, mostly second lieutenants. I replaced a first lieutenant by the name of Eddie Fry, who had been made operations officer of VM-121. Fry had been well liked by his men, so the new assignment caused some hard feelings at first, and the men took it out on me. I had a thousand more flying hours than Eddie, but that alone was not enough to forge a working relationship with them. Fortunately I'd inherited some of my father's ability to turn a bad situation around, and I immediately looked for ways to divert the potential divisiveness into teamwork. I visited with each man in the squadron and tried to build a friendly rapport. I always treated my junior men as I would like to be treated, and I never asked anyone to do anything I wouldn't do myself. Before long I had developed a good relationship with my squadron.

On August 1, 1942, I entered Camp Kearney as the executive officer of VMF-121. On August 11, I was promoted to captain. On September 11, I was on my way to an undisclosed destination in the southwest Pacific.

When Colonel Parmly had offered me the VMF-121 assignment, he had paused at one point and looked at me seriously. "Didn't you get married a couple weeks ago?"

"Yes, sir."

"You know, if you take this job you'll be on your way to a hot outfit."

"Hot outfit" was military lingo for a unit heading into the thick of it. It meant that many of the fliers in that squadron would almost certainly not be coming home.

PART TWO
The Cactus
Air Force

The names of Guadalcanal, Midway, and Normandy can still bring chills of apprehension to those who survived them. . . . To many historians, Midway is now in the category of one of the great, decisive battles of the world. The Battle of Normandy also has a special niche in history. And to those of us who fought through Europe, our memories of the cold, gray, winter days of the Ardennes will always be vivid. But all of the later triumphs would not even have been possible if we had not won our first offensive campaign of all: the Battle of Guadalcanal.

—Lt. Gen. James M. Gavin
The Cactus Air Force

Chapter 7

Crossing
the Pacific

For over six months the U.S. forces in the Pacific had played cat and mouse with the Japanese, which had mostly amounted to retreat and defeat for our forces. Then on August 7, 1942, we had finally launched the first U.S. offensive of the war in the Pacific with an assault on the island of Guadalcanal. The First Marine Division landed and seized a Japanese airfield, which the Americans renamed Henderson Field after Major Henderson, one of the heroes of Wake Island.

Guadalcanal was one of the southernmost of the Solomon Islands, and whoever controlled it was in an advantageous position either to attack or protect the supply lanes from America to Australia. Thus, the Japanese were determined to recapture it. That was where we came in.

VMF-121 sailed from San Diego on September 1 aboard the troop transport *Matsonia,* while our planes shipped out ahead of us on the escort carrier *Copahee*. Once we were out to sea we learned that our destination was Guadalcanal, and we were given briefings on the situation there. I wasn't worried about where we were heading. I just wanted to get there and get started. What did worry me was the fact that the men in my squadron had never flown together as a unit. In flight time logged they averaged only 213 hours apiece, in contrast to the thousand hours I'd had in instruction time alone. This gave me a lot to think about as the San Diego naval yards faded and the Pacific opened up before us.

A Proud American

The number one man in our outfit—the skipper—was Major Leonard (Duke) Davis, an Annapolis graduate and a gifted tactician. He was an outspoken, wiry little guy who never gave you reason to doubt where he stood on any subject or issue. As the executive officer, I was in charge of the actual day-to-day business of the squadron, which meant I saw that the skipper's every command was carried out. To my group of eighteen to twenty-three-year-olds I was "Old Foos," and I soon became "Smokey Joe," thanks to my cigar smoking. We all had nicknames. There was "Jughead" Haberman, "Nemo" Loesch, "Guts" Morontate, "Bilious Big Bill" Freeman, "Boot" Furlow, "Legal Eagle" Bate, "Hunkey" Palko, "Casey" Brandon, and "Danny" Doyle.

My quarters were located forward on the starboard side in "the Lily Pons suite." Her name was on the door when we arrived; apparently the famous soprano had rented it once for a cruise. Eight of us were quartered there, and the bunks were set four high in the low-ceilinged room. It was a nice place to get in out of the rain, but that's about all I could say for it. Everything was battened down, and we couldn't show any light so all the portholes were locked. The weather was hot, and fresh water was rationed to a bucket a day per man, making our cramped, airless quarters even more unpleasant. I welcomed the occasional cloudburst, day or night, and would stand out on deck enjoying a freshwater shower.

As soon as we had settled into the naval regimen—chow on a rigid schedule and boat and fire drills—the skipper began teaching us fighter tactics. We talked strategy and studied Lieutenant Commander Jimmy Flatley's *Fighter Doctrine,* a pamphlet that set forth the Flatley-Thach crossweave. This would become the primary American fighter strategy of the Second World War, a maneuver first used by American mercenaries fighting for the Chinese against the Japanese before the U.S. entered the war.

Squadrons usually consisted of eighteen to twenty-seven planes, with as many as forty pilots, but the crossweave maneuver required only sixteen planes separated into two "flights" of eight planes each. When nearing a combat area, each flight would slow to only a knot or so above stall speed and pair off in twos. In this "buddy system," each flyer had a wingman he depended on to cover his back. This was accomplished by flying constantly back and forth in opposite directions, in overlapping figure eights, one slightly under the other. Also, each pair in the flight flew at slightly varying altitudes to avoid collision. Thus, with guns pointed in both directions at all times, at least one of the two planes in each pair could immediately face the enemy no matter what direction he came from. Using this tactic, a flight could move across the skies together without abandoning the crossweave, or they could remain stationary over one position. Of course, when combat began, they would nose up and split into the chaos of the classic dogfight.

Besides studying tactics, our primary diversions were shuffleboard and poker. Before long I was heavily tanned from playing shuffleboard for hours in swimming trunks. I soon grew bored with the game and began spending my free time playing poker. You could find a game going in some corner of the ship almost any time, day or night. All told I won about $2,500, no mean sum back then, and sent most of it home to June so she could buy an insurance policy for us.

I also took advantage of the downtime by having the squadron's surgeon, Dr. Rodney K. Peterson, remove a ganglion growth on my knee caused by the crash at Pensacola. The injury had been bothering me, but I'd kept quiet about it because I didn't want to jeopardize my shot at combat.

On September 29 we sailed into the harbor of Nouméa on the island of New Caledonia, where we were reunited with our Wildcats aboard the *Copahee* and prepared to be catapulted, a new experience for all of us. Practicing takeoffs and landings on the runway mockup back on base was a far cry from actually being catapulted from the pitching decks of a carrier. We all had butterflies.

"Man all flight quarters stations," came the orders.

"Ready room from flight control. Pilots, man your planes."

The skipper volunteered to take off first, and I went last, to see that everyone got off okay.

With its wings unfolded and locked into place, the lead plane was ready to go.

"Stand clear of propellers."

"Start engines."

When it was my turn, the deck crew hooked the catapult cable to the attachment on the belly of my plane, as I kept my weight crammed down on the foot brake.

With the cable in place, I slowly moved the throttle forward, keeping the catapult officer in the corner of my eye, watching for his signal. The Wildcat's powerful engine revved faster and louder until it reached a high-pitched roar and the plane vibrated severely. When the officer's arm dropped sharply, I relaxed my legs and released the brakes at the exact moment the catapult yanked the screaming Wildcat down the flight deck for forty yards and thrust it into the air, out and beyond the carrier's bow.

Once in the air we moved into formation and, following our orders, flew to a landing strip at Tontouta on New Caledonia, where we would have a chance to warm up a bit flying together before we moved into real action. We landed in heavy winds, and Bill Freeman tipped slightly at touchdown, catching a wing tip on the ground. The plane ground-looped and Freeman barely avoided hitting an oil dump before he ran the plane into a rock pile. Fortunately he walked away from the crash.

Bill reported to me first, and I sympathized with his embarrassment; then he went to Major Davis, as though wanting to be disciplined. Instead, the skipper listened and merely said, "That's sure a tough wind out there." For the next week Bill practically disappeared from sight, using every spare moment to put his plane back together, salvaging parts from the mechanics and the junkyard.

While we waited for our orders to move up to Guadalcanal, we practiced all the theories and exercises we had studied on board ship by flying combat drills—short flights to a mock target where we practiced dives and strafing attacks.

Reports arrived daily on conditions in the Solomons, and if you believed all the stories, it could really throw a scare into you. We heard fantastic reports about the Japanese fighter plane, the Mitsubishi Zero, or Zeke—some of them true, some exaggerated—about its super speed (almost fifty miles per hour faster at combat altitude than the Wildcat) and advanced maneuverability. The Zekes turned much sharper and climbed significantly faster than anything we could throw up against them. It was also true, though, that the Zeros were less armored and more prone to exploding if they were hit. Their two slow-firing cannon of low muzzle velocity and two .29 caliber machine guns did not compare to our Wildcats with their six .50 caliber guns.

While we lacked the combat experience the Japanese had gained since their invasion of China, we had been well trained in fighter tactics and believed we were better pilots. We knew our Wildcats well and had a lot of confidence in them. Most of all we were fighting mad over Pearl Harbor and couldn't wait to get revenge. We were ready to take on the Zeros or anything else the Japs wanted to throw at us.

We also heard that progress by the American forces on Guadalcanal was slow and costly, in terms of equipment and supplies and lives lost. When the Marines had landed on August 7, following the Navy's effective shelling of the enemy airfield and installations along the coast, the Japanese had nearly finished construction of the airfield at the northern tip of the island. After our invasion, our seabees completed the job in only two weeks. However, for those two weeks the Marines had to survive without any land-based air support. They had the airfield, but the Japanese had the rest of the island.

As we gathered around the campfire after supper, the mood would sometimes turn somber and fearful. Occasionally all conversation just stopped and the men sat staring into the flames. I knew what they were thinking, and that was my cue to launch into a story and try to snap them out of it. One topic that was always good was hunting season. Back home the first of October meant the opening of duck and goose season, and all of us talked about the good times we'd had hunting. Just thinking about it made us homesick. Nobody complained much, though, because we knew that soon it would be open season on Zeros.

On October 6 we were ordered aboard the carrier *Long Island,* which headed northwest toward the Solomons. We were on our way at last, edging into the hot zone.

The first morning we were up at 4:20, on alert, waiting for

Zeros to show up, but they never came. This was a letdown, because we were itching to go after the enemy.

On the second day we were up at 4:20 again. This time the radar picked up a "bogey"—an unidentified airplane blip on the screen—and had the whole ship preparing for combat. Moments later it was identified as an American reconnaissance plane.

As we steamed closer and closer to Guadalcanal, everybody got quieter and quieter. We played cards without seeing the spots and listened to the phonograph without hearing the music. There was only one thing on our minds.

Finally on the third morning we were told to pack our bags. We were taking off. They had planned to take us closer to the island, but half a dozen Japanese submarines had been sighted in the area, and the skipper decided it would be better to launch our planes early rather than risk losing them if the carrier took a hit.

On deck the Wildcats' wings, folded back in transport position, were being unfolded. Each plane had been checked for any possible mechanical flaw and cleaned inside and out. Dirt on the outside surface might slow the plane down the fraction of a knot that could make the difference between life and death. Loose dirt on the inside of the aircraft could lodge in a pilot's eye at a critical moment and lead to disaster. The Wildcats were painted dark blue on top to match the color of the sea and light grayish blue on the bottom to match the sky, camouflaged from either direction.

After checking out the tires, gas cap, and guns, I climbed into the cockpit, strapped myself in, and looked out across the flight deck crammed with tightly packed Wildcats. Our Pratt and Whitney engines required a shotgun shell-like starter, inserted into the engine and triggered by the pilot, creating an explosion that fired the engine. The blast of starters followed by the roar of engines created a thunderous din on deck. Exhaust fumes filled the air with a haze of blue-gray smoke that was almost intoxicating in our incredibly charged-up state.

When the carrier had turned into the wind and reached full speed, we were pushed into launch position, one by one. The plane ahead of me was piloted by a guy from Chicago named Bob Simpson, and the catapult hook broke during his launch.

His plane skidded overboard, and Simpson had to climb out of the cockpit and run across the wing of his sinking plane. The Navy photographers captured it all on film, and Simpson's narrow escape has been seen over and over again in still pictures and war movies ever since.

Then it was my turn. Once I was in the air I banked slightly, looked back at the receding carrier with its short, flat deck ruled off like a Ping-Pong table, and then began climbing in a counterclockwise pattern until I had caught up with the rest of my flight. They had been circling until we were all joined in formation. The skipper had already moved off with his group, and we followed.

In a little over three hours, the island of Guadalcanal appeared on the horizon. Shaped like a fat letter S about seventy-five miles long, it looked like a jungle paradise. Surf foamed along its jagged coastline beaches. Ringing the island was brilliant light blue water, while further out it shaded to a deep, dark blue. I could see coconut palms waving peacefully in the ocean breeze and even spotted some cows grazing in a green meadow. The whole thing looked like one of those tropical islands in a Dorothy Lamour picture, only Dorothy wasn't there. Close up, I could understand why.

As we circled and peeled off for our approach to Henderson Field, the scenery changed quickly. The landing field was little more than a dirt strip carved out of the dense jungle. Pockmarks were evident everywhere, the result of Japanese bombings and shellings. Just before touching down, I caught glimpses of foxholes and trenches laced together, and off to the side of the runway I spotted an airplane parking area. Even in a swift glance I could tell that most of the planes were heavily damaged.

I set down on the runway, oblivious to the screeches and puffs of white smoke as my speeding plane's rubber tires contacted the steel marston matting, then taxied across the field—dirt covered with thick, perforated metal sheets that cut the weight of the heavy planes so they wouldn't sink into the ground when the rains turned the dirt to mud.

As soon as we stopped, bearded men in worn and faded fatigues swarmed out of the dense foliage cheering enthusiastically. Antiaircraft gunners, bomber and scout bomber

crews, torpedo bombers—everything but fighters.[1] This rough
and rugged bunch climbed onto the wings of our planes, helping us out of the cockpits. They looked like they were ready
to kiss us.

Like all newcomers, we felt we were prepared for whatever
the enemy had in store for us, and this enthusiastic reception
only buoyed our self-confidence. It didn't take long for someone to knock a notch out of our cockiness, and our come-
uppance came from none other than Major John Lucien
Smith, one of the most famous aces of the day. He would be
credited with nineteen victories during his seven weeks on
Guadalcanal.

Major Smith drove out in a jeep to greet us, and he
promptly and sarcastically informed us that we had landed in
the wrong place. We had come in on the bomber runway
rather than the coral fighter strip about three quarters of a
mile away. "Smitty" obviously enjoyed putting us in our
place.

After we had sheepishly taxied our planes over to the "cow
pasture," also known as Fighter One, we finally met the veteran pilots of VMF-223, who began warning us about what
to expect: grim land fighting all around, nerve-shattering daily
air raids, shellings from Japanese battleships, artillery, sniper
fire, and dogfights. Supplies and aircraft replacement parts
were scarce. Weary ground crews worked miracles just to
keep the planes in the air. "Cactus" was the code name for
Guadalcanal, and this was what it meant to be part of the
"Cactus Air Force."

Their no-holds-barred indoctrination did not deter me. I
was champing at the bit for excitement. The circus was about
to begin.

---

[1] Fighter squadrons were designated with the letters VMF: V
meaning heavier than air; M meaning Marine; and F meaning fighter.
There were also Marine scout bombing squadrons (VMSB), pursuit
squadrons, scouting squadrons (VS), fighting squadrons (VF), torpedo squadrons (VT), bombing squadrons (VB).

Chapter 8
Henderson Field

The island of Guadalcanal was a rude shock for a guy from the plains of South Dakota. Graceful flying fish skimmed the turquoise coastal waters, and man-eating sharks infested the coral reefs below. Rushing streams zigzagged through the jungle floor of the island. Sleepy crocodiles sunned themselves on muddy riverbanks, while brightly colored birds of every species fluttered among the branches. It was a tropic paradise plunged into war.

Since we landed on the island right after a bombing raid, however, it looked more like what the Australians called it —"a bloody stinking hole." We also arrived during the rainy season, which lasted from November to March. Actually there were only two seasons: wet, hot, and steamy, and wetter, hotter, and steamier. Between the rain and the humidity nothing ever dried out, including us. I'd never seen so much rain and mud in my life.

A writer for *Life* magazine would extol, "Guadalcanal is an exciting place . . . botanically, meteorologically and zoologically speaking. . . . There are butterflies the size of birds and spiders that spin webs as thick as chewing gum."[1] All I knew was that there were mosquitoes as thick as termites in a woodpile. I'm allergic to mosquito bites anyway, and these

---

[1] John Field, *Life*, 7 June 1943.

buggers were the sticking kind. They'd swarm over your face
so thick you had to wipe them off, and before you were done,
they'd be covering the other side of your face. I think they
even got hooked on the repellent we used.

Two battles were raging over Guadalcanal when we arrived:
one between American and Japanese troops, and the other
between forces within the American military who disagreed
fiercely over the wisdom of supporting the Guadalcanal campaign. While some wanted to strengthen our position, others
wanted to pull out entirely. Those of us doing the fighting
were caught in the middle, poorly equipped and often confused by the actions of our superiors.

Scavenged from divisions all over the Pacific, the men on
Guadalcanal were mostly a mixture of experienced misfits—
career soldiers with little hope of promotion—and raw recruits. So far, despite inferior equipment and support, they
had held their ground and beaten the odds, surprising both
Japanese and Americans. Salty veterans provided the sea-
soning the untested soldiers needed and gave them a sense
of Marine tradition and honor that couldn't be taught in boot
camp. But it became increasingly clear that they could not
endure without reinforced air power. The first wave of pilots
and planes to follow the infantry landing had suffered high
losses, and rapid reinforcements were needed if the ground
forces were to survive.

There was no consensus, however, that such reinforcements
should be sent. From the beginning, Vice Admiral Robert L.
Ghormley, chosen to execute the campaign, considered holding Guadalcanal a futile impossibility, and circumstances combined to complicate the already poorly planned effort.

In Wellington, New Zealand, the longshoremen's union
went on strike just before the campaign began; they refused
to load materials needed for the front, leaving soldiers with
only days of ammunition. When the food they carried in their
ration packs ran out, the men were forced to subsist on anything they could raid from the Japanese positions they captured. Elsewhere, sixty U.S. Merchant Marine vessels, on the
advice of their union, refused to deliver supplies and ammunition without an impossibly extravagant hazard bonus,

although they were already earning more than those who were actually targets of the Japanese attacks.

Available pilots and planes in other Pacific regions were held back from Guadalcanal by commanders who would not give up their forces to what they considered a suicide mission. Eventually, many historians would accuse at least one admiral of desertion in the face of battle for the cavalier failure to support the Marines on the beleaguered island.

The Yanks on Guadalcanal were hard-pressed to decide who we resented more, the unions or our own brass. We did agree that we hated the Japanese most of all and were willing to pay the price to win if we could get the air support we needed. Our precarious situation inspired numerous songs and poems, recited and sung wherever Marines gathered to swap scuttlebutt. One raunchy ballad began, "Say a prayer for your pal on Guadalcanal."

The men of VMF-223, the fighter squadron we were replacing, had been on Guadalcanal for six weeks, hanging on to Henderson Field and fighting the Japanese for control of the rest of the island. Many of the men were sick with malaria and trembling with exhaustion, and I wanted to let these guys know how much I appreciated them for proving that American pilots could hold out against greatly superior Japanese odds. I also wanted to pick up any tips they could give, so I talked to as many as possible as they prepared to leave. I was particularly impressed by Major John Smith and Captain Marion Carl. Smith and Carl, along with Major Robert Galer, had been labeled "The Three Flying Fools of Guadalcanal." All told, the three of them shot down forty-six Japanese planes and were decorated by Admiral Nimitz, Commander of the Pacific Fleet.

The enemy believed they could take the island back from the Allies like a piece of cake and move on to Australia and New Zealand. These guys had stopped them cold, and now it was our turn.

One of the first men I met after I landed on Guadalcanal was First Lieutenant Ben Finney, a Marine I'd gotten acquainted with shortly before we shipped out for the South Pacific. Outside of the skipper, Finney, already in his forties, was the only officer in the squadron older than I was, and we hit it off immediately. I'd already made something of a reputation for myself as a joker and raconteur, but I was an amateur compared to old Finney. Seeing his mug among the palms was a welcome sight.

Finney was descended from an old and once wealthy aristocratic Southern family whose ancestors had emigrated from Ireland. Ben used to joke that he came from the wrong part of two countries: the north of Ireland and the south of the United States. Some said he'd managed to go through life without working a day. Actually he just made work look like play. He'd been an actor, a film producer, a screenwriter, and a skillful investor and entrepreneur. A veteran of World War I, where he had served in France, Finney had later returned and almost singlehandedly turned the Riviera into "the" place to be. His closest friends included F. Scott and Zelda Fitzgerald, Ernest Hemingway, Harpo Marx, Alexander Woolcott, Noël Coward, Cole Porter, William Powell, Ronald Coleman, and Charlie MacArthur. He hobnobbed with bootleggers, movie stars, politicians, royalty, and practically anybody else who was part of the "lost generation." Finney managed to spend much of his life on the most luxurious private yachts in the world, attested to years later in his autobiography, *Feet First.*[2]

Soon after Pearl Harbor, Ben interrupted his society lifestyle to reenlist in the Marines. This was not easy, since he'd been given a Purple Heart and a disability discharge in 1919. In his own words, he "began to feel that the Corps took a dim view of taking on a 'retread.' " But nothing deterred old Finney, and through some rather bizarre circumstances he ended up being ordered to Guadalcanal as a ground installation officer for our unit, where he found himself in the middle of some of the most torrid action of the war.

Finney didn't know what a ground installation job was, but he did his best. He always said, "I was moved from a job I knew little about to one that I knew nothing about."

Finney was an anachronism. Besides being a veteran of the

[2] Ben Finney, *Feet First,* foreword by John O'Hara (New York: Crown Publishers, 1971).

last war, he always looked like he was going to lunch in Beverly Hills—a decided contrast to his bearded, scruffy compatriots. The skipper didn't know what to do with this debonair, middle-aged, nonflying officer who'd been assigned to our unit.

"Well, I do need a ground installation officer," Duke finally said. "You're in charge of everything from security to where we put the tents."

That would turn out to be one of the best decisions the skipper ever made.

Approximately ten ground Marines were required to keep

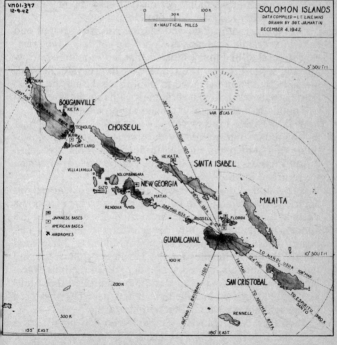

My hunting grounds from October 9, 1942 to January 6, 1943.
(Map courtesy of U.S. Navy)

each pilot in the air, so our squadron numbered well over four hundred when we were fully operational. A dive bomber outfit had arrived on Guadalcanal the same day we did, commanded by Eddy Miller, my former instruments instructor from Pensacola. Both squadrons were assigned living areas in a palm grove jungle between the landing strip and the beach. A few yards away was the latrine—a shallow trench with a log slung over it. The bathtub was the Lunga River, complete with an endless supply of running water and an occasional crocodile audience.

Miller's unit quickly set up their tents, stowed their gear, and went walking about, checking the area and gabbing with the veterans, but we didn't get off that easy. Finney put us to work digging foxholes near our tents.

Due to alternating rain and blazing sun, the ground had baked to ceramic hardness, and once we got below the crust, we hit coral. But Finney insisted that we shouldn't burrow into the softer ground. If dirt was easy to excavate, he said, it was because water tended to pool there during the rains. During an attack, a foxhole brimming with rainwater and mud was about as much use as a second tail on a tomcat.

While we slaved and sweltered away in the suffocating heat and humidity, interrupted by the frequent torrential downpours that sent rivers running through our tents, we heard lots of smartass comments from the bomber squadron, which we returned in kind.

By the end of the day we were all physically exhausted but emotionally exhilarated to be in the center of the action. As daylight faded we could hear the mortars and small arms fire announcing that the nightly struggle for the perimeter had begun. The vets had warned us about "Millimeter Mike" and "Pistol Pete," nicknames for the Japanese artillery fire and the enemy gunners located somewhere up in the hills above Henderson Field. At the moment they controlled those hills and could lob a shell into the base at any time. They pestered the airfield nightly with rocket and mortar fire.

Then there was "Maytag Charlie," who flew nightly raids over the field in a plane with unsynchronized twin-engine props that made a peculiar grating sound like an old gas-engine washing machine. Probably more than one pilot flew this nightly nuisance mission and possibly more than one air-craft, but to us he became one and the same. Usually Charlie made one pass over the field, dropping bottles that whistled like bombs. Just to make it interesting and keep us awake, however, he occasionally lobbed the real thing blindly into our dark camp, and he did score some direct hits.

We quickly learned that a whistle meant an incoming bomb or shell, which meant you jumped for cover, and even then you weren't entirely safe. Not long after we arrived I was standing talking with four other Marines when the familiar descending whistle sounded—the whistle dropped in pitch as the bomb or shell doppler shifted toward you. There were two bomb craters nearby, so I jumped into one with another soldier, and the other three men leaped into the other one. When the deafening explosion passed, and with ears still ring-ing, I crawled out of the pit and looked for the other Marines. The shell had scored a direct hit on their foxhole and cut the heads off all three.

Throughout most of my first night on Guadalcanal shells streamed above our tents in both directions as Japanese ships in the channel targeted our artillerymen on the island, who returned the fire. Twice we had to hit our foxholes—the ones Finney had driven us so hard to finish that first day. The veterans of the island struggle, who enjoyed their sardonic one-upmanship, assured us that the night's shelling was "light."

I was up at 4:00 the next morning, but didn't make my first combat mission until that afternoon, flying escort for dive bombers on a run up "the slot." The Solomon Islands, of which Guadalcanal is a part, are an archipelago that stretches over four hundred miles in a generally straight line northwest from San Cristobal at the bottom to Bougainville at the top. Running through the middle of the chain of islands is a long, thin trench of ocean we called "the slot," down which the Japanese attacking forces came with bitter regularity. My eight-plane flight flew high cover that first day and kept a sharp lookout for Zeros. We didn't spot any, but the bombers located a Japanese destroyer and scored a direct hit, sending a mushrooming explosion of fire and smoke high into the sky.

The next day, October 11, we scrambled to intercept

twenty-eight Japanese bombers and twenty-one Zeros that were rapidly approaching Henderson Field from their base on Bougainville Island, to the northwest. These attacks, I would soon learn, were an almost daily routine. For some reason, this time the enemy miscalculated and dropped their bombs two miles behind their own lines, probably killing many of their own infantrymen. They turned and headed back to their base, but not before our squadron downed two bombers and one Zero. The dogfight ended almost as quickly as it had started, and I didn't get close enough to fire a single shot.

That night there was a terrific naval engagement off Cape Esperance at the northwest hump of the island. Sleep was impossible. By morning heavy oil and debris covered the surf while the Navy picked up swimming sailors—Americans and Japanese. The light cruiser *Boise,* armed with only small six-inch guns, had sunk six enemy ships in only thirty minutes, earning itself the title of "The One Ship Navy." The Japs lost two heavy cruisers, one light cruiser, and three destroyers. We lost one destroyer and 107 officers and men from the *Boise*. Despite their heavy casualties, the Japanese did succeed in landing thousands of troops on the island.

The third morning, October 12, we took off before dawn, heading up the slot, again escorting dive bombers going in to chase off Japanese ships still in the area following the previous night's battle. Just off the coast of New Georgia we spotted two Japanese destroyers. My flight went in first to divert the antiaircraft fire away from our torpedo planes, and our attacking bombers scored a square hit on one of the destroyers and sank a cruiser. We returned to Henderson without a scratch.

After a relatively quiet night when we actually got some sleep, we returned to the air to intercept twenty-two approaching enemy bombers, but they changed course and we never fired a shot. A scant two hours later we got the call, "Eighteen bombers headed yours," which meant a second flight of eighteen enemy bombers had been sighted on a direct course toward Henderson Field.

We scrambled and climbed high and to the left of the big bombers and spotted six Zero escorts off to the right. I led my men along the edge of some clouds, hoping the Zekes would not see us. The old adrenaline was pumping now, as I sensed the real thing closing in. I just wanted one good shot at a Zero. Just give me one.

Suddenly I spotted my wingman, Greg Loesch, in close, waving urgently and pointing upward.

I smiled and waved acknowledgment. "I've already seen them," I yelled. In my excitement I didn't notice that my radio wasn't working.

Just then Loesch dived out of formation. I looked around and saw that all my men had scattered. Then a shower of fiery tracers sprayed over my head.

Hell. Loesch hadn't been waving with excitement. He'd been trying to warn me. At that moment a crazy little jingle raced through my head:

> *Zero and me,*
> *Down in the sea,*
> *You really should flee!*

That bird came by like a freight train and gave me a good sprinkling, but I knew I had him. I pulled up and gave him a short burst, and down he went. *Glad to get rid of that one!* I thought. *That's one less Zero we have to worry about.*

I felt charged with electricity—my hair standing on end and my mouth dry as cotton. I'd just gotten my first Zero. Straining against my lap belt to stand as erect as possible in the cramped cockpit, I yelled a victory war whoop at the top of my lungs.

Busy celebrating, I failed to see the three Zekes lining up on me—until I found myself in the midst of streaming tracers.

"Got to head out of here, fast!" I said aloud. I jammed the stick forward and went into a screaming dive from 22,000 feet. I'd read that a Zero couldn't follow such a dive; its wings would come off trying to pull out. Well, whoever wrote that was a fiction writer, because those boys just kept on my tail, pumping lead!

Two shells entered my fuselage. Dark, smoky oil spewed out the right oil cooler. With its lubrication pouring into the air, the high-speed engine froze almost instantly. Clouds of smoke replaced oil, pierced by tracers from the three planes on my tail.

When the engine seized, the reduction gear between the propeller and the engine was wrenched off and the prop became a free agent, causing extreme vibrations. Between the wind shrieking through the holes in the canopy and the rotating prop with its ruined connections, the noise level was deafening. And if that wasn't enough to get my attention, through the side of the canopy I stared wide-eyed at a gaping hole in my wing where a 20 mm cannon shell had exploded. I could see the ocean through it.

In an almost vertical dive, picking up airspeed rapidly, violent vibrations set in, and sharp pressure and pain began to build in my ears. I knew other pilots in the same situation had suffered burst and hemorrhaged eardrums. Mine held, but it was a wild ride.

When the earth took up most of my field of vision, I pulled back on the stick with all my strength, hoping the tail assembly was still functional, and leveled out just over the ground. Streaking dead stick just above the trees, I headed for the field, at the same time worrying about keeping as much distance as possible between myself and the closing Zeros.

It was just about then I asked myself, *Why did I ever leave the farm? Sitting on a plow, staring at a horse's tail, is a whole lot safer than this!*

By now I was only 150 feet off the ground, my pursuers hot on me, still sending sizzling streamers in my direction. I was coming in much too fast—150 knots when 90 was considered the maximum for a safe landing—but if I slowed down they'd blast me out of the sky. The piercing, penetrating racket increased, and the vibrations were unbelievable. The vacuum flaps designed to slow the plane refused to deploy at 150 knots. Only the landing gear that I had dropped was slowing me down.

In a desperate attempt to line up with the runway, I sideslipped the Wildcat. It set down, hitting hard, but kept upright. I managed to turn forty-five degrees into the palm grove and was fortunate enough to go bumping down the only row between the palm trees that was clear of barrels or trenches.

When I finally came to a stop, I just sat there thinking, *The score is tied—I'm ready to be a farmer again.*

The antiaircraft batteries surrounding the field did a good job of chasing away my pursuers, and the next thing I knew, an ambulance with red lights flashing and siren screaming was racing to the scene.

I climbed out of my plane, flustered, embarrassed, and mad as hops. I'd bagged my first Zero, but I'd also made a boob of myself, which almost cost me my life. My bad mood didn't last long though. When the rest of the squadron got down, the young bucks swarmed around yelling congratulations and beating me on the back.

"Congratulations, skipper!"

"Boy, you got one of the sonsabitches."

They went on and on, looking up to the old man, and that charged my battery up again. The further I got from the actual fight, the more I was thinking, *Boy, I really am good.*

Actually, though, I learned two important lessons that day. I had been indelibly reminded that I had to stay alert to stay alive, and no one ever caught me asleep at the switch again or so intent on an attack that I failed to keep looking around. In fact, from then on I looked around so much that the guys soon started calling me "Swivel-neck Joe."

The second lesson was a result of what happened to Lieutenant Bill Freeman, a drawling engineer from Bonham, Texas. Separated from Duke Davis's flight, Bill had dived alone into a V formation of bombers and shot down the leader, which made him an easy target for every side gunner in the group. Fortunately he squeezed through without being shot down and survived to share his rather obvious discovery: Always start an attack at the rear of a formation and move progressively forward.[3]

---

[3] In the 1943 book *Joe Foss, Flying Marine: The Story of His Flying Circus,* as told to Walter Simmons, much of the story of that day was omitted because it was written during wartime and subject to military censors. Though I was straightforward about my disappointments and failures, the powers that be made sure my experiences were painted in a manner more conducive to recruitment efforts. The censors also objected, of course, to the publication of any exact dates or names

That night, huddled in the meager shelter of a shallow, muddy foxhole, bombarded by enemy fire, all I could think about was the plane I'd shot down, its pilot, and the war. *Why was I here and what was I doing?* After all my eagerness to enter the fray, I had suddenly experienced the real thing. I'd killed and almost been killed.

Suddenly I wasn't so sure about this war business. Then I thought about the attack on Pearl Harbor, and I got upset all over again. The Japanese were our enemies, and they had some ideas I didn't like. They wanted to do away with our great country, and I liked America. And that's when I finally realized, for real, that if I didn't do my part in the war, I wouldn't have a farm to go back to.

After that first night I never again thought about putting my tail between my legs and running back to the farm. I was where I was supposed to be, come what may, and I accepted it.

of harbors and ships that might be useful to Japanese intelligence. An astute reader could find areas of the book that don't flow together well, as if whole sections had been deleted just before the book went to press—which was exactly what happened.

Chapter 9
Fill'er Up
with High Test
✯ ✯ ✯

Finney was telling stories, the thing he did best. I don't remember exactly which one he regaled us with that time. It could have been about fishing for marlin with Ernest Hemingway off Cuba's Morro Castle, or about Izzy and Moe, two born comedians who, as prohibition agents, "poured out enough beer to float the Atlantic fleet," or perhaps it was his duck hunting adventures on the Whangpoo River below Shanghai. Whatever the story, his punchlines were punctuated by occasional bursts from mortars and machine guns.

We were under a blackout order, stretched out on our cots under our mosquito netting inside the tent we shared with the skipper and Soupy Campbell, a Marine major from another squadron. I couldn't even smoke a cigar, since the slightest flicker of light might aid a sniper or bomber in aiming into the camp. Then, about a half hour before midnight, all hell broke loose.

Moving shadows appeared on the tent canvas, backlit by a bright and burning sky, forecasting a naval shelling. The burning brightness came from star shells floating down over the airfield, further lighted by our spotlights that turned the night into day. Star shells were powerful flares the Japanese attached to parachutes and dropped from a bomber.

I was pulling on my khaki pants and stuffing my feet into my boots when I heard the shrill, descending whistle. Without even buttoning my shirt, I grabbed my helmet, ran outside, and jumped into one of the eighteen-inch-high foxholes we'd dug next to the tent. The skipper was already there. The ground shook as thunder and lightning issued from ground level only hundreds of feet away. Seconds later debris showered down on us.

Armor-piercing rounds blew out craters big enough to bury a jeep, while the explosive shells sent shrapnel shooting horizontally for yards. One shell fell in the midst of some captured Japanese gasoline drums about a hundred yards from our position and set off a chain of explosions as stacks of gas barrels heated and blew. The barrage also hit the munitions dump, where our scarce and precious ammunition was stored, showering everything with a fireworks display of multicolored flashes and streamers.

The worst of the shelling lasted from one to three o'clock in the morning, as over nine hundred shells landed on the island, mostly on and around the airfield and the palm grove where our quarters were located. Droning Japanese bombers circled the field endlessly. Offshore a flotilla of Japanese ships poured their munitions and their fourteen- and sixteen-inch shells on the field.

For minutes at a time the roar of explosives was so loud and the pain in my ears so intense that I could do nothing but hold my hands over my ears and cringe. Screams pierced the air when someone was hit. Those two hours were indescribable. Unless you've been through it, you just can't imagine what it's like. And the rest of the night wasn't much better. Large bombs made more noise, but the smaller antipersonnel bombs sent ragged metal out in all directions. Shrapnel whizzed over our heads, sometimes cutting deep gashes into the earth beside us or tearing tents from the ground.

The skipper and I stayed in the foxhole all night, covered by dust, sweat, and mosquitoes. At one point I found myself unconsciously humming a Dorsey brothers tune in time to the explosions, drumming my fingers on Davis's helmet. Finally he could stand it no longer.

"For God's sake, stop that!" he snarled. "It makes me nervous!"

When the ear-ringing barrage on Henderson Field finally

ceased, the screams and sobs we heard were even more terrible.

The dive bomber outfit across the road had neglected to provide themselves with adequate foxholes in which to hide, and they had been ravaged by the deadly shards of metal that filled the air during the bombardment. Dozens died, including two of my buddies from Pensacola and a camp doctor. Ben Finney's insistence on digging foxholes for our squadron had saved VMF-121 from the same fate.

As soon as it was clear that the bombardment had really stopped, we climbed out and stared disbelievingly at the devastation. Henderson Field was a shambles.

Lieutenant Simpson, a fellow from Chicago, began shouting furious and colorful curses at the enemy. He had hung his laundry on an old rope the day before, and jagged shrapnel had gone straight through his entire wardrobe, leaving only shredded rags.

The mechanics and metalsmiths rigged lights and went to work immediately, rebuilding whole planes out of the pieces of the ruined ones. Since our main fuel dump had been hit and destroyed, others set out searching for gasoline.

Finney was as innovative as ever. Fearing that Japanese observers would report the success of their attack and incite an instant return to finish the job, Ben gathered anybody who wasn't needed elsewhere and began building a paper air force at the end of the runway. Using bits and pieces of the wrecks, cardboard from cargo boxes, and bamboo salvaged from the sheds built by the Japanese laborers who had started the airfield, he engineered the construction of rows of mock airplanes before the sun came up. No way were the Japanese going to learn how helpless we were to resist another attack.

The first alert sounded before we could even grab a running breakfast. Hordes of Zeros were on their way. There was only one problem. Only seven of our squadron's Wildcats were in condition to fly. The skipper pulled rank to command the first mission.

A swarm of Zeros screamed out of the clouds before the guys were away from the ground, trying to destroy them before they could take off. All seven escaped to engage the enemy only hundreds of feet up. This kind of action would prove the norm, not the exception during that time at Henderson.

Unlike the other arenas of the air, much of the battle for Guadalcanal took place over the airfield. In other air battles, the claims of pilots and their kill records were sometimes questionable simply because dogfights were too intense for accurate accounting when you were in the midst of them, and there were usually no unengaged observers to keep the tally. Kills were verified by others or by gun camera when it worked. Pilots flying a mission would sometimes be unable to stay on target long enough to know whether smoke meant the plane was going down, because they would have to cut over to another target. On Guadalcanal, however, a high percentage of the action was within sight of the field. Time after time, spectators on the ground with field glasses and telescopes kept the score. It was great for the morale of all the troops.

The lethal effectiveness of our remaining planes, combined with Finney's decoy air force, apparently convinced the Imperial strategists that their night-long attack had been less successful than they thought. They couldn't have been more wrong. A determined, continued pounding could have ended our control of Henderson Field that very day.

Meanwhile, the mechanics and "tin peckers," as I nick-named the metalsmiths, frantically patched the rest of our planes together as best they could, cannibalizing from those that would never fly again; they even checked Japanese aircraft shot down over the field for usable parts. Normally the support crews made the most of every daylight hour and even beyond when it was safe to use lights. After the destruction of that night's bombing they pushed even harder. Without their determination, stamina, and ingenuity, we would have been lost.

Besides an extraordinary array of birds, animals, and reptiles, the jungle also concealed Nipponese marksmen who would try to crawl past our lines to shoot into the base. Officially the mechs and other support personnel were not supposed to go after snipers, but they were on the island to win the war, not comply with official, sometimes unrealistic, policies.

That morning of October 14, I was standing around watching the ground crew reassemble my plane, trying to give them at least my verbal encouragement, when the crack of a carbine broke the air. I ducked my head instinctively and watched the ground crews jump into trenches and foxholes as the round struck home in the mechanics' area. Before anyone could send for regular infantry support, an angry young mechanic from Tennessee cocked his pistol and ran into the jungle. Apparently he was an experienced hunter and tracker, because it wasn't long before we heard another shot, and in a few minutes our boy returned carrying a Japanese rifle. He had picked the sharpshooter right out of a tree behind Operations, the strategic command and communication center of Henderson Field.

Fortunately for us the Japanese were not as skilled with small arms as the Americans or the Australians. Their relative incompetence as sharpshooters probably stemmed from their culture's historic restrictions on civilian gun ownership. Marksmanship in intense, real-life situations cannot be learned properly in the mere months of standard military training. It comes from years of familiarity with firearms.

Every man, from ordnance to medic, was overworked, but we were doing more than fighting for our country; we were fighting for our lives. During every spare moment, men dug their foxholes deeper than ever before, lining them with sandbags and covering them with metal plating salvaged from wrecked planes. The dirt was really flying.

Nearly all our fuel dumps, which had already been scarce at best, had been destroyed. Without fuel, we were powerless to protect our own airspace, and the coastwatchers reported a major Japanese convoy heading our way. Major General Vandegrift, in charge of the Allied forces on the island, sent out pleas for gasoline, and we started scrounging for every fluid ounce in Allied controlled territory, including the tanks of wrecked enemy planes.

We established a large gasoline holding tank away from the field up a jungle hill where it was hoped artillery and bombs would be least likely to fall. Every can of siphoned fuel and a few scarce fifty-gallon drums were emptied into the tank. The Marines hired natives from Guadalcanal, Florida Island, and Malaita to carry and roll the metal gas drums up the hill and drain them into the tank hidden under the palm trees and camouflage netting.

Midmorning on the day after the bombing of Henderson, coastwatchers sighted an armada of Betty bombers coming down the slot. Our planes had been repaired, so I scrambled my flight and headed into the clouds. In some ways I felt I was mounting the horse that had just thrown and trampled me. The preceding twenty-four hours, with the all-but-calamitous duel that had almost dropped me end up on the runway, followed by the horrendous all-night fusillade, had shaken my confidence. It's been said that all young men believe they are immortal. By that standard, at least, I was no longer a young man.

Fear churned in my stomach as we rose above the lowest cloud layer and caught sight of the bomber escort—several dozen Zeroes. One day earlier I hadn't known firsthand what I was getting into when I faced the emperor's best. Today I knew too well what was coming at me. But along with some genuine dread, the old adrenal started pumping, sending me eagerly out for the hunt and vengeance.

Suddenly my engine coughed, and for a brief moment the power faltered. It kicked back in again and I returned my attention to the sky. Once more the powerful Pratt and Whitney engine barked and stalled. I pulled back on the throttle and dropped a few yards in altitude. Again the power revived and I returned to elevation. I shoved the stick forward and the engine revved, only to die. Slamming my left fist into my thigh and gritting my teeth in angry frustration, I tried several more times to get power from the stuttering engine.

Finally I had to fish or cut bait. "I've got engine problems," I radioed Loesch. "Take over."

The bombers were already dropping their freight; I could see flowers of smoke blossoming on the runway far below. Stuck between the battle and the base, I headed for the shelter of an immense cloud over the mountains. Much as I hated to do it, I had to hide while I nursed my ailing machine and waited for the bombing to cease. Like a wounded shark just below the surface, I circled the inside edge of the cloud, helpless, watching the struggle through the thin borders of mist. This sense of helplessness did nothing for my rattled confidence. Slower and less maneuverable than the Zero even when performing optimally, my wounded Wildcat would be easy prey if spotted. In a word, I was scared.

Hollywood has fostered the fable that dogfights are extended affairs affording pilots plenty of time to discuss political philosophies and shake their fists at one another. Well, you can haul all that away in the honey wagon. Dogfights are normally over in a matter of seconds. If you blink, you could miss the fight. If you blink during the fight, you could die. That, in fact, is the trick to aerial combat. There is virtually no time to think about acting or reacting. The impulse and the act must be one. Skilled fighter pilots have one thing in common: They are fast. The airplane becomes an extension of your body, like an arm or a leg. If somebody's coming at you with a red-hot poker, you instinctively get out of the way. You don't have to think about it. You just do it. In the air, whoever acts smartest and fastest is going to be the survivor. As the Red Baron said, "It's not the crate, it's the man sitting in it." If it were not so, the Grumman Wildcat would have been a flying coffin.

Later in the war, planes under development in the United States, especially the P-51 Mustang, would give the technological edge to the Americans. On October 14, 1942, however, the only advantage the Cactus Air Force had was mental, and I knew it.

Then fate intervened. A Wildcat plunged, banked sharply to fly into the clouds that concealed me, and the Zero stuck to his tail turned directly in front of me, trying to line up his guns on my fleeing buddy before he jumped into the cloud. They were so close I was lucky they hadn't collided with me.

I nudged my right rudder delicately and pulled the trigger at precisely the right moment. Six guns functioned flawlessly and sent one of the Zero's wings soaring away from the rest of the plane. I never got an easier kill.

The battle in the sky was nearly over by now and the empty bombers were fleeing for their base in Rabaul. Returning to the field, I saw the Zeke I'd hit burning on a hill above Henderson.

Despite the downed Zero, I was angry and frustrated about the engine failure and stomped over to the maintenance tent. When they looked into the engine, they discovered that the carburetor was plugged. It wasn't the mechs' fault; it was dirty fuel.

Several others had experienced the same problem, which got me curious, and I started snooping around and asking questions. We determined that it had to be coming from the fuel storage tank on the hill, but we couldn't figure out how in tarnation any sediment was getting into it. A lot of the fuel was salvaged from various sources, but we'd strained the stuff carefully before we stored it.

Some dogged sleuthing finally solved the mystery, and the solution was indicative of the bizarre conditions on Guadalcanal. The ground where the barefoot natives rolled the gasoline drums up the mountain was packed hard. The heavy barrels had compressed the earth, which then soaked up the searing tropical sun, so that walking on it was like walking on an unshaded beach on a blistering hot day. Once they got the precious barrels up to the holding tank, the natives would take the stopper from the metal cask and pour the gasoline into a wooden trough leading to the tank. Then they'd dip their feet in the gas trough, and when the gasoline on their skin hit the air, the evaporation would cool their feet. When their feet got hot again, they'd stick them back in the trough, and the dirt and coral on the bottom of their feet would wash right down into the tank. That's what was gumming up our engines.

From that time on we strained all of the gasoline used in the airplanes, tanks, and trucks—especially the aviation fuel.

The Japanese convoy—a group of transports loaded with war materials and thousands of Japanese soldiers—steamed closer and closer as the day went on.

The number one Marine aviator on the island was General Geiger, a brave and gregarious man. He sent one of his aides, Colonel Toby Munn, over to the fighter strip to spread the word that the last fuel would be used in an attempt to stop the convoy. "After that," he said matter-of-factly, "you'll have to attach yourselves to one of the infantry divisions. Good-bye and good luck." Twice during that little speech, Munn had to kiss dust when artillery shells exploded close at hand.

After lunch a group of hastily patched dive bombers and torpedo planes were pronounced fit for combat, and it was decided that I would take a flight of Wildcats out to escort the SBDs. The SBD was the standard Marine and Navy dive bomber in the Pacific at the time, a comparatively slow plane that carried one powerful thousand-pound bomb.

We found the six troop transports skirting the edge of Santa Isabel, an island north and across the slot from Guadalcanal. They were traveling single file, approximately a hundred yards apart, with heavily armed destroyers on either side. We would make a strafing run to distract the antiaircraft gunners long enough for the dive bombers to get in close and drop their loads.

I quickly checked the surrounding sky, gestured for my men to follow, and veered over to start the run. Antiaircraft shells burst in deep black patterns as the gunners on the transports and destroyers split their fire between the dive bombers and our Wildcats, while we separated one at a time from formation to attack the transports.

Dodging flak, we worked our way forward from the rear, raking lead across the floating targets. The troops in the open transports were sitting ducks, but the AA gunners sacrificed the lives of individual soldiers on the transports to protect the entire convoy from the dive bombers. Failing to penetrate the thick flak, the bombers managed to sink only one transport before the attack was halted.

I had just enough fuel to get me back to the field, so after strafing the last transport, I raced away from the antiaircraft fire. Only then did I have time to check on the rest of my flight. One pilot was hit and bleeding but able to fly. Another, Lieutenant Paul Rutledge, a big easygoing guy, had crashed amid the convoy, where the gunners on deck took leisurely aim at him.

Then I looked over my shoulder and spotted Andy Andrews, a happy-go-lucky little daredevil from Liberty, Nebraska, headed back into the inferno, obviously determined to avenge Rutledge. The odds were bad enough when the enemy gunners had a dozen evasive targets. By himself, Andrew drew the focus of all their fire.

Andrews performed a wild exhibition of totally mad flying. Dropping down to sea level, he flew directly at the bow of the first transport firing all six of his guns across its deck. At the last minute he pulled up the Wildcat's nose, barely missing the top of the transport, and immediately dropped back down off the stern to fly straight at the next ship, guns blazing again.

Actually he was crazy like a fox. If gunners on either transport fired at him and missed, they'd hit their own ships. And if the destroyers shot, they could hit their own ships with the crossfire. Andrews repeated the maneuver until he'd raked all six transports twice.

Despite his bravery and derring-do, I really chewed him out when we got back to the field.

"Leave the heroics to Hollywood, Andrews," I snapped. "The Marine Corps has more in mind for you than a dramatic exit dying for your country."

Flamboyant mavericks might go down in a blaze of glory, but we needed men who would live to fight another day. It was teamwork and consistency day after day that won air wars. Besides, too many good fliers were dying in the natural course of battle without taking extra chances.

Back at Henderson the ground crew drained the gas tanks of two wrecked B-17s. That, combined with the last dregs of fuel in our Wildcats, would allow us one more attempt at the convoy. While the skipper took up the last flight, I waited nervously, hoping for either the arrival of a shipment of gasoline or word that the Japanese ships had been routed. Good news did not come. The second flight was beaten back by intense antiaircraft fire and Thompson, another airman from my squadron, was killed.

The mood in the ready tent, where pilots waited in vain for the order to scramble, was damp that evening. I'd been keeping a diary—something I did throughout my tour of duty—and that night my closing entry reported, "I'm deep in a foxhole for the night." The tension was as thick as the heat. With no gas for the surviving planes, we were now the sitting ducks.

Whenever the bombing eased enough for the mechanics and ground crews to leave their dugouts, they carried on a frenzied gasoline scavenger hunt all through the night. Many also foraged successfully for rifles to augment the .45 caliber pistols and six-inch blades they carried, convinced that the Cactus Air Force would soon become the Cactus Infantry. Some had already walked up the hill behind the strip, where the 7th Marines were holding back the Japanese, to determine where they would be most useful when the final ground assaults began.

The top-ranking officers huddled together, racking their brains for some solution to the fuel problem. Meanwhile the nightly barrage arrived with fervor at about 2:00 A.M., and within thirty minutes, over 750 eight-inch shells tumbled onto the bomber strip and Fighter One, the base for the Army, Navy, and Marine fighters, taking further toll of the Cactus Air Force. A naval battle in the slot partially distracted the warships from their usual target—us—but in the pandemonium of battle, at least 4,000 Japanese troops along with tanks and heavy artillery landed on Guadalcanal only ten miles from the airfield.

"A poor omen for the future," I wrote in my diary.

As the equatorial sun rose on October 15, one of General Geiger's aides was feverishly digging up buried treasure uncomfortably close to the perimeter of American controlled territory. Earlier, as the officers were chewing over our dilemma, the aide had suddenly recollected vague rumors of emergency fuel caches buried on the island during the original battle that had wrenched control of the airstrip from the Japanese. General Geiger ordered an immediate search.

As the day went on they unearthed over 450 barrels of fuel from half a dozen subterranean hoards—two days' supply of gasoline, if we scrambled only to meet larger aerial raids. In a bizarre plot twist, the general later discovered an unopened letter in one of his shirt pockets; it contained directions to the locations of the buried gasoline. Geiger, an accomplished and highly regarded general, simply hadn't had time to read his mail!

Chapter 10
Daily Life

✯ ✯ ✯

About the time they were pouring the first of the recovered fuel into our planes, someone yelled, "Five Zeros on the way!"

I strained my eyes to see the five enemy planes through a gap in the clouds. Flying single file several miles above the camp, they were much too high to be endangered by our antiaircraft batteries. When they were directly over the field, the leader of the Japanese flight banked leisurely to the left and the other four followed in precision, forming a counter-clockwise circle. *What in the blazes were they up to?* I wondered.

Though there were no other planes at their altitude, a trail of smoke appeared behind the first of the Zekes as if it had taken a shot in the fuel line. Then one by one the other planes began to spew tails of white smoke, like skywriters. A large broken circle slowly took shape above the field, and the Zeros dispersed as suddenly as they'd appeared. Only then did the word reach us that waves of Japanese bombers were headed for Henderson Field.

I realized at once what those guys had done. They'd painted a gigantic bull's-eye! When the bombardiers reached us, they'd just drop their payloads through the giant bombsight in the sky.

Although still concerned about our limited gas supply, I

scrambled fourteen F4F fliers to meet the bombers. We went up as fast as possible while maintaining the scissoring buddy system of the Flatley-Thach drill. As we ascended past breathable atmosphere I slipped on my mask and opened the oxygen valve to the right of my seat. These oxygen masks were a necessary nuisance. We had to have them above 10,000 feet, but they were made of hard white rubber and were very uncomfortable.

Though I had two Zeros on my scorecard, neither had resulted from the kind of test I felt proved my mettle. Was I finally going to confront the Imperial fighter pilots face-to-face?

Rising through the white frosting of the successive cloud strata, I finally broke through the top of a cloud band and found myself in a parking lot filled with twenty-eight bombers and sixty-four Zeros. The old adrenaline started pumping as I soared between the bombers and their Zero escort. Old Swivelneck lived up to his name. I snapped my head about constantly, checking every bit of sky, looking for the optimum point of attack; but the decision was snatched from me when eight hidden Zeros dove from their fleecy cover onto our formation. I saw them coming and warned the crew, "Bogeys at nine high. Comin' in fast!" even as I pushed my stick forward. We scattered for the dogfight, and I jerked my head around to watch the hounding Zekes over my shoulder. . . . Suddenly . . .

I was back in the living room in South Dakota, sitting in Pop's old comfortable chair beside the radio. Mother was mending a coat with needle and thread. Cliff and little sister were engrossed in the adventures of the Green Hornet. I struggled to hear the scratchy radio drama through the static. The old radio was fading out just when the story seemed to reach a peak. The actor was shouting something, but I couldn't make it out. Why didn't somebody adjust the knob? . . .

"Pull out! Pull out! Pull out!" I shook my head trying to figure out the drama, but my body wanted to float in cozy bewilderment.

"Pull out, Joe! Please! Pull out of it! Pull out!"

I fought to open my eyes, and a jungle mountain filled my vision.

"Pull out! Joe, pull out!" It was Greg Loesch, flying just off my wing and bellowing into his radio at the top of his lungs.

Heart pounding, I reached forward to grab the stick, pulled back, and the shaking plane began to level out. I was still headed into the mountainside, but I kept pressure on the stick until the plane nosed up and barely skimmed over the top of the mountain. Using the four hundred miles per hour velocity I had attained in the dive, far beyond the official limits of the Wildcat, I angled up and shot into the clouds with Loesch right behind me.

Still coming back to my senses, I noticed my oxygen mask coupling hanging loose across my shoulder and quickly hooked the hose back in place. Apparently while I was swiveling around to watch the enemy, the coupling had slipped out, cutting off my oxygen supply, and I'd passed out. Once my dive sent me down to the oxygen-rich lower altitude I'd recovered enough to hear Loesch's determined screaming and then regained consciousness before I hit the mountain. I was lucky. Hypoxia is no laughing matter. You just get goofy. We lost too many men that way.

Racing through the air, I angled up to rejoin the fight, but the deadly skirmish was over, so Loesch and I headed back to land.

In the meantime the tin peckers at the bomber strip had patched a handful of dive bombers from the wrecks, so the mechanics and ordnance men began refueling and arming our group as soon as we touched down and rolled to a stop. Twenty minutes later we were off again, escorting three of the SBDs in an attempt at five transports that had landed the night before and were still unloading supplies. Japanese transports came every few nights, using the area that extended northwest of Henderson up to Cape Esperance for the purpose of dropping off soldiers and supplies.

The dive bombers separated from our flight and flew low over the island, while I took my team in from the coastline and descended on the transports just offshore. The ships were no longer packed full of soldiers, but men were busy unloading the materials to be used in their assault on Henderson. A little farther out the guard dogs, eight destroyers, turned their

antiaircraft guns on us, the same AA fire that had claimed
Paul Rutledge the day before. The flak was so thick that the
air was black.

We returned fire, and the Japanese soldiers on the ground
took any available cover they could find behind drums and
machinery. Where our .50 caliber shells missed their targets
and hit the water, white water rings as large as wading pools
exploded outward. In a matter of minutes we had fired thousands of rounds into the transports and beach installations.

When the Japanese gunners were totally absorbed by our
attack, our dive bombers came in low over the mountains and
released their payloads onto the transports. They left two
ships burning as they fled the AA fire.

While we were pressing our attack, one of General Geiger's
top aides, Major Jack Cram, was having the mechanics con-
vert the general's personal transport plane, a relatively large
twin-engine PBY-5A amphibian, into a fighting machine. The
mechs rigged a harness under the wings for two torpedoes,
triggered by a manual wire release that ran to the cockpit.
The plane had practically no aerobatic capabilities and its
maximum cruising speed with its makeshift armaments was
well under a hundred miles an hour.

Cram had no experience with torpedoes, but he took a full
crew of five, including four gunners, and set out without escort
to join the attack on the transports. He sank one of the transports and, though his craft was seriously damaged, fled for
home.

I had just landed from my sortie when Cram appeared over
the fighter strip with four Zeros on his tail. The Wildcats who
were still in the air brought down three of them, but the
tenacious fourth followed Cram down onto the field.

Roger Haberman, who was tougher than whang leather
without a backward bone in his body, had just dropped his
landing gear and was setting his Wildcat down when he saw
Geiger's PBY with Cram at the stick coming in spouting oil
where the Zeros' bullets had pierced the engine. Haberman's
plane wasn't in much better condition. He had scores of punctures and was spreading smoke from the oil line, but without
bothering to crank up his gear, he pulled back on his stick
and went after the fourth Zero. On the second pass he put a

tracer into the Japanese plane's gas tank and the craft exploded in a ball of fire.

When Haberman set down and climbed out of his battered Grumman, the ground crew walked toward him applauding. Old Rog bowed and then bellowed a Tarzan victory cry that echoed across the field where the wreck was burning. It was his first Zero.

As Rog and I walked together to the dining tent to have breakfast, I congratulated him. Our day had just begun.

I had already established the habit of arriving at the dining tent before first light to drink cocoa and watch the activity on the field. Seeing everyone going at full bore, day or night, made me proud to be an American—the mechanics starting the engines and inspecting the planes, the ordnance men checking the guns and filling the ammunition pans. The amazing thing was that in the midst of going at full power all the time, everyone seemed to see the humorous side of things and to forget about the danger. That morning the maintenance boys were already near the end of their second twenty-four hours of emergency repair without sleep. Bathing and shaving weren't even on the schedule.

Breakfast—which meant cereal and dehydrated eggs—was served about eight o'clock. I hated dehydrated eggs. We all hated dehydrated eggs. They stunk so bad we had to turn our faces away when we ate them.

After breakfast I went to the ready tent, which was large enough for thirty to forty people. At all times a minimum of two full flights of eight men each waited for the siren that would signal an emergency scramble. Right now, however, the calls to scramble were few. Geiger had ordered that unless we sighted fifteen or more bogeys, the antiaircraft guns dug in around the field were to take them out. There was simply not enough fuel for us to send up aircraft for anything less threatening to the security of the base.

The ready tent, which was nothing more than a piece of canvas over a pole, without sides, captured the hot, humid air, but it was a shelter from the sun and the rain, and there were cots where you could stretch out and catch up on the sleep you'd missed during the night. When bombing raids made sleep almost impossible at night, it was not difficult to nod off in the day. A night in a foxhole is not the same as a sleepless night in bed. Playing the part of a target takes much more out of a man than a few hours of insomnia after a strenuous day of farm work.

The most common method of passing the nervous time between flights or enemy attacks was either swapping stories or talking tactics. We analyzed the successes and failures of our missions by the hour. A phonograph in one corner of the tent played scratchy well-worn records, mostly big band tunes that reminded us of the days before the war. A pinup of Betty Grable, chaste by modern standards, hung on the tent wall. Dog-eared, months-old newspapers and magazines, hand-carried by arriving pilots, were spread around the tent. Decks of cards, checkerboards with makeshift checkers, a cribbage board, and dice also helped pass the time. I loved to gamble and was considered lucky at blackjack, poker, and craps. To keep my luck, I carried two red dice at all times. When I lost those, I got a pair of green dice—for the Irish.

For more recent "news" and music, there was Toyko Rose. Given the moniker by American soldiers in the South Pacific, the most famous disk jockey of World War II was actually Iva Ikuko Toguri D'Aquino, an American citizen of Japanese descent with a degree in zoology from UCLA. From her post in a Tokyo radio station, she broadcast programming designed to demoralize the American soldiers with a blend of popular music and propaganda. Her sexy voice, with no trace of a Japanese accent, was well known to the troops of Guadalcanal—and we were well known to her. She often referred to the events of the day on Guadalcanal, painting them in the worst possible light. She'd try to tempt us with descriptions and details about the life we'd left back in the U.S., including the fact that our girlfriends and wives were betraying us with civilian men. Thirty years later she would be imprisoned for treason in an American prison until, on the last day of his presidency, Gerald Ford granted her a presidential pardon.

For the most part, I found Toyko Rose amusing. There were no USO shows in the Solomon Islands, and at least the music was good.

Major Jack Cram dropped by the ready tent after lunch that day to talk and laugh about his attack on the transports and his frantic flight back to the field. "As soon as I hit the ground," he said, "I get this message that Geiger wants to see me immediately, and that he's steaming."

General Geiger had called him on the carpet and managed to keep a straight face, Cram admitted, "while he chewed me out for getting his personal plane filled with bullet holes." The general even threatened Cram with a court-martial for destruction of government property. When Cram caught on to the joke, Geiger wrote the order to grant him the Navy Cross for his heroism.

Cram was not the only high-ranking officer to leave his relatively safe bunker to join the fray. At one point Geiger himself, either to bolster morale or because he thought it would be fun, took a dive bomber up onto a ridge where Japanese soldiers were prevailing and personally installed a bomb crater squarely in their midst.

Throughout the afternoon our dive bombers and Wildcats continued the onslaught on the transports. The combined attacks finally convinced the enemy to pull out and try to offload the three remaining transports another time. A considerable victory for the Allies.

A group of us had begun spending our evenings together playing cards. As our membership grew, we became known as the Short Snorters—a short snort being a small drink, which we occasionally managed. We did enjoy a beer or a Scotch now and then, since it was military policy to provide some alcohol to fliers to combat the terrible stress they endured. Whereas many of us had the ability to relax completely in stressful conditions—an ability that has served many good fliers well—some of the pilots were so affected by the pressure of combat that they found it almost impossible to sleep, even when things were quiet. But the drinks were relatively infrequent. Stories of hard-drinking pilots were popular and circulated after the war, but there was scant room on the occasional cargo plane for whiskey, and I knew of no heavy drinkers on Guadalcanal.

The Short Snorters adjourned about midnight, and that

night the bombing was about half as bad as usual, which was still really bad. Near morning, when the worst was over, a lone Mitsubishi bomber flew over and dropped its load, then turned back to fly in low over the fighter strip to strafe the field and our planes.

Angry and frustrated after another night spent hugging the earth at the bottom of their foxholes, the men suddenly erupted everywhere, as if on cue. Pilots, mechanics, cooks, and radio men all were up and running, pistols and rifles blazing at the sole invader, cursing the ancestors that brought forth the Asian invaders.

It was hilarious, and I started to laugh as the bomber fled from the crazed swarm of indignant ground warriors. As the last shots faded, some of the guys around me stopped and stared at me in puzzlement as I held my stomach and roared. Then I walked over to the parking area to check on the planes and saw my number 53. Though it was largely undamaged, the throttle stick had been cleanly severed from its base. Now that was getting personal!

Chapter 11
The Takeoff Point

★ ★ ★

There are aces, and there are aces.

Technically any pilot who shoots down five enemy planes is an ace, but there are varying levels of mastery in aerial combat. Certain fliers go far beyond expertise to attain almost superhuman combat capabilities. A select few, or so the theory goes, undergo a change in the midst of battle that catapults them to a state of near invincibility. Some call the moment when a fighter pilot takes that quantum leap in martial proficiency the "takeoff point."

"The right stuff" has entered our vocabulary in recent years, thanks to Tom Wolfe, denoting the quality or combination of qualities possessed by the very best test pilots. Test pilots are not the only ones who need that stuff. Combat pilots have to draw on the same abilities that test pilots depend upon: the power to think clearly and make instantaneous decisions while performing maneuvers intended to take both aircraft and aviator to the razor-sharp edge of physical failure.

A fighter pilot must go one step further if he is to survive. He must test the right stuff in the presence of an additional element—the enemy dedicated to his destruction. The stuff not only has to be right, it has to be better than his opponents—day after day, mission after mission. Pilots like Eddie Rickenbacker, Joe Bauer, John Smith, Marion Carl, Bob Galer, Gabby Gabreski, Dick Bong, Dave McCampbell,

Chuck Yeager and I had a great time on Dick Carlsberg's goose hunt in northern California in November of 1987. (Photo by Bob Allen)

Chuck Yeager, Jack Purdy, Duke Davis, Joe Palko, Roger Haberman, Tommy McGuire—the list could go on and on—were examples of the right stuff fighter pilots I knew and admired.

Yet no pilot enters combat as a great warrior. Even the most complex and exacting training and simulation cannot fully prepare you for the almost inconceivable realities of the dogfight. The early engagements with the enemy can be so bewildering and terrifying that only luck or providence bring the flier through alive. If a combat pilot survives the fledgling stages of his career and possesses the appropriate qualities and character, then he may undergo the transformation from a novice to a truly great fighter pilot. If time and chance place such a person where his skills can be exercised to their utmost, he may become an ace of aces and claim a place in the history books.

One distinguishing mark of the fighter pilot is his attitude toward the joust. Fear is the inevitable and natural response to any sort of mortal combat, and everybody on Guadalcanal felt that fear to one degree or another. Yet accomplished fighter pilots overcome the debilitating effects of that fear and harness their reaction to danger for their own purposes. Great fighter pilots may even grow to crave the dogfight.

I was not yet at that point. A little over a week into action, I was not at all sure that I would live through this assignment. My first fights had been mostly haphazard affairs, and my confidence was far from secure. By October 16, I still hadn't faced a Zero head-on, even though I'd shot down two.

Along with this, I had to deal with the reaction of those around me. More than one member of VMF-121 was falling apart before my eyes. The daily hell that was life on Guadalcanal—the nerve-shattering, life-or-death missions, combined with malaria and dysentery and poor food—was simply too much for some men.

One morning I found one of the squadron huddled near the edge of the palms, shaking as if he were in the Antarctic instead of the tropics. The prevailing term for this crippling condition was "the jerks." I spent time with the guy, but he was broken. Ultimately I could do little except get him scheduled for evacuation.

Other players in the Guadalcanal game were struggling with their own hand. Thousands more Japanese troops and additional equipment had landed, causing Vice Admiral Robert Ghormley to lose faith in his ability to defend the island. He sent a memo to Admiral Chester Nimitz announcing his conviction that his forces were "totally inadequate" to deal with the enemy forces.

The Japanese army, with the supplies unloaded from the barges not destroyed, was beginning to make its way through the rain forest toward Henderson Field. The valley a few miles west of us was turning into a Japanese supply dump, in preparation for their ground assault on the airfield. Deadly anti-aircraft guns were concentrated around the stockpiles of tanks, heavy artillery, machinery, fuel, food, and ammunition.

Meanwhile, our gasoline was running precariously low again, although three R4Ds did manage to fly in from Espíritu Santo with twelve 55-gallon drums each. One drum would buy one hour of flight time for one Wildcat.

For all these reasons, things seemed muted in the dim morning light of October 16 when the fresh dawn scent of tropical flowers was overpowered by gasoline fumes as I prepared to take off and lead my flight in the first attack of the day. Mechanics scurried about the planes, performing last-minute checks and removing wheel blocks. I climbed up onto the wing, eased into the cockpit, and started down the runway.

At the end of the field, where I would normally have climbed for height, our flight leveled out and turned away from the sun. Skimming barely five feet above the treetops, the eight of us dropped into the island valleys and all but brushed the hilltops as we hugged the contour of the land. This close to the ground our relatively slow cruising speed seemed far faster than the greater speeds we reached high above the earth. The countryside appeared as still as an oil painting.

Less than five minutes later I dropped over the summit of a hill and saw the Japs below me turn, wide-eyed, as the roar of eight Pratt and Whitney engines filled their valley. Staying low and below the AA fire, we savagely strafed the area. Somehow that destruction had more of an emotional impact on me than the dramatic death in the sky. Miles above the earth a wounded or lifeless pilot was insulated from sight, shrouded in his own metal coffin. Just above the ground, I could actually see the rank markings on the uniforms of the soldiers I attacked. When our .50 caliber shells happened to hit a man, they almost literally turned him wrong side out.

Distracted by our cavalry charge, the Japanese gunners barely saw the dive bombers hurtling down from the clouds to drop their explosives on the AA positions. Several AA guns were destroyed and hundreds of the enemy killed, at the cost of only one American bomber.

Returning to base, we had a twenty-minute break before our planes were reloaded and recharged. This time we flew to the shore where the hollow barges were beached. We riddled the transport rafts until they were beyond repair and left them lolling on the shoreline, where they would still rest half a century later, rusted monuments to the war.

After those runs, we settled back for a relatively calm afternoon. A naval task force, led by the carrier *Hornet,* had been sent into the neighborhood to aid our attacks on ground troops threatening the Allied outpost. Japanese aerial efforts focused on the naval group, taking some of the pressure off Henderson Field and allowing us to preserve the few precious gallons of fuel we had left.

Over our supper of Spam and rice we were buoyed by reports that a shipment of gasoline, torpedo bombs, and other ammunition was slipping through the dusk toward the island. Our optimism was short-lived.

Out at sea the Japanese had lost track of the *Hornet* and its companions. As the Nipponese dive bombers searched for them, nine Val bombers chanced upon the modified destroyer *McFarland,* anchored at the mouth of the Lunga River near Henderson Field, loaded with 40,000 gallons of gasoline and desperately needed ammunition. It had dashed from Espíritu Santo to deliver its cargo to the Cactus Air Force.

In a matter of moments, the Val bombers, which were remarkably maneuverable and fast for their class, left the ship blazing and dozens of sailors dead. The exploding ammunition and fuel attracted the attention of Lieutenant Colonel Harold W. (Indian Joe) Bauer, the leader of a veteran squadron on Guadalcanal. He and his men from VMF-212 were returning from a mission across the slot and saw the blasts and the fleeing bombers. Bauer's group caught four of the fleeing bombers as they entered the airspace above the fighter strip. Within seconds Bauer had downed all four enemy planes.

Bauer's resolve and audacious response to the situation was an incredible performance, and I witnessed the whole thing. I'd run into the open when I'd heard the first explosions from the *McFarland* thundering over the airfield and saw the conflagration lighting the darkening sky.

That night I mulled over the lessons of the day as I dropped off to sleep—a sleep undisturbed until the arrival of morning was announced by the cockcrow of .20 caliber Japanese guns in counterpoint with our American guns.

Stumbling outside, I looked straight up to see a burning Zero falling toward the ocean. Duke Davis and his flight were dogfighting directly over my tent. I watched with great satisfaction as our boys vanquished six bombers and four Zeroes.

* * *

The following morning I finally got the fight I'd been itching for.

The sun was almost straight up when I led my flight out to meet a group of bombers reported heading toward the field. The sixth man to begin his run down the strip, cratered from the previous night's shelling, was Andy Andrews, the young flier who had strafed the Japanese barges by himself. Somehow he lost control of his plane and swerved into a Wildcat parked along the strip. Even from the air it was obvious that one of our most dauntless and well-liked fliers could not have lived through the explosion and fire.

We scissored upward, waiting for the remaining two members of our flight, Bill Marontate and Danny Doyle, who were delayed until the ground crew could clear some of the wreckage from the runway. Later I would learn that my plane captain, the number one mechanic in charge of aircraft maintenance, was working on the plane that Andrews swerved into and had been seriously injured.

Marontate and Doyle finally got off the strip, but when I looked down as I banked for a turn, I saw five planes instead of two, several thousand feet below. Three Zeros had come straight in behind Bill and Danny and were jockeying for the perfect position before firing. Converting my turn into a dive, I led the rest of the flight down and slid gently in behind the enemy.

I picked the Zero farthest to the left and started shooting. My first tracers set him afire, and he tipped over into a spin and went in. The tracer shells that missed the Zero flew past Bill and Danny, alerting them to the predators on their tails. They spun away, out of the line of fire, and we took out the two remaining Zeros.

We didn't have time to gloat, because while we were concentrating on the Zeros sneaking up on Doyle and Marontate, another group of Japanese fighters were coming down on us. That's the way the layers within layers of air combat work. You just polished off one Jap and the rounds from another would whip past your wing tip.

The attacking planes had the advantage of greater speed from their drop out of higher altitudes, but I turned to the side and headed toward a Zeke coming at me from above.

To turn away for a more advantageous approach would have presented the enemy with an easy target. The Zeke twisted out of the way before I could line up on him, and I followed him, turning in and down toward the right, the direction he was flying. The enemy was adjusting even faster, however, and we chased each other away from the center of the melee.

I turned again, trying to cut left into his trajectory. Instead, the Jap pivoted to the right and nosed over to pick up speed in a short dive. Unable to follow with the Mitsubishi's speed, I began to recognize that I was not up against an inexperienced pilot. I'd seen plenty of good and bad Japanese fliers, and this was one of the best.

I nosed over, leaning on the rudder, until both of us were flying upside down in a broad circle. As we continued our jockeying contortions, I searched for the slightest momentary advantage. More than a dozen other planes were dueling with equal abandon, so I also had to worry about an accidental collision. Moreover, there were unengaged Japanese planes in the air who were more than willing to pick off an American pilot too focused on one opponent.

In that situation, you're inside time. Maneuvers that last only a fraction of a second seem to stretch out forever.

I clenched my teeth, straining through wringing instantaneous moves until I saw the opportunity I needed, aimed, and shot ahead of the Zero. The trajectories of my ordnance converged perfectly with the other plane. From my perspective my shots seemed to enter the cockpit, but the smoke from the Zero's engine indicated that my aim had been low but effective. The plane tilted over and fled.

In less frantic circumstances I would have pursued the crippled Zero, guaranteeing that he didn't limp back to Rabaul, but there wasn't time, so this one would never be credited to my official record. Too many Zeros yet to fight.

I spotted another one coming up behind a Wildcat and flew directly at it. The Jap turned to face me, and we flew toward each other in a deadly game of chicken, my trigger finger tensed to fire. As I expected, the Zero banked away at the last minute. The angle was near perfect for a shot, but just then I caught sight of another plane flying by behind the Zero, the blue and gray of my own squadron. I eased off the trigger and twisted the stick forcibly to the right and forward. The Zero and I passed so closely that if my landing gear had been down we'd have struck each other. Both of us circled back hard for another run.

On my second approach the Zero's pilot opened fire while we were still hundreds of yards apart. His aim was off, and the tracers provided a clear visual indication of the plane's flight path. I flew onward, holding back until I was nearly on top of him. He pulled up and only then did I clamp down on the trigger.

The Mitsubishi burst into flames with the first round. He did a tight wingover and headed down. I banked to my left and looked down over my shoulder to see the burning debris falling toward sea level. No question about that one being a notch on my gun.

Then I looked up over my right shoulder and saw the eight Betty bombers the Zeros were escorting, flying a V formation. The twin-engined Type I bombers were a remarkable piece of engineering, perhaps the finest bomber of the war. Faster at its unhurried cruising speed than the Grumman at full bore, the Betty sprouted defensive guns in most directions and was manned by a crew of seven. Its two 600-gallon gas tanks provided vast range, as well as its most vulnerable attack point.

I climbed to meet them on a 180-degree course and made a run on the right rear bomber. As I came down in a vertical dive, making my run and ready to shoot, he suddenly blew up. One of the other guys had taken care of him, and I had to do some fancy flying to avoid the burning debris while lining up on the next bomber in line.

By that time I was too close for anything but a short burst, which started smoke but produced no fire or explosion, so I dove down and away from the bombers' guns at full throttle to pick up speed. A thousand feet below, I suddenly turned back up and headed toward the belly of the last plane on the left wing of the V echelon. Directly under the bomber, nose pointed straight up, I waited until my plane had lost almost all of its speed and I was on the verge of stalling before I pulled the trigger.

I scored a direct hit on a gas tank and fire spewed down at

me. At the top of my stall, poised beneath the flaming bomber, the intense radiant heat from the gasoline fire flashed over my forehead and cheeks.

The burning bomber flew on past me as I used the last of my velocity to nose slowly over the top of my stall and regain maneuverability, my finger still tight on the trigger though my ammunition was long gone.

The fire died out as quickly as it started and burst forth again in another cloud of flame, then died down and exploded once again as the Betty's left wing separated from its fuselage. The plane went into a spin and plummeted into the Pacific.

In all the excitement I barely noticed my engine cough and lapse into silence after my final climb. Conveniently, the rest of the Japanese planes were gone, most in the sea, and I could concentrate on the difficult task of piloting my Wildcat dead stick—as pilots call it when the power quits—onto Fighter One.

From that moment on I was officially an ace.

Chapter 12
The
Flying Circus

✮ ✮ ✮

About the time I was adding a fifth Japanese plane to my
tally, the American command of Guadalcanal changed hands.
Admiral Ghormley was relieved by Vice Admiral William F.
Halsey, who took command of the South Pacific Area and
the South Pacific forces. When ordered to this command,
Halsey's response was reported to be, "Jesus Christ and General Jackson! This is the hottest potato they ever handed me!"

"Bull" Halsey was already well known to the men on Guadalcanal for his command of the first attacks on the Gilbert
and Marshall Islands. In fact, his successful obstruction of the
larger Japanese fleet had made the beachhead on Guadalcanal
possible. Halsey had earned his nickname not only for his
bullet-spitting, hard-charging fighting style, but also for his
bulldoglike features. The report that he was taking charge of
the battle was enthusiastically received by all of us on the
island, although at that point, to be honest, we would have
considered any change in management a good sign.

The next day a new load of pilots arrived bringing, among
other things, chocolate bars, and since I had some time off
that afternoon I took the short hike to the front lines to visit
with the ground troops and pass out candy. I'd been flying
morning, noon, and night, and we were short of planes, so it
was my turn to get a break. The Japanese were in the last
stages of preparation for their "final assault" on Henderson

Field, and the rumors of their strength, powerful enough in reality, were impossibly exaggerated as reports and scuttlebutt traversed the American-controlled sector. As I made my way through the perimeter I was surprised to find that most of the soldiers knew who I was. Before long I would also learn from arriving pilots that as one of the newest aces, my name was beginning to appear in publications back home.

After swapping stories and jokes for a while, I walked back to our squadron encampment, grabbed my duffel of dirty clothes, and headed for the Lunga River, where we did our best to wash the tropical sweat and grime from our clothing. At one time this had probably been an idyllic tropical setting, but heavy foot traffic had turned the site into a muddy outdoor laundry room. As I stood in the cool, silty water, using a fallen jungle tree like Mom's washboard back home, I realized this primitive procedure was not working. There had to be a better way.

Leaving the stream, I picked the leeches off my feet and then carried the soaking laundry back to my tent. There I scavenged a large metal can from the mechanics and filled it with water. I built a fire near my foxhole, set the can over the flames, and tossed my clothes in with some dark brown homemade soap my mother had sent.

Soon the water and the clothing, including a cheap pair of burgundy socks, were boiling away. Feeling cocky about my jerry-rigged Maytag, I took the laundry off the fire only to discover that although my clothes were clean, they were also a vivid shade of pink.

Ben Finney happened by just as I was hanging my fresh pink underwear on a line between a palm and my tent.

"Nice, Joe," he commented as he stopped to watch. "Very attractive, though hardly GI."

"Thanks, Ben." I grinned. "I'll do yours as soon as I have time."

By the end of the first week I had become accustomed to Maytag Charlie and the nightly shellings, and even the daily scrambles to ward off the bombing attacks by the Japanese air force. But I never did get used to the miserable muddy foxholes, high humidity, and unbearable heat.

Except for the dogfights, there was little excitement. News from home could bring out the melancholy in a man, but we still looked forward to mail call. My mother and June were faithful letter writers, even though I seldom wrote. Truth be told, I often felt a strange kind of detachment from people back home, especially June. We'd only been husband and wife a couple weeks before I'd left, so in some ways I didn't really feel married. June and South Dakota seemed like another world.

At night, when the Japs weren't shelling us, the Short Snorters would congregate in the bivouac area and unwind with tall tales, whiskey, brandy, strong Australian beer, or fruit juice—in that order of preference—when we could get our hands on it. The rare quart of whiskey could bring a hundred bucks. We'd sit around swapping stories or making postwar plans, which usually meant go home, return to a job, go hunting and fishing.

One subject we never discussed was death. When one of the guys failed to return from a flight, we tightened our jaws but said nothing. We never did anything special for the guys who were killed. The chaplain did, but we would just sit around and talk about "what a great guy ol' so and so was. I hope he went to heaven or gets back." Somebody always had a glimmer of hope that the guys would get back.

Most of us were pretty fatalistic, though, figuring if our number was up, we were going to get it even if we were in a bombproof shelter ten feet underground. Besides, thinking about death in that situation was a good way to go nuts.

Some of the men read Bibles, and all of us thought more about God, no doubt about that. I reasoned that if there was a heaven I would surely go there because I was an honest, moral, hardworking guy. I always encouraged my men to attend their respective religious services—Jewish, Catholic, or Protestant—and I went myself whenever I could. I never gave serious thought to why. It just seemed like the thing to do.

When we were not intercepting enemy planes, we went after enemy ships and land convoys. Day after day we took to the air, and we seldom came back without bagging something. My own personal tally was beginning to add up: I'd downed my first Zero on October 13, and the next day I got my second; on October 15 I'd shot down two Zeros and a Betty bomber; on October 20 I downed two Zeros; on October 23 I got four more, and two days later I got five. That made sixteen in all. Not bad for twelve days' work.

Night after night we wearily sought shelter in the bottoms of our foxholes, exhausted and haggard. We now knew first-hand why VMF-223 had greeted us so eagerly when we'd arrived a few weeks earlier. Relief had to come soon. Munitions were almost always in short supply and had to be brought in by sea after dark.

By now our flight, consisting of Roger Haberman, Danny Doyle, Bill Marontate, Rudy Ruddell, Greg Loesch, Boot Furlow, Bill Freeman, and Oscar Bate, had become known as "Foss's Flying Circus." Joe Bauer, one of the Cactus Air Force's legendary pilots, first gave us the nickname about three weeks after we got there because of our aerobatic escapades against the enemy. But our guys weren't the only ones whose daredevil antics saved the day.

Like the ploy used by Lieutenant Jack E. Conger, who had also been one of my high school buddies back in Sioux Falls. On one of his runs Jack ran out of ammunition just as he was closing in on a Zero. Determined to knock the Zeke out of the sky, Jack dove straight at the enemy plane and rammed it, and miraculously managed to parachute to safety, as did the enemy pilot.

Crashing into a Zero wasn't something they taught in our flight manual, but old Jack made it work. Actually it was a tactic used on several occasions during the war by pilots of various nationalities, particularly the Soviets.

War is a do-or-die situation, and if you're going to do, you very quickly learn survival techniques. For example, the enemy is never seen as an individual. You're not shooting down pilots—men—you're shooting down death-dealing flying machines. You get them before they get you or your buddies. And we never called them Japanese; they were Japs, Nips, Jappies, Slant Eyes, or some other slur. Yet we had an unwritten code of respect once a plane was disabled. I never shot at a Japanese pilot in a parachute, and I personally only

knew of one American pilot who did. He was reprimanded
severely for the act, but after he did the same thing again the
following day he was himself killed by a Japanese pilot. If an
enemy plane crashed on the island, it usually attracted trophy
hunters who combed the wreckage in search of samurai
swords, guns, flags, currency, photographs, uniforms, or anything else of value. I could never bring myself to join the
scavengers; somehow it seemed below the dignity of a Marine
flier, and most of the men felt the same way.

Japanese pilots hardly ever flew in formation; instead they
wandered around independently. When it came to combat
tactics, we were better trained and quickly cashed in on our
foes' errors.

When the Japanese had you outnumbered, they would do
fancy tricks to show you that their planes were faster and
more maneuverable. They'd swarm around you and get close
enough to flaunt the capabilities of the Zero and their flight
skills. I've always said that if I were their leader I could have
won the air war in the South Pacific for the Japanese. I would
have told them to stay away from those American birds except
when they could get near them at high speeds from altitude.
The Japanese could have come racing down shooting at point-
blank range and then cleared out, never doing extravagant
rolls or other complex maneuvers to show off or try to intim-
idate us. High-speed hit-and-run would have been my tactic.

What the enemy lacked in tactical skill, however, was more
than compensated for by the superiority of the Zero fighter.
At the time, it was the best fighting plane in the world. It
could beat our Wildcats in interception, maneuverability,
climb, and speed. A Zero could turn on a dime and climb
like a scared monkey on a rope. I could take any one of my
pilots and put him in a Zero and he would shoot the hell out
of me in no time.

None of our pilots wanted to fly a Zero, though; they were
too vulnerable. When hit in the wing mount area they almost
always exploded or quickly became "smokers" or "torches."
Our Wildcats were much safer. I never heard of one exploding, and only once did I learn of one torching. In back of the
pilot's seat was a heavy steel plate that could deflect enemy
fire, and the plane also had superior armament. The six .50

caliber guns on a Wildcat were really more than were needed. They could rip anything apart. At least four times I had Zeros in my sights, only to run out of ammo before I could shoot them down. Then I got smart and saved ammo by cutting out two guns and using only four at a time. In short, they beat us on speed and maneuverability; we beat them in fire power and durability.

Experience put the finishing touch on my fighter pilot training. I quickly learned that best results came when I flew close to a Zero before opening fire. I always tried to surprise the enemy by coming up on his tail, but if I ended up playing a game of chicken with him, I would wait until the Zero pulled up to avoid a collision and then I'd send a short burst into his wing base. Side shots—deflection shooting we called it— required good marksmanship. To a farm boy it was like shooting a pheasant on the fly.

Because I usually shot from very close range, the Zeros almost always exploded, which was quite a sight. There was a bright flash when the gas tanks blew and the engine would spin off by itself in a lopsided whirl. The pilot, usually still buckled in his seat, popped out of the cockpit and the air was showered with thousands of little pieces of the plane. What was left of the wing fell like a giant burning leaf. When a Zero blew up in front of you there was nowhere to go except right through all the debris. All you could do was duck and hope you missed any big pieces.

No matter how daredevil or wild your aerial maneuvers might be, however, the one thing you couldn't afford to be was stupid or greedy. The morning after I downed my seventh plane, a flock of parrots—our slang for a large group of Zeros—drew every available plane into the air. Scheduled for a later flight, I was forced to sit this one out. So I stood near operations monitoring the battle. Listening to the radio reports, my pulse accelerated as a situation developed. Fourteen Japanese dive bombers, without escort, were sneaking in while the Wildcats were occupied with the Zeros. If I could just get into the air before the bombers arrived to drop their loads on Henderson, there was a chance I could bring down the entire flight. I could just picture myself dispatching all fourteen. That's the one time I got greedy.

Looking down the field, I spotted a lone Grumman parked beside Fighter One. Its engine was new and it had never been flown.

"Hey, Sarge, do you know why this plane is grounded?" I asked.

The sergeant in charge said the craft had been grounded by a certain lieutenant because of excessive magneto drop. The guy he named was a flier I considered less than eager about getting into combat and I figured it was just an excuse, so I ran for the Wildcat.

I buckled in and fired the Pratt and Whitney to life, listening to the engine and testing the rudders before pulling on my helmet. The plane sounded a bit anemic but operational, so I revved the engine and turned into the wind from the mountains. I had difficulty reaching takeoff speed and cut the throttle to taxi back for a second attempt; this time I achieved the speed I needed but knew as soon as I left the ground that I'd never make the climb over the trees.

Figuring the engine just needed blowing out, I gunned the motor a few times, then shoveled on the coal and went the other way.

In the middle of my turn the engine quit entirely. Barely seventy-five feet off the ground and lacking the speed to make it back to the landing strip, I looked down at the palm grove and realized I'd made a serious mistake. I'd managed dead-stick landings both in training and in battle, but never from such a low altitude or into such a treacherous spot. I figured I probably wasn't going to do too well on this one.

As I went down I tried to avoid hitting a tree directly, but when I hit the top of one the impact hurtled me into another square on. I was thrown forward and knocked unconscious as the plane continued to travel, turning slowly as it tilted to the right. A wing tip caught on a tree, was severed, and skipped away. Another tree sheared off the landing gear and sent the Wildcat spinning on its belly, skidding forward, leaving pieces of metal like torn paper on the shattered trees.

I was far from dead, but I might have slept on until the medics revived me, except that the enemy beat them to it.

The bombers had arrived, and one of them dropped a load only yards away from my left wing tip. The explosion startled me into shaken grogginess. Wiping blood from my eyes, I looked out through my shattered canopy as dust and debris settled onto my head. Worried that the remaining fuel in the Wildcat might catch fire, I crawled out of the ruined plane and stumbled away to sit down in a nearby trench. I pulled off my helmet and stared at the blood and the gaping puncture in my headgear.

Moments later the ambulance arrived with Doc Peterson, the doctor who had operated on my knee during our voyage out. Doc and the ambulance driver climbed onto the remaining wing of the plane, checking the cockpit for my corpse. They both jumped a mile when I yelled, "Hey, Doc, here I am."

Joe Bauer was waiting when we got back. It was the only time I ever saw him really mad.

"You damn fool!" he yelled as I stumbled, dazed and bleeding, out of the ambulance. "You could have been killed. You should have been killed. Anybody that dumb—to take off in that plane."

The dive bombers were still at it, but Bauer refused to be distracted by falling bombs. "The mag drop on that plane was too great!" he yelled. "You've just demolished an airplane that could have been fixed. You think we write up requisitions and these things appear like eggs on Easter morning? You think trained pilots grow on trees?" The colonel eventually sputtered to a frustrated finish and spun around to march away.

I respected Bauer, "the one man gang," as much as anyone on the island, so it was doubly humiliating to be chewed out by him.

When they finished bandaging my head—the wound was not serious, mostly bloody from a gash on top of my head inflicted by flying glass—I was ready to get airborne immediately.

Later when Walt Simmons wrote a wartime book on my experiences on Guadalcanal, the censors eliminated the details of my crash amid the palm trees and Colonel Bauer's response. The Navy department wanted us to look totally heroic for the homefront, rather than telling the whole truth about the realities of war.

Despite this lapse in judgment, I really wasn't flying to set records or impress others. The heat of battle was forging my purpose and my aerial mastery. I knew why I was on the island, although I didn't spend much time thinking about political and philosophical issues. I lived to fight Zeros. I grew more determined than ever, obsessed with my mission. When I wasn't flying I was talking about flying, and when I slept I often dreamt about flying. The fight had become an end in itself.

By now, however, I had scored ten planes, and the journalists were beginning to chronicle my exploits for their civilian readers. The day I brought my score to eleven, several reporters climbed onto the wing of my plane even before my propeller had whirled to a stop.

The day my score rose to thirteen, I landed particularly pleased with myself. While shooting down three Zeros I had escaped the melee without catching even one bullet. Danny Doyle, wearing a goatee identical to mine, was nearby when I landed and heard me bragging that I'd come through the dogfights unscathed.

"What do you call those?" Doyle asked with an odd expression, pointing to the thick headrest that cushioned the back of my skull during the flight. It had been shredded by several Japanese shells.

That was also the day Jack Conger went down.

When I was in high school my cousin Jake and I once sneaked in through the back door of the Dakota movie theater in Sioux Falls. We sat down quietly near the front of the house hoping no one would notice us, but we'd only been there a few minutes when an usher, a high school kid even younger than we were, walked up behind us and firmly escorted us outside. That usher was Jack Conger. Now we were fighting for our lives together.

On this particular day, October 25, eight Japanese fighters attacked Henderson, and Jack Conger was one of the four Wildcats who met them overhead. Locked in extended combat with an equally determined and capable Japanese pilot,

Jack could not get in a killing shot. When he ran out of ammunition, he was so caught up in the passion of battle that he turned his Grumman straight up as the Zero flew over, intending to use his propeller as a buzz saw to take off the enemy's tail rudder.

I was only about 1,500 feet below on the ground at the time, watching as Conger misjudged and hit halfway between the tail and the cockpit, chewing at least five feet of the Zero's tail before both planes started falling toward the water off the beach we controlled. Both pilots clambered out of their cockpits and pulled their ripcords. I jumped into a nearby jeep and raced for the beach, where I found a group of sailors and Marines already going after the two pilots in a small higgins boat, a squarish rough-iron vessel with a bow that would lower to the beach when landing.

The Japanese flier was closest to the shore and the boat started for him, but he pointed out toward Conger and gestured for them to go for him first. When the rescuers got to Conger, one of the sailors laughed and said, "Your friend back there said to pick you up first."

"Well, he's a real sport," said Conger. "There is a little chivalry left in the war at that."

With Conger in the boat, they turned back toward the Japanese pilot. The Marines wanted to finish the enemy at a distance, but Conger insisted on rescuing the man. I could hear the heated argument clearly from where I stood knee-high in the surf.

Conger won the debate and personally reached down to grab the enemy airman's life vest to pull him into the boat. The pilot smiled and extended an arm up to Conger. As the two clasped hands, the Japanese pilot whipped his other arm around with a cocked 8 mm Nambu pistol, rammed the barrel between Conger's eyes, and pulled the trigger.

The gun misfired with only a wet click, but Conger threw himself backward against the other side of the boat so violently that he was plagued with back problems for the rest of his life. The Japanese pilot then turned the pistol to his own head, and the wet ammunition misfired again. Conger grabbed a five-gallon gasoline can and hit the Jap over the head with it.

As the Japanese pilot passed me, he spit at me, and I wanted to shoot that sucker.

An interesting footnote to this event would occur years later, in April 1990, when Jack Conger once again met the Japanese pilot, Shiro Ishikawa, and the two veterans shook hands and talked for the first time since this incident forty-eight years earlier. After being shot down and captured, Ishikawa, a member of the Second Air Group of the Imperial Japanese Navy, spent the rest of the war in a prisoner of war camp in New Zealand.

Significant moments like this may be locked in history, but time heals and God can give us a forgiving heart. Suburo Sakai, the top surviving Japanese ace, with whom I often share platforms at university symposiums, recently told me that I am his best friend in America.

Chapter 13

Saved for Another Day

It was November 7, 1942. To date over 5,000 Japanese soldiers had died on Guadalcanal trying to take back the Imperial outpost. The mood on the island was guardedly optimistic. Tokyo Rose's arrogant predictions, accurately reflecting the Japanese command's belief that the Americans were doomed, had gone unfulfilled. We had held our ground.

The day started quietly, but for some reason I felt a bit uneasy, anxious. Religion was something I'd always taken for granted but not on a very personal basis, although I would at times repeat the Lord's Prayer, the only way I knew how to pray. Late that afternoon I found myself repeating it more than usual before we left to strafe the group of ten Japanese destroyers and a light cruiser spotted about 150 miles north steaming in toward the island. We would act as decoys to provide cover while the torpedo planes struck the flotilla.

One reason for my anxiety was Danny Doyle. I was worried about him. Doyle's best friend, Casey Brandon, had been shot down and killed a few days earlier, and this was the first time I'd allowed Doyle to fly since then. Brandon and Doyle had been inseparable. Brandon was an opinionated and articulate Irish-Norwegian farm boy from Grand Rapids, Minnesota, who had finished high school at sixteen and gone on to graduate from the University of Minnesota with high honors. He'd been offered a postgraduate post in aeronautical engineering at Annapolis but turned it down in favor of more direct participation in the war.

Danny Doyle, two years younger than Brandon, was also from a Minnesota farm. All Irish, he was dark, wiry, full of sauce, and afraid of nothing. He had graduated from State Teachers' College in Mankato, Minnesota, and intended to teach after the war. His passion as a child had been the rare coconut his mother bought and hid from him for fear he would eat it all before the rest of the family had a share. Danny found it particularly funny that he was now camped in the middle of a coconut plantation.

I never minded the pair's irreverent wisecracks and practical jokes. They were good at what they did and were excellent for the squadron's morale. Even their nicknames reflected their friendship; Doyle's tag, the code name used when flying, was Fool, and Brandon's was Ish—the Foolish Twins.

I couldn't forget Danny's reaction the night Brandon didn't return. Doyle's plane had been grounded that day with mechanical problems, and Brandon flew into combat for the first time without his usual wingman. No one saw him die, but as the hours passed without word of the downed flier, Doyle grew from grimly pensive to raving with hatred. "Those goonies are going to pay if it's the last thing I do," he vowed.

Seeing how disturbed he was by the loss of his friend, I'd grounded him for fear he'd do something truly foolish. Finally, however, I had to let him fly again, although his despondency showed no real signs of abating.

When we sighted the Japanese flotilla, they had company —six float Zeros, equipped with pontoons for water takeoffs and landings—directly in front of and below us, in hot pursuit of another flight led by Major Paul Fontana.

"Don't look now, but I think we have something here," I radioed to my wingman, Boot Furlow.

We pulled up behind the Zeros, and Boot slipped right in under my wing just as I fired a short burst. The deadly spray ripped into the wing mount of one of the Zeros and blew the plane into a thousand pieces.

We peeled off in opposite directions to avoid hitting each other and the exploding wreckage. Boot trailed a second plane and shot it down in a flaming arc, while I looked to the left and saw my premonition come true. Danny Doyle was flying unswervingly toward a Zero, and I knew how the game would end. Without firing a shot, Danny flew straight through the enemy plane, demolishing both planes and ending his own life.

Later it would take me some time to get over Danny's death. I took all our losses hard—all the men were very close to me—but Danny's death hit me harder because I had let him fly when he was still upset. For now, however, in the heat of battle, I had to grit my teeth and let him go.

I whipped into a quick wingover and accelerated toward the buzzing swarm, looking around for another shot. But it was over; all six had been blasted out of the sky, leaving only a few pieces of falling debris and five blossoming parachutes with empty harnesses. When I spotted the sixth it was about 2,000 feet above me, and the Japanese pilot was struggling out of the harness. Pulling free, he plunged past my plane, falling headfirst into the sea. Apparently the other five had committed suicide in the same way, and I wondered what strange vow they had taken.

With the Zeros out of the way we went after the ships, our original target, who were already peppering the air with AA fire. I signaled my flight to join with Fontana's squadron in reverse order, leaving me to fly the tail-end position. As I lined up to dive for a strafing run, I swiveled my head for one of my habitual cloud scans. Lucky I did, because I spotted the float of a Japanese plane, like an inverted shark fin, protruding through the bottom of a cloud. *Better get rid of this baby so he doesn't follow us down,* I thought.

Circling away from the group, I flew upward to get above the bogey, still cloaked by the clouds. When he emerged from the mists I made a diving run for my prey, figuring this was duck soup, but I'd overestimated my adversary. The plane I was stalking was not the swift and nimble Zero but a scout ship with a rear gunner. The slow-moving plane seemed to be standing almost stationary in the clouds.

I dove in too fast and had to roll on my side to avoid crashing into the rear of the plane. The quick-thinking pilot of the scout plane rolled as well, giving his tail gunner a perfect shot at me, at nearly point-blank range. That little squeak in the back seat just riveted me with that putt-putt-putt gun, and several of the .29 caliber shells pierced the left side of my engine cowling and shattered on through the side of the canopy three or four inches from my face—right across and out the other side. That really got my attention, I can tell you. I glanced around at the wings and tail, then checked my instruments. Despite the shrieking wind roaring through the holes in the canopy, it appeared there was no serious damage.

"This is red leader," I radioed. "Continue your attack."

When we came in view of the enemy fleet, Oscar Bate was in a perfect position, so he led the attack. Because of the condition of my canopy, I was unable to dive, but on my second pass I made a belly shot into the scout, sending a stream of shells into the base of the plane's right wing. It burst into flame almost at once. As the smoking plane spiraled toward the sea, I spotted a second scout, its pilot apparently unaware that his companion had been knocked out of the clouds. Circling behind him, I pulled up for an unhurried belly shot, and sent my nineteenth victim to join his buddy in the drink.

Leveling off, I looked for my squadron. Then I spotted the rest of the flight, maybe a mile and a half away, streaking out of range of the ships' guns to regroup and head back to base.

I tried to call the rest of my flight, but couldn't raise anyone. Apparently my radio was dead, which wasn't unusual. The radios in the Wildcats were inclined to frequent failure, especially mine. Bad radios plagued me. Probably this time one of the Japanese shells had damaged my aerial, but I continued calling for help just in case my radio was transmitting and I was being heard.

Just then my plane started to miss and backfire, burping out puffs of white smoke. Heading for the rendezvous point, I throttled back repeatedly to prevent the engine from conking out or vibrating off its mounts. A few moments later it quit again. I pulled back and shoved her on; it quit and started again.

At this point I started getting nervous. The other planes had long since regrouped and headed back, and I was alone in the clouds without friends—a dangerous predicament. The wind screamed through my shattered canopy as the speed increased. It sounded like the canopy was going to come off.

Suddenly I sighted a lone Wildcat. It was Jake Stub, who was having engine trouble too. He was flying even slower than I was, and we were both losing altitude. Then we ran into some rain squalls and heavy clouds, which separated us.

Breaking out of the clouds in heavy rain, with Stub nowhere in sight, I could make out the silhouette of two islands up ahead and steered for them.[1] Flying on feeling instead of watching my compass, I mistook them for the gateway to Guadalcanal.

I was gaining and losing altitude sporadically as my engine cut out and recovered. Soon the stops got closer than the starts, and I realized I wasn't going to make it back to Henderson. Checking my compass, I saw that I was 30 degrees off course, with nightfall rapidly approaching.

Viscous sheets of another squall appeared dead ahead, and I flew left to circumvent it. Just as I came abreast of the storm, a plume of smoke swirled out of my motor, and the engine stopped cold. No amount of urgent manipulation of the throttle would bring it back to life. Now all I could hear was the whistling of the wind rushing over the plane's outer skin and through the hole in the canopy.

The storm was growing, and if I landed in the water my chances of being spotted from the air were minimal if not nonexistent. Suddenly I keenly lamented the fact that I had never learned to swim!

I began rocking to and fro in the cockpit in the motion a child uses to move a kiddie car forward foot by foot, as though I could propel the plane physically. Bathed in sweat, I felt like my hair was standing up so straight it would raise the helmet right off my head.

I spotted an island off to my left and set a glide path for it. Fortunately I was at about 13,000 feet; I figured I should have plenty of altitude to make the distance. I'd ditch the plane in the water directly offshore and paddle to land with

---

[1] Later I would learn that Jake got shot down shortly after I had seen him. It took him five days to get back to home base. Jake had spotted Zeros chasing me that I had not seen, but apparently they lost me when I went into the clouds.

the aid of my Mae West, the bulky life vests we wore at all times when we flew.

As I circled in over the deserted shoreline, looking for a smooth, sandy beach on which to land, I miscalculated: The maneuver had cost me considerable altitude, and when I circled back out to sea to make another landing approach, I rapidly ran out of elevation and speed. Now I had no choice. I was going down in the water almost five miles from land.

The thought of having to swim five miles was terrifying; the single test I'd failed during flight training was the basic swimming test. Adding to my woes was the storm, now in full force, whipping up the sea and ruining my visibility.

I opened the canopy and pushed it back so I could climb out when I hit the surface. As the water rose to meet me, I pulled the plane's nose up, intending to skip the machine like a rock on a pond, but the tail section bashed against the water and bounced up above the front of the plane. When I hit the water a second time, I nosed into the Pacific like a torpedo from a dive bomber. The impact threw the canopy forward and slammed it shut. Water poured through the rents in the canopy with the force of a wave breaking on a beach.

The Grumman manual promised that the plane would float at least thirty seconds, but the heavily armored machine sank immediately. Gliding into the depths, I found myself in utter darkness with water gushing into the cockpit through the fist-sized punctures in the canopy. Only then did I remember my training: Even when every precaution is taken, a water landing is a dangerous maneuver—and in my excitement and panic I had neglected two precautions. I forgot that I was supposed to jettison the canopy entirely before hitting the water, and I forgot to release the snaps on the leg straps of my parachute harness.

Trapped in the dark plane, numb with fear and cold, I forced myself to act. *Listen, dope,* I told myself. *If you don't quiet down, you're going to spend a long time inside this bird on the bottom of the ocean!*

Water filled the cockpit as I felt for the latches that held the canopy, unfastened them, and pushed it open with all my strength. I fought to maintain consciousness, but momentarily blacked out and sucked in brackish sea water

Just like the old story goes, my whole life passed before my eyes as I lost track of the real world. I saw my buddies gathered around the Short Snorters table, sorting and distributing my personal belongings among themselves and talking about what a fine fellow old Joe had been. I had a lot of things I loved, like my sewing kit, and I could just see those punks sitting around there having a good time with it. It irritated the daylights out of me and snapped me back to reality.

Forcing myself to action was agony, and I restrained my gagging cough, a reaction to the ingested sea water, through sheer force of will. I had no idea how long I'd been under the water, but my body was screaming for oxygen. Reaching down, I unhooked my leg straps, swallowing more sea water in the process.

No longer locked to the plane, I was pulled upward toward the surface by the current streaming past the rapidly sinking Wildcat and by my buoyant parachute pack and life preserver. Fortunately I had remembered to crack the air cylinders on my Mae West, and the life jacket's buoyancy, along with my floatable parachute pack, began to pull me toward the surface—fanny up.

Suddenly my left foot caught and wedged under the cockpit seat, trapping me and holding me fast as the Wildcat continued its descent into the deep. For a moment I thrashed helplessly in the water. Then, using the fabric of my flight suit for a grip, I pulled my way, hand over hand, toward my captured foot. The need to breathe was almost uncontrollable, but I tapped the last of my strength to free my foot. Finally, disengaged from the airplane, I felt the crushing pressure of the cold water as I shot upward.

The passage seemed an eternity. My craving for air was pure pain. When I finally reached the surface, it was backside first, the parachute pack on my back pushing my face underwater. The boxing matches of my youth were child's play compared with the fight I waged with my own safety gear as I struggled to undo the stubborn straps of the parachute harness that had twisted with the fastenings of the Mae West, all the time swallowing more sea water.

I got one strap unbuckled and twisted the chute around

under my stomach. At least now I could keep my head above water. Then at last I unsnapped the remaining strap, only to have the loose-fitting Mae West float up over my ears. I pulled the adjustment straps tighter, and all of a sudden I was floating peacefully.

Now all I had to do was swim five miles to shore through a raging storm!

Gasping and coughing and shaking, I remembered the instructions: Relax and try to swim calmly. Thinking I should get rid of all excess weight, I unlaced my boots and let them sink. Instantly I regretted doing this. *I know I'm going to need them on that island; the coral will tear my feet to shreds.* I didn't scuttle my parachute, figuring I could use it as a cover after reaching shore.

But the odds of making it to the island were slight, and I knew it. Between the storm and the rapidly approaching darkness, it was difficult to see clearly. Also, it seemed like the current was carrying me out to sea.

I started thrashing my arms and doing some kind of ridiculous bicycle-pedaling motion with my legs, which all amounted to a crazy kind of jig with a lot of splashing and little progress. *Sure glad nobody's here to see this,* I thought.

Suddenly a stone's throw away something caught my eye. "Shark fins!" I think I yelled it out loud. *What a way to go. After all I've been through, I'm going to check out as a hunk of shark bait.*

Now, trying to swim became doubly fearful. Every time I reached an arm out to paddle I was afraid I'd draw back a stub. Though sharks normally don't bother humans, many in the area had developed a taste for human flesh because of the numerous naval and aerial battles that left men bleeding in the waters of the slot. Men from both sides had fallen prey to the carnivorous sea creatures, and I was terrified.

Then I remembered the chlorine. My flight suit was equipped with little capsules of chlorine shark repellant. (It's a good thing I didn't know, as would later be proven, that chlorine doesn't protect swimmers from shark attacks.)

I broke one open, hoping the sharks disliked the smell as much as I did. Then I started praying harder than I'd ever prayed in my life. I confessed every sin I could remember and kept praying, "God help me!"

I had never felt more alone or more helpless.

Four or five hours drifted by, and I was growing weaker struggling against the sea. Then, through the black night around me, I heard something. *Voices!* I turned my head in the direction of the sounds. *Canoe paddles?*

Two flickers of light moved in an odd pattern across the water. *Japs!* I thought. *They saw me hit the drink!*

I stopped swimming and floated silently as the splashing of oars grew louder and louder. It appeared there were two boats traveling toward me. The boatmen were carrying on a mumbled conversation, but I couldn't make out any words or accents.

When the light was only yards away I could see that they were outrigger canoes, heading straight at me. I held my breath, afraid the noisy thumping of my wildly beating heart would give me away.

The clumsy Mae West made it impossible to duck underwater, so I desperately tried to push myself silently to one side. The canoes skimmed by, too close for comfort, but even then I couldn't discern the nationality of the murmurs and low-pitched conversation.

The searchers combed the waters, back and forth, but somehow I escaped their notice. Finally someone yelled, "Let's look over 'ere."

It was an Australian accent and the most welcome sound I'd ever heard.

"Hey!" I yelled. "Over here!"

The lights headed toward me immediately and circled. When I finally saw the faces of the men, they were grotesquely highlighted by the lanterns. Almost all were natives, and they were armed with war clubs.

"Hey, get me out of here!" I yelled. "I'm an American . . . friend . . . birdman . . . flier . . . pilot . . . I got shot down."

A hand reached out of the darkness to pull me into the outrigger. It was the hand of Father Dan Stuyvenberg, a Catholic priest.

My parachute was waterlogged and weighed a ton.

"You must be a superman to drag anything like that along with you," said the other white man. Later I would learn that he was Tommy Mason Robertson, a sawmill owner from the island of Malaita.

As the natives paddled back to shore, Robertson held his lantern higher to get a better look at me. In a flash something struck the lantern from his hand and sent it clanking across the bottom of the boat. The something that had knocked the lamp from his grip was flipping in the bottom of the boat: a slender garlike fish, about twenty inches long, with a sharp, pointed nose.

"I should've kept the lantern down," Tommy apologized. "Guess I got careless in all the excitement. Plenty of men have lost their eyes at night doing that. These jumping fish go toward light. Even the reflection of your eyes will attract them."

That was enough to convince me, and until we landed I kept my hands over my face and peeked through my fingers.

The men also pointed out that the jut of land I'd been swimming toward was overpopulated with man-eating crocodiles. If somehow I'd made it to land, I'd probably have been somebody's supper. Talk about an obstacle course!

The island was Malaita, and my rescuers were from the Catholic mission there. The mission colony consisted of two compounds, one for the women and another for the men, as well as a scattering of native dwellings.

When we landed, I stumbled from the beach to a campfire where the islanders had gathered to wait for the searchers' return. The welcoming party included two bishops, four fathers, two brothers, and eight sisters. The place was a regular melting pot of nationalities. The missionaries were from France, the Netherlands, Norway, Russia, Italy, and even a brother from Emmetsburg, Iowa, and a sister from Boston. Most of them had escaped to Malaita when the Japanese invaded neighboring islands. Some of their fellow workers had not been so fortunate; the Japanese had an ugly fetish for bayoneting missionaries through the throat, and two nuns had been raped and killed by a group of Japanese soldiers.

A Proud American

I was exhausted and feeling sick from the sea water I'd swallowed, but my rescuers were anxious to hear what was going on in the outside world. Their only sources of news were Tommy Robertson's tiny radio aboard his scow and meager reports from natives who crossed the channel from one of the other islands. One of the sisters had been in the islands for forty years. Though she had seen the airplanes that strafed and bombed the islands, she had never seen an automobile.

Dry clothes and an excellent meal revived me. Steak—the first fresh meat I'd had in weeks—eggs, papaya, pineapple, and a delicious dark bread. No supplies had arrived on the island for months, but they gave me the best they had.

They kept me awake for some time, fascinated by my stories about the war and other progress in the outside world. When I finally hit the sack it was a thatch mat with a pillow that felt more like a hundred-pound bag of rock salt, but I was so exhausted I could have slept on a bed of nails. And I slept well, except for one bout of nausea from all the sea water I'd swallowed.

The sound of hymns woke me the next morning. I ached from head to toe, and when I stood up, my shaky legs brought my crash landing vividly to mind. I rubbed the sleep out of my eyes and left the long, narrow one-room thatched building. Following the sound, I came upon an open-sided thatched hut which was obviously a church; the altar was made of carved bamboo and coconut shells, and before it stood one of the priests leading a congregation of seminaked natives. Some of the older natives were a fearful sight, clad in red loincloths and savage-looking jewelry made from shells and animal teeth, their mouths stained red from chewing betel nuts, and their hair standing out like it was charged with electricity. The missionaries had told me the night before that this particular tribe had a reputation for being hostile, but here they were, singing hymns.

After the service Father Dan arranged a reception and breakfast near his living quarters so that everyone could shake hands with me. The entire village turned out. Again, though food was in short supply, they brought out their best—eggs, fresh goat's milk, papaya and other exotic fruits I didn't recognize, and more of that delicious bread.

I had once joked with my men, "If I get shot down, don't come looking for me for a couple weeks, because I'll be fishing." With their fine hospitality and the surf fishing I could do, a couple weeks here would seem like heaven.

But there was a war on, and somehow I had to get back to my outfit. After breakfast I stretched out my chute in a clearing, knowing that any circling American plane would recognize it as a distress signal.

The missionaries told me about an airplane that had crashed on the side of the mountain not far from the village and wanted me to go with them to investigate. They were unsure which country it belonged to. Minutes later we started up the steep trail to find the site of the crash. As we moved through the jungle we heard an airplane approaching, and the party started to scatter.

"It's a Grumman F4F. Probably looking for me," I said, and ran into a clearing. As the plane turned, the pilot looked right down at me. I recognized Dutch Bruggeman from our squadron, and he recognized me. When he turned and headed for home, I told the priests that it wouldn't be long before someone came back for me.

After a short time, a PBY appeared on the horizon. The pilot set the flying boat down far out at sea and cruised in toward the bay, so that any enemy observers would have a hard time pinpointing where he was heading.

I hurriedly said good-bye to my new friends and gave my chute to the nuns to make vestments for the church. I understand that to this day that parachute silk adorns the altar of the Catholic church on Malaita, with the letters U.S. still clearly visible.

Two native rowers gave me a swift ride out to the plane, and once aboard I made my way to the cockpit, where I found two old friends at the controls: Major Jack Cram and his copilot, Major Charles Parker. They were flying General Geiger's plane again!

Homecoming was a raucous event—sort of like someone coming back from the dead. Someone said I came back "dressed in a pair of sailor's white trousers, smoking a cigar, and talking a mile a minute."[2] That's the way I remember it, too.

I went straight to the fighter ready tent to find my men.

"Joe!" they shouted. "We thought for sure you were a goner!"

Once more I was kept awake telling stories, but this time I was the one catching up on what had happened while I'd been gone. Several good men and friends had died, and despite my fatigue, we talked for hours. I even did my popular impression of a befuddled Jap commander calling roll after we'd wiped out his entire flight.

We camouflaged our feelings with laughter, rather than think too hard about our fallen comrades and our own narrow escapes. Of the original eight in my flight, half were gone forever, and many of the guys had silently given me up for dead before word arrived that I'd been sighted on Malaita.

That night I wrote in my diary: "Glad to be back again. Thankful is the word. Yesterday I prayed more than I ever prayed in my life."

One thought kept running through my mind as I lay on my cot and stared into the darkness: *I've been saved for another day—for some reason.*

---

[2] Thomas G. Miller, Jr., *The Cactus Air Force* (New York: Harper & Row, 1969), p. 179.

Chapter 14

More Than One
Kind of Battle

The next morning I slept in till six o'clock, then climbed into my flight suit, grabbed my helmet, and headed for Operations. Vice Admiral Halsey, the new naval commander in the South Pacific, had ordered a special awards ceremony for Bill Freeman, Lieutenant Wallace Wethe, another member of our squadron, and me. Even for this auspicious occasion we wore our working duds, since we were on alert.

The three of us stood at attention in the jungle shade outside the command dugout while the admiral made some brief remarks and then awarded each of us the Distinguished Flying Cross. My citation read:

> For extraordinary achievement while participating in aerial flights with Marine Fighting Squadron 121 in the Solomon Islands area. During the period October 13, to October 20, 1942, inclusive, Captain Foss shot down six enemy Zero fighters and one enemy bomber in aerial combat. His constant aggressiveness, skill, and leadership during these engagements were worthy of the highest tradition of the Naval Service.[1]

---

[1] The paperwork for the award had gone through when I had seven planes to my credit; on the day of the ceremony my total was nineteen.

My boys in the Flying Circus VMF-121, Guadalcanal, the hot spot of the South Pacific. These men shot down 73 planes, flying Grumman F4F Wildcats. To my left: Greg Loesch, Bill Freeman, Guts Marontate, Boot Furlow, Oscar Bate, Roger Haberman, and Frank Presley.

In my opinion, everything there could have been said of the other men in the Flying Circus.

Later that same day Admiral Halsey called all available fliers together for a short pep talk. He was aware that the Marines on the island were indignant that the dreaded Toyko Express, otherwise known as the Japanese fleet, was operating so unmolested in the waters off Guadalcanal. As we saw it, the U.S. Navy could and should have waited for the enemy to sail into the slot, then circled in with a pincer from both sides and put an end to them. Instead, the Japs had destroyed another of our fuel dumps and a barge loaded with gasoline on its way to Guadalcanal; along with all our other shortages, we were nearly out of fuel again. Morale was high, considering the critical situation, but we were frustrated with the Navy brass. In retrospect, I suppose they simply didn't have the ships to do the job, but at the time few of us on the front line had any real perspective on that. So the gist of Admiral Halsey's speech that day was "I know you don't like the U.S. Navy right now, but Guadalcanal has to be held. And I promise you I'll give you everything I've got. Gentlemen, there is going to be some fighting!"

"Give 'em hell" Halsey, with his bulldog jaw and bushy eyebrows, was just what the doctor ordered. Admiral Nimitz had wanted a more aggressive commander, and he'd gotten one. As one historian would rightly comment: "The flamboyant, fun-loving 'Bull' Halsey proved to be a shot in the arm when the patient seemed in danger of passing away."[2]

After flying a combat mission the next day, I prepared to take a group of recently arrived pilots on a guided tour of the islands, a kind of general area orientation we gave new arrivals. Before leaving, I stuffed a duffel with candy bars, razor blades, tobacco, and the newest three-month-old magazines, and rigged it to the outside of my plane. I also threw in a few cans of Spam. We were always looking for an excuse to get rid of a little Spam.

During the orientation flight, I led the formation of newcomers to the island of Malaita and flew directly over the missionaries' compound, where I pulled the rope releasing

---

[2] Robert Sherrod, *History of Marine Corps Aviation in World War II* (Washington: Combat Forces Press, 1952), p. 106. Also, on November 7, 1942, Brigadier General Louis Woods replaced General Roy (Jiggs) Geiger as Commander Air, Guadalcanal. "By early November, it was clear to all that Roy Geiger, the rock-hard old airman, was suffering from a bad case of combat fatigue. Two months and four days of seeing his always outnumbered young men killed or evacuated, unable to fight any more, had finally broken down even his constitution. . . . In a way it was a tragedy for Jiggs Geiger to be sent back to run his air wing from a desk six hundred miles from the fighting. He knew that he was about to miss the final battle for the island. But for the Cactus Air Force, it was the best thing that could have happened. Fresh, relatively rested, ten years younger than Geiger, changed by his promotion, as he said, 'from a kindly old colonel to a blood-thirsty brigadier general,' Louis Woods stepped into the direct command of Guadalcanal's air power at the most crucial hour of its short, tumultuous history." (Miller, *Cactus Air Force,* p. 177).

the package. Fourteen years later when I was the guest of honor on Ralph Edwards's *This Is Your Life,* Tommy Mason Robertson recalled the incident, including the welcome contents of the package.

On November 11, I rose at 4:30 A.M. to lead a strafing mission. Then Boot Furlow and I set out alone hunting a flying boat. We returned just as the rest of the squadron was scrambling to intercept a swarm of fifty Japanese planes chasing the American fleet. The mechanics didn't have enough gasoline left to refuel the two of us, so Boot and I borrowed a truck and raced off in search of gasoline. We found a gas truck with sufficient fuel for the mission, but were delayed gassing up and left the ground well after the rest of the flight. Flying at top speed toward the squadron, I listened to the clear sound of machine-gun fire over the scratchy radio and the men calling for help or in warning. I knew every one of their voices without hearing their names—we all knew each other's voices. I gritted my teeth and pushed the throttle as if metal stress might get me to the fight faster.

That air battle ended up being one of the most brutal to date, and there was nothing I could do to help. The Japanese lost eleven bombers and Zeros, but we lost seven planes and five pilots—an unusually high loss for us. Our boys had plenty of experience on their side, but one more airplane always made a difference, and mine wasn't around when they needed it.

Our skipper, Duke Davis, and my good friend Roger Haberman were both wounded. A shell exploded in the skipper's cockpit and shrapnel permeated his right side. He had the medics bandage his jaw and shoulder carefully so he could still wear his oxygen mask when he flew out to fight again that night.

Haberman entered camp on a stretcher, bleeding like a stuck hog. A Japanese belly shot had penetrated his plane's fuselage and entered the inside of his thigh just above his knee, traveled up inside his leg, and come to rest near his scrotum. After field surgery they airlifted him to the hospital on Espíritu Santo for further treatment and recovery.

A few days later I was surprised to see Haberman limping

into the ready tent in his flight suit. "I'm ready to fly, Joe. I'm released."

I thought the big German-American looked a little fragile, but since the medics had released him, I put him to work. Later I got a report that Haberman had deserted. Actually what had happened was that he couldn't stand to stay in bed and recuperate, so he'd simply walked out of the hospital and bluffed his way onto a military transport back to Guadalcanal. We knew where he was, but as far as the hospital was concerned, he'd gone AWOL.

Early on November 12, a coastwatcher high in the mountains of southern Bougainville reported Bettys on their way. I took my flight up to 29,000 feet, where we circled the cloud-covered harbor, waiting for the enemy to arrive. We figured they would try to surprise us by launching their attack from the clouds that hung over nearby Florida Island, which is exactly what they did. Nineteen Bettys came out of the clouds at about 500 feet, peeling off for their torpedo runs on the ships.

"All right, boys, let's go get them," I radioed.

It was a long way down from 29,000 feet, and we dove at full throttle, reaching a speed of 600 knots, way past the redline of 300 knots. As we entered the warmer, humid air, the planes began to ice up; our canopies frosted over, and I had to scrape the frost from the inside of my windshield to see. The air pressure from the rushing wind ruptured my cockpit hood and tore some pads from the edge of the fuselage.

The sky was black with antiaircraft fire from twenty-seven warships as the Flying Circus pulled up behind the Japanese planes and started picking them off before they could make a run for it. Major Paul Fontana's flight from VMF-112 had also joined the fray, along with eight P-39s from the 67th Pursuit Squadron of the Army Air Corps.

I swung in about a hundred yards behind a Betty bomber and cut loose with four of my guns. The bomber's right engine burst into flames, and the plane went into a crazy cartwheel, then plopped into the water on its belly.

I pulled up to look for another target and spotted several

bombers trailing smoke and fire on the way to their watery graves. Lining up on a bomber, I flew near the ships to get into a better position. Just as I was about to squeeze the trigger, a Zero seemed to jump at me out of nowhere. I pulled up abruptly and let the speeding plane fly by, then swung onto his tail and gave him a short burst dead into the wing mount area. The Zero blew only a few feet above the water, scattering its debris over the surface.

Going back to where I was so rudely interrupted, I approached the bomber from a rear angle, keeping my distance from its tail gunners. I fired and missed—probably because I was swiveling around like crazy, watching for more maverick Zeros. On my second pass at the bomber, my shots went home, right at the base of the wing, firing the left engine and bringing the plane down.

In less than eight minutes our fighters and AA fire had shot down all but two of the Japanese bombers and a Zeke.

Something big was coming; it was in the air. Rear Admiral Aubrey W. Fitch, Commander Air Force South Pacific, had been sending any aircraft reinforcements he could find into Henderson as fast as he could: P-39s, SBDs, an Army B-26 squadron loaded with torpedoes; F4Fs escorting TBFs, P-38s. At Fighter One and the bomber strip, maintenance crews worked flat out, trying to get as many damaged planes as possible in fighting trim.

The tension broke at 1:30 in the morning on November 13 when the air-raid siren went off, echoed by horns, bells, and sirens at every location. Ten minutes later we heard the rumble of naval guns in the distance, growing to a muffled roar. Those of us who had lived through the night of October 13–14 knew what it meant. The Japanese naval forces were closing in on the island.

No shells fell on Henderson that night, but the northern horizon was so bright it reminded me of the aurora borealis on a winter night in South Dakota. The Battle of Guadalcanal had begun.

I was sent out alone at dawn to assess the damage to our own ships in the night's battle.

The Japanese had planned to bombard Henderson Field

early that morning, with the battleships *Hiei* and *Kirishima* providing the firepower, along with a light cruiser and eleven destroyers. Before they could strike, eight American destroyers and five cruisers had intercepted them at point-blank range in the sound between Guadalcanal and Savo. One Japanese destroyer and two American destroyers had been sunk outright. Five miles off Lunga Point, I spotted the shattered light cruiser *Atlanta,* and halfway between Lunga Point and Savo the destroyers *Cushing* and *Monssen* were burning, as was the Japanese destroyer *Yudachi*. The stern of the heavy cruiser *Portland* had been damaged and twisted by torpedoes, but even as I watched, the crippled *Portland* opened fire and finished off the *Yudachi*.

I also located the *Hiei,* which had taken scores of hits and was being protected by three destroyers. Finally we had an enemy battleship at our mercy!

When I got back to base with that word, the Cactus Air Force scrambled as quickly as the ground crews could get us armed and gassed. We were to go in over the enemy fleet at 12,000 feet, doing vertical dives on the battlewagon and anything else out there. As we were diving on the ships, with all the enemy guns trained on us, the torpedo planes were to come around Savo Island. Once the torpedo attack was rolling along, down would come the real dive bombers. We'd have them firing in every direction as we attacked from high above and at ocean level.

A little after 10:00 that morning my flight of eight Wildcats roared down on the *Hiei*. We made our vertical dives one at a time, peeling off. I was bouncing .50 calibers off the decks of the battleship as the pom-pom guns on deck pumped away at me, evidently shooting below me because my dive was so vertical. I got so caught up in the action that I almost flew into the ship. When it was time to pull out, I had to lift my left wing to avoid hitting the superstructure on the ship. As I flew out, taking evasive action, I called back to my boys, "Keep the dives steep. Keep the dives steep."

We all made it out of there in good shape and had just gotten back to the field when General Geiger came down, congratulated us, and said, "I'd like to have the same group go out again and give them another good blasting." So as soon as we were refueled and rearmed, the same outfits took off again and repeated the act.

I would classify that mission as about the most dangerous we ever flew. It made my hair stand on end more than any other because of the amount of flak that was thrown at us. Geysers spurted up all around us as the big shells hit the water, and if we had run into one of those fountains, it would have knocked us to kingdom come. But we had a successful mission, and by sunset the battleship *Hiei* lay sinking off the backside of Savo Island. What some would later call "one of the fiercest naval battles ever fought," was over.

Later it would also be reported: "Although the terrible sacrifices of the cruiser and destroyer sailors had given them the opportunity, it should be recorded that the first battleship to be sunk by Americans in the Second World War was sunk because of the attacks of a handful of Marine and Navy aircraft."[3]

That night was a real bear cat as the Japs shelled us mercilessly from dusk to dawn. Maytag Charlie started it off, followed by some 1,000 rounds of eight-inch shells from two heavy cruisers. Fighter One was hit, we lost two Wildcats, and fifteen others were hit by shrapnel.

All of this was paving the way for the arrival of a reinforcement Japanese convoy of cruisers, destroyers, and transports, which had been headed for Guadalcanal and had turned back after the night battle of November 13. Now they were steaming in again.

Despite the exhausting, nonstop battle the day before, followed by a tense, sleepless night—and bad weather—in the morning we took to the air. We were determined to blow the bastards out of the water.

By late that afternoon the Cactus Air Force had destroyed or crippled most of the Japanese convoy, and I was ordered to take a flight up to provide cover for the final attacks as our dive bombers and torpedo planes went after the surviving transports.

Colonel Joe Bauer said, "I'm going with you, Joe." Usually

---

[3] Miller, *Cactus Air Force,* pp. 183, 188.

grounded now by his duties as flight director, Bauer used the excuse that he was taking the place of a tired pilot. I knew he just wanted to get into the game. As flight director of VMF-212, Bauer was one of the top strategists in determining which squadron would be on scramble alert, who would give air ground support, and who would carry out search missions. We all worshiped him. "Put me on the team, Coach," pilots would plead when they wanted to go on a strike.[4]

"No, sir," I said that day. "You lead, Coach."

Bauer agreed, but his Grumman wouldn't start, so I told Greg Loesch, "Shove on!" giving him command of the flight. Boot Furlow and I held back to accompany Bauer.

When the three of us finally headed north up the slot, I was on the right side of the colonel and Boot was on the left. As we got to the other side of Russell Island, we spotted our squadron coming back and smoke rising from five of the eight remaining transports. At that point, a normal man would have turned back, but not Coach. He led us right up to the enemy fleet for a final strafing run.

Once when a lieutenant landed jubilantly and cried, "I got two!" Bauer roared at him: "Get the hell back up there! You've still got gas and guns, haven't you?" Bauer himself sometimes landed without enough gas to taxi up to the line.[5]

Now Bauer gave the signal, and we followed him in a steep dive into the middle of the fleet. Racing around in there, picking our separate targets like we were shooting sitting ducks, we kept just high enough so our props cleared the water, but low enough that they couldn't shoot at us or they'd shoot each other.

Throughout the day, General Woods had ordered all the fighters to fly their cover at high altitudes; the Japanese fighters hadn't shown their wings, and he expected a surprise attack at any moment. Now, suddenly, here they came, a flock of eight Zeros descending on us like a snowstorm. They couldn't really get at us, though, because we were so low.

Bauer, an excellent pilot with eleven enemy planes to his

---

[4] Richard G. Hubler and John A. DeChant, *Flying Leathernecks* (Garden City, N.Y.: Doubleday, Doran & Co., Inc., 1944), p. 97.

[5] Ibid.

credit, turned into the nearest bogey and annihilated it while I chased another. I was concentrating so completely, weaving around the ships just off the water, that I barely noticed I was headed straight into the side of an enemy destroyer. I almost ran into the superstructure of the ship, and when I pulled up the Zero got away.

I quickly chose another target and shot it down, then turned back in time to see Boot knock a Zero out of the sky. My radio had gone out again, as usual, and antiaircraft was coming at us from all sides. Boot and I joined up, ready to get the hell out of there, and looked around for Bauer.

Heading out into the slot, we spotted a long oil slick spreading in the water, and swimming out of the center of it was the Coach. I pulled the toggle behind my head to drop my life raft, but it wouldn't release. The colonel waved us on. He was a good swimmer and probably figured he was safe in the water until we could get back with a rescue plane, as long as we didn't draw the enemy's attention to him.

Boot radioed to Henderson that the colonel was down, and when we got back, Colonel Joe Renner had readied a Grumman Duck J2F, capable of landing on the water. Renner, like Bauer, was a big man with American Indian blood in his veins. Both were photogenic characters and either could have walked off the set of a western movie. The guys always said, since I was a dead ringer for John Wayne, that the three of us made an ideal fighting group.

I gave a quick explanation of where I'd last seen the Coach, and Renner climbed into the cockpit while I pulled myself into the bottom of the plane to make certain the bilge-camera porthole, where they placed the camera on photographic missions, was fastened. If we landed on the water to pick up Bauer, I didn't want to sink. Renner hit the gas and had just gained a good flying speed when about halfway down the runway a B-25 taxied out in front of the Duck. Later the guys on the ground told us they'd braced themselves for an explosion, but Renner had enough speed to send the plane on a desperate hop, barely clearing the bomber.

I had no idea what was going on because I was still crawling toward the cockpit, bouncing around like a loose goose. The Duck dipped back to the ground, but Renner didn't even slow. He took off again and just missed the tips of the palm trees at the end of the runway.

A bit bruised and bewildered, I pulled myself into the rear seat and directed Renner back to where I'd last seen Bauer. When we left Henderson it was still daylight, but by the time we arrived at the position where the Coach had gone down it was pitch dark. We spotted the battle site long before we got there; the five or six flaming, exploding transports scattered about the area lighted the sky like a beacon. Outside of that, however, it was black as the inside of your hat. We couldn't see a thing as Renner kept cruising closer and closer to the fires, flying at such a low altitude, only a few feet above the water, I was afraid we might hit a lifeboat on the water. The Japanese were searching the waters for their own survivors, and in the confusion and darkness it was impossible to see anything. In fact, we almost ran into a destroyer running without lights. They probably wondered who this nut was flying around in the middle of the enemy fleet.

I began pleading with Renner to go back to the field. "There's no use hanging around here. We'll run into something and we'll all get killed. We should go back, and I'll bring my flight up here in the morning. We'll arrive before daylight so we'll be on station here. Then you can bring the Duck in, and if we find him you can pick him up."

I took a bearing, and come daylight, my flight was on station above the area. By now all the ships had sunk, and the sea was scattered with life jackets and other debris. Before we could even begin searching, in pulled six Zeros, skimming down across the water. I called, "Let's go!" to my flight, and we got all six of them.

Then we lined up eight abreast, close enough so we could scan the territory in between each plane, and began flying back and forth looking for signs of life. Back and forth, north to south, south to north; east to west, west to east. But outside of the debris on the water, we couldn't see anyone or anything. We stayed there on station until our fuel supply was down to a point where we just made it back to Fighter One by the skin of our teeth.

We never saw Lieutenant Colonel Joe Bauer again.

That night I fell asleep as soon as I hit my cot, despite the shelling and gunfire close at hand. Several hours past midnight I woke up covered with sweat and aching all over. It seemed to take forever for morning to arrive, and when it did I had a full-blown case of malaria, a particularly malevolent variety that had resisted the standard dosage of quinine and Atabrine we all took in the tropics. To make matters worse, I'd also contracted a serious case of dysentery. Drenched with sweat and shaking with chills, I turned my executive duties over to Bill Marontate.

The medics put me on a strong diet of quinine—forty-five grains the first five days—which alleviated some of the roller-coaster symptoms, but periodically I'd collapse into trembling delirium. Between bouts of freezing to death and burning up, the side effects of the quinine treatment—severe double vision and a constant ringing sensation in my ears—barred me from almost everything but forced rest.

Those blasted mosquitoes had accomplished what the Imperial air force had failed to achieve. I was out of action.

But so was Japanese supremacy in the southern Solomons. The four-day Battle of Guadalcanal had turned the tide in that area of the Pacific—and perhaps elsewhere. As Admiral Halsey wrote several years later: "If our ships and planes had been routed in this battle, if we had lost it, our troops on Guadalcanal would have been trapped as were our troops on Bataan. . . . Unobstructed, the enemy would have driven south, cut our supply lines to New Zealand and Australia and enveloped them."[6]

On November 19 the authorities decided our flight should be pulled out for some rest and recuperation. They sent us south to Noumea, New Caledonia, where I landed in what we called the aviatorium—the garage for aviators who needed a rest and a tune-up. Several others from our squadron who'd been devastated by the same disease, including Ben Finney, were in there at the same time. The stuff they doctored me with turned me yellow as a piece of butter, but eventually the medication began to take effect and my condition improved.

---

[6] Quoted in Robert Sherrod, *History of Marine Corps Aviation in World War II* (Washington: Combat Forces Press, 1952), p. 117.

One day while I was recuperating, I got a call from the shore patrol saying they had arrested seven men who were out of uniform and who claimed they were Marines from my outfit. When he named them, I said, "Yes, those are my men. I'll be right there. Just wait there."

I remembered that when he had decorated me, Admiral Halsey had told me if I ever needed anything to just call him. *Well,* I thought, *his headquarters are here and I need him right now.* So I went down to his office, and he happened to be there—a miracle in itself, since he was a very busy man.

"Well, what can I do for you, Captain Foss?"

I told him my men were being held by the APs for being out of uniform, and he laughed and told his administrative assistant, "Get me that commander on the phone."

Halsey told the commander to bring the men personally over to his headquarters, which the man did. Of course by that time my boys were really glad to see me. When they'd arrived for their R and R, they'd needed some clean clothing and had happened on some Aussie or New Zealand shorts and shirts. That's what they were wearing, along with their Marine insignias. The admiral just laughed about the whole thing.

"These are fighting men," he said to the commander. Then he asked, "How long have you been out here?"

The commander said he'd just arrived a week or two before, and Halsey said, "I'll see that you get some experience. Now don't bother these men. They're all right. They just needed some clean clothes."

From that day on I thought the admiral was a close relative of mine, and until he passed away I would see him from time to time. In fact, when I was governor he came out from his home in New York City and spent almost a week with me in Sioux Falls. It was during the dedication of Joe Foss Field, and when it was advertised that Admiral Halsey would be there, soldiers and sailors and Marines from all over the Midwest came up to see him—that's how popular he was.

On November 30, Finney and I flew to Sydney, Australia, for two more weeks of rest and recuperation. From the moment we set foot on the island, Finney's contacts rolled out the red carpet treatment. Restaurateurs, civic leaders, and war correspondents fell over themselves to pour on the hospitality. The first day we were there, Finney even introduced me to His Lordship the Mayor.

Finney was famous with the glamour crowd, so his welcome didn't surprise me. What did shock me was that the public knew who I was. Japanese plans for conquering Australia, after they had cleaned up the Pacific islands, were well known there, so it was small wonder that the Aussies were following the action in the Solomons with fearful immediacy. If they'd been around, *Nightline* and CNN would have had a field day. Apparently my contributions to the war effort had been regular front-page news "down under," and they treated me like a full-fledged hero. People even offered us the use of their homes and apartments. We never spent a dime while we were there, and I was in the papers almost every day. I didn't mind at all.

One of the first privileges I claimed was a hot bath and a shave, and for the first few days I ate steak three times a day—good-bye Spam and rice.

When I met up with a group of my buddies from VMF-121 who'd arrived in Sydney while I was convalescing in Noumea, they didn't recognize this lean, yellow-skinned fellow without the goatee. A few also ribbed me about a quote falsely attributed to me in a newspaper story. Some jokester of a flier had told a gullible reporter that on one of his ventures the "smoke was a-pourin', the rivets were a-poppin', and then the wings fell off. But the old ship made it." The comment had been erroneously credited to me, and the guys labeled me "the only man in the world who ever landed a ship without wings."

When I was not being feted by the locals, Finney was escorting me through the best restaurants, nightclubs, and beaches Sydney had to offer, helping me put back some of the weight I'd lost. But the malaria was still with me, and periodically I'd relapse into chills and fever.

On December 7, 1942, I wrote in my diary: "One year ago today the Dirty Rats went to work. I bet they wonder a bit now. That day I was O.D. (officer of the day) of Saufley Field at Pensacola. A lot of blood has gone under the bridge. Gosh

I wish my boys who are gone were here for the rest they worked for."

Bad weather on the anniversary of Pearl Harbor kept me from the one thing I really wanted to do while in Australia, which was fly the new British Spitfire I'd heard so much about. A number of Australian fighter pilots who had recently come home from the desert war in North Africa sought me out to learn what they could about fighting the Japanese. The Aussies, including the famous "Killer" Caldwell, were headed into battle with the emperor's air force and planned to sustain their winning streak. In return for any tips I could give them, they promised me a turn in the cockpit of the new Spitfire fighter, which was supposed to be an equal match for the maneuverable Zero.

The African air war against the German Luftwaffe was an altogether different contest from the air war in the Pacific, and I was equally curious about their experiences. The only contact I'd ever had with a German pilot was an odd incident a few weeks earlier when one lone Zero flew in low over the bomber strip at Henderson to strafe the bigger planes. Dozens of men working around the field drew their handguns and opened fire.

Somebody must have hit the pilot in the head or the back, because he did a loop and splattered. The most intact thing I saw was his boot with his foot still in it. It was a black boot like the German pilots wore and the skin of the foot inside was white. We'd speculated that the flier was a German instructor working with the Japanese.

Finally the weather cooperated and I got a chance to check out the British Spitfire. While I was at the airbase outside Sydney they asked me to speak with a group of their top flyers headed into Pacific combat. Though I had no formal speech to give, I shared my experiences, sipped coffee, and smoked cigars as the pilots asked me about tactics.

From the beginning it was clear that the leather-jacketed RAF pilots draped casually over their chairs were indifferent toward the Flatley-Thach crossweave. They were much more interested in the glamorous tricks of individual combat. When I tried to underscore the value of the crossweave, a few traded

In 1943 I visited the factory where the faithful Grumman Wildcat I flew for all my aerial combat was built. (Photo by Peter Kirkup, courtesy of Grumman History Center)

blatant yawns. I gripped my cigar in my teeth and thought, *You clowns! Just wait till you get out there.*

"You know," I finally told them, "I didn't come out here to give a lecture anyhow. I came out here to fly a Spitfire. I know exactly what you're thinking. You're thinking that if that old duck up there can shoot down twenty-three planes with a Grumman F4F Wildcat that weighs 8,900 pounds against a Zero that weighs between 5,600 and 5,900 pounds, then you can take the Spitfire that weighs 6,200 or 6,300 pounds and go out there and blast them out of the sky. Well, it doesn't work that way. If you try to dogfight a Zero, he'll eat you for lunch.

"Two things save us," I went on, ignoring their grins of

skepticism. "We use the weave so there are eyes and guns pointed in all directions at all times. And we have a very durable airplane with greater firepower than anything they have. We don't worry about points for style; we just blast them out of the sky."

"Well, mate," a young flier asked, "how would you handle a Zero one-on-one?"

"We have a saying at Guadalcanal," I replied. "If you're alone and you meet a Zero, you're outnumbered. Run like hell is my advice."

A low murmur of amused disdain spread through the room. "That's not quite sporting, is it now?" one Aussie asked.

"It may not be sporting," I replied, "but it's smart!"

They just went "ho-hum."

When I finally flew the Spitfire, I had a wonderful ninety-minute hop. With its speed and maneuverability, that baby really handled. Then I made a perfect landing and showed the Aussies I could fly a little.

A week or two later those pilots went off to combat in the New Guinea area and ran into those measly little Zeros that could just wink at you, make a turn, and go the other way. Speedwise, Zeros were equal to or better than the Spit. And those guys tried to dogfight the Japanese one-to-one instead of scissoring the whole team like mad the way we did, and they really got blistered. Umpteen of them got shot down. A few days later they went out again and got another shellacking that just knocked their block off. They really and truly fought a bad war. They didn't listen to me at all.

When my leave was up on December 16, I flew to New Caledonia to wait for orders to report back to Guadalcanal. While I waited, I spent most of my time at the intelligence office reading bulletins and talking to the officers in charge of gathering information about Japanese air power and strategy. I also spent a day at a prison camp questioning a Jap fighter pilot and got quite a bit of interesting dope from him. I was loaded with information, my guns were cleaned, and I was ready to move.

Some mail caught up with me there, just in time for Christmas: three letters from June and a knitted sweater from my sister, Mary Flora, who was now working at the Lockheed Aircraft factory in Burbank, California.

The day before Christmas I wrote in my diary: "A year ago I was flying students. Today I'm just thinking a good fight is the thing I need most to make me really feel O.K.—I'm convinced of that. This eve I just spent thinking of June and Mother and all my other good friends back home."

Chapter 15
Scramble Everything!

Rested, reorganized, and recuperated, my flight was ordered to Guadalcanal for another tour. I received my orders on New Year's Eve, hopped on a DC-3, spent all night flying, and the next morning, January 1, 1943, I was back on the island. But things had changed at Henderson Field.

The muddy "cow pasture" that had been Fighter One was now a landing strip with a steel mat runway. There were more people and vehicles, regular supplies, new roads, telephone poles, and movies for the troops every night. The field had suffered no multiple bombing attacks since we'd left, and no bombing of any kind since December 14. In short, there was no excitement.

All that was left of VMF-121 was our eight-man Flying Circus and the enlisted men. The rest of the pilots in our squadron had been transferred to Samoa to reform as a new unit; they'd been replaced by a new air group on Guadalcanal. Five of the original members of the Flying Circus were gone forever: Andy Andrews, Casey Brandon, Danny Doyle, Gene Nuwer, and Joe Palko. Now our flight consisted of Oscar Bate, Boot Furlow, Bill Freeman, Rog Haberman, Greg Loesch, Bill Marontate, and Frank (Skeezix) Presley, along with our sixty support personnel. We also had a new group commander, Lieutenant Colonel Sam Jack, who welcomed our experienced crew, although I don't think he was sure why we were there.

It was generally assumed that our company would soon go on to join the squadron on Samoa; assumed by everyone but the Flying Circus. I fought for the right to stay and fight on Guadalcanal—a game I was becoming an old hand at—and once again my tenacity won the day. Colonel Sam Jack made me commanding officer of VMF-121, which put me in charge of the Circus pilots, our support crew, and several Navy pilots we adopted after their carrier sank and they landed on the island.

Our old quarters in "Mosquito Grove" were occupied, so we set up camp in a new area only fifty feet from the big guns aimed out into the slot. A makeshift sign posted on a palm tree identified the area as Muddy Valley, with good reason. Between the mud and the nightlong pounding of artillery barrages, it was almost like old times. "And they told me things had quieted down," I said in the morning.

After one night of that, we moved to a high ridge overlooking the ocean. At the back of our two four-man tents, the edge of a steep cliff funneled the incoming sea breezes and provided the closest thing to air conditioning on the island. The site was far enough from the airstrip to provide some sense of security from bombing and a sufficient distance from the big guns to lessen the noise. We were, however, directly underneath those guns' ballistic trajectory, so that shells making their way into the slot whistled eerily over our tents.

On January 3 my diary reflected my increasing impatience toward anything that stood between me and the enemy. "Again all the days seem the same. Last night Jap bomber came over and dropped his load but we never even woke up in our tent. If the bombs are to hit you they'll get you wherever you are so why get up? General Mulcahy introduced me to Admiral Towers and some other admiral. They asked a lot of irrelevant questions." I was weary and restless with much of the day-to-day situation. I thrived on aerial combat and just wanted to get in there and win the war.

We did fly regular missions, but most of our targets were Japanese cargo ships. Occasionally we scrambled to intercept approaching planes, and on one sortie I sank a Japanese schooner equipped with a radio station that was sending intelligence about local air movements to Japanese headquarters. The ship was camouflaged with netting and anchored under an overhanging cliff on the other side of the island. To get a shot at it, I had to fly directly at the cliff, headed straight for the target. I put several long lines of .50 calibers into the wooden hull at the water line, then pulled straight up and seconds later actually mowed the tops of trees on the bluff. When I flew past the next day, only the mast protruded from the water.

On January 15 one of our squadron's Catalina seaplanes encountered five Japanese destroyers about sixteen miles northeast of the Russell Islands, sixty miles northwest of Guadalcanal. The Catalina was credited with one sure hit, and as the day wore on, a force of our dive bombers, escorted by Wildcats, ran across nine more Japanese destroyers about 140 miles from Guadalcanal. Two of the ships were hit and the Japanese sent up some Zeros to drive off our forces. By the time the skirmish was over the Japanese had lost eleven Zeros and we had lost four planes. Closer to Guadalcanal, a plane on patrol ran across three Zeros and shot them all down.

"Things are starting to look more like old times," I remarked, as battle reports came in through my post as assistant operations officer, a position I held concurrent with my duty as CO of VMF-121.

That afternoon our flight, along with some Army Air Corps P-39s, flew escort for dive bombers moving out to attack two Japanese warships north of Guadalcanal. No sooner did we spot the two ships than we were jumped by a group of the new square-wing Zeros, said to climb better and fly faster—the first time we'd encountered these new mosquitoes.

I sent three of my men to take on the Zeros while the rest of us stayed high, keeping an eye on a second group of Zekes that were standing by for action. Within a short time our men had shot down several Zeros, but I spotted a Wildcat with a missing left wing spinning toward the ocean.

Who is it? I asked myself anxiously. Before I could check it out, the dogfight moved into my vicinity. I lined up on a

.Zero, fired, missed, and as it scurried away, I saw Oscar Bate zooming at me with a swarm of angry Zekes in hot pursuit.

I pulled around to line up on the enemy planes, and just then a Zero dove right in front of me. Maneuvering slightly to bring him into my sights, I squeezed the trigger and disintegrated the Zero into an exploding ball of fire.

Then another Wildcat dove in front of me, followed by a determined Zero. I easily lined up for a shot at almost point-blank range and sent the enemy in a slow, flaming spin toward the water.

I didn't stick around to sightsee, however, because off to my right, Bate was trying to dodge a Zero that wouldn't get off his tail. I got that bird in my sights and fired, sending a stream of bullets in front of his nose. The Japanese pilot pulled up short and turned in my direction. We flew straight at each other, both firing with everything we had. My tracers went over his hood, missing by inches; he did the same for me. Our planes got so close I could clearly see the enemy pilot and the vivid markings on the plane—the no-glare strip of green in front of the windshield and the bright red cowling. At the last minute we curved around each other, avoiding a head-on collision and jockeying for good firing angles. I knew I was up against one of the best Japanese pilots I'd yet encountered. Everything was pumping inside me, my heart beating rapidly, my mouth dry.

The Zeke leveled off, made a turning climb, and came back, and I climbed to meet him in another head-on run. At the last possible moment the Zero pulled up into a tight turn to the right to avoid hitting me, which gave me just the chance I needed, and I peppered his cockpit area.

The Zero dove down and past me a few thousand feet, then circled back for a third attack.

Why won't he go down? I wondered, as I prepared to go after him again. Then I spotted several of his buddies closing in as their wounded comrade finally started coughing smoke. Outnumbered, I headed straight for some cloud cover. When I was about half a mile away the Zero finally burst into flames and headed for the drink.

I managed to get back to the field without running into any more enemy planes, but more trouble greeted me there; the

Japanese were bombing the field, which made for a rather tricky landing.

On the ground, to my dismay, I discovered that the Wildcat I'd seen go down was my close friend, Bill Marontate. As we pieced together what had happened—which we always did after battle—Presley and Bate reported that they had seen Bill shoot down a Zero; then apparently he'd had a head-on crash with another, shearing off his wing. A gunner in one of our dive bombers reported seeing Bill bail out safely. Altogether, six American chutes had been spotted, and they had landed in the vicinity of a Japanese destroyer. We all hoped that Bill had survived and at worst was a prisoner.

For the rest of that day and the following, we flew back and forth over the area where Bill had last been seen. We never gave up hope that he'd return. We kept his bunk ready for him right up until our last day on Guadalcanal, but Bill was never heard of again.

That January 15 dogfight kicked my score up to twenty-six planes, equaling Eddie Rickenbacker's American record held since 1918. Next to Charles Lindbergh, Rickenbacker had been my biggest childhood hero and my principal inspiration during the hours I spent learning to fly at Rickenbacker Field near Sioux City, Iowa. Later I learned that Rickenbacker, "ace of aces," had sent me a letter of congratulations and a case of Scotch. Both disappeared in transit, and I never received them. I would also learn later that folks back home were following my tally as eagerly as they had followed Joe DiMaggio's fifty-six-game hitting streak a year and a half earlier. Folks were laying bets on the date I'd break Rickenbacker's longstanding record.

Actually I was unaware of my record-setting accomplishment until I read about it in a newspaper article written by one of the war correspondents stationed with us on the island. Since the mail rarely got through now, it was amazing what we learned from old newspapers.

The Japanese had obliged my longing for action by stepping up their aerial activity, although most of it was still night bombing. Daily dogfights over the fighter strip were a thing of the past. Yet as much as I wanted action, it was probably a good thing I didn't get more of it; I was running on nerves and secretly fighting malaria. The disease had refused to go away, so I stoically concealed my symptoms, fearing I would be forced off the island for further treatment. When the doctors inquired about my health, I just plain lied. On those rare occasions when I did meet the enemy propeller to propeller, the aches and weariness that plagued me on the ground disappeared completely. My nerves burned with electrical energy, my senses sharpened.

As assistant operations officer, I spent every other day at the communications center—a covered hole in the ground—scheduling flights and overseeing daily operations. In fact, it was this job that led to my showdown with Major General Francis P. Mulcahy, who had relieved General Woods on December 26 as commander of Allied land-based aircraft.

The intelligence boys and the top brass were all but celebrating the victory of Guadalcanal. Our antiaircraft fire had finally taken out Maytag Charlie, Pistol Pete had been eliminated, and our forces were keeping the Japanese ground troops restricted to the northern end of the island, where they were fighting for their lives at terrible cost. Thanks to the code breakers, the Tokyo Express no longer held dominion over the ocean, making it more and more difficult for the enemy to land reinforcements and supplies on the island.

But I had seen many of the intelligence reports myself while recuperating in Sydney and New Caledonia, and I interpreted the situation differently. I was convinced that the Japanese had no intention of giving up Guadalcanal. Yamamoto, the man who had masterminded the bombing of Pearl Harbor, would not simply fade away and leave us the field. But I seemed to be the only man on the island who believed the enemy was going to make another major run at us.

Meanwhile, General Mulcahy had taken to running the Cactus Air Force like he was a traffic coordinator at a stateside airport. He kept every available pilot busy supporting the ground troops and assailing the Japanese navy—usually some distance from Henderson—but nobody was guarding home base, where all the equipment not in use was lined up in neat, straight rows like a doggone parking lot.

I would walk around the newly constructed airstrips and stare at the neatly organized equipment. Then I'd turn and look up into the mountains where I knew the Japanese spies watched back through their telescopes and binoculars, and I would almost shudder.

What would I do if I were running the Jap air force? I asked myself. I decided that I'd take some time to regroup and let the Americans get cocky. When they were sure they had nothing to worry about and had dropped their guard, I'd send in a whole slew of dive bombers and wipe them and their airfield off the map.

As the days passed, I grew increasingly convinced that the defensive war was not over, and I decided that if the general wouldn't take some action, I would. With Colonel Sam Jack's permission, I hid eight Grummans in the palm trees at the end of the fighter runway, ready to fly at a moment's notice to protect the field while the rest of the Wildcats were out on missions. Camouflaged by the foliage, the craft were concealed from both the Japanese and Mulcahy.

When the general drove by one day and discovered what I'd done, I was handed my walking papers in the scene recorded at the beginning of this book. This was more than a simple reprimand. Mulcahy's rebuke could mar my record and signal the end of what I had decided would be my career. If it weren't for my Distinguished Flying Cross and my reputation, I might even have faced serious charges for my insubordination. As it was, I figured Mulcahy's censure signaled the end of my hopes for the confidence of my superiors and quick promotion.

Nonetheless, I knew I was right, and the consequences were not unexpected. When I made the decision to hide the eight Wildcats, I knew the risk I was taking. But I've always believed that when something is right, it's worth the risk, no matter what the cost.

And the very next morning after the conversation with Colonel Sam Jack and General Mulcahy, I was proved right.

January 25, 1943. While waiting for my last push-off from the island I'd arrived on a little more than three months earlier, I was in the right place at the right time and heard the voice of a Navy lieutenant ask over the radio static, "Say, have we got any planes around Savo Island? We're picking something up on radar."

The Japs were doing just what I'd expected; they were moving their aerial armada down the slot in a last-ditch effort to hold on to Guadalcanal. They were going to devastate Henderson Field and then blast our fighters out of the sky.

I scrambled the Flying Circus long before any official call to arms—an audacious act for a guy being sent off the island merely because of a difference of opinion. We climbed to about 18,000 feet, just below the clouds, and moved in our standard formation toward Savo Island, the direction in which the enemy planes had been reported.

Moments later twelve Zeros appeared in the distance low over Savo. I ordered my flight to continue climbing, and I called for the next flight to be scrambled, which happened to be Peters and Livingston's flight. We continued our scissoring figure eights and watched the confusing flurrying of enemy craft. After a few minutes, four swift P-38s from another squadron joined us and I said, "Okay, gang, let's go and get the SOBs."

When the enemy was still about a mile away, I nosed up through the overcast and found myself between two flat layers of cloud extending in all directions. Conditions around and over Guadalcanal produced bizarre weather and cloud patterns, and on that particular day at least six distinct cloud strata, like multiple layers of frosting, provided shelter for hundreds of planes if they wanted to hide—and they did.

In the clear space between the bottom two strata I saw what I feared most—a sky black with an enemy armada. There were sixty-plus Zeros, at least two dozen Betty bombers, and eighteen dive bombers, and in the far distance another whole swarm headed toward me. It was the attack I'd been expecting.

Now I knew for certain that the twelve Zeros at this altitude were hoping to draw the Flying Circus into the concentrated distraction of combat. If we attacked, the Zeros would signal their rapidly increasing forces above the cloud ceiling to begin the assault on the field. Bombers would scream down with full fighter escort to bomb Henderson Field off the face of the earth.

"Scramble everything!" I radioed to the base. "Right now! There's a whole shitpot of airplanes up here."

My first breaking of the no-profanity-over-the-air rule called up an immediate reprimand from the ground: "Can't you speak English, Marine?"

I radioed back frantically, alerting them to clear everything away from the landing strips—people, planes, and equipment. "Because these bombers mean business!"

The race was on, and it was up to us to carry the day. The planes lined up neatly downstairs could never get into the air in time.

"Stay in formation and circle," I ordered. "They want us to attack those Zeros so the gang above can send its dive bombers right to the field while we're busy."

Two of the P-38s circled to one side of our group, and the other two took the other flank. Like a coherent swarm of wasps, we fought the temptation to go after the half-dozen crazily maneuvering Zeros who flew in close in an effort to draw us into battle.

I had to grit my teeth. Oh, how I yearned for just one shot at those SOBs. I could almost taste blood and it was maddening. The heat of battle and my hatred for the aggressor built to a fever pitch, and I split from the formation and started for the closest Zero. Moments later I came to my senses and pulled back from the easy kill.

Bewildered by the lack of response to their orchestrated carelessness, the Japanese fliers flew directly into our gunsights, wagging their wings in a ludicrous, sacrificial challenge. My trigger finger tensed, but I refused to fire. I did, however, give the nod to the four P-38s to pick off the fliers who grew too bold.

Suddenly I noticed a lone Zero flit down from the cloud stratum above and then climb immediately back through the cloud canopy. Instantly I reckoned that the Japanese planes above were positioning themselves to drop down en masse to take our flight.

"We're moving," I radioed curtly and led the group away. Moments later, a large group of Zeros descended from the same section of cloud, expecting to come down over and behind us. But their prey had moved.

I've never been able to emphasize enough the fact that in combat you must know your enemy, and this was certainly a critical example. I knew how the Japanese thought and fought. I had seen, too often, a small group of flamboyant fliers offered as bait. The famed kamikazes, the suicidal "Divine Wind" that did so much damage later in the war, were not yet known to the world, but I was fully aware of the Japanese sacrifice play.

Hopelessly outnumbered, some flight leaders would have retreated to avoid wasting their planes and lives; others would have plunged into combat to inflict at least symbolic damage before dying. Instead of doing either, I waited.

Waiting was almost more difficult than active combat, but if the Zeros were decoys, so were we. If their attention was on us and we could delay the fight as long as possible, it would give our planes on the ground a chance to take off. And when the attack did begin, I didn't intend to waste time on Zeros. I planned to go after the bombers. They were the ones who could inflict the greatest damage on the airfield.

Once again a Zero darted down from the canopy above. Once again we changed position. And once again when the mass of Zeros appeared, we were far from the spot they expected.

In the meantime, the P-38s had picked off their first Zero while we stuck to our formation. Another Zero made the mistake of following a twin-tailed P-38 into a pillarlike cloud below. A short while later the Mitsubishi slanted out toward the ground trailing black smoke.

Later we would learn that back on the ground General Mulcahy was bent over the radio at Operations listening to every word from his men in the sky, his knuckles white. Every officer who wasn't busy pushing plane after plane off the end of the runways and into the air was watching the sky and listening to the radio.

The previous evening the general had mocked my notion that the Japanese could still muster a force of any magnitude. "It's over!" he'd told me.

The one slim chance I'd seen, to turn the tables and keep

the enemy swarm in the air long enough for the planes on the ground to scramble, was paying off, but things could still go awry.

The Japanese air commander had planned the attack precisely, perhaps overplanned. When we refused to go along with his plan, a sort of paralysis captured the huge enemy force. Also, multiple layers of thick clouds that had worked to their advantage also worked to our psychological advantage. The Japanese could not be sure that we did not have other planes playing hide-and-seek somewhere in the sky. By refusing to run away when the odds were clearly and overwhelmingly against us, we instilled the deep suspicion that we must have many more planes in the air. When another squadron managed to get into the air and engage a group of twenty Zeros in between two other cloud layers, the idea was firmly implanted.

"Just continue wheeling and keep your eyes on them," I told my now-nervous flight. "Keep your finger in the dike and hope the sharks don't bite it off!" Seconds seemed like minutes and minutes like hours as we kept raising the bid.

Finally the Zeros circling the Flying Circus made one last ostentatious but unsuccessful attempt at picking a fight. Then they veered away and the enemy fliers at all levels turned and headed back up the slot toward their home bases on Bougainville and Munda.

The hundreds of poker games I'd won during the long hours of military waiting were nothing compared to the extraordinary bluff I'd just pulled off—without firing a shot. Old Foos had played the greatest empty hand of his life.

Some writers later speculated that I had nobly placed the importance of the mission over bettering my score in the record books, but nothing like that even entered my mind—that's something the boys in the press corps dreamed up. For me it was not a matter of notches on my belt, but of averting the death and destruction of our airfield.

When we landed, the story of what some called my "tactical brilliance" had already made its way around the base, and our tiny squadron was greeted with the kind of vehement appreciation that can only be shared in life-or-death combat. Less than an hour later, a torrential downpour hit the island, turning everything into a quagmire and protecting us from further attack by air.

Slithering and splashing his jeep from the fighter strip, Colonel Jack went to see General Mulcahy, and the two decided to evacuate our flight the next morning.

When Major John Smith, whose VMF-223 had been the first squadron on Guadalcanal and the one we'd relieved back in October, had applied for more combat duty, he was told, "Not until you have trained 150 John Smiths," which was pretty much the sentiment among the brass. So it wasn't surprising that Colonel Jack's response to our request to stay was, "You've fought your war here and earned a good, long rest. You can do more good teaching other pilots what you know about air fighting and by training combat teams than you can by continuing to risk your neck several times a day here. There'll be plenty of other chances in other campaigns for you to shoot down more Japs."

General Mulcahy agreed and the next day sent a full report to General Geiger, now commanding general of the First Marine Air Wing and senior aviation officer in the area, recommending me for the Congressional Medal of Honor. General Geiger in turn wrote to Washington, recommending that I be awarded the highest honor in the United States "for repeated acts of heroism and intrepidy at the risk of his life far beyond the call of duty and without detriment to his mission."

I knew nothing about all this. All I knew was that tomorrow morning the boys and I would be outward bound on a DC-3. I'd flown my last combat mission over Guadalcanal.

In an April 3, 1943, story for the *Saturday Evening Post,* Marine Captain Garrett Graham reported the events of January 25. Though he focused on my contribution to the effort, I prefer to read this as a final resounding tribute to the outstanding pilots of the Flying Circus:

> They were a grimly confident young lot, dauntless in the face of odds which might be five or six to one against them. In [an] hour and a half they were to create one of the most brilliant tactical chapters in American war

flying. . . . Everyone on the field was counting as they came in. Twelve had gone up and here were—three, five, six, nine, ten, twelve back! Lieutenant Colonel S. S. Jack, commanding officer of the fighter strip and himself one of the finest fighter pilots and aerial tacticians in the service, gathered the twelve pilots together as they climbed from their cockpits. What had happened? It was Joe Foss all the way—Foss and his generalship. Colonel Jack, his superior, and the men who fought under him, said unanimously it was only his shrewd leadership and knowledge of combat tactics that saved the Americans and their precious airfield from a hail of destruction. It was Joe Foss's farewell to Guadalcanal.

Chapter 16

The Dancing Bear Act

✫ ✫ ✫

"Look at him. He'll be weighted down and sent to the bottom before we cross the dateline." The voice drifted toward me through cobwebs of time and space, and I tried to summon some superhuman effort to argue with it.

"It's a waste of good canvas, if you ask me," a second voice complained. "There's a war on, you know. Every time we bury one of these guys at sea they wrap 'em up in brand-new canvas that ought to be used for tents or duffel bags."

"What are you moaning for, buddy?" the first voice complained. "I'm the poor stiff that's got to sew him in before they push him over."

These two sounded like nattering crows out in the cornfield. I wished they'd just go away.

Slowly I drifted into an awareness of my surroundings. First I felt the slow monotonous roll of the transport ship, and then the smell of sweat, leather, and fuel oil in the darkened cabin where I lay curled beneath the scratchy khaki blankets, knees drawn to my chest against the shivery chills.

I remembered the rainy flight from Guadalcanal and standing at attention before General Geiger at Wing Headquarters on Espíritu Santo, five hundred miles south of Henderson Field, only days after leaving the combat zone. Geiger, affectionately known as Jiggs because of his resemblance to the short, heavyset character in the popular Jiggs and Maggie cartoon strip, had amicably asked what I planned to do in the future.

"A regular commission in the United States Marine Corps, sir," I'd said. "I'd like to make it a career, but I just have a reserve commission."

"That's no problem at all," the general assured me.

"I was two weeks too old to get a regular commission when I signed up," I said.

"Don't worry about that. I'm sure we can waive the rule in your case."

In the nearly two hours we talked, the general clued me in on several things, particularly what would be awaiting me stateside.

"You're a hero, Joe," he said, "and people back home want to see you and hear you. And needless to say, the Marine Corps is proud of you and wants to show you off to America."

"You mean the Marines want me to put on a dancing bear act?"

The general chuckled. "There's a lot more to it than entertaining people, Joe. You can make a real contribution to the war effort if you want to. Now listen, let me give you some advice: I don't want you embarrassing God and country, yourself—or the United States Marine Corps. So don't join any organization until you know it's a patriotic one."

I never forgot that piece of advice, and much later when the American Legion invited me to become a member, even offering me a free membership, I gave those legionnaires the third degree. They were a little taken aback at first, but then we all became friends and I joined. Some organizations didn't pass the patriotic acid test, though, so I wouldn't join.

While we had waited around on Espíritu Santo for transportation back to the States, my malaria, complicated by gastroenteritis, threatened to return with greater force than ever. Despite this, however, I'd spent several happy days with Lieutenant Commander James H. (Jimmy) Flatley, one of the two men for whom the Flatley-Thach crossweave was named. Jimmy had been serving as a fighter pilot with carriers in the southwest Pacific, and the two of us discussed the art of fighter flying for hours on end.

Ben Finney also turned up on Espíritu Santo, as did Major Gregory (Pappy) Boyington, who had just come in from the States. He'd been serving with the AVG (American Volunteer Group) in China, so this was his first action in the Pacific. It was on Espíritu Santo, shortly thereafter, that Pappy put together his Black Sheep squadron, made up largely of replacements and remnants of various units which had moved elsewhere. I'd first met Boyington in Pensacola where he was an instructor. Playing poker with Pappy one dark rainy day I lost thirty dollars, then changed to dice and won it back plus another sixty-five.

I also spent time with an old friend, Major General Nathan Twining, one of the top commanders in the Army Air Corps and a pheasant-hunting buddy back in South Dakota before the war. And I made some new friends, including General Louis Woods and screen actor Robert Montgomery, who was serving as a Navy officer in the southwest Pacific.

Colonel Pinky Passmore at Pensacola had told me that there are two things a good commander never loses sight of—his men and his baggage. So when I finally got my orders to leave for home, without accompanying orders for my men, I drove a jeep to island headquarters to do some lobbying. A publicity tour was in the works for me back in the States and I couldn't delay my departure, but I was determined not to leave my men behind. At HQ some in-the-know officers steered me in the right direction.

"Who knows something about transportation around here?" I asked. "Somebody has got to be able to get transportation for my whole outfit."

One of the older officers smiled and said, "There's a lieutenant who's handling this stuff for the Navy. If anybody can do the trick, he can. He's up there above the bomber strip."

It had been raining, as usual, and the road to the strip was a muddy river. Between trying not to get stuck and working the hand-powered windshield wiper, driving was quite a maneuver. As I reached the quonset huts connected by wooden sidewalks at the top of the hill, the rain stopped abruptly, the sun broke through, and within minutes the place was an outdoor steam room. It was miserable, hot, and humid, but it would have looked nice on a postcard. Even the grass was cut.

Spotting a Navy lieutenant coming out of one of the huts, I jumped out of the jeep to ask directions. He was a thin man wearing baggy trousers, an oversize shirt, and a hat that was too big. He looked like a sack of potatoes.

"I'm looking for a transportation officer," I said after hailing him down. "A Lieutenant Richard Nixon. Any idea where I might find him?"

"I'm Lieutenant Nixon," he said. "Can I help you?" Then he broke into a broad grin. "Say, you're Joe Foss, aren't you?"

"Yeah, I am," I said, and we shook hands.

Back at the lieutenant's office, I explained how I had been sitting around Espíritu Santo for nearly two weeks now, waiting for transportation.

"I've had a good time visiting with some old friends and some new ones. General Geiger and Major Cram took me on a one-day visit to some islands the other day, and helped

I was proud to serve as chairman of Veterans for Nixon in 1968. (Photo by Donna Wild Foss)

break the monotony. But about the only thing new around here is the latest coconuts that drop off."

The lieutenant alternated between congratulating me for my aerial accomplishments and explaining how he would get my men off the island within two or three days, a task I'd begun to believe impossible. He agreed to look into our transportation personally, and as I left his office I thought, *Now there's a guy who knows how to get things done!*

This incident began what was to become a lifelong friendship with Richard Milhous Nixon. Later I would be one who encouraged him to run for the governorship of California, even though Nixon's own aides advised him against it, saying he would probably lose.

"Who cares?" I told him. "You've got to get into a fight before you can get scratched. I've known guys who ran seven times before they were elected. If you really want the job, you go after it." However, I didn't advise him to tell off the press at the end of it!

And when he ran for president, I served as national chairman of Veterans for Nixon.

That was all to come much later. For now, Lieutenant Nixon had come through with transportation as promised, and on March 25, 1943, Bate, Freeman, Furlow, Haberman, Loesch, Presley, and I—the remaining members of the Flying Circus—boarded a liberty ship, *Juan Cabrillo,* carrying wool and a few passengers.

I'd looked forward to the days at sea filled with nonstop card games and sitting in the sun, but two days out the malaria hit me with renewed vengeance. As I moaned and rolled in my bunk, I kept thinking about the irony of life. I was going to die at sea of malaria after escaping death so many times on Guadalcanal. To everyone's surprise, including mine, after four tormented days, the massive doses of quinine and Atabrine did the job and pulled me through the dangerous relapse.

The ship docked at the naval base at Long Beach, California, on April 19, and from there I was driven to Camp Kearney at San Diego. That night all my baggage was stolen, and the next day I boarded a C-46 for Washington wearing a rumpled uniform—the only one I now owned.

The fact that I was a hero seemed to impress everyone but me. I paid about as much attention to all that hero talk as I do to a barking dog. I was just thankful I'd made it back alive. As far as I was concerned, there were many good men who had lost their lives doing the same job I'd been called on to do. I was just lucky and downed a few more enemy planes, that's all.

But regardless of what I thought, the Marine Corps was determined to see me as some kind of superhero. The *Saturday Evening Post* called me "America's greatest fighter pilot of all time" and *Esquire* named me to its "Hall of Heroes" for "the twenty-seventh Zero that he did not shoot down to break [Rickenbacker's] record, and for the twenty-eight, and twenty-ninth, that would have sent him far into the lead, and made him the ace of aces." Apparently the story of my strategic restraint and bluff had established me as more than a hotshot pilot, and that part was all right with me.

In Washington I was greeted by General Robert Denig, head of Marine public relations; Frank Knox, Secretary of the Navy; Admiral E. J. King, Chief of Naval Operations; Admiral Jack McCain, Vice Chief of Naval Operations; Colonel Jerry Jerome, one of the Marine pilots who had inspired me to become a Marine flyer; and a host of other military leaders. They even took me to the Pentagon to give a lecture for Army Intelligence officers. One of the things I told them was my conviction that the Japanese were not yet finished with Guadalcanal. I spoke to the men at the Marine base at Quantico, Virginia, the midshipmen at Annapolis, and was guest of honor at the National Press Club in Washington.

The dancing bear act had begun, and before it closed I would travel almost nonstop around the United States making public appearances, selling bonds, recruiting for the armed forces, and encouraging the men and women who powered the industrial forces of the American military effort.

My health had improved despite the rigorous schedule, I was eating well and sleeping on a mattress, and I'd been reunited with June.

On Easter Sunday, April 25, June and I were accompanied to the First Presbyterian Church in Washington by a small contingent of Pentagon brass, but to me it was mostly a ceremonial gesture. Although I believed in God, somehow I just didn't make the connection in my mind that God had anything to do with what had been happening in my life. I went to church simply because I thought it was the right thing to do.

One highlight of the publicity tour was a visit to the Grumman aircraft plant at Bethpage, Long Island, where I was thrilled to be able to thank the folks who had built the F4F Wildcats I'd flown. The reliable Grumman had saved my hide more than once, and I told the men and women who built it what a good job they had done. Leroy Grumman and Jake Swirbel, who ran the Grumman plant, gave me a tour of the place. They were making some slight changes in the Wildcat's design and armament, so I was interested to see how it was going to stack up against the Zero.

The first stop of my countrywide speaking tour was Sioux Falls, South Dakota, on May 4, where family and friends greeted me at the airport, along with Mayor Cliff Whitfield and my old band, the Washington High School band, playing John Philip Sousa. I told the cheering crowd how much I enjoyed being home and how much it meant to be an American. Then I was the guest of honor in a parade led by 2,000 uniformed marching men and women and viewed by more than 75,000 spectators.

Later that day June and my mother and I were interviewed on a nationwide radio broadcast on NBC, after which there was a public reception at the Howard Wood baseball field. The only regret I had was that my father wasn't there to see it.

The tour was more than simply a hero-worship, sightseeing event; I was promoting war bonds and giving pep talks to the factory workers, encouraging everyone to give their best for the war effort, and wherever I went I was deeply touched by the hospitality shown me. Then when I got to Chicago something really special happened. I was told that when I returned to Washington I would have a personal meeting with President Roosevelt!

On May 18, 1943, I rode to the White House in a limousine along with June and my mother. When we stepped out, we were greeted by General Geiger, the Marine Corps Com-

The Dancing Bear Act

mandant, General Thomas Holcomb, and several other officers and civilians, including Secretary of State Cordell Hull, Navy Secretary Frank Knox, and New York Governor Lehman. Actually, with all that brass and prestige around I felt out of my league, and in some ways, even though I was there to be honored, I felt like a bit of a bystander.

After about twenty minutes General Watson, one of the president's aides, led us into the Oval Office.

President Franklin Delano Roosevelt was seated at his desk wearing a rather rumpled seersucker suit, looking just the way he had in so many newsreels. The president's wheelchair was concealed by the desk, and I later learned that the press always cooperated in the angle of their picture-taking to minimize his handicap.

After the president had greeted everyone, he turned to me. "I've got something for you, Captain Foss," he said with a smile. Then he picked up an official-looking document, adjusted his glasses, and began to read:

For outstanding heroism and courage above and beyond the call of duty as executive officer of Marine Fighting Squadron 121, at Guadalcanal, Solomon Islands. Engaging in almost daily combat with the enemy from October 9 to November 19, 1942, Captain Foss personally shot down 23 Japanese planes and damaged others so severely that their destruction was extremely probable. In addition, during this period he successfully led a large number of escort missions, skillfully covering reconnaissance, bombing and photographic planes as well as surface craft. On January 15, 1943, he added three more enemy planes to his already brilliant successes for a record of aerial combat achievement unsurpassed in this war. Boldly searching out an approaching enemy force on January 25, Captain Foss led his eight F4F marine planes and four army P-38s into action and, undaunted by tremendously superior numbers, intercepted and struck with such force that four Japanese fighters were shot down and the bombers turned back without releasing a single bomb. His remarkable flying skill, inspiring leadership and indomi-

Here I am receiving the Congressional Medal of
Honor from President Franklin D. Roosevelt while my
admiring mother looks on, May 1943. (Photo by
June Foss)

table fighting spirit were distinctive factors in the defense of strategic American positions on Guadalcanal.

Franklin D. Roosevelt
President, United States

While this was the proudest moment of my life, it was also
embarrassing to listen to these words of praise. When he had
finished reading the citation, the president asked me to stand
beside him, and I leaned forward slightly as he placed the
ribbon bearing the Congressional Medal of Honor around my
neck.

Mother, the longtime, dedicated Roosevelt supporter and
the Foss family diehard Democrat, beamed sternly throughout the presentation. She was wearing a new print dress and
a felt hat with a feather in it. Being a lady of very few words,
her comment to the press was, "I'm proud of my son."

From Washington, I resumed my tour of American cities

CAPTAIN FOSS, U.S.M.C.
AMERICA'S NO. 1 ACE

LIFE

JUNE 7, 1943 10 CENTS
YEARLY SUBSCRIPTION $4.50

Being on the cover of *Life* magazine was an
exciting experience for this country boy.

like Newark, Chapel Hill, Jacksonville, Pensacola, New Or-
leans, Corpus Christi, Los Angeles, Chicago, Des Moines,
San Diego, and San Francisco. I think I appeared on every
major radio show in the country, including Kay Kyser, Vox
Pop, and Paul Whiteman, and for the boy from the South
Dakota cornfields, it was pretty heady stuff.

My first public appearances were nervous, self-conscious
affairs. I felt uncomfortable talking to such large groups of
people; I wasn't a speaker and knew it. Then I got some good
advice from an unexpected source.

It was the "I Am an American" celebration in New York
City, and for three days I'd raced around the city with Mayor
Fiorello La Guardia, giving speeches to men and women in-

volved in the war effort. The culmination was a major rally in Central Park with the vice president of the United States, Henry A. Wallace, the cardinal of New York, and a host of other celebrities, and I was supposed to be the guest of honor.

I was sitting on the podium between the actor Raymond Massey and General David Sarnoff, an Army general who in civilian life was head of RCA (Radio Corporation of America). Waiting to talk, looking out over Central Park and a hundred thousand people, I was nervous as hell. Knowing Massey was a major in the Canadian services, I turned to him. "Boy, I'd rather be in combat than here."

"Don't be nervous," he said. "Just tell them something they'd like to hear."

I asked him what that might be, and he said, "Just be yourself. Get up there and tell them some little story and sit down. Make it short and to the point."

All this time General Sarnoff was also reassuring me. "Don't be nervous. People are people. Just remember every man puts his pants on one leg at a time."

When Mayor La Guardia stood up to introduce me, he kept going on and on in his distinctive, high-pitched voice about my accomplishments, many of them unknown to me until that moment. Finally he just sort of stuttered and said, "And now . . . and now . . . ," and I knew he'd forgotten my name. So he just said, "I want to introduce you to the only man who ever lived through a head-on collision with a Zero."

Every eye was riveted on me, and it suddenly struck me as funny that the mayor had forgotten my name, and that put me completely at ease.

"Ladies and gentlemen, I don't know who the mayor's talking about, but my name is Joe Foss. I never had a head-on collision with a Zero, and I never want one!"

Everyone laughed, and when the applause died down, I told a few war stories about shooting down Zeros—and about Zeros shooting me down. Massey and Sarnoff were right; they loved the stories. That day I gave twenty-three more speeches and almost lost my voice, but I'd learned a valuable lesson. Just about the time I'd start believing the introductions and press notices about how great I was, I'd remember Mayor La Guardia forgetting my name—or one of a number of similar incidents. Like those occasions when someone would come up to me and say, "Can I have your autograph, Mr. Wayne? I love your movies." For the rest of my life, I'd either be mistaken for him or have people tell me I looked like him.

Throughout the tour I met old friends and picked up reports about guys I'd known overseas. In Chicago I saw Roger Haberman, and met up with Oscar Bate in Newark at the Curtiss-Wright plant. Along with the publicity obligations, I also had telephone calls to make, letters to write, and personal visits to pay to the parents and widows of men I had known who had been killed in action. It reminded me of my old days on funeral duty that had helped get me into all this in the first place.

On July 4 they took me off dancing bear duty and sent me to the Marine base at Santa Barbara, California, to do what I wanted to do most: head up and train another squadron bound for the Pacific war. After Guadalcanal and the rigors of the road, the Santa Barbara Goleta Marine Air Station seemed a welcome relief.

June and I rented a beautiful house that belonged to the actor Ronald Coleman, up on the side of a hill with about forty acres of olive trees. He let us have it for peanuts and the price even included a cleaning lady once or twice a week.

I was able to choose my top officers for the new VMF-115 and I got Greg Loesch as my executive officer and Bill Freeman as my engineering officer. Loesch had been my second-in-command in the Flying Circus and had more common horse sense than anyone in the old outfit. Freeman was a big Texan with thin sandy hair where he had hair at all. He had three engineering degrees—mechanical, electrical, and aeronautical—and was the most conscientious man in the world. I was also privileged to have Jacob A. O. Stub for Operations, Bob Kingsbury, John King, Roger Haberman, and Bill Bacheler—all veterans.

Any success I've had as an administrator, starting back in those wartime years, has been founded on my personal philosophy of management, which is based on the delegation of authority. I've always had people who were smarter than me around, and I wanted it that way. In the service I was blessed with men who could keep airplanes flying despite unbelievably stressful conditions. My aircraft availability rating was as high as anybody's.

To start with, I had ninety-some pilots in the outfit, twice the number I needed, and these were new kids. We were issued the new F4U Corsairs, which were gradually replacing the Wildcat that had earned its place in history in the South Pacific. We had forty-eight airplanes plus some utility crafts, so everybody got to fly, fly, fly. But we were also having trouble with the Corsair. It tended to cut out above 21,000 or 22,000 feet, and when you've got a 14,000-pound airplane with a glide path like a brick, you've got trouble in River City. Many guys jumped out; others tried to land on the highway and disintegrated. Some got out alive and one guy even landed in a bean patch and lived, but three or four guys were killed, so I went over to see my CO, Colonel Lawson M. (Sandy) Sanderson, who had been one of the Marine pilots who came to Sioux Falls for the stunt exhibitions in the 1933 air show that had so impressed me. He was also an All-American football player from Van Camp's early team.

"Colonel, what we need is an expert to get those things fixed up," I said.

"Well, I'll call up General Bill Wallace," the colonel said. Wallace had been on Guadalcanal and was now Commanding General of Marine Aviation for the West Coast, located in San Diego. After Sanderson exchanged pleasantries with General Wallace, he handed me the phone.

"General, I'm having a terrible time with these Corsairs," I said, getting right to the point.

"You'll have an expert tomorrow," the general promised.

I thanked him and hung up and went about my business. If I was lucky, I figured I'd hear from somebody within a few weeks.

Two days later I was sitting in my office, which was just about the size of a small desk, when someone knocked on the door. I called out, "Come in," and a tall slender man in plain khakis with no military insignia appeared.

"Major Foss," he said with a smile, extending his hand, "it's good to meet you. I'm Charles Lindbergh."

"The real Charles A. Lindbergh?" I asked. I couldn't believe it.

Lindbergh smiled and assured me that he was the real Charles Lindbergh.

"Come in, come in!" Then just to be sure I wasn't hearing and seeing things, I asked, "Charlie Lindbergh?"

"Yes, sir."

"Well, sit down!" I said enthusiastically. "When I was a kid I wanted to meet you in the worst way when you flew into South Dakota, but the cops threw me off the stand. And here you are. Gosh!" I was thrilled and just about speechless—for me.

Lindbergh smiled and looked a bit embarrassed. "General Wallace sent me over to see if I can help you solve the Corsair problem."

It didn't take me long to learn that Lindbergh never liked to talk about himself, so we started talking about the things that were going wrong with the Corsair and how the plane acted.

"I'm ready to go right now," Charlie said, and told me he wanted to take one up and really try it out, fly a lot, and asked for a map of the area. I had one of the boys come in and give him a briefing on the area, and he went right to work.

Lindbergh's talents as an aeronautical engineer were awesome, and almost immediately he began unraveling the mechanical problems that plagued the Corsair. Charlie, as he insisted on being called, moved into the Coleman house with us, and I was in hog heaven. Not only had I finally met my lifelong idol, but I was actually working with him. We ate meals together, spent our evenings together, and even rode to work together. Soon we were fast friends.

Charlie was one of the most conscientious men I'd ever worked with. He solved every problem that had developed with the Corsair, which had to do with the whole electrical ignition system, plus many additional problems. He made those Pratt and Whitneys purr, and we still had time to pal around or just sit and watch the planes come in. Once we were watching an old TBF torpedo plane and Charlie said, "As an engineer, I've never figured how that plane flies. It

185

looks like a bumblebee, and they're not supposed to fly either," and we both laughed.

I also learned the story behind his fight with President Roosevelt.

Before World War II, Charlie had made a trip to Europe where he was decorated by just about everybody—including Germany—for his contribution to aviation. When he came back, the reporters huddled around and asked him how he'd rate the air powers of the world, and he said, "Germany number one. Great Britain number two." As I recall, he rated the United States number three.

Well, his comments just tore up this great country of ours, which could never settle for being second to anyone. About the same time, Senator Burton K. Wheeler of Montana was involved with a group called "America First" and got Charlie to go out and make speeches urging the government to keep its cotton-pickin' fingers out of foreign entanglements and to build up our own outfit first if we were going to create a strong bastion here. They probably had some high-sounding resolution covering this, but that was the heart of the matter.

Perhaps Lindbergh's greatest offense, from FDR's point of view, was his claim that the president was covertly maneuvering the U.S. into war without consulting or informing the people. Since then, responsible historians have concurred that Roosevelt did hide many of his efforts from the American public, and his private conversations about Lindbergh were astonishingly vitriolic.

FDR got so mad that he took Charlie's colonel status away from him and threw him out of the reserves. Charlie went to work for United Aircraft, but Roosevelt brought enough pressure on them that they had to get rid of him. FDR would probably have a rougher time getting away with that today, but the way he handled things makes today's presidents look like boy scouts. "Fire that guy Lindbergh!" he said. "Get him out of there or you won't get any war contracts!" Of course United wanted those war contracts, so they got rid of Charlie.

A little while later James Newton, Charlie's closest friend, ran into his friend Henry Ford and said, "You ought to hire Charlie Lindbergh."

"Is he available?" asked Ford. Learning that he was, Ford

immediately called Charlie to have lunch. During the course of the meal Ford asked Charlie, "How would you like to work for me at the new bomber plant we're building at Willow Run outside Detroit?"

"I'd love it," said Lindbergh, "but I don't think you'll want to hire me. The president of the United States will be right after you and you wouldn't get any war contracts."

"I don't worry about things like that," Henry Ford said. "Do you want to work for me?" So they consummated the deal, and Charlie went to work for Ford, and that's how he got into testing military aircraft. High-ranking men in the military who admired him and respected his ability began to ask quietly for his help—and Charlie never took any money for the work he did for the military.

A lesser man might have been embittered by the president's rejection of his help, but Lindbergh gave his all to the American cause, though he never changed his mind about the wisdom of entering World War II. He believed strongly that the Japanese would not have attacked Pearl Harbor if Roosevelt had handled them differently in the diplomatic sphere.

The criticism heaped upon Charlie for associating with prewar Germany was particularly bitter and woefully unfair. According to General Truman Smith, the military attaché in Germany, Lindbergh had been gathering information about German power at the request of the U.S. government. Furthermore, Charlie had seen the handwriting on the wall and had urged the German Jews he knew to flee Germany while they still could. In Germany he had even worked, unsuccessfully, to change the policy that prohibited Jewish emigrants from taking their possessions with them, one of the primary reasons so many resisted leaving until it was too late.

Lindbergh also warned, contrary to the forecasts of contemporary "experts," that American involvement in the European war would only serve to benefit the Soviet Union. In his opinion Soviet domination of Europe was something to be feared. America, he said, "should not involve itself in the internal affairs of Europe. They never were and never will be carried on according to our desires."

Charlie could have publicly blamed Roosevelt for not disclosing his true activities in Germany, but it was not in his character to undercut the president in time of war. As a result he was stuck with an anti-Semite and unpatriotic label that stung him deeply throughout his entire life.

After working with us for a month, Charlie ironed out the problems we were having with the Corsair and had to move on. I really hated to see him go. Charlie was a really fun guy, a good-natured guy. The only time he ever got a little irritated was when we would go to some hash house to eat and some dame would come running up to him screaming, "Lindy! Lindy!" That would really chill old Charlie. He wanted to be known either as Slim or Charlie. Only the people who didn't know him called him Charles or Lucky Lindy.

Before he left Charlie said, "I'd like to talk to the men."

I ordered all the officers and enlisted men to assemble beside the hangar, and when they had gathered I climbed up on one of the rolling stairways used to board large planes. "Colonel Lindbergh needs no introduction. You've been working with him." The ovation was thundering.

"I just want to thank you for your generous support of my efforts here," Charlie said to the group. "I've really enjoyed working with you, and there's only one more thing I'd really like to do," he added. "I'd like to fly tail-end Charlie with this outfit."

Tail-end Charlie was the last man in a flight—a dangerous spot because an enemy pilot coming up from behind could pick you off first without warning.

When the applause died away, I assured him, "You've got a job flying with us any time you show up. But if I have anything to do with it, you won't be flying tail-end Charlie. I want you up the line."

Chapter 17
Second
Time Out

While training the VMF-115 in Santa Barbara, I continued doing public appearances whenever I could spare the time. Occasionally I was asked to visit training centers to talk to student fighter pilots, but my speeches were not the cheerful rah-rah-rah that many, especially those who sent me to speak, expected.

The missions we'd flown over Guadalcanal were still fresh in my mind, and I described some of our bloody encounters. Frequently I told them about one mission my guys flew with eight planes from another squadron. I'd given this other commander the mission of flying high cover, but twenty-four Zeros came down from high altitude onto us with all guns firing. My flight was swirling around dogfighting when out of the corner of my eye I saw the other guys headed nose-down toward Guadalcanal—the wrong direction. Their leader had chickened out, leaving the eight of us alone and outnumbered over three to one. Although no American lives were lost that day, two of our planes were shot down.

Before I landed, I planned to walk over and just shoot the guy. Leaving a fight was bad enough, but to leave eight to fight twenty-four Zeros! By the time I set down, however, I'd cooled off some and didn't even say a word to him. I just never depended on him after that.[1]

After I told the story, I'd look straight out at the audience and say, "If you're planning on this being an easy job, you've got another think coming. You can end up dead in this line of work. War is dangerous! If you have any thought of chickening out, now's the time to do it. Being any kind of pilot in enemy territory means having your life threatened on every mission."

As word got around about my speeches, the brass asked me to tone it down. After one of my talks, they said, thirty-six fliers bailed out of the program. I didn't lose any sleep over that; in fact, I was glad my strategy had gotten results. I wanted these young trainees to understand what they were getting into. A lot of these young pups thought war was some glamorous air show with a Hollywood sound track. So I just kept on telling it straight and never heard anymore about it.

Frequently I traveled to Hollywood to speak at Lakeside Country Club, Rotary, Lions, Kiwanis, and various clubs in the Hollywood area. It was a short hop by air, and I could fly into Burbank or one of the other little strips. In those days you didn't have to go through all the rigmarole and red tape to land an airplane. It was like putting on roller skates at the front door and you were gone; and when you got to your destination you just took them off. If it was a noon talk, I'd fly down and back the same day so I wouldn't lose a lot of time from the squadron. If it was a banquet, I'd stay overnight. Even then, however, the base had to know where I was every minute because I was on call twenty-four-hours a day.

Many times when I spoke, people in the audience would ask if there was anything I wanted or needed for the squadron. A lot of those folks were well-heeled, so when I went overseas the second time I had the best-equipped squadron that ever sailed. We had a portable sawmill, an ice cream machine and

---

[1] To this day I've never told anything more specific about that day, lest some military scholar reconstruct the battles from the records and determine the identity of the commander. I figured he knew who he was and had probably suffered his share of torment about the incident through the years.

about a ton of ice cream mix, six shotguns—because I had remembered all those big, fat wild pigeons out there on the islands—ammunition, fishing rods and tackle, and refrigerators. The boys and I went first-class.

Many of the men I met during those Hollywood visits became lifelong friends, including Bing Crosby, Gary Cooper, Bob Hope, Sammy Kaye, and Robert Taylor. Some of the guys began calling me "Hollywood Joe" because of my show business connections.

One evening when I got back to base after one of these Hollywood receptions, some of the young lieutenants asked, "Who were some of the stars you met?" So I named them, including Jane Russell, whom I'd met for the first time and found very nice and a pleasure to talk to; she had been born in Minnesota, and we had reminisced about some of the things we had in common as midwesterners.

Then Lieutenants Steve Warren and Swede Larson and Norm Gourley, who went on to become a Major General in the United States Marine Corps, said, "Wow, we'd sure like to meet some of those people. Do you think you could get us a date with any of those starlets?"

"Why, sure," I said. "I can line that up for you." The reason I was so cocksure I could do this was that Bill Frawley, who became famous for his role as Fred on *I Love Lucy*, had said, "If there's ever anything I can do for you, you just give me a call." Fred and I had really hit it off; I'd even been to his home and met his family. So I figured, okay, I'll take him up on that. I called Fred and told him about my lieutenants and that I wanted to show them I could really get things done.

"Sure," said Fred. "I'll see what I can do." And he arranged to have Jane Russell and two of her friends drive to the base and meet the young men. When I told Norm and Swede and Steve they had a date with Jane Russell and her friends that Saturday, they thought I was joshing; and on Saturday afternoon when a convertible rolled in carrying three beautiful women, they couldn't believe their eyes. From then on, as far as they were concerned, old Joe could really get things done. In fact, then the whole group wanted dates!

I also managed to get Bob Hope and his troop to come up and entertain the base. Gary Cooper came one time, Bing

Crosby another, and Kay Kyser put on a full show. The Hollywood folks really went the extra mile and deserved a lot of credit for all that they did for the morale of the troops.

During one of my trips to Hollywood I met Walt Disney, and when word of this spread through the squadron, the guys wanted me to ask the famous cartoonist to create an insignia for VMF-115. My old outfit had been the Flying Circus, and these kids wanted some moniker like that. They finally came up with Joe's Jokers. So I contacted Walt, who had his people submit several different versions—most of which ran along the lines of a happy Corsair topped with helmet and goggles, smoking a cigar. In those days I was always smoking a cigar, so it had become my trademark.

And it wasn't just the people from the film industry who helped us. Football Hall of Famer Ernie Nevers, who was a member of the Marine Corps, did everything he could to assist with the physical training program of the Marines at Goleta. But Ernie wanted to get into the war. He became commander of the service squadron and did an outstanding job in the southwest Pacific, proving that he was both a great football player and a great leader.

In spite of the considerable satisfaction I was experiencing, both with the squadron and in finally having a real married life with June, those days were not free of tragedy.

One afternoon I was observing a flier who was worrying me. The young pilot did everything by the book, but he just didn't seem to have a feel for the job. Through no fault of their own, some guys just lacked the right kind of coordination for fighter flying, and I was convinced that was the case with this fellow.

"I'm going to ground him," I told Greg Loesch.

"Maybe you're just working too hard, Joe," said Loesch. "Why don't you let me go up and check him out."

"Fine with me," I said.

Not long after that I saw the two of them flying in from the ocean side of Goleta. They'd been doing maneuvers and aerobatics and Greg gave the command for right echelon. Suddenly the young flier crossed directly into Greg's plane. Both pilots bailed out. Their chutes were just opening as they hit,

My good friends Bob Hope and Gary Cooper came to entertain the troops at the Marine Corps Air Station, Goleta, California.

With my ever-present cigar, sitting next to my Corsair on the island of Emirau in the Pacific, May 30, 1944. The emblem on the side of my plane was designed by Walt Disney for my squadron, VMF-115. (Photo courtesy of U.S. Navy)

and the force of the fall drove their bodies fourteen feet into the swamp.

Greg Loesch's death was a tremendous loss to me, although I could never express how I felt and I know I didn't show it on the surface. I'm sure to some I appeared callous, but I never did—maybe never could—allow myself the luxury of emotional indulgences not directly related to the goals at hand. Actually, this is quite typical of all the fighter pilots I've ever known; we don't wear our emotions on our sleeves. Perhaps because a kind of emotional detachment is necessary to that kind of work. So there's an element of truth to the competitive, self-assured, often arrogant, seemingly uncaring or emotionless characters portrayed in movies like *Top Gun*.

Despite the loss of my best friend, and the best executive officer a man could ever have, I was getting increasingly anxious to get back to the war. Finally, after our departure date had been put off about three times, we got our orders to leave for the South Pacific, and we departed on the *Copahee* in January 1944.

A lot had happened in the months I'd been home. We had won the lengthy battle for Guadalcanal, and the war had moved closer to Japan. Emotions were at a fever pitch.

Our first act of duty when we arrived with VMF-115 was to fly the new Corsairs from Guadalcanal to Bougainville, where the war was still going strong. The enemy had surrounded the airport at Torokina on the southwest side of the island, and just as we landed puffs of dirt were going up.

"Looks like the war is still going on," I radioed to the men.

Word came from the tower that enemy artillery was giving us a reception. So, dodging bomb craters and zigzagging to avoid enemy fire, we landed and hurriedly taxied the shiny new Corsairs back down the runway to the base's operations tents.

After a night's sleep at Bougainville, our next hop was to fly the old war-weary F4U Corsairs south to Espíritu Santo, stopping en route at Guadalcanal to refuel. When we landed at Henderson, I was told that I had to go to a meeting there and should get somebody else to fly my plane on down to Espíritu Santo. I'd been flying an old Corsair called the "Eight

Ball," which everybody got a big hoot out of, heckling me that I was behind the eight ball.

One of my lieutenants, Steve Warren, said, "Skipper, I'd like to take the Eight Ball the rest of the way."

"Well, you've been a good boy," I kidded, "so I'll let you take it."

Warren climbed in, strapped on his helmet, triggered the starter shell, and waited a few moments, revving the engine, before finally heading down the strip. Shortly after takeoff, when he had his wheels up and flaps down, that baby blew up. Steve did a fast roll, turned the plane upside down, gave the stick a kick, and dropped out. Fortunately he had enough altitude for the chute to open before he hit the ground—and miraculously he escaped without a scratch.

No two men fly exactly alike. The timing, angle of takeoff, and a hundred other variables define every pilot. If I'd been flying that buggy, I might have taken off later and been at a lower altitude—and thus less likely to walk away.

Trying to understand why life worked the way it did was about like trying to milk a moose on a dark night, but I must admit as I stood and watched that burning Corsair, I wondered for a moment whether there was some reason I was still walking around. On the other hand, the incident seemed pretty funny after it ended safely.

Steve Warren lives in Texas today, and he still jokes about it. "You knew that was going to happen, didn't you? That's why you let me take the old Eight Ball!"

When the boys came back we picked up another set of new Corsairs and headed north again for Bougainville and stayed there for some time. With the shuttle runs completed, we were assigned to make strikes on Rabaul, New Britain, from the base on Bougainville, and it was there I met another military man destined to change our country's history.

The Japs were holed up in Rabaul's big harbor, and we were hitting them at least once, sometimes twice, a day. The battle was fierce, and our losses were heavy among the dive bombers and torpedo planes going into Rabaul because they had to go right down onto the target.

Our intelligence officer was a Marine reserve captain from Wisconsin, Captain Joseph R. McCarthy, and one day when he was giving a briefing, he said, "You know, we should change these times around a little bit. We always attack at the same time. Their antiaircraft at Rabaul can just sleep in because they know exactly when we're coming."

Major General Ralph J. Mitchell, the commanding general at the time, responded, "Captain, you're the briefing officer. Just confine your remarks to the briefing. You're not the strategist. You don't know what you're talking about. You've never been out there."

"Yes, sir," said McCarthy. But in order to prove his point, Joe decided to start riding in the rear seat of the SBD dive bombers. He rode thirty-some missions, which was no minor thing, because, at that point, out of a flight of eight we were losing maybe two, sometimes four, dive bombers and torpedo planes per mission. He was willing to take that chance, and as a result of his flying missions he proved his point and some of the times were changed, so he probably saved some necks.

We were close to the front lines, so when we weren't flying we stayed off the surface as much as possible, away from stray bullets. At night we played poker in our foxholes, and Joe frequently joined our game. While we were shooting the bull one night he told us that when he got back to Wisconsin he was going to run for the U.S. Senate. We had a lot of fun razzing him about that. We just laughed and said, "Who you gonna run against," and he said, "Senator Robert La Follette." I knew enough about La Follette to know how tough he was in the political field and figured McCarthy had about as much chance as a cat in a dog pound. But he kept his word, and was elected to the Senate in 1946.

After the war all the services adopted a policy whereby you could submit your logbook, and if you had so many missions you'd get an air medal, and if you had so many more you'd get a Distinguished Flying Cross.

Joe, who was a U.S. senator at the time, asked me if I had sent in my logbook, and I said, "No way José. I'm not about to get any medal that way. And if you do, you'll get your neck in the wringer." And he did. Drew Pearson and some others criticized him for this. But the true story was never told. Joe did fly those missions, and he was willing to die for his country, which was more than you could say for a lot of his critics. They were great debaters far out of the combat zone. But Joe never ducked anything. He went full speed ahead and as a result got in a lot of trouble.

No matter what anyone thinks about his later actions with the Un-American Activities Committee, when it came to battle, Joe McCarthy was a dedicated American who was willing to put his life on the line in actual combat, and I was there to witness it.

After Bougainville we set up base at Green Island until another squadron relieved us, and then we went on to Emirau Island, where we settled in for constant search and destroy missions, involving mostly dive bombing and strafing land and sea targets at Kavieng, New Ireland.

Emirau was a pleasant place compared to Green or Bougainville. On Bougainville the enemy was always firing at us, and on Green there was no fresh water. All we had was what ran off the top of our tents into barrels, and the mosquitoes used that for reproducing, so our drinks had mosquito larvae in them.

Emirau, which had once been used as a leper colony, had plenty of pure spring water and enough game and fish to keep us eating as well as most hunting lodges. With the hunting and fishing tackle we'd been given, we had fish, pigeons, doves, and wild chickens—a pleasant change from Spam and other GI rations. The guys even planted flowers around the mess tent with seeds some of the Hollywood folks had given us. We had ice cream a couple times a week and used the portable sawmill to cut some planks for decking outside our tents.

This is not to say that life was all mangoes and cream. Although dogfights were still the order of the day in some arenas, I never again saw the kind of aerial combat I'd had on Guadalcanal, but our missions were still dangerous. With VMF-115 we were hitting ground or sea targets; or flying night missions where we'd have to get right down on the water and fly along and look for the little lights on the trucks. During those raids the planes I got were planes on the ground at Kavieng and some sea planes parked in the harbor.

The flight schedule was frenzied, and flying the Corsair in battle was a whole new experience. The Corsair was a dive bomber, not a fighter like the Wildcat, and it required a completely different approach to aerial warfare. I'd lead the squadron in at a high altitude until we were within striking distance of the target. Then the guys would peel off, rolling over onto their backs for power dives at the targets below.

Dive bombing did not hold the same excitement and challenge that dogfights did, but it was no less dangerous. Night attacks were particularly hazardous.

On one of my first night missions flying the Corsair, I was streaking down toward a convoy of enemy trucks along the coast highway. Closing in fast on a truck, only hundreds of feet and a fraction of a second from the ground, I triggered my machine guns to strafe the vehicle.

With the first burst, the guns lit the night sky as bright as the sun, and even though there were covers over the gun barrels meant to shield the pilot's eyes, all I could see was the afterimage of the six .50 caliber gun blasts. I pulled up on the stick blindly, managing to avoid colliding with the other planes in my flight until my vision returned. The worst of the blindness passed within seconds, but it seemed like an eternity before my night vision returned. After that, I learned to squint my eyes when I fired my guns at night. My wingman Dick Cline had a close call that night also, and the next night we lost Mit Hall on the same type of mission, when he was probably blinded by the flash.

War is no place for heroes or glamour boys. As a matter of fact the very word "hero" turned our stomachs, especially when applied to us. We were frequently scared and we admitted it. Once Bob Cromie, a *Chicago Tribune* correspondent, asked me if I was ever frightened during battle. "Hell, yes!" I said. "Anybody who says he isn't scared when bullets start tearing through his plane is obviously a liar." But a man must be able to conquer that fear somehow; the fellow who stays scared doesn't belong in the business.

Once we were settled in, we got an unexpected and pleasant surprise. Charlie Lindbergh showed up to make me keep my word.

"You remember what you said, Joe?" Lindbergh reminded. "You promised I could fly with you."

My friend Charlie Lindbergh showed up to make me keep my word: "You promised I could fly with you, Joe."

"Consider yourself on duty right now!" I said.

So for the next month Charlie flew every mission with our squadron, searching for ships and ground targets. He flew from morning till night, and he taught us some tricks—like how to extend our range significantly. That's one that saved a lot of lives. He also taught our whole outfit to be thorough.

A plane is like a gun; you never assume it is in the same condition that it was in when you last saw it. You check it and recheck it. Before every flight, Charlie checked everything on his airplane from start to finish, and he did it fast. He didn't take chances. And he was never without a map. That's important, because you can get careless, especially at night, and get lost.

Charlie was no coward. I remember one time we were bombing Kavieng, going after an oil dump that had been spotted there. We knew the general location, but since we didn't know exactly where the oil was, we strafed the target area with .50 caliber guns and swept a wide expanse with napalm. Napalm was a mixture of gunpowder and gasoline the consistency of gelatin put into drop tanks underneath the planes. When dropped as a bomb, this mixture scattered and caused furious fire everywhere it hit.

The area was heavily fortified and the hidden entrenchment of antiaircraft fire was intense. The order was to drop our loads and get the hell out of there. I looked back and saw number eight—Charlie—turn around and go back for a second round. When he was coming down the first time he'd noticed a major dump hidden off to the side, so he made a swing around for a second run by himself with all that AA fire concentrated solely on him. Apparently he hit something, because there was a big explosion and clouds of smoke billowed.

When we got back to base, I jumped out of my plane and walked over to chew him out. "Charlie, you just don't do that. There's no way you're supposed to go back after a target alone. It's a sure way of dying young."

The thing about Charlie, the most pleasant individual who ever came down the pike, if you corrected him and he was wrong, he admitted it.

One day when I walked out of the mess hall with Lindbergh, a photographer snapped our picture. When the photo was published in *Parade* magazine, the supplement that went in Sunday papers all over America, letters began to pour into Emirau addressed to Major Foss. I think we got about seven hundred of them.

Whereas I was this war hero, Lindbergh was considered a traitor by much of the country for his opposition to the war, an opposition that he still maintained to be one hundred percent correct. In general, the letters told me that I was keeping very bad company and asked if I really knew who this guy Lindbergh was. They were giving me a bad time and telling me not to associate with Charlie.

I was furious, as was the rest of the squadron, and the men and I answered every single letter. We pointed out that in America opposition to a war was not only the right of the individual but evidence of the functioning of a democratic system. Among other things, I said, "Lindbergh's out here fighting a war at his own expense while you're at home!"

* * *

In the fall of 1944 we got word that our squadron would fly on to the Philippines and possible action, but about that time the frequency of my ever-present malarial attacks increased. None of the medications they gave me seemed to work, and I could no longer hide the symptoms. Also, the doctors were afraid I would develop a usually fatal complication called black water fever, so they ordered me to return to the States.

Before I left I was able to take a flight to New Guinea for a briefing by General Mitchell and a meeting with Marine air strategists for the Philippine campaign.

Too sick to walk, I was sitting on the ground waiting for a ride home when someone came up behind me and pushed down on my shoulder. When I tried to turn around or get up, he just pushed me back down and kicked me in the rear, not hard enough to hurt but with just enough force to keep me off-balance.

It was Charlie. He was still there and working hard. Later on, he was flying a P-38 as an observer with a P-38 squadron when they were jumped by some Jap fighters. One of them headed straight for Charlie, and he fired a burst at the plane, making several hits. The plane flew under him, almost colliding, rolled over, and crashed into the sea.

Whenever a plane was shot down, an official report had to be filed, and as soon as General Douglas MacArthur saw that Lindbergh was actually fighting, Charlie was sent home. MacArthur went by the Versailles Treaty, which says civilians aren't supposed to be out there fighting.[2]

Back in the U.S. of A., weighing only 150 pounds, I was passed from specialist to specialist in search of a cure, until I ended up at the Tropical Medicine Center in Klamath Falls, Oregon, under the care of an expert in tropical diseases. Under his close personal attention and treatment, my health began to improve, to the point where I was never bothered by malaria again.

---

[2] Our friendship lasted until Charlie's death in 1974. I first met his wife, Anne, and his children when I was cochairman of the Lindbergh Foundation, the environmentally oriented, nonprofit organization that was formed after his death.

During the six months I spent in Oregon, to facilitate the Marine Corps' plans for my eventual promotion as a career officer, I was appointed Commander of the Second Battalion Marine Base in Klamath Falls. Planning a career for me as a regular officer, they figured I should have a complete background. When I protested that I'd never had all that infantry ground-pounder stuff, they just laughed and handed me a book on U.S. Marine Corps Regulations. That manual worried me more than the war. Nevertheless, I had a wonderful time up there as I began feeling better.

Since housing was scarce in the area, the Lieutenant Governor, Marshall Coronet, who was living in Salem because the legislature was in session, offered his spacious and beautifully furnished house in Klamath Falls so that June could join me, along with our daughter, Cheryl, who had been born on June 16, 1944, while I was overseas.

My boss in Oregon, the commanding colonel of the Marine base at Klamath Falls, was a record-holding marksman and sniper, George Van Orden, who was famous for developing equipment and strategies for snipers. I had a great time working with George, a short, stocky guy who looked like the cartoon character "The Little King." He had about a sixty-inch chest and the rest of the body to go with it.

Van Orden was a major sportsman, and the two of us often hunted duck and geese in the morning before work began at eight o'clock. On weekends we were sometimes joined by Governor Snell, Lieutenant Governor Marshall Coronet, Secretary of State Cliff Hoag, and the movie star and singer Dennis Morgan. Dennis was the guy who introduced me to big-time football when he got me tickets to the Rose Bowl in 1945, the first major game I'd ever attended. Only later did I learn that he'd given me his own tickets. I also met and hunted with FBI agent Willis Woods, who'd lost his toe during a shootout with John Dillinger. Hoover was so PO'd when Dillinger got away that he sent Willis west.

Snell and Coronet often flew to a ranch situated northeast of Lakeview, Oregon, and they asked me to go with them. I'd never turn down a chance to hunt, but after making one trip with them, I always declined these invites. They would fly in a light plane out the east leg of the Lakeview Range, then make a sharp right turn and let down to find a landing strip. The unpredictable weather in the range made it downright stupid. A high overcast often developed in that area, and when that happened it was no place to be in a small plane. It was just too risky.

I know this may sound strange coming from a guy who'd been dogfighting Zeros, strafing battleships, and dodging antiaircraft fire. But if there's one thing all that teaches you, it's that while sometimes life thrusts you into dangerous situations you can't avoid, you don't go looking for them. You keep sticking your neck out and there's gonna be a hatchet somewhere to take care of it.

Anyway, not long after I left Oregon, Snell and Coronet went on one of these fly-in hunting trips and began to let down in the heavy overcast, executing one of the landings I'd specifically advised them against. They misjudged their location and flew directly into the side of a mountain. The plane exploded on impact, killing both men.

While I was in Oregon the word came down that I couldn't be a regular officer because I was too old when I signed up; I was going to be a reserve officer. General Geiger must have really snorted when he heard that; he'd told me that the regulations wouldn't matter in my case. But that's the way it was, so I started planning to get out.

After six months in Oregon my health had improved and they sent me back to the Marine Air Station at Goleta near Santa Barbara as director of operations. While I was there, President Roosevelt died, Harry S. Truman became president, and the armed forces went on immediate alert. Many feared that our enemies might attempt some surprise offensive during the time of turmoil because of the death of our commander in chief.

I remained at Santa Barbara until the Japanese surrendered to General Douglas MacArthur on the battleship *Missouri*. At that point I was called to Washington by the Marine Corps to discuss remaining in the military, and I explained to them that my request for a regular commission had been turned down because of my age. I was surprised to learn that Secretary of the Navy Frank Knox had given me a regular commission during the war, but for some unknown reason it never made its way to me in the South Pacific. This didn't change my mind, however; I had decided to return to civilian life, and at Christmastime, 1945, I was relieved from active duty.

PART THREE
Full Speed Ahead

If you get into something, get into it all the way.

—Joe Foss

If I had to pick out one trait that stands out through all the years I've known Joe, it would be *tenacity*— in everything he does.

—Duke Corning

Chapter 18
Home Again

When we were sitting around in our tents on Guadalcanal, spinning yarns about hunting and fishing, someone would invariably ask, "Joe, are you going back to the farm after the war?"

"Vell," I'd respond in my best Norwegian accent, "I tink dat I vill run for sheriff. It's a good yob—the highest payin' yob in Minnehaha County, you know."

Joking about it was the extent to which I considered the future. I never worried about the future—still don't. It just upsets your metabolism, and then you bother the people around you. Plus, in wartime the military brass did all our planning for us, and besides, none of us really knew if we would even live out the day. So why worry and plan. Whenever anyone asks me what my plan is for the day, I usually say, "I just think I'll let it happen."

But now the war was over, and I had a family to support. Actually, I turned down a number of private sector jobs on the east coast that would have paid handsome salaries, including one from Grumman, mainly because I wanted to live in the wide open spaces. I wanted to start my own aviation business, but that took much more money than I had, so essentially what I did was take off for about the next ten months to hunt and fish and gamble with my buddy Duke

Corning. We hunted all day, and at night we shot dice at various clubs.

Duke and I had known each other since high school and college days when we had worked together at Roy Tollefson's filling station. We'd played football together, and even started learning to fly at the same time out at Sioux Skyways. When I'd joined the Marines I tried to get Duke to join, too, but he went into the Navy and ended up flying B-24s in England in the same squadron with young Joe Kennedy. The two of them got to be good friends, flying scout missions together over the coast of Europe. Later Duke flew Corsair night fighters.

We were the two luckiest monkeys in the world, making just enough gambling with our crap-shooting buddies at the local clubs to keep bread and butter on the table. We never won big, but we would pick up a few bucks and then hunt or fish the rest of the time, keeping the freezers full of meat, so there was always food on the table.

Everything took a backseat to hunting, including our families. Duke and I bought an Air Corps surplus barracks and converted it into living quarters for our two families, just in time for the birth of my second daughter, Mary Joe, on September 7, 1945. Our wives and children were together, but Duke and I were often gone for ten days at a time, mostly within the state, although we did go to Nebraska, North Dakota, and Canada for game birds, and to Wyoming for elk. It wasn't that we had any less love for our families; we just knew they were going to be there when we got back. We weren't being bad guys; we just didn't recognize that what we were doing was a little goofy.

We made out like gangbusters hunting. We never planned anything—just took off into the country and let the chips fall where they may. Like the time we went up toward the Slim Buttes area, which had been closed to hunting for several years. It had recently been opened, and we had licenses, so I called Duke one night and said, "Let's go hunting up there tomorrow."

"We don't have any place to hunt," Duke said.

"Oh, we can find a place."

We drove all night, so we'd get there just before dawn.

When we got to the area, we decided we'd stop at the first light we saw and ask to hunt. When we noticed a light in the kitchen of a ranch house, we pulled into the yard and went up to the door and knocked.

"We're looking for a place to hunt deer," we said when the rancher came to the door.

"Come on in and have some breakfast," the man said with a broad smile, reaching out to shake our hands. He told us his name was Vic and said, "I've been wondering if I'd find somebody to hunt with."

After a hearty rancher's breakfast of pancakes and bacon and eggs, Vic took us out in his own vehicle and gave us advice on what not to shoot. "Don't shoot the first buck you see 'cause there's some monsters in this country. First time it's been open in fifteen or twenty years."

We each got five-point bucks right away, and Vic chortled, "You dummies. You shoot those little ones." And he was right. Before noon we'd seen twenty bucks bigger than the ones we shot. But we had a great time, as well as providing plenty of meat for the table.

When we weren't hunting or shooting craps, we were flying or doing odd jobs. After the war the military began establishing reserve squadrons around the country, and they offered me command of the Marine Aviation Reserves at Minneapolis, Minnesota. The job required weekend commutes of 260 miles from Sioux Falls and paid almost nothing after expenses, but I was flying.

I managed to buy a tractor, trailer, and hay baler for a few hundred dollars and occasionally did contract work for local farmers. Duke bought a load of house paint at bargain rates; he sold some of it to make a profit and used the rest to paint houses. But neither of us let work interfere with our hunting and fishing.

At one point Bill Schmidt, Duke's father-in-law, asked me to try to talk Duke into getting a steady job. "You're probably the closest friend Duke has," Bill said in his slow German accent. "You have a great influence on him, Joe. Could you get him to find a job of some kind? I think you could convince him."

"Don't worry about Duke," I said. "He's going to make it."

Then I went to Duke and said, "You know, if you get too much painting work, it will screw up our hunting and fishing."

Between my gambling winnings and odd jobs, we probably could have begun to accumulate enough to get started in business, but our first child, Cheryl, had been diagnosed as having incurable and crippling cerebral palsy. We consulted with specialists to seek a cure, but finally had to accept that her condition was permanent. June, too, was having health problems, as she had suffered from diabetes since her early teens. So I cashed in my savings bonds and emptied my bank account to cover the medical bills and therapeutic treatments.

Coming out of a combat zone into the normal world is something like emerging from the twilight zone. Probably no veterans and their postcombat fatigue and stress have received more attention and coverage than the Vietnam vets, for a number of reasons, but the truth is that men in combat suffer more or less the same after all wars. Everyone works it out —or doesn't—in his own way, and I guess mine was to retreat into carefree boyhood and roam the countryside I loved. I wanted to make up for all my lost hunting time.

After about a year of this roving life, however, Duke and I turned our attention to the flying service. Since between us we had just about enough money to buy a ham sandwich, our first stop was the bank.

"Well, boys, what can I do for you?" asked Ralph Watson, president of the Northwest Security National Bank in Sioux Falls.

"We want to borrow some money," I said.

"How much do you need?" Watson asked, chewing on the stub of a cigar and spitting the tobacco juice into an empty Coke bottle.

"Seventy-five thousand dollars," I said, and I swear that cigar popped right out of his mouth. Seventy-five thousand was real money in those days.

"What?" exclaimed Watson. "What are you going to do with it?"

"We want to go into the aviation business."

"Seventy-five thousand!" he repeated. "What do you have for security?"

"Just our faces," Duke said, "and a wife and two kids each."

"You're both smart enough to know that you have to have something for security if you're going to borrow that kind of money," said Watson.

"Well, we took money and banking courses in college," I said, "and we were taught that since banks are part of the business world, they try to get new business started."

"This is highly irregular," Ralph grumbled.

"You're always asking us what you can do for us. Everybody's asked that same dumb question since we've been home, but I guess nobody meant it. It's a different ballgame when the war's over."

The following day the phone rang at our barracks. When I answered it, Watson growled, "Come on down, you two. Come and sign for the seventy-five thousand. The board okayed it."

So Duke and I went down and put our names on the dotted line. We had three years to pay the sucker off, and I know old Ralph was really wondering if we'd make it.

Although we called the business "Foss's Flying Service," capitalizing on my name recognition, Duke and I were equal partners. It was always fifty-fifty with Duke and me, even though we never had anything in writing. We were friends and trusted each other, and nobody could ask for a better business partner and friend than Duke Corning.

We started with one airplane and an office in a tarpaper shack, and at first it was catch as catch can. We had a lot of great ideas, but aviation hadn't really caught on yet. Everybody was waiting for what's happened since—the executive flying and that sort of thing. So at first we did a little instruction—Duke taught instruments and I taught flying—and we had a few charters. Not many at first, because our planes weren't good enough.

Then Taylorcraft Corporation asked us to distribute their airplanes, and Duke and I went to Chicago to take delivery on our first demonstrator, a two-seater light plane. But I'll let old Duker tell the story, since he brings a little different perspective to it:

We headed back home with our first plane, and, typical of Foss, he only flew high enough to clear things. He never flew to 2,500 or 3,000. Oh, no, you gotta stay down there where the air's rough and the wind's blowing so you can see everything—the pheasants on the ground and the chickens and the pigs. That's the way he flew all the time.

It was hot and choppy and he was chewing a dead cigar, wet about four inches down. Well, we bounced along like this for a couple hours until finally I said, "Joe, you got a choice."

"What'er you talking about?" he growled.

"Either throw the cigar out the window or I'm gonna vomit in your lap."

Well, I can tell you, that cigar went out the window real fast—I guess I was looking green enough that he believed me. But when we opened both the windows to get some fresh air, our map blew back into the tail section, so we had no way to tell where we were.

About dark we figured we should be close to Sioux Falls, but we didn't recognize a thing and were running low on fuel. So we set down in a farmer's hog lot.

"What are you guys doing here?" the farmer said. We told him we needed some gas and then casually asked, like we were asking the time, "How far is Sioux Falls?" He told us we were nine or ten miles away and sold us five gallons of gas.

He was about to pour it into the airplane when we said, "Hey, wait a minute, maybe we'd better strain that." And it was a good thing we did, because we strained out a double handful of algae and straw and every kind of crud. We'd never have made it with that dirty fuel.

My wife, Katherine, has given me a hard time ever since about not being able to find my way home in an airplane.

As business picked up, we hired Mary Rohn to be our secretary. We also began to buy more planes—Piper Cubs, Luscombs, Taylorcrafts, and a twin-engine Cessna Bobcat, which was little more than woodpecker bait because it was made of plywood. At one time we had a fleet of thirty-five assorted planes. We bought and sold them, offered a maintenance and repair service, ran a flying school and a charter service, and even did some crop spraying until we sold out in 1956.

Between flying charters and spending one weekend a month flying F4U Corsairs with the reserve squadron in Minneapolis, I maintained my air time and my edge as a pilot.

Then in 1947 I was approached by Brigadier General Ted Arndt, the commanding officer of South Dakota, and a regular Air Force colonel, Fred Grey, about this wonderful thing called the Air National Guard that would be affiliated with the newly created U.S. Air Force (the old Army Air Corp). They proposed starting an Air National Guard unit in South Dakota with great airplanes like F-51 Mustangs for the fighter squadron, C-45s and C-47s for the utility squadron, and they wanted me to head it up.

"Who'll pick the pilots?" was my first question. "Who'll run it?"

"You'll be it, Joe," said General Arndt. "You can pick your own people and run your own show."

"So what do you say, Joe?" asked Colonel Grey.

"When do we start?"

I resigned from the Marine reserves and immediately began to form the South Dakota Air National Guard, with the rank of lieutenant colonel, all of which caused considerable consternation in the Marines, who had assumed I'd be one of them until the day I died. A lot of Marines didn't much like the Air Force or the Army Air Corps that it was based on. At that time a political cartoon came out showing two cleaning ladies outside a door bearing the Marine seal. Some sort of ruckus was taking place behind the door, and one of the cleaning ladies was saying to the other, "The National Guard just trumped one of their aces."

The formation of the Air National Guard in Sioux Falls was big news in South Dakota. For me it meant I could be

213

closer to home and the business and could get to fly more. For others it provided a unique opportunity to continue to serve their country. Word spread quickly, and former members of all branches of the armed services turned out for the initial meeting at City Hall in Sioux Falls, and I began hand-picking my men.

The first man I selected, of course, was former Navy pilot Duke Corning, and I appointed him the executive officer, my second-in-command. Other key members and their responsibilities were: Lieutenant Colonel Iver Tufty, operations and training; Major Fred A. Brazee, inspector; Major Donald R. Clancey, supply and evacuation; Major John Davies, public information. And then there were John Schilt, Stan Rollag, Garney Nelson, Voy Winders, Harold Ledgerwood, Ken Lane, Oscar Fladmark, Doug Wilson, and Kenny Miller. We also had a cross section of enlisted men from the various branches of the service, such as Clark Baker, Dutch Meier, Howard Joyce, Lyle Sheldon, Don Campbell, Swede Stenholtz, Herbie Creighton, and First Sergeant Harry Tunge, administrative assistant, who worked closely with me during all my years as CO of the South Dakota Air National Guard and would become a particularly valuable part of my life.

Our unit, the 175th, was a composite wing, which meant we had a fighter squadron, a weather squadron, a maintenance squadron, and a medical squadron. A composite wing is set up to operate independently, so nobody has to come and save your bacon in a time of national emergency. You have the whole show, even public relations. It's organized much like the Marine Corps—an outfit that can get going and move fast.

Having men from the different branches gave us a good mix and the potential to become a great outfit. I told my men we could have the best unit in the world if we'd just get out there and work. Once again I tried to bring in the best people to run the administrative and technical departments and operations, surrounding myself with the most qualified men and women I could find. I'm proud to say that, to this day, the 175th still wins as many awards and commendations as any other Air National Guard unit in the country.

A number of our early awards were won by the unit's precision jet flying team, "The Red Devils," which Duke and I organized. It was one of the country's first Air Guard precision jet flying teams and was composed of Justin Berger, Robert Reid, William Downey, and me. The team quickly progressed to the most advanced aerobatics and participated in exhibitions and competitions throughout the state and around the country. The press often referred to the group as "Joe's Flying Circus," in remembrance of my Guadalcanal crew.

Not everyone saw things the way we did, though. I remember our first annual inspection, which was carried out for the National Guard by the regular Air Force. They sent in some guys from the 10th Air Force out of Selfridge Field, Oscoda, Michigan. Again, I think Duke tells the story best:

> Joe figured I was the Operations Officer, so I could babysit these guys. And they really gave me a hard time. They were critical of everything we were doing—the way we flew airplanes, everything. So I kept complaining to Joe, "These guys are impossible!" And he kept saying, "Aw, take it easy. They'll be gone in a couple days and everything will be okay. They just act tough."
>
> Joe showed up for a half hour every day or so and then disappeared, leaving me stuck with these turkeys all day long while they went through our books and everything else.
>
> So on this one particular day I was standing talking to the two of them. They had their backs to the door, and Joe came in just at the moment they were discussing the Marine Corps. Now Joe's an old Marine, and Marines never change; they just stay Marines. And one of these Air Force guys says to the other, "They [meaning the Marines] couldn't fight, but they had the best public relations outfit in the world."
>
> Well, I could see Joe's ears perk up at that, but he didn't say a word. Just went right straight up the stairs to his office.
>
> A minute later the phone rang. It was Joe.
>
> "Send those guys up here," he snapped. I did, and went along with them, not wanting to miss this.
>
> As we stepped through the door to his office, Joe said, "You guys are out of uniform."

One looked at the other, and they looked back and forth and said, "What do you mean, sir?"

"You should be wearing a polka dot suit with a peaked cap," Joe snapped. "You're a couple of clowns. Now get the hell off the base." Not because I'd said these jerks were a pain but because they'd said the Marine Corps was not a fighting unit!

Of course, that wasn't quite the end of it. The Air Force guys immediately ran to the commanding general at Selfridge, Major General Williams, who called me and said, "Hey, Joe, the boys that were over there on an inspection are complaining that they didn't get treated very well." At which point I really unloaded on him: I told him those guys shouldn't be running around loose, that they didn't know what they were talking about to start with and that they didn't know what a fighting outfit was.

Some time later I ran into another guy from that same 10th Air Force inspection team. We were at some National Guard deal in Columbus when this lieutenant colonel came up to me and said, "Foss, I don't like the way you run that outfit. I heard some of your men call you Joe, and you can't have any military courtesy and discipline if men working for you don't address you as colonel."

"Now just a minute," I said. "I've told the men in my outfit—many of whom I've grown up with—that it's absolutely all right to call me Joe when there are no strangers around. But if there are strangers around, call me strictly by rank and have your military courtesy and bearing because they wouldn't understand. As long as everybody does their job, I don't care what they call me, just so they call me in time for dinner."

Then this guy said, "You're nothing but a socialist Communist," and he stood up and swung at me and missed. So I had to tap him one on the chin. He landed on a table at which the folks had just been served their steaks; food flew in every direction. And that was the last I saw of any of those guys from that inspection team. My fuse could be short in those days, and I was always ready to fight, literally or figuratively, for what I believed in. Of course, socking someone seldom proves anything, but sometimes you do need to get their attention.

In 1949 President Harry Truman was eyeing a $13 billion defense budget, which would have reduced the required flight time of pilots in all of the services. When I heard they were considering three proposals—one that would cut the flight requirement to 130-some hours, another that would cut it to just over a hundred hours, and a third that might possibly take it down to sixty-some hours—I got hot under the collar. I'd always figured a pilot should have at least 150 hours a year to be safe to handle the aircraft. So I decided to fly down to Washington to talk personally to Secretary of Defense Louis Johnson. I had gotten to know him the previous year, 1948, when I had served as Vice Chairman of the National Aeronautics Committee, which later became the National Aeronautics and Space Committee.

From Sioux Falls, South Dakota, I flew an F-51 to Bowling Field. Upon arrival I discovered that I'd forgotten to put my suitcase in the pod. I was somewhat embarrassed because I was sweaty from the flight, and in those days you didn't leave the area of operations in your flight suit. But I figured it wasn't something they'd shoot you for, so I rode the nickel snatcher across to the river entrance of the Pentagon.

I was trying to get past the guard, showing him my credentials, when a Marine who'd been on Guadalcanal came up and recognized me. "Captain Foss, what're you doing here?" Whenever I met any of the boys who'd been on Guadalcanal they always called me "captain," because that was the rank they had known me as.

"I'd like to see the Secretary of Defense."

"Sure, I'll run you up there," he said. He took me up to the secretary's office, and lo and behold, there we met another Marine who'd been on Guadalcanal and recognized me.

"The secretary's out right now," he said, "but you can wait in his office." So I was waiting there in the secretary's office, looking at all the memorabilia, when in walked Steve Early, whom I recognized immediately. He had been President Roosevelt's press secretary when I'd received the Medal of Honor. He looked a bit startled, and I started to introduce myself.

"Oh, I remember you," he said.

He wanted to know what I was doing now, so we visited for a few minutes. I was sitting in a big chair and Early was perched on the corner of the desk, when in walked Secretary of Defense Louis Johnson. He, too, looked startled to see this guy in a flight suit sitting in his office, and I quickly explained about forgetting my suitcase.

"What can I do for you, Joe?"

"I hear you're going to be making a decision about the hours of flight time for a pilot per year."

"Yes," he said, "the papers are right there on my desk. We're going to make that decision very shortly."

"Well, I'm concerned," I said bluntly. "If you're serious about limiting pilots to sixty-five hours of flying a year, it will be a big mistake. A lot of good pilots will be killed. I've always maintained that a pilot should have at least 150 hours. I sure wouldn't want to ride with anyone who flies any less than that."

Secretary Johnson turned to Steve Early and said, "You know, the colonel has a good point. I don't think you or I would like to fly with someone that we think isn't safe for solo." When I heard that, I was confident he would change it, which he did.

But then he surprised the socks off me. "I'm ready to leave here shortly for Philadelphia, and I want you to go with me," he said. "I'm going up there to speak to the American Legion convention."

"I don't have any clothes, sir."

"That doesn't make any difference. You're absolutely all right. You just come with me."

So I accompanied Secretary Johnson and his entourage up to Philadelphia, where he introduced me from the stage. My luggage finally caught up to me, and I ended up staying at the convention for a few days as a guest of the legionnaires.

The machine guns of my Wildcat were silent now, but I was learning to fight a new kind of battle—how to make government do the best for the people it represents—with an incredibly powerful weapon called politics.

Chapter 19

A Reluctant
Politician

"**J**oe, have you ever thought about getting into politics?"
Pierce McDowell had asked me one day back in early 1948.
Pierce, a nonpracticing attorney, was vice president of North-
west Security National Bank, the bank that had financed
Foss's Flying Service, and I often stopped in to chat with him.
We also ran into each other frequently at the Elks Club and
on social occasions. This time, however, he'd made a special
trip out to see me at our flying service office.

"Yeah, I've thought about it some," I said. "It would be
the most boring thing in the world. The most uninteresting
thing I could do."

Pierce chuckled, accustomed to my directness, then explained that he was the spokesman for a small but enthusiastic
group of businessmen who would be willing to back my candidacy financially for the state legislature—Frances Reagan,
an insurance agency owner and a Democrat; John Griffith,
who owned half of the Lewis Drug chain; and Milt Pay, who
was in the investment business. My success in organizing and
commanding the South Dakota Air National Guard had not
gone unnoticed, he said, and this group felt I could be the
man to guide the state into a prosperous postwar future.

Looking at McDowell across the desk, I leaned back in my
chair, stretched out my legs, folded my arms over my chest,
and said reflectively, "You know, my pop always used to say

that if a man gets involved in politics, and he's honest, all he'll end up with is a shiny blue serge suit! Well, I'm an honest man, and I don't want a shiny blue suit."

After appealing once more to my sense of patriotism, Pierce left me with the assurance that he wasn't taking "no" for an answer. "Think it over some more, Joe," he said. "I'll be back."

In the following days several other friends went out of their way to urge me to run for office, but my response was always the same: "Not interested." I believed in good government, but I didn't want to take responsibility for it. I was like a chipped molar. I just wanted to ride along and let someone else carry the burden.

Even old Duker laughed at the idea and told me he didn't believe I could be elected. I agreed.

Friends and community leaders continued to press me, however, and eventually Pierce and his group approached me with a petition to get my name on the ballot for the House of Representatives.

"We'll circulate the petition," they said. "You won't have to do a thing, Joe. Just leave it to us."

Their persistence left me feeling not only a bit puzzled, but also somewhat guilty that I'd let them down if I didn't go along. So finally I said, "All right. Only because you guys want me to. But I'm not making any promises, I'm not giving any speeches, and I'm sure not going to spend any of my own money!" When it came right down to it, I was willing to run for office, but I didn't want any part of politics.

They assured me they'd handle all the finances. All I had to do, they said, was make a few public appearances.

Well, I did end up spending some of my own money on the election. It cost me twenty-five bucks to print up little cards with my name and picture on them, and a line that said I was a Republican candidate for the legislature.

Seventeen candidates were running in the Republican primary that year, and despite my passive approach to the whole thing, I came in first. Maybe the moral of the story was that people were tired of baloney, and I didn't give them any. Whatever the reason, no one could have been more surprised by the vote than I was.

Boy, I've really done it now, I thought. What was I doing running for office? Now I really had to get with it and learn what was going on in the state. Until now I had not paid that much attention. Then I remembered some of the politicians who had visited the troops in the South Pacific during the war. Most of those guys had backgrounds as shallow as the Missouri River. When I thought about it, I figured I could do at least as well as they did.

From that day on I started taking my candidacy seriously. Once I became involved, my eyes were opened, and I really began to feel that I wanted a part in good government and that I had a responsibility to make the government work for the good of our great country. Suddenly I realized that politics was very much my responsibility and was as much a part of defending and protecting my country as my military career.

I began reading every current newspaper I could get my hands on, trying to get a good feel for what the job involved, what was happening in the state, and what people were thinking. I also began making personal appearances around the county, getting to know the people and what they wanted.

That fall the people of South Dakota voted me into the state House of Representatives, and overnight, politics became the number one priority in my life.

I arrived in Pierre, South Dakota, the state's capital, in January 1949 and started talking to old-timers in the government, devouring the daily newspapers, and listening to every newscast, trying to learn what the job of a state representative was all about. The first thing I did after the election was go to see one of the older men in the legislature, Senator Arthur Fanibus, and he gave me some great advice.

"Don't say anything until you know what you're talking about," he said. "Don't make up your mind until you've heard all the sides. And don't start introducing bills."

In other words, don't go off half-cocked. Taking his words of wisdom to heart, I didn't introduce any bills or talk much the first session. Whenever somebody asked me a question I couldn't answer, I just told them I didn't know, but that I'd try to find out. I didn't lead anyone on, and I never made promises I couldn't keep. I was almost surprised to find myself enjoying the job.

One of the new Super Cubs that my partner Duke Corning and I used in our spraying operation. (Photo by Duke Corning)

The post paid zilch, but Foss's Flying Service was beginning to generate a comfortable income. In our second year Duke and I had paid off the three-year loan from the bank and were prosperous enough to move our families out of the barracks and into our own individual homes in Sioux Falls. Besides charters and lessons, we had expanded into crop-dusting, so the flying service took most of my time when I wasn't doing legislature business. Also, that year, 1949, Duke and I were able to purchase a Packard-Studebaker dealership in Sioux Falls.

Besides, I didn't mind the low pay. As far as I'm concerned, political jobs pay too much. If you need a job, you shouldn't be in politics. You should go into politics for the welfare of the county, state, and country, but a lot of politicians show more concern for their own little kingdoms than they do for the people who have elected them. The only way to enjoy an office is not to give a hang about reelection. Trouble is, too many elected officials start campaigning for the next election as soon as they're in office, and as a result, they're not concerned with the real business of the people.

I've never been quite sure what accounted for it, whether it was the "war hero" status or my down-home, forthright personality, but I felt as though most people welcomed my entry into government. However, "most people" did not include my wife.

At first, like me, June had not taken my candidacy very seriously, and when I was elected she showed even less enthusiasm for my newest venture. When the legislature was in session, to save money, I lived in a tiny room on the third floor of the St. Charles Hotel in Pierre, while June and the children remained in Sioux Falls. Added to this was the fact that June had never been very realistic about my future. June's hero was Albert Schweitzer, and she was never truly happy to see me in business or in politics. Her growing dissatisfaction, coupled with my devotion to the job, created a rising tension in our relationship.

For another thing, June's politics were exactly opposite of mine. And whereas I had grown up in a household of conflicting political philosophies where we did not find that a personal problem, June found it increasingly difficult to accommodate my political stance. My position was that the government was taking over too much of what communities and the private sector did best. Actually I joked with the legislature that we ought to have one session dedicated to fixing all the problems they'd created in the past.

In government the stated purpose of a program rarely had much to do with the real results of the program, but that's difficult to understand if you haven't taken the time to study the way government actually works. So it's natural that people who care a lot about the unfortunate think that you can solve more problems than you create when you start taking money from some people for the benefit of others. Bureaucratic programs designed to help the needy usually end up padding the pockets of the greedy. June didn't see it that way, though, and as time went on, she grew more and more unhappy with my job.

President Dwight D. Eisenhower greeting the
Easter Seal Child of 1961 during my tenure as
President of the National Society of Crippled
Children and Adults, 1961. (Photo courtesy of
National Easter Seal Society)

I threw myself into the legislature heart and soul—full
speed ahead—to the exclusion of just about everything else.
All I could see at the time was that the people had given me
a job to do in government and that responsibility came first.

From the very beginning, my involvement in politics gave
me an opportunity to influence a special interest that would
become a lifelong commitment. During my first year in office
I helped organize the Crippled Children's Hospital and School
at Sioux Falls. This was a very personal concern for me because of Cheryl's cerebral palsy. Little was known then about

the illness, and we could only hope and pray that medical science would eventually come up with some answers. Turning my energies into this positive outlet was something I could do to provide support for others in the same situation.

There were tough times along the way, but Cheryl made it through school; she even sang in choirs. Along with all the joy and happiness she brought us, Cheryl gave a deeper, more purposeful meaning to my life. Her disability opened my eyes to the great need of the many handicapped children and adults in our state and country. June found strength in Christianity; I found strength in activity.

I always had to feel I was tackling the problem, affecting the outcome of the battle, and in this case seeing what I could accomplish through the legislature. In 1954 I would become president of the South Dakota Society of Crippled Children and Adults, and in 1956 I would be elected president of the national organization. Years later I would be a member of the White House Conference on Handicapped Individuals.

My friends had pulled me into politics. Now they couldn't get me out. In November 1949, after looking around at the potential gubernatorial candidates and figuring I could do a better job than any of them, I announced that I was going to run for governor—without consulting anyone. Well, that straightened the kinks in the telephone wires.

Immediately my supporters were on the phone. "You can't do that, Joe. You've haven't been Speaker of the House yet, you have no organization, no real platform—"

"I don't want to be Speaker of the House," I said. "As for a platform, I'll make one up. The election's way down the road. The platform will take shape by then."

I'd announced on a Wednesday, and the *Daily Argus-Leader* carried it as the front-page lead. That was another thing the boys in the back room were steamed about. Wednesday was a bad day, they said, because that was the day all the stores chocked the paper full of their advertising. Besides, said the critical experts, my decision had been announced much too far in advance of the election. Some of the small papers endorsed me immediately; others called me a glamour boy and asked what right I had to represent the state. Some

225

said I was a lousy orator, and some said I was a good one. Others said that, at thirty-four, I was too young. All of which goes to prove that you can't please all of the people all of the time.

The Republican party officials were less than pleased with my independence and my homespun campaigning. The GOP was planning to run one of their favorite sons, the popular Attorney General, Sigurd Anderson. Today, looking back, I can see both the humor of the situation as well as my own arrogance. There I was, a pip-squeak who had only limited experience in the legislature and nobody backing me. Anderson announced his candidacy a short time afterward, and two others threw their hats in the ring, making a total of four Republican candidates.

Despite my bucking the system, the polls showed me leading the Republican pack; it looked like I might step directly from the House into the governor's mansion. Then I got a call from Boyd Leedom, from Rapid City. Boyd was a highly respected and successful state senator and one of my good friends in the legislature.

On our way to lunch one day, Boyd had said, "Joe, if you ever run for governor, I'll support you."

But Boyd was not calling to reaffirm his support; instead, he told me, he'd decided to run for governor himself and wanted to know if I would mind if he did.

"If you want to run, go ahead," I said. "But I don't think you'll win. You'll just goof it up for me. But you do whatever you want to. It's a free country."

Leedom was from the Rapid City-Black Hills area of the state, where I was stronger than horseradish; I told him he'd probably take just enough of the vote away from me so that the second-place candidate, Sigurd Anderson, would win. Within a few days of the primary the political know-it-alls came out with their version of the race, which was exactly the same as the analysis I'd given Boyd. And that's what happened. I ended up in second place, 2,352 votes shy of the winner, Sigurd Anderson, and Boyd came in third. In the fall campaign it was Sig Anderson against the Democratic candidate, Joe Robbie, an old schoolmate of mine. Anderson won the vote and his defeated opponent moved to Minneapolis and started a law practice. People have had a way of cropping up again and again in my life, and that was the case with Joe Robbie. We would meet up again years later when I was with the American Football League.

At the end of my two-year term in the House, I returned to Sioux Falls and resumed working full-time at the flying service. Then came the Korean call-up.

In 1950, when armed conflict broke out in Korea and the United States committed to provide a military "policing action," South Dakota's 175th Air National Guard was called to active duty by the Air Force as an Air Defense Command Unit and assigned as a group to Rapid City, South Dakota. Because I had been promoted to a full colonel in 1950, I was too senior with too much experience to stay with my unit and was assigned to the Central Air Defense Command (regular Air Force) at Kansas City as Director of Operations and Training for a twenty-state area. Duke Corning took over as commanding officer of the 175th, and we left the flying service in the capable hands of several civilian pilots.

I desperately wanted to fly missions in Korea. I knew I was an even better pilot in 1951 than I had been in 1943, with many more hours in the air than most of the pilots sent to do the fighting, and I wanted to contribute to the effort in Asia. But when I asked for a transfer to combat, I was told that no recipient of the Congressional Medal of Honor would be allowed inside a combat zone. There was nothing humanitarian about it; it was all public relations. A killed or captured medal recipient would be considered a disaster for America and a propaganda coup for the enemy. I not only disagreed; I was furious. Once again I flew to Washington. This time to plead for a chance to fight.

Knowing it would be a sensitive dispute, I wanted to put my case directly before General Hoyt Vandenberg, Chief of Staff USAF, without the knowledge and resultant spotlight of the Washington press corps.

The day before my appointment with the general I ran into Senator Francis Case from South Dakota, who asked why I was in town. I told the senator, in confidence, why I was there. The next morning when I glanced at the newspaper at the breakfast table, I was mortified to see my photograph in the *Washington Post* with the headline, "Ace Wants to Go to Combat." Obviously the senator had ignored my off-the-record disclaimer and talked to the press.

When I walked into General Vandenberg's office, the four-star general greeted me with, "Glad to see you, Joe, but the answer's no!" If Washington made an exception in my case, he said, then other medal of honor recipients might feel obligated to volunteer, and the government believed we could better serve our country by remaining in the States to help build up the nation's defense. I returned to the base to channel my energies elsewhere. Though I was bitterly disappointed, that was not the greatest misfortune to touch me during the Korean conflict.

I began my duty with the Air Force in Kansas City on March 14, 1951. On August 9 of that year, our son, Joseph Frank Foss, was born, and shortly after that June became an instructor of nutrition and diet therapy at the Sioux Falls Hospital. During her teaching term in 1952, a polio epidemic hit, killing or crippling scores of children in the Sioux Falls area. All but essential medical activities were suspended, and employees were moved around where they were needed. Since nutrition was her specialty, June went to work in the hospital's kitchen during the emergency.

One night, exhausted from a long day, she returned home to find her housekeeper pacing anxiously with the baby. Frankie was barely breathing, and the left side of his mouth was paralyzed.

Later in an interview with *Household* magazine, June confessed her fear that she had brought the disease home with her from the hospital. "I worked day and night," she said. "In fact, everybody did, for the polio-ridden hospital was overflowing. I thought I was careful when I came home nights. I washed my hands—hung my clothes out in the air."

Probably her hospital work had nothing to do with Frankie's contracting bulbar polio. Many children were afflicted whose parents had no contact with the hospital. But June took it hard. She resigned her dietician post and kept a constant vigil beside Frankie's hospital bed. When he was sleeping, she

My good friend Ted Williams, one of the greatest
batting champions of all time. Ted's baseball
career with the Boston Red Sox was interrupted
when he was called to active duty as a fighter
pilot for the United States Marine Corps during
the Korean conflict.

assisted the nurses with the other patients—changing diapers,
fetching water, and telling stories.

I was relieved that, as usual, June had everything under
control. I always felt useless when someone was sick, but
seeing Frankie tore me apart because he was so helpless.
There was nothing I could do to make my little baby better.
I've always been a man of action, and I'll take whatever action
is necessary to get the job done, but this problem was beyond
me. Thankfully, Frankie eventually made a full recovery.

After the Korean conflict ended, I resumed my role as
president of Foss Motors, the Packard-Studebaker dealership,
which Chuck Steinmetz managed for us. I was also itching to
get back into politics, and in November of that year I was
elected to another two-year term in the House of Representatives. I also served as Chief of Staff of the South Dakota

Air National Guard, and Duke and I still had Foss's Flying Service, although not without the occasional setback.

Back in 1951, a heavy spring runoff from melting snow and torrential rains had flooded the Sioux River and swept more than three feet of water into our hangar at the airfield. The damage amounted to over $30,000, but because it was an "act of God" our insurance covered very little. I immediately contacted Lloyd's of London to take out an insurance policy against future flood damage. When we learned how high the premiums would be, Duke and I decided that the odds against another freak flood were long. We gambled and lost. The very next year the Sioux River flooded again, and this time the water rose even higher.

At least we had learned something from history, and reacted quickly when the waters began to threaten. We sandbagged the hangar and flew our planes out to my brother's farm—the old Foss homestead—where Cliff had a runway for his private plane.

Surely there could never be a third such natural disaster, we reasoned. The flying business was doing well. We had thirty-six planes, three mechanics, and a nice hangar. Counting Duke and me, we had eight pilots and a full-time accountant. From time to time we even had to hire extra pilots. We were rolling.

"You know," Duke said to me, "why should we pay out good money for insurance we'll probably never see again."

"I agree," I said. "Why don't we just carry our own insurance?"

So instead of paying premiums to an insurance company, we planned to put the equivalent into an escrow account each month to be used in case of emergency.

Three months later, I was standing before the South Dakota House of Representatives discussing an upcoming bill when a page approached from behind and whispered over my shoulder, "There's an emergency phone call for you, Mr. Foss."

After requesting and receiving permission from the Chair to leave the chamber I hurried to the phone outside. It was Duke.

"Hi, Duker. What's the problem?"

"The roof just fell in on the business," he said. "Everything is on fire and the roof just caved in."

"Did anybody get killed?" I asked.

"No."

"Well, we have something to be thankful for then," I said stoically.

"The weather is bad," Duke said, "so not many planes were flying. Some dummy parked the Beechcraft Bonanza up against the door, locked the brakes, and went to lunch. By the time we got it moved out of there, it was too late to save anything." We had lost nine customers' planes and fourteen of our own.

After the investigators got through, they determined that the cause was an unextinguished cigarette left by some school kids who had crawled into an empty plane to sneak a smoke. Since we had yet to put the third of our payments into our insurance escrow account, we were knocked down for a temporary count. But we got back on our feet and borrowed money so we could rebuild and continue to operate.[1]

During my second term in the House I concentrated on trying to bring new business into South Dakota and on improving the road system and universities. I was also getting interested in the water situation, since South Dakota is a dry state.

My popularity quotient was high, my reputation as a legislator was growing, and my influential political friends knew it. I was welcomed as a rising star among the GOP legislators, and this time they asked me to be their candidate for governor.

---

[1] We kept the business going until 1956 when we sold the sales, repair, and charter service. In 1955 we sold the spraying service and Foss Motors.

Chapter 20

Governor
Joe

✯   ✯   ✯

"**G**eneral Foss! General Foss!" The group of reporters vied for attention and recognition as I stood before a microphone-cluttered podium.

"General Foss, why do you think being a war hero qualifies you to be governor?" one newshound asked.

I smiled politely but shook my head in mild irritation. I'd been campaigning for governor for nearly half of 1954, and this inane question still came up at every opportunity. My answer was always the same, but that never stopped the press from badgering the hell out of me.

"I don't think being a war hero does qualify me for governor," I said. "It's what I'm made of that enabled me to do what I did during the war." Then I added with a grin, "Being a war hero just means that fewer people ask, 'Joe who?' "

I had announced my candidacy earlier that year on January 5, and the following day the front-page story in the *Daily Argus-Leader* quoted me as saying, "As the primary campaign develops I will outline my ideas on the issues as I see them and as I call them. That has been my policy in the past, and it hasn't changed."

My name was in the papers again on January 14, this time announcing my promotion from colonel to brigadier general in the South Dakota Air National Guard, a commission I held jointly with being a brigadier general in the Air Force reserve. This publicity didn't hurt my campaigning, of course.

During the hectic whirlwind months, I did my best to maintain a no-nonsense line with both the people and the press, and tried to be consistently straightforward about my view of government and the responsibilities of the job.

"To me a governor has a job that is just plain hard work and long hours," I said. "And a lot of his success depends upon the caliber of men and women he has working for him. As for my philosophy, whether it was in the Marines, in business, or in public service, I have always tried to bring the best administrators and technicians on board to get the job done."

In that vein, I selected Hoadley Dean as my campaign manager. I figured I'd lost my first bid for governor because I hadn't had a veteran campaign manager, and Hoadley Dean was every bit a veteran. He had been an administrative assistant to two of South Dakota's ranking public servants— United States Senator Harlan Bushfield and Congressman Harold Lovre.

I'd first met Hoadley when I was playing football at the University of South Dakota; he was a skinny little guy who worked as a reporter for the school newspaper, always coming around with his clipboard, asking questions and taking notes for some story.

In those days, Hoadley's opinion of me hadn't been terribly complimentary. "Joe was no campus bigshot at Vermillion," he once told a writer doing an article for *The Saturday Evening Post.* "He went out for some campus activities, but he wasn't at all outstanding. We never would have elected him 'most likely to succeed.' "

Hoadley was in favor of an aggressive campaign at the grass roots level, and since I was no longer reluctant to hit the campaign trail, he scheduled me for as many speeches and public appearances as possible. The two of us crisscrossed the state in a private plane, the first time in South Dakota politics that a gubernatorial candidate campaigned by airplane. We traveled 15,000 miles by car and more than 10,000 by plane —which sometimes landed us in interesting situations.

While I was giving a speech in White River, a heavy rainstorm came up. After finishing an interview with a newspaper writer, I went to the airport and climbed into my Piper Super Cub. What I didn't realize was how much the rain had softened the ground. As we rolled down the field, the wheels picked up the gumbo so that we couldn't clear the woven wire fence at the end of the runway and ended up in a hog pen belonging to a local Democrat! After a short delay we managed to take off on a grassy field and were on our way to the next appointment.

Hoadley's campaign strategy was simple: I was to shake hands personally with everyone I could and ask them for their support, which was fine with me. I've always preferred what I call "hand-to-hand combat"—looking voters straight in the eye and asking for their vote. Furthermore, I refused to take part in the numerous debates normally scheduled for candidates. You just can't afford to go around and debate everyone. It takes too much time and doesn't really matter that much. It's mostly a lot of hot air anyway. When it comes right down to it, our country was built by doers, not talkers. Debates are tailor-made for slick talkers who make good speeches but bomb out when it comes to getting the job done.

Politicians tell people that they'll cut taxes and increase services. It's a lie, but people believe it. Running a government is like running a business, if you do it well. But a number of people in office aren't interested in cutting costs or in managing the people's money responsibly. So they make impossible promises and then raise taxes. After years of this, people have gotten so disillusioned that they won't do their homework anymore. A great percentage don't even vote. They don't ask the hard questions—the questions the media won't raise because they're trained to support the politicians' attitude that you can spend your way out of any problem.

The Republican voters gave me a decisive victory in the primaries, and I scored almost 10,000 votes more than the second- and third-place candidates combined. Coming out of that, my Democratic opponent was Ed C. Martin, a rancher from Chamberlain, and as we entered the home stretch, the pace quickened. Hoadley and I flew into even the smallest of towns to campaign. If there was no airport, we landed in a nearby field, meeting with as few as five people. It was rigorous, but I loved to get out and talk to the people this way; sometimes I would even get up a couple hours early to go duck hunting with some of the locals.

I told the people that I believed the state's economy was overly dependent upon agriculture and proposed an aggressive industrial development and expansion program. Essentially my program was to create new jobs and halt the mass exodus of young people from the state.

By the time my family and I gathered at home to watch the election returns on television, I was exhausted but exhilarated. We'd done all we could. Now the moment of truth rested with the voters.

When the vote was counted, I had 31,301 more votes than my opponent, making me at age thirty-nine the youngest man ever to serve as South Dakota's governor up to that time. The polls had predicted my victory, but the analysts were surprised at the margin, especially since the rest of the election leaned overwhelmingly in the Democrats' favor; they reduced the GOP legislative margin by twenty-two seats.

"South Dakota Draws an Ace," declared the headlines of the *Minneapolis Sunday Tribune,* and the subhead described me as "Joe Foss: Governor Elect, War Hero, Family Man and Humanitarian."

I'm sure June took exception to the "family man" description, given our situation at home, which was probably more accurately described by the headline from an article in the *Daily Argus-Leader,* "Mrs. Foss Wonders If She'll See More of Her Husband as Governor."

From the start I bucked tradition. At the news conference following the election, I was asked about plans for the inaugural ball.

"Tell everyone they're invited and welcome to come," I announced boldly.

"It's their state and I'm their governor. Why shouldn't everyone be able to come and have a good time?" I argued with my surprised staff later when they challenged me about this plan.

"That eliminates the question of whose names get on the invitation list," quipped one staffer.

"And there's no need to send out costly engraved invitations either," added another.

"Now you're talking." I grinned.

"What will people wear?" asked one of the women in the group.

"I don't care as long as they're comfortable. It'll suit me fine if the men wear overalls, cowboy gear, business suits, or tuxedos."

The news media had a field day with my open invitation to the inauguration. The story made front-page headlines in newspapers from one end of the state to the other and led to some interesting speculation. I had a reputation for liking my shot of whiskey and my cigars, which prompted some to predict freewheeling revelry. One columnist even likened the upcoming event to the shocking free-for-all staged by President Andrew Jackson at his inauguration.

When inauguration day came, January 11, 1955, my mother was there as I took the oath of office, and someone reported that she said to the man next to her, "Joe has always been a good boy." I was pleased that I had made my mother proud, and I hoped my dad was somewhere up there watching, too.

More than 7,500 people gathered that evening at the Capitol Rotunda and the Pierre National Guard Armory for the celebration. Contrary to journalistic conjecture, it was not a wild, raucous affair. I donned a tux and June wore an elegant white gown, and the highlight of the evening came when our ten-year-old Cheryl put her crutches aside and danced with her white-haired grandfather, Oscar Shakstad. Even three-year-old Frankie took an unscheduled part. As part of the inaugural ceremony, Cheryl and nine-year-old Mary Joe walked down the aisle to present June with bouquets of flowers as South Dakota's new first lady. Noticing that there were no flowers for his dad, Frankie ran up and indignantly snatched Cheryl's bouquet and presented it to me. The press loved it.

At one point in the evening red-haired Mary Joe protested to a startled guest, "I don't like for you to call my daddy 'governor.' His name is daddy or Joe."

Later our friends Harry and Vera Bradshaw would tell

Household magazine, "Mary Joe's humility, Cheryl's courage and determination to conquer her immobile legs, and Frankie's will to see that everyone was treated fairly are merely reflections of their parents' deep-rooted virtues."

Certainly if those virtues did exist in our lives, they had been borne out of our own experiences. We had faced death; battled polio, cerebral palsy, and diabetes; lost our life savings; and been separated by two wars. But that which made us strong also came at great cost to our marriage and family relationships.

My first day in the governor's office began when I walked the two blocks from the governor's mansion to the capitol building. Walking to work became a routine for me, and whenever I sighted ducks on the pond next to the governor's mansion the old hunter instinct would course through my blood. I'd carry a duck call in my pocket, and before long the neighbors got used to hearing me quacking at the ducks.

Although I had been in and out of the governor's office many times over the years, I was never particularly impressed by the high ceiling, lavishly draped windows, highly polished wood paneling, monolithic oak desk, and luxurious royal blue carpet. The first personal item I brought into the office was a scale model of the Wildcat, which the Grumman Aircraft Corporation had built and presented to me in recognition of my combat record. It was the first of many model planes I would place on display there.

Security was never a big deal during my administration. I walked unaccompanied to and from the office every day—often late at night—and my office door was always open. I never turned anyone away.

Once in a while an irate citizen would storm in and unleash a verbal attack over some issue, but I'd just tell him firmly, "Now either settle down and act like a gentleman (or a lady, as the case might be), or I'll have to ask you to leave. And if you don't leave, I'm going to see how far I can throw you!" After that they'd usually settle down, although in a couple instances I had to show out-of-order visitors the door. Threats I wouldn't sit still for; disagreement was another matter. I would hear anyone out, whether they liked the way I did business or not.

This open-door policy meant that I usually had to do my paperwork after normal business hours; fortunately I had Harry Tunge, my personnel director, Bob Lee, my administrative assistant, and Maxine Isenberg, my executive secretary, who were as dedicated to working long hours as I was.

Hoadley Dean had recruited Maxine Isenberg from a court reporter's job, and it wasn't long before I couldn't function without her; as far as I was concerned, she held the office together, and we began a working relationship that would last for eleven years.

Looking back, years later, Maxine recalls some of her initial impressions from those early days:

> Although Joe had been active in the state legislature and Republican politics and I had known him slightly, I was not well acquainted with him. Joe was a war hero and highly publicized. As a World War II widow, I had occasion to resent him for all the understandable reasons. I didn't initially follow the masses into total admiration. In those days I had a lot of chips on my shoulders, and I also felt that Hoadley, who was a master choreographer in politics, had thought it might not be an image hurter to have the war hero hire a widow. I resented that a lot. Also, I soon learned it wasn't true.
>
> My wounds took a long time healing. But my attitude then was: What the heck, I don't know where this guy is going, but who cares; it's a four-year stint and it could be fun. And it was fun, and the whole experience a great healer of wounds. I found out I had worth. Joe treated me as an equal and constantly praised me. He gave everyone a feeling of worth and value. That's what Joe did best.

Maxine's words mean a great deal to me, both because she is someone I have worked closely with and because those are qualities I prize highly and have tried to instill in those around me as well as myself.

However, the thing that drove Maxine nuts in the early days, she says, was my work habits.

Joe always let somebody else pick up the details so he could get on with the "big picture." At first I thought his work habits were the pits. Later I realized they worked for him and it was all a matter of style. The man drove me nuts with his unorthodox work habits, but I simply had to learn that there may be a hundred ways to get to a solution or the bottom of a problem. That was the Foss style. It may have been a very circuitous route, but he did get to the bottom of problems—and he cut a lot of red tape. As the song goes, he did it his way—which was not always by the times on the office calendar or in my appointment book. My hair colorist today must thank Joe Foss a thousand times over!

Joe did not like detail. Somebody else pick up the pieces, if you please, and let him get on with the broad canvas. Stuff that bugged Joe was the nonmeaningful paperwork that bogged us all down. He usually buck-slipped it on and gave us carte blanche on handling it.

One of the funnier examples of his attitude toward detail involved a "who's who" listing. These annual publications contained biographical material on Joe and were often sent to him for updating, which he didn't want to bother with and passed on to me. As a famous World War II ace, Joe was given a rather large paragraph in the *Who's Who in Britain* volume. Now Joe's long-time friend Duane Corning goes by the nickname Duke. When this particular paragraph came through from the British publication for editing, I noted that good old buddy Duke was listed as "the Duke of Corning." When I checked the material with Joe for a big laugh, he just grinned and said, "Let's leave it in." And to this day, as far as I know, the Adjutant General of the State of South Dakota is probably believed to be the Duke of Corning.

The military had taught me to be a big-picture man—to delegate routine administrative and technical matters to

subordinates—and early on I made my philosophy of executive leadership clear to my staff.

"I'm not interested in negative people who have all kinds
of excuses why something can't be done," I told them. "I
want people who can figure out a way of doing it. So I won't
be leaning over your shoulders. You won't see me in your
office unless you're in trouble, and then I'll be there to help
you out of it."

Harry Tunge, who still worked full-time in the office of the
South Dakota Air National Guard, took a four-year leave of
absence from his position to work with me in the governor's
office as personnel director. While there, he set up the personnel department for the state patterned after the Air Force
and General Motors. (Later Harry, who, along with his wonderful wife, Faith, has been our treasured friend for years,
would be there again when I needed him, once more taking
a leave of absence and coming to Dallas for a year while we
were setting up the American Football League operation.)

In those early days Maxine worried about getting every
single letter answered, never hurting feelings, and taking it
personally if I didn't make an engagement or turned up hours
late. She felt it was her failure. Both she and Bob Lee, my
administrative assistant, fretted a lot about such details. Finally I guess they just figured I wasn't going to change, so
they learned to cope with a new recipe.

Actually, Bob shouldered the toughest responsibilities of
anyone on the staff; he deserved his own Medal of Honor for
juggling and coping with my schedule. He took the flak from
organizations, constituents, state and federal politicians, to
say nothing of all my "old buddies" who seemed to crawl out
of the woodwork and were all given a certain priority on the
Foss list. Whether it be a general or a buck private from long
ago, there was never any rank in my book. Maxine always
said that if she'd known about my "buddy list" before she
went to work for me, she might have said, "Buzz off, who
needs it?"

Upon taking office in January 1955, I presented a legislative
program that called for creating an Industrial Development
and Expansion Agency (IDEA) that would cooperate with

Chambers of Commerce, community clubs, and civic and service organizations in attracting new industry and encouraging existing businesses to expand. I also recommended a long-range building program for the state's institutions of higher learning; enactment of a Korean veterans' bonus plan; endorsement of the Little Hoover and Legislative Research Council proposals for reorganization of the Highway Department, the Game, Fish and Parks Department, and the Health Department; and pay raises for state employees on a merit basis to retain the best talent and attract young people into government service. I also urged removal of laws that were discriminatory against the Native American Indians of our state.

I proposed halting the practice of spending beyond the state's income at the expense of the General Fund surplus and requested sufficient funding for a "reasonable surplus for unforeseen emergencies"—large enough to offset any loss of income from drought, business recession, or other severe changes in the state's economy. Fulfilling one of my campaign promises, I did not propose any new permanent taxes; I did, however, suggest revising the tax structure "so the burden of taxes does not fall unfairly on any one group of taxpayers."

The headline "No New Taxes" overshadowed the coverage of the inaugural, and it was a promise I would keep. Later I would confound the state bureaucracy when I terminated a tax previously passed as a temporary measure, even though the tax measure was written in such a way that I could have extended it through simple inaction. When word spread that I intended to cut revenues, emergency requests for additional monies inundated my office, demonstrating Foss's Law: "The need for government services always expands to exceed available revenues." I made my point more personally when I refused a four-hundred-dollar-a-year increase in the governor's salary because I had voted on the raise when I was a legislator.

Emphasizing my intention to seek bipartisan cooperation, I stirred controversy from day one. In my search for the best possible choices for my cabinet, I showed more concern about the quality of the appointees than their political affiliations.

I remember sitting at my desk in those early days discussing political appointments with a room full of advisors and friends.

"Now, for the water resources executive director," I said, my hands crossed behind my head, "I want Joe Grimes if I can get him to leave his job with the federal government."

"Do you know he's a Democrat?" a concerned GOP loyalist asked.

"He's the best water man there is," I answered.

The objections flew thick as snowflakes in January. I should be loyal to the Republican party, which meant not giving government jobs to Democrats.

"Don't get your afterburners hot," I said. "He knows surface water, ground water, and the laws of the entire Midwest. And the U.S. for that matter. Can you think of anybody better?" They couldn't.

The same sort of opposition arose when I named the members of the Fish and Game Department and chose a mix of personnel that evenly represented rural, urban, Republican, and Democratic populations.

On another occasion a man who had supported my campaign approached me privately and asked me to appoint his candidate as tax director.

"No way," I said. "He's not qualified. Besides, the guy's a crook!"

"Have you forgotten that I gave five hundred dollars to your campaign?"

I reached into my pocket and pulled out my personal checkbook. "You want your money back?" At which point the guy launched into a four-letter-word explanation of how the real world worked.

I listened for a few moments, then said calmly, "You're causing me to lose my sense of humor."

"You can't talk to me like that after what I did for you!" By now he was swearing at me in a rage.

I opened the side door and said, "Get out before I throw you out!" He didn't, so I helped him a little.

I tried never to lose sight of the fact that the government existed for the good of the people, and sometimes I needed to remind others in government of this important truth. To expedite this, I sat in on as many board and commission meetings as my schedule would permit so I could keep abreast of the workings of government. In this regard, I recall a highway commission meeting where several petitioners voiced the need for new bridges and wider roads, among other things. At the conclusion of their presentation the commission's engineer—a capable though sharp-tongued man—proceeded to sarcastically ridicule the requests.

"Cut that out!" I shouted, angered by this personal attack. Evidently the engineer didn't think I was serious, because he resumed his tirade.

I banged the gavel so hard the handle broke. "I said cut that out!" My voice boomed through the chambers and a deathly hush fell over the meeting. Every eye was on me now.

"You listen to this," I said sharply, gesturing with the handle stub, "and don't ever forget it again. We're here to serve the people of this state, not to humiliate them. If you can't understand that, get yourself another job."

Some years later in a profile of me included in the book *South Dakota's Governors,* Bob Lee wrote, "It wasn't uncommon during the sessions to find the Governor in the Senate or House chambers after a day's proceedings, sitting at one of the legislator's desks, his feet on the desk, chatting with his former colleagues—of both parties—about the issues of the day, or about their mutual hunting and fishing experiences. Foss was best when 'just visiting' with people, individually or in small groups, and his informal style, his accessibility and candor won him many supporters."

I'd come a long way from those first dancing-bear days when I dreaded speaking in public, but I'd never go down in history as a great orator. The only prepared speeches I read while in office were those required for publishing in the legislative journals—my inaugural addresses. Bob Lee always said that what I lacked in oratorical skill I more than compensated for with colorful language, folksiness, and straightforward sincerity.

If I was good at anything, it was public relations. I enjoyed a good working relationship with the press, mainly because I dealt directly with them as often as possible. They called me a "curbstone correspondent" because I talked to everybody

—Willy the riveter, Jake the farmer, the president of the bank, or the janitor. And I still do that. People make up the world, and if you just talk to those who can afford the good clothes or if you just talk to those at the other end of the spectrum, you're not doing a job for everybody.

Once a reporter asked me if my Medal of Honor had helped me in my postwar career. I told him that it had opened many doors to me, then added, "Once inside, it was up to me to prove myself."

Another thing I had going was that I was a natural-born salesman. I especially enjoyed the prospect of bringing business into the state. Since I had many contacts throughout the aircraft industry and in national and international circles, my role in that area was a great challenge and one I worked at tirelessly. I always kept the long-range view in sight. As a result, perhaps I didn't always follow protocol, but I got things done.

I flew around the country, presenting South Dakota as an option for development and emphasizing the quality of life in the state and the extremely low tax rates. Some critics, mostly politically inspired, accused me of traveling too much, a claim I did not take seriously as IDEA began to earn a return.

I was not so successful, however, against their charges that my participation in the Air Guard's Red Devils aerobatics team was too risky for a governor. In the end, I grudgingly gave up my precision flying.

The thing that saved me and my staff in the pressure cooker of all this was my crazy sense of humor—what Maxine called my "zaniness." I loved to mimic people and was pretty good at it; I could impersonate a walk, an attitude, or a voice. I also liked to give people nicknames. The first few times I asked Maxine to get me Pete the Pugilist or Dandy Dodo on the phone, she thought I was goofy. But before long she learned my vocabulary and, as she said, "The weird part was Joe's nicknames made sense."

Probably one of the biggest headaches to my staff was the well-known fact that I could not tell time. I was usually late for planes, running through the airport a mile a minute. Most of the time I did make it to my engagements, but not always. And when I didn't, my staff always covered for me. Maxine's favorite line in answer to where I could be reached was, "The Governor is en route."

She admits she stole that line from Bob Lee and carried it over to our time together in the professional football business. To this day there is a writer in New York who, when he sees Maxine, asks, "Is Commissioner Foss still en route?"

I firmly believed that one of the greatest attractions South Dakota offered businesses was a quality of life, enriched by its fine hunting and fishing. This conviction led to the formation of the South Dakota Sports Club, which was funded entirely by some of my hunting and fishing buddies. Among other things, the club established a special fund from which I could buy complimentary nonresident hunting and fishing licenses for well-heeled out-of-state executives who were promising prospects for establishing new business in our state. The courtesy of the unsolicited license, coupled with enjoyable hunting and fishing trips, gave these executives a favorable impression of the state and its people. I usually served as their personal hunting and fishing guide. Later when I left office, the Sports Club went out of existence, but it had created an immeasurable amount of goodwill toward South Dakota, without spending a single tax dollar.

Chapter 21
Personal and Private

During my second year as governor I was named President of the National Society of Crippled Children and Adults, and along with the trips I made for the state, I also made personal appearances at charitable functions and other special events. I even dressed up as a clown and marched in the annual Shriners parade to raise money for crippled children. Nationally I conducted a campaign coast to coast as spokesman for the Easter Seal campaign, and was among the first to call for changing institutions for the handicapped from places of confinement to rehabilitation.

As part of this promotional tour I traveled to Los Angeles, where I made personal appearances on *The Ernie Kovacs Show* and *The Lawrence Welk Show*. The latter was actually a television special produced on location at the Ambassador Hotel, where a hundred-dollar-a-plate fund-raiser was held for the benefit of the Society. At this gala occasion I was interviewed by Lawrence Welk. Many celebrities participated, and I was particularly pleased to see my old friends Bob Hope and Danny Thomas. I had gotten acquainted with both of them when they came to the Marine base at Santa Barbara. I had also seen Hope when he came to the South Pacific to entertain the troops.

Television was still rather unfamiliar to me, since at that time—1956—Pierre did not have its own television station and we were too distant from the cities to enjoy good reception.

On the following evening, after I had addressed another L.A. group regarding the Easter Seal Society, I was told that California's Governor Goodwin Knight wanted to see me. Excusing myself, I followed the messenger outside, where a helicopter awaited me. I climbed into the craft, and the pilot took us up and headed across the night sky. I noticed the beam of a large searchlight piercing the sky ahead, reflecting off the cloud cover.

Over the intercom the pilot pointed out the light and announced, "That's where the governor is."

When we set down near the base of the beam, I was greeted by Governor Knight and his entourage. We visited for a few moments, and then the governor led me toward a large building, which we entered through an unlit back door. Once inside there was barely enough light to illuminate a narrow, winding pathway through what appeared to be a storage area for movie sets and props.

Someone opened a door, and we stepped into blinding light. A smiling man walked briskly up to me, shook my hand, and said, "Hello, Governor Foss, I'm Ralph Edwards, and this is your life."

"Yeah, I know it is," I quipped, thinking I was being given some sort of new California greeting. At that time I had never seen the popular television program nor even heard the well-known phrase, "This Is Your Life."

I heard hearty applause and cheers from what was obviously some kind of audience beyond the blinding lights, and as my eyes and brain slowly adjusted, I realized I was on a television program that was honoring me. Ralph Edwards told the audience about my early days on the farm in South Dakota, and then the television personality surprised me by calling out on stage his first guest—my mother. That was only the beginning! Next came June and the kids, then my first flight instructor, Roy Lanning, several of my war buddies, including Roger Haberman, Boot Furlow, and even Tommy Mason Robertson, the man who was with Father Dan Stuyvenberg when they pulled me out of the sea back in the Solomons. After that night, I was one of the leading proponents for getting television to Pierre.

The program focused not only on my accomplishments during the war and in politics, but also on my personal life and family, presenting a balanced life with the right priorities given to career, charitable work, and family. That's the public image I had. But the truth was—although I didn't recognize this until years later—that while I was doing a good job as governor and went out of my way to help charities and old friends, I was far from being the ideal husband and father.

Because of my open-door policy, I spent the good part of each day listening to the stream of constituents who filed into my office all day long. Only after the office officially closed for the day did my staff and I get down to the business of running the state.

One of the South Dakotans who benefited from my accessibility was a young man named Tom Brokaw, who wanted to be a reporter. Years later, Tom would remark, "For me, Joe Foss was not only a Congressional Medal of Honor winner and governor of my home state, he was a pal. That was a pretty heady experience for a seventeen-year-old, to have a man of Joe's stature interested in my life and opinions. I learned from him the qualities that make him special: a love of people and the outdoors, plain talk, and a zest for life. My life is richer for having known Joe during my formative years."

Unfortunately, that which made me accessible to the people often made me inaccessible to my family.

I felt I had to be on duty all the time. I'd work in the office from early morning until I had to jump into my plane at night and fly off somewhere to give a speech. Then I'd turn around and fly back to Pierre. Usually I wouldn't get into bed until after midnight. Night after night I did this.

During legislative sessions I worked sixteen hours a day. I read every single bill and held endless briefing meetings. I was always sitting down with my budget director, Morris Hallock, going over the numbers, so I knew everything on the budget.

The real irony of it is that while I'd take time to talk with anybody who came into my office, I never discussed official business with June. Anything she knew about my governorship she picked up out of the newspapers, and my misplaced priorities put a tremendous strain on our relationship.

If you're family oriented, politics is the wrong place to be. You're gone, gone, gone. There's just no way you can be around to run the show at home.

Also, June's politics were more quiet. She thought I was too loud. I've always been a fighter, and it makes some people think I've got a chip on my shoulder. Of course, I wasn't as mellow then as I am today—not by a long shot. If somebody did something I didn't like, I'd shout, "Fire that sucker!" June and some others objected to that approach.

Our conversation became difficult and superficial. We didn't agree on my role as a husband and father, and we didn't agree on the philosophy of government. That didn't leave us much to talk about that wouldn't lead to an argument.

By mid-1957 my campaign for reelection was in full swing. IDEA was getting off to an encouraging start; the legislature was working in harmony with my office on most matters; and the reorganization of several top departments was well underway. I had also dealt a death blow to any serious plans by organized gambling in the state.

Early in my term two men had walked into my office whom I recognized immediately as proprietors of the largest and most successful gambling house in the state. I recognized them because I was an experienced and capable gambler, although I had quit several years earlier as soon as I entered the fishbowl of public service. My familiarity with unlawful casinos extended back to my college days, when I had worked briefly as a bouncer in the back of a private club.

I knew why they had come as soon as they walked through my door. They thought they could make an arrangement to slip a share of their profits to an old gambler like me and get the law off their backs. I looked them straight in the eye and said, "I'm telling you right now to make tracks between you and me. And you'd better close down or I'll have my boys on you like a blanket."

Either they didn't believe me or thought I was just saying it for effect, because the betting house didn't close down. On the contrary, the owners flouted the law more blatantly than ever, believing they would have it easy under my administration.

I called for a raid, but when the police arrived at the club they found no evidence of illegal activity. Apparently at least one person on the force was on the take. Another surprise raid ended the same way, so I called my attorney general, Phil Saunders, who was also an old friend and college classmate.

"Phil, don't tell a soul," I said. "Just pick your agents at the last minute so no one will have a chance to make any phone calls. Then make the raid."

Late one evening, Phil gathered his party. He called each man individually and asked him to join him at the office for "a personal matter." When the entire group was assembled, Phil loaded them into cars and told them where they were going.

That's what it took. Phil and his boys raided the place and closed them up for good.

Enforcement of the tax codes proved a much thornier problem than the gambling laws and became a critical issue in the election.

When the Board of Equalization's report detailing the wildly irregular collection of real and personal property taxes arrived on my desk in 1956, I knew my life would be much easier if I simply swept it under the rug. The report described the inequities resulting from a system in which each county seemed to have its own procedure for assessed evaluation of personal property for taxes. A tractor in one part of the state could cost the owner many times more in taxes than an identical tractor in another part of the state. The revenues in question accrued entirely to local governments, so the state budget presided over by my office was unaffected by the collection methods. The issue for me was entirely one of fairness and the law.

It would have been a simple matter to release a statement wrapped in impenetrable boilerplate, passing the buck to some future administration, but that was not my way. I hadn't balked at hiding a flight of Wildcats in the jungle when I knew it was the right thing to do, and I wasn't about to run away from this situation. So I took the bull by the horns.

"Follow the law," was my straightforward decree. "If the legislature doesn't like its own laws, it can change them next session."

Unfortunately, many county governments, when given the order to equalize tax assessments, used the opportunity to juggle their budgets instead of lowering their levies. As local property taxes rose, some dramatically, the blame fell squarely on me.

The tax equalization controversy, combined with growing discontent with Republican President Eisenhower's farm policies, threatened all of South Dakota's Republican candidates in the upcoming elections, and some analysts predicted my defeat.

I had tried, unsuccessfully, to influence Eisenhower's farm policies. This issue was not an easy one for me because I believed the government had no right interfering with business in any way. The moral dilemma was created by prior interference in many other areas of the economy that injured the farmers of our state. Many of them were struggling to survive, and some were losing the battle. They found it difficult to understand, for example, why they should pay federally mandated minimum wage levels to benefit other workers' standards of living when their own was slipping into bankruptcy.

My position was that government should keep its hands out altogether, but if the politicians in Washington raised our farmers' costs, they should at least make sure that we didn't go broke because of it. Therefore, I backed a proposed solution that would guarantee some level of parity, meaning a minimum price level for agricultural products to make up for the costs imposed on farmers by government.

Eisenhower believed that the burdens placed on agriculture were wrong, but he also believed that more interference to offset those burdens would only compound the problem. I was sympathetic to his view, but I had been elected to protect my own constituency's well-being.

To try and accomplish that, I joined with a group of governors from agricultural states and headed toward Washington, D.C., via New York, where I was scheduled to appear on *The Today Show* with Dave Garroway.

I arrived at Rockefeller Center early in the morning, and while we were getting ready, Dave Garroway asked me, "Is there any subject that you don't want to talk about?" I should have known better, but I was a naive country boy who took the guy at his word. "Yes," I said, "I'd appreciate it if you wouldn't bring up the subject of agriculture."

"Why's that?" Garroway asked, and I explained that I was going to meet with the president later that day, and a public discussion of the issues before the meeting would give the appearance that I was trying to pressure rather than cooperate with the president.

Garroway assured me that I had nothing to worry about, and we went on the air. After the introductions had been made, Garroway turned to me and asked, "Governor Foss, just how do you stand on the farm problem? Do you favor parity?"

I couldn't back out, and Garroway wouldn't change the subject. Throughout the entire interview, he cross-examined me on agricultural policies.

Later that afternoon our governors' group arrived at the White House, where we met first with Sherm Adams, the president's administrative assistant.

"Boy, the president is waiting for you," he told me. "He heard the broadcast you did this morning, and he's really upset."

I was just a member of the governors' agricultural committee, not the chairman, but when we walked in to talk to Eisenhower, he didn't see anybody else. Old Ike's eyes just beaded in on me and the first thing he said was, "How's my television star?"

He was so mad he was ready to explode, and when Ike got hot under the collar, he really got hot. Anything we brought up, he took the other side. It was like talking to a block of dry ice, and we didn't get anywhere on the parity issue.

Later I would win back Eisenhower's favor in the most unlikeliest of circumstances. During the inauguration parade for his second term I rode in an open convertible, as part of the procession that rolled past the president's reviewing stand.

Before the spectacle began, somebody had pushed a camera into my hands, asking me to take a picture of the president, so when we came up even with the reviewing stand, I told the driver to stop the car while I snapped some pictures. While I was snapping shots of the president, photographers were snapping shots of me. A photographer from *Life* magazine asked for my roll of film. I gave it to him, and the magazine later published some of my shots, along with their photographer's pictures of me photographing Ike and Nixon.

Ike got a charge out of the whole thing and started laughing, and we got along well after that. In an interesting juxtaposition, an April 1956 article on me in *Saga* magazine stated:

> A lot of people in South Dakota like to compare Joe with President Eisenhower. "He may not be the smartest speaker in the world," says Paul Kretschmar, a powerful lawyer in the state, "but he speaks from the heart and that's why the people love him. In that respect he is a lot like President Eisenhower. And he is a lot like Mr. Eisenhower in regard to executive ability too.[1]

Back in South Dakota things heated up on the homefront when June threatened to leave me if I ran for reelection. I told my closest friends and advisors, who pleaded with her to reconsider. In those days divorce was an automatic obstacle to any elective office. Ultimately I persuaded her to stay with me if I were reelected, but without any real reconciliation between us.

When election day arrived, political passions ran high. Although I was reelected by over 25,000 votes, my margin of victory over my Democratic opponent was 5,000 votes lower than my margin of victory in my first term. Elsewhere in the state, Democrats gained ten more seats in the Republican-controlled house and Republicans controlled the senate by only a one-seat advantage. Five-time incumbent Republican Harold Lovre lost his congressional seat to a relative newcomer, Democrat George McGovern.

---

[1] "Joe Foss, An American Saga," *Saga,* April 1956, pp. 9–11. Brumby, Robert Mongin.

As expected, the legislature immediately tackled the controversial and emotional issue of tax reform, stripping the Board of Equalization of most of its authority. In time the controversy abated and passions cooled, and later legislative sessions gradually reversed this gross overreaction. Eventually the dispute would become so troublesome that South Dakota would do away with personal property taxes entirely.

To me, getting reelected meant the opportunity to carry on the important programs I'd begun during my first term. In my inaugural speech to the 35th legislative session in 1957, I pointed out that "there has been progress and there has been opposition. I sincerely believe the state is stronger because of it." I concluded with the observation that "South Dakota is a sparsely settled state and it has too few people to share the tax burden" (at that time the population was about 667,000). No property should be exempt from taxation, I urged, adding that all revenue from property taxes should be reserved exclusively for the local governmental subdivisions.

With the equalization fight behind me, my second term was less contentious than the first, despite the increase in Democratic party strength. As a result of my unbiased and nonpartisan appointments, my working relationship with the Democrats in the state house and senate was unprecedented.

Power struggles between the two parties can hurt the people. When politicians forget they're working for the people and start thinking they work for their parties, things can go haywire.

Before I left office I would be presented with a mock award—the front half of a toy elephant attached to the back half of a toy donkey—representing my refusal to use my position to profit the party loyal. I was accused of being either a Republicrat or a Demopublican.

This is not to say that I was not an ideological conservative. I was. But the day-to-day business of government has less to do with ideology than with management skills and integrity, fairness, honesty, and leadership of all the people.

Furthermore, I had no desire to serve in any office beyond the two-term limit South Dakota placed on its governors. I made it known that I would not run for another office, and with no reason to think about the upcoming election, I enjoyed the job immensely.

Get rid of politicians after they've served a couple of terms, that's what I've always said. Nobody should stay in there for a lifetime. It's the worst mistake the founding fathers made; they should have limited senators to two terms, and set two four-year terms for Congress. Then you go on home and live under the laws you've legislated. See how you like it.

During my second term a Hollywood film producer, Hall Barlett, approached me about making a major motion picture based on my life, focusing on my Guadalcanal experiences. He had interested John Wayne in playing the title role, which was great casting. We resembled each other in physical appearance as well as in our politics, our "true grit" styles, and our western drawls. I liked the idea, and the $750,000 they offered me for the film rights would mean a comfortable nest egg for the first time in my life.

They flew me to Hollywood, where I met with Hall Barlett, John Wayne, and a writer at the Beverly Hills Hotel to discuss the project. The Duke and I hit it off right away, and he seemed eager to do the movie. The large-budget film would pay him a million dollars—big money at that time. He wanted the role and the money.

Everything was going along slicker than butter on a hot pan—until I read the script. Though the sequence of events followed my life in a vague way, most of it had very little to do with my experiences. Many of the men in my flight were to be portrayed as insecure and anxious, filled with resentment or fear, while my character was uncertain of the validity of his own actions. Nothing could have been further from the truth. Moreover, the story centered around an entirely fictitious romance. When I read that, I said, "No deal."

I figured there was more than enough drama in the real story of my experiences to make an exciting, inspiring movie, but the writer insisted that all the baloney they put into the script was necessary to sell the film to the public. Well, I've never been one to stake my life on baloney. I didn't believe it then, and I don't believe it now.

Wayne and I remained friends, however. We did some dove

hunting together at his ranch in Arizona and saw each other on a number of social occasions. Also, I would continue to be mistaken for him through the years. In fact, while I was in Beverly Hills for that meeting, three teenagers came up and asked me for my autograph, thinking I was John Wayne.

As my tenure as governor drew to a close, I began to look around for new challenges and announced my intention to return to the private sector. Well, you'd think I'd run off like a spooked cat at a dog kennel. The Republican leaders argued that I was obligated to the party because of the strong support they'd given me, and they exerted intense pressure for me to run against the freshman Democratic Congressman, George McGovern. I'd never turned my back on a friend or an obligation, so I agreed to seek election to Congress from the First District.

Once again I hit the campaign trail, this time building my platform on my experience in agriculture and business.

"To ignore the problems of agriculture is to court economic ruin," I warned the voters. "To learn about labor and business, work with your own hands and invest your own money," both of which I'd done.

In a congressional race the entire state does not vote, of course, only the appropriate district, and I missed the vote from the rural areas of the state where my popularity was the greatest. McGovern won reelection by polling 107,202 votes to my 93,388. Privately, I was relieved.

In January 1959, I addressed the legislature for the last time, during which I noted that the state now enjoyed one of the lowest per capita tax burdens in the nation and that the surplus in the General Fund was larger than when I'd taken office four years earlier, reflecting improved economic conditions. I had led the government without deficit spending for four years by strictly following the state's long-standing pay-as-you-go policy.

One thing I didn't include in my farewell address was my spittoon legacy.

June was always trying to get me to improve myself, and one thing she harped on was my cigar smoking. My cigar habit probably aggravated a lot of people. I'd chew those stogies down to soggy butts, and when you do that your mouth has a way of producing too much saliva. But while I was in office, Harry Tunge and I came up with a solution for that.

Harry liked to rummage around in the bowels of the Capitol Building, and one day he unearthed some old brass spittoons that hadn't been used in decades. We polished them up and put them everywhere—in my office, in the senate, on the floor of the house. It must have offended a lot of cultured people, although I never heard a single complaint directly.

When I left office, the new administration dispensed with all the spittoons!

Chapter 22
A Real Job

As my family and I were leaving the statehouse one day during my second term as governor, eight-year-old Frank looked up at me and said, "Dad, when are you going to get a real job?"

"I have a real job," I told him.

"Well, I don't like this political stuff," he said. "Some people don't like you."

At the end of my second term, over thirty "real" job offers came my way, including two Defense Department positions. President Eisenhower offered me the posts of Assistant Secretary of the Air Force and Assistant of the Department of Defense for Legislative Liaison, but since no number one spot was available I declined; I did not want to be an assistant. One initially tempting offer came from fellow fighter pilot Eddie Rickenbacker, who wanted me to work for his company, Eastern Airlines.

Through the years, Eddie and I had become good friends. In the late 1940s we had worked closely together when Eddie was chairman and I was vice chairman of the American Legion's group, Air Power Is Peace Power. I admired Eddie; he was an outstanding leader as well as a convincing speaker. His offer was not one I took lightly.

Eddie asked me to meet him in Chicago to discuss the job.

A Real Job

Our conference began over dinner, and at two in the morning we were still yelling at each other in his suite.

Early on I said, "Eddie, what chance do I have of ever becoming president of Eastern Airlines?"

"That's all programmed," he said, and told me who was going to be the next president.

"That ends it for me," I said. "I'm not interested in any way, shape, or form if I don't have a shot at the driver's seat." I thanked him for the offer and said, "Let's just be friends."

That didn't make him happy, so I explained further. "What you've got is a one-man company, Eddie. You run the whole thing. You know everybody and their dog by their first names, from baggage handlers on up. You even know their wives and their kids' birthdays. That's wonderful. But when you step out of there, the whole thing's going to crash. You've got a lot of guys that you figured you had to keep a string on, and the guy you've chosen to take your place will lose you nothing but money because he can't think for himself."

That really blew his cork, but I was right. That was exactly what happened when Eddie retired. The company wouldn't work without him because he had set it up that way.

I also turned down the position of Vice President of Public Relations for Western Airlines. I sat down with the president of the company, Terry Drinkwater—I always called him Terrible Terry—and we were talking about the job and the great salary he was going to pay me when it suddenly dawned on me. "You know, Terry, I could never work for you. I've seen the way you tangle with your people. The first time you did that with me there'd be a head-on collision. Let's just stay good friends."

Eventually I decided to go with Raven Industries, a company that manufactured high-altitude research balloons and had located in South Dakota in response to my IDEA program. They offered me the kind of responsibility I was looking for, along with a good salary and stock options.

I'd put in about seven months as vice president of this successful young firm, when in the fall of 1959 business took me to the Los Angeles area. Raven's major investor, H. P. Skogland, president and controlling stockholder of North American Life and Casualty, was headed in the same direction to attend an owners' meeting of the novice American Football League, so I hitched a ride in his company plane.

Before we parted to go to our separate rooms at the Beverly Hilton, Skogland turned to me and said, "They're having a cocktail party for this football thing. Why don't you drop in if you haven't got anything better to do."

I went to the gathering and then on to dinner with a group of the club owners. During the course of the evening, the subject of their need for a league commissioner came up, and someone asked me if I'd be interested in the job. They were looking for a well-known face to promote the new league, they said.

I told them I honestly wasn't informed enough to know whether I was interested or not, but that I was intrigued enough to submit to an interview. I loved football, both playing it and watching it, so the thought of being a commissioner of one of my favorite sports certainly had its appeal.

The following evening the owners met with me at the hotel, this time to grill me. The first thing they seemed to want to determine was whether I knew a football from a bale of hay.

"How much football have you played, Mr. Foss?"

"I played at Sioux Falls College and the University of South Dakota."

"What position did you play?"

"Tackle and guard, but I never made first string. Most of the time I just ran in carrying plays. The coach used to lean on my shoulder and yell, 'Tell that idiot to keep his hands down,' or something like that. So I'd usually go in for one play and come right back out."

"Have you ever coached?"

"Well, I took coaching from Rube Hoy, the athletic director at the University of South Dakota. I never intended to coach, but I took coaching from him just to hear his basic philosophy of life, which has always influenced the way I deal with people. He was an outstanding leader of young men. He always pointed you in the right direction and believed in you and gave you the feeling, 'Yes, I can do it whatever it is.' And I did coach fighter pilots. The scoreboard didn't light up at the end of the field out there—the score was kept in life or death. But if all you're looking for is a good football coach, wait for the season to get started. Everybody can't win, and there will be plenty of good unemployed coaches available."

That comment raised a few hackles, and there was a dead silence, eventually broken by another question. "How many pro football games have you seen?"

"Actually I've only seen two in the flesh."

"How about on television?"

"Oh, maybe thirty-some. The TV transmission is so poor in Pierre that it's usually like watching a static storm."

Finally one of the owners asked bluntly, "Why do you think you would be qualified?"

Hell, this sounded just like the old political grilling—"Do you really think you're qualified to be governor?"

I paused for a moment, staring at the faces before me, then plunged in. "Seems to me what you need is somebody who has the ability to open doors and pump life into a dead horse."

A few of them sat back, startled at my candor, but that didn't stop me. "From what I've heard, the National Football League has a forty-year head start, and right now you're being confused with the new continental baseball league that's trying to get started. If you're going to be successful, you've got to have somebody who's willing to travel the length and breadth of this land to talk to people in person and get attention for the league."

Well, that ended the meeting. I figured I'd made about as much of an impression as a speck of dust on the eyeball of time. Besides, knowing that among the candidates for the job were such gridiron luminaries as Notre Dame's Francis Leahy and Admiral Jones Ingram, the last commissioner of the foundered All-American Conference, I knew I had about as much chance as last year's snowman. However, I had learned a great deal more about the real situation with the would-be league.

The American Football League had germinated in 1956 when Lamar Hunt, the son of preeminent oilman H. L. Hunt, began to shop for a professional football team to add to the family's balance sheet. Lamar's brother Bunker shared his predilection for the gridiron and fully backed his efforts to purchase the Chicago Cardinals, a team suffering from a pitiful record and rumored to be on the auction block. The owners of the Cardinals, however, only wanted to bring additional capital into the club; the most they would part with was a minority interest.

Hunt was not simply looking for an investment opportunity. In fact, anyone looking for a routine return on investment would never consider a professional football team. The young Texan wanted to play the game, which meant managing the organization toward athletic as well as financial excellence.

Football had not yet taken over as America's favorite spectator sport, but it was growing steadily in popularity. The obvious markets—the major American cities—already had local teams, and television with its lucrative advertising revenues was expanding in importance as well.

The biggest obstacle to Hunt's participation in professional ball was the owners of the National Football League teams, who for the past decade had refused to admit additional franchises into the game. Believing that additional teams would simply split the existing football pie into smaller pieces, the NFL owners saw no reason to share their revenues. Furthermore, the players earned less than the coaches in those days, and more teams meant unwelcome competition for star players.

In their defense, even established NFL teams had failed financially, without additional rivalry, so it was understandable that the veteran owners were not very confident that the market would bear more clubs. No new league had succeeded since the turn of the century, when the American Baseball League came into existence.

When Hunt had approached NFL officials with his desire to launch a team in his hometown of Dallas, his overtures were rejected. Lamar Hunt was not, however, the sort of man to abandon a dream just because no one was selling what he wanted to buy. Thus was born his audacious scheme to completely circumvent the NFL by establishing a separate football league.

During his search for an available team Hunt had learned of another prospective club owner, K. S. (Bud) Adams, Jr., who had also bid without success for the Cardinals. The two men had never met, but in January 1959 Hunt flew to Houston to meet Adams. The two Lone Star citizens provided a fascinating contrast.

The unassuming and hard-working Hunt, at twenty-six, was a conservative dresser and a careful man with his money. Some would even say the lean tycoon went beyond frugal. Thirty-six-year-old Adams, whose father was chairman of the board of Phillips Petroleum, was part of another, more rakish tradition of Texas oilmen. He sported a cocked white Stetson, enjoyed spending the fortune he made from the oil business, and his large frame reflected an affection for Tex-Mex cuisine.

For more than three hours the two businessmen sized one another up. Finally, as Adams drove him to the Houston airport, Hunt said, "If I could get people in four other cities to sponsor teams in another professional football league, would you join us?"

Adams agreed, and Hunt began the search for others whose efforts to procure an NFL franchise had failed. He pitched his idea to Bob Howsam, the brilliant Denver Bears baseball executive, and H. P. Skogland, the president and major owner of North American Life and Casualty in Minneapolis. Both responded eagerly.

Max Winter, also from Minneapolis and a noted sportsman, reacted similarly, as did the well-known and flamboyant sports announcer and Redskins stockholder from New York, Harry Wismer. Hunt also talked to Barron Hilton of the hotel Hiltons, who expressed interest but harbored doubts about the viability of the endeavor.

Armed with six potential team sponsors, Hunt sent an invitation to the popular and respected commissioner of the National Football League, Bert Bell, asking him to serve as commissioner to both the NFL and the new league, to be called the American Football League.

The commissioner of a professional sports league is in a somewhat tenuous position. Though endowed with authority, he is, in the final analysis, an employee of the team owners. The balance of powers can be effective, but extremely fragile. In Bell's case, a decision to act as commissioner for Hunt's proposed organization would signal an endorsement of competition unwelcomed by most of the NFL owners who paid Bell's salary.

When Commissioner Bell responded two weeks later, his reply arrived in the form of an invitation for Lamar Hunt to attend meetings of a congressional committee that was investigating charges that the twelve-team NFL league had engaged in exclusionary antitrust violations. Bert Bell was to testify.

His testimony was a tremendous encouragement to Hunt.

"The more football there is and the more advertisement of pro football, the better off we are. We are in favor of this new league," Bell told the committee. And when asked about his league's monopoly, the commissioner promised the congressional committee that he was "all for the league and would help nurture it."

After the hearing Hunt joined Bell at his farm near Atlantic City for in-depth discussions about the new league. Bell made his own plans clear, assuring Hunt that the NFL would not expand until its existing teams were more equally balanced, which would be several years down the road. Several of the NFL teams didn't have as much talent as the others. Talent was procured by dollars, and some teams had more operating capital. Also, because of these unequal resources, the teams did not have an equal distribution of radio and television receipts.

Hunt returned to Dallas, confident that nothing stood in the way of a second football league. Nine days later, he and Bud Adams called a press conference in Houston and announced that both Houston and Dallas would host new AFL teams. They told the several dozen sportswriters present that they would soon name the other franchise cities. Given such decisive progress, Barron Hilton threw his hat in the ring.

With six of the planned eight teams in place, an organizational meeting was held on August 14, 1959, at the Conrad Hilton Hotel in Chicago, where the six franchises were announced: Lamar Hunt, as principal owner, would head the Dallas team; Bud Adams would do the same for the Houston club; Bob Howsam's team would play in Denver; Barron Hilton's organization would operate out of Los Angeles; Harry Wismer would have New York; and H. P. Skogland and William Boyer (another Minneapolis businessman, an automobile dealer) as the two principal owners, along with Max Winter, would guide the Minneapolis team.

Eight days later the AFL owners met again, this time in Dallas. The new league's rulebook and the articles of association were approved, and it was agreed that each owner would put up a $100,000 performance bond and contribute $25,000 earnest money to the league.

During the flurry of August activity, others who had previously believed that ownership of a pro club was out of the question because of NFL policies began to reconsider. One of these was Ralph C. Wilson, Jr., the Detroit trucking and insurance magnate, who owned a small part of the Detroit Lions franchise. He wrote a letter to Hunt outlining his belief that the growing city of Miami could support a professional football team.

Wilson was not the only one to notice this rapid headway. Despite Commissioner Bell's pledge of support for the AFL, owners in the NFL decided to circumvent their own commissioner and head the upstarts off at the pass. Suddenly the long-standing resistance to NFL expansion disappeared, as both Hunt and Adams were approached discreetly by representatives of the NFL who offered to grant them NFL franchises for Dallas and Houston, while Hilton was offered the opportunity to buy a major share of the stock in the Los Angeles Rams. All of this was on the condition that they abandon their efforts to challenge NFL dominion.

Lamar Hunt spoke for himself, Hilton, and Adams when he told the NFL agents that the AFL owners had pledged their support for the entire group—all for one and one for all. They were willing to drop the AFL only if all six teams were accepted into the organization. However, most of the NFL owners were adamant that their league not locate additional teams in New York, Los Angeles, or Denver, so that was the end of the matter.

Shortly afterward, George Halas, the great coach and owner of the Chicago Bears, who served as chairman of the NFL expansion committee, and Art Rooney, owner of the Pittsburgh Steelers, announced provisional plans for two new NFL franchises. It could hardly be coincidence that the clubs were to be located in Dallas and Houston, where they would compete with Hunt and Adams for limited ticket revenues.

Apparently there was going to be a battle royal, and the determined entrepreneurs of the AFL geared up to challenge the giant. Ralph Wilson officially came on board, although local resistance led him to discard his plans for a Miami team. Instead he located his organization in Buffalo.

With seven teams in place, the owners scheduled a November 22, 1959, player draft in Minneapolis, to be supervised by Francis William Leahy, the great Notre Dame coach who had been hired to work with Barron Hilton's Los Angeles Chargers. And soon an eighth team, owned by William Sullivan, would be established in Boston. Sullivan had been public relations director for Notre Dame. Now, as president of a large company in Boston, Metropolitan Coal and Oil, he headed up the group of investors forming the Boston Patriots.

These new owners had no illusions that the contest against the entrenched National Football League would be an easy one, but they figured they had an ace in the hole: NFL Commissioner Bert Bell. With his help, at least they were playing on a level field. Then on October 11, 1959, while on business in Philadelphia where the NFL's office was located, Commissioner Bell died.

That was the situation the day I left my interview with the AFL owners, convinced they were not interested in me. The next day my suspicions were confirmed when a brief story appeared in the sports section of *The Los Angeles Times*.

"According to Thomas Eddy, administrative assistant to Barron Hilton, owner of the Los Angeles Chargers," the article reported, "the American Football League is certain of one thing and that is that Joe Foss will not be commissioner."

So I told Skogland I wasn't interested in the job and went on about my business for Raven Industries in L.A.

The next day the same story went out over the wire service, and when I got back to my office in Sioux Falls, Cy Hoigard, the president of Raven Industries, said, "I see by the papers that you've been out looking for a new job. Don't you like it here?"

"Yeah," I said, "but I've never turned down an interview.

I even tell my people—'anytime you can better yourself, tell me, and I'll help you.' "

"Well, you didn't get it anyway," he said, "but I just wanted to know."

We were both wrong. Apparently when I told Skogland that I was no longer interested in the position, the owners started to reconsider my worth. I don't know whether my cavalier dismissal bugged them or what. Whatever it was, within a few weeks Lamar Hunt called and asked if I would reconsider the job.

"I might," I said, "if certain conditions are met." Hunt asked if I could be available for a four o'clock conference call to discuss them with the selection team.

"I'll make a point of being near the phone," I said.

When the call came, Bob Howsam, Lamar Hunt, and Bud Adams were on the line, and they officially offered me the job. They also told me I could decide where the AFL office would be located, although it was evident at that time that the owners preferred Dallas. The location was a big concern to me, because, as I told the press later, "You couldn't pay me enough to live in New York."

We agreed on a salary of about $30,000 a year. This was no better than my stock options and salary at Raven Industries, but the job did provide the kind of challenge and environment that appealed to me. I also asked for and received assurances that the entire group was in the game for the long run and was committed to the goal of an operating, profitable league.

With these matters hammered out, I agreed to a three-year contract. They offered me a longer contract, but I believed that was long enough to do the job. If I couldn't take the league to success within that time, I would not hold the organization to any obligations beyond that period.

"When does the job start?" I asked.

"Right now."

"I can't do that," I said. "I have to give some notice to Raven. This is October. What about the first of January?"

That generated a howl of protest. "There's too much to do and not enough time." So I promised to get to Dallas as soon as I could.

My contract arrived in the mail a few days later, and on November 30, 1959, my appointment as commissioner of the AFL was officially announced.

The press release announcing my appointment stated that my selection had been unanimous. That was not the case. It was a public relations ploy I knew nothing about until months later when Harry Wismer, owner of the New York club, complained to the press that he had never backed me. Wismer called me "a hick" and told a reporter I was "not a football kind of guy." This was an early indication that although I was to have more than enough opposition outside the league, I was also to have a dedicated antagonist on the inside.

Chapter 23

On the Gridiron

Raven Industries let me give two weeks' notice, and I set up shop in Dallas. While this signaled a major and welcome change in direction for me personally, it also signaled the beginning of the end of my marriage.

June thought football was a total waste of time. I wasn't contributing to the success of society and I was wasting my talent, she said—if I had any. I thought the sport was a great profession, and I enjoyed it. But then I've enjoyed just about every job I ever had. I had been telling June for years that if she didn't stop humiliating me, trying to destroy every career I tackled, I would leave.

As things got more unpleasant at home, I reacted by flitting away from the whole thing like a crayfish. The two of us drifted further and further apart until we came apart. You always want to stay together for the family, but it was actually worse trying to do that. Finally in November 1959 we began going separate ways.

As soon as I became commissioner, I was on the job morning, noon, and night. Harry Tunge took another year's leave from the South Dakota Air National Guard and came down to set up our small office on the eleventh floor of the Southland Center in Dallas. After some pleading, I also convinced Maxine Isenberg to join us. Later T. V. King, assistant to Sargeant Shriver, called me and suggested I interview Milt Woodard, executive vice president of the Western Golf Association in Chicago, Illinois, to act as assistant commissioner. I did so, and Milt proved an able and loyal associate.

From the start, the appointment of an ex-governor and war hero as commissioner generated great publicity for the new league. Sportswriters loved to play up my cowboy/fighter pilot image as a perfect complement to the owners, who were seen by many as wealthy young swashbucklers. Coverage of my appointment dominated sports pages for weeks as I swung into gear. What nobody seemed to notice was that I had long thought in terms of football. My fliers had called me their "quarterback," and I had often compared combat strategy to the game.

Of course, there were also those who questioned my qualifications, and during my first month as skipper of the new league the press relished a series of subtly hostile exchanges with George Halas, the NFL's leading critic of the AFL. But even that kept us in the public eye, and we needed public interest in the league. I had something going every day for the sportswriters to jangle about, and I loved every minute of it.

One of the most urgent of a number of pressing matters I faced immediately was the selection of an eighth team, since Minneapolis had abandoned the AFL for the NFL shortly before I took charge.

The owners, then without a commissioner, had been gathering in Minneapolis in November for the draft meeting when Harry Wismer stalked into the conference room, flanked by his two legal associates, and threw a stack of newspapers on the table. As they scattered, various headlines told the same story: "Minneapolis to Get NFL Franchise."

"Okay, you guys," Wismer proclaimed. "This is it. This is the last supper!"

All eyes turned to H. P. Skogland and his three partners, Max Winter, William Boyer, and Ole Haugsrude.

"It's not true!" Skog protested.

But the story didn't die. That same day a local radio station reported that Austin Gunsel, acting commissioner of the NFL, had leaked the story that the Minneapolis group had defected from the AFL to apply for an NFL franchise.

Days later the Minneapolis group requested the return of their $25,000 earnest payment, confirming the earlier rumors. They had, indeed, begun negotiations with Halas to join the NFL, although his assurances were in violation of the NFL's own bylaws requiring unanimous approval by team owners for league expansion. I don't know why Skogland had denied this earlier, unless he wanted to be sure of the NFL before he slammed the door on the AFL.

At least one NFL member was firmly against the move. George Preston Marshall, owner of the Washington Redskins, told Frank Blauschild of the *New York Mirror*, "The only reason for expansion I've heard from other owners is that we could destroy the new league. If that's the only reason, then we are guilty of monopolistic practices. No one can give me an intelligent reason for adding a couple more franchises."

Meanwhile, the remaining AFL owners were outraged at the Minneapolis group's request for a refund and most argued that the deserters should forfeit their money. When I came on board, I chose to give it back. I wrote the group a check and told them if they didn't want to be with us they should go on their way. Later the club owners would make sure that defectors would suffer, instituting a $1,400,000 fine in the bylaws for any team that switched to the NFL. But at the time this happened there was nothing like that in writing.

Wismer was furious that I would give the money back to Skogland, the man who had first recommended me to the group as a potential commissioner. Later I would realize that this incident just fueled his animosity toward me.

Another bone of contention was the matter of competition for star athletes among the AFL, the NFL, and the Canadian Football League. Salaries were already going up, and rumors circulated of NFL threats that any players who contemplated signing with the AFL would be blackballed when the new league failed. As a result, that first year top grid stars often had to decide between higher salaries in the AFL and the security of the established NFL.

Occasionally, however, a player signed with both leagues. The most publicized conflict raged over All-American halfback Billy Cannon from Louisiana State University. Both the NFL's Los Angeles Rams and the AFL's Houston Oilers drafted the Heisman Trophy winner. For some reason he signed contracts with both clubs under hotly debated circumstances. Likewise, both the NFL's New York Giants and the AFL's Los Angeles Chargers signed the gifted Charlie Flowers, Mississippi All-American fullback. At least four cases of double signing headed to court, and several lawyers attended the first meeting after my official installation as commissioner.

At thàt first meeting, I hung a chart on the wall detailing the league as I envisioned it. But before we got to the future we had to deal with the present, which meant the many problems facing the new organization. One of the biggest headaches was the disagreement about the optimum size of the league. I believed in expansion, but from the very outset most of the owners wanted to stick to an eight-team loop.

Actually, the question of rapid growth was somewhat premature. Several of our teams were even unsure of finding stadiums in time for the start of the season. To help deal with objections raised by reporters who doubted our ability to secure suitable facilities, I had gone to a local sporting goods store before the meeting and bought a football. When I approached our meeting room, I held up the pigskin. "At least we have a ball," I said, grinning at the reporters waiting outside.

The proceedings extended into a second day when a group of investors from San Francisco made a last-minute plea for the eighth-team position. Because San Francisco already had an NFL team, the two cities considered most seriously for the eighth franchise were Atlanta and Oakland, with St. Louis and Miami a distant third and fourth. I would have brought in both Atlanta and Oakland myself, but the owners didn't want to get too big too fast.

Oakland eventually won out over Atlanta because it was thought that, with Barron Hilton's Chargers already in L.A., a team in northern California would create a natural rivalry. Despite Hilton's best efforts, however, including well-publicized open tryouts for the team, the community never supported the Los Angeles Chargers, and about a year later the team became the San Diego Chargers.

We had people waiting in line for franchises, but we had to be careful because a league is like a family. You didn't want to bring in some brother-in-law who would cause problems later; some wise bird who would refuse to work with the rest of the group and cause nothing but trouble. When anybody made application I really took a close look at them, and the owners did the same.

Our first meeting adjourned on a high note when we learned that Johnny Unitas, the legendary and nationally loved quarterback who played with the NFL's Baltimore Colts, had given his endorsement to the AFL that very day. Unitas was in Philadelphia, home of the NFL, to receive that city's sportswriters' award as America's outstanding athlete. In the course of his statements he surprised the press when he said, "The more teams the better. I don't think the league will be hurt as much as everybody says. With more pro teams and a greater demand for players, it means that some of the veterans will be able to play maybe two more years than they normally would." In fact, he went so far as to say, "I'll tell you something. If the AFL was looking for players when I was getting out of Louisville University, I'd probably be playing in the AFL today."

Our good humor did not last long. The day after our meetings ended, the newly elected commissioner of the National Football League, Pete Rozelle, announced that Dallas and Minneapolis were to be granted NFL franchises.

Thirty-three-year-old Pete Rozelle had been hired away from his post as general manager of the Los Angeles Rams to replace Commissioner Bell, and his appointment as head of the NFL provoked nearly as much skepticism as my selection to the AFL. Though experienced in professional football, because of his relative youth Rozelle was considered by a certain contingent of sportswriters to be a purposely weak selection. They saw it as a ploy by dominant owners who wanted a tractable administrator to yield to their policies.

On the other hand, as general manager of the Rams, Rozelle had successfully juggled the often dissonant demands of five of the most disputatious owners in the National Football League, an experience that would serve him well as commissioner of the NFL.

Within a few weeks of Rozelle's appointment early in 1960,

the two of us met to talk over potential problems that might arise if either league tried to hire signed players away from the other organization. A "no raiding" agreement was announced publicly, but the NFL was still far from affectionate toward us.

The spearhead of the NFL attack was the placement of a competing team in Dallas, our headquarters. If Lamar Hunt's popular and well-funded team could be forced out of the local market by a strong National League club, the future of the entire AFL would be jeopardized.

Sportswriters, intrigued by my combat record, seemed addicted to military metaphors in their press coverage, so I played along. I called the NFL move an "act of war" and threatened to take the battle to the Justice Department if the NFL followed up on its threat. Dallas columnist Gary Cartwright wrote: "Joe Foss is sweeping to a reputation as a word merchant. Latest Fossism, 'The National Football League moving into Dallas (where an AFL team already claims squatter's rights) is like putting a Christmas tree on a birthday cake.' "

Headlines heralding my warning spread across the tops of sports pages, but I did not limit my tactics to the legal arena. If this was a dogfight, I was going to have my guns crossweaving, not all pointed in the same direction. In the wake of the NFL's announced expansion, I stepped up our promotional activities, flying all over the country to bring the AFL message to reporters and anybody else who wanted a nationally known speaker with a purpose. I talked to anybody who would listen—hair-burners, riveters, plumbers, political conventions, the elks, the moose, or the owls. Turning the double signings and the Dallas turf battle into assets rather than liabilities, I exploited the controversies to assure that sports fans never lost interest in our entry into professional football.

On the morning of March 9, 1960, I settled behind my desk at the AFL office in Dallas with a dozen reporters and cameramen before me. Maxine Isenberg distributed an eight-page statement to the group, and I then gave them time to look over the copy. As the reporters leafed through the press release detailing the alleged injuries inflicted upon our league by the NFL, their initial reaction was puzzlement; they saw nothing they had not seen or heard from me before.

Bill Rives of *The Dallas Morning News* later wrote, "The newsmen threw glances at each other, which meant, 'What kind of deal is this? It's the same old stuff.' "

Ed Fite, sportswriter for UPI, asked the obvious question, "Joe, where's the meat in this thing?"

I smiled and pointed to the top of page one, overlooked by the eager reporters as they skimmed the statement for a scoop. Pages rustled as they turned back to read: "City of Washington, District of Columbia. Joe Foss, being duly sworn, deposes. . . ."

In sportswriters' parlance, I had "triggered a bomb." Within the record of my testimony before the Department of Justice's antitrust division in Washington, D.C., I had asked for antitrust action against the NFL, based on actions that included the establishment of the team in Dallas that would eventually become the Cowboys. I had cited:

Attempts to persuade members and prospective members of the new league to abandon or refuse franchises by promising them permission to join the NFL.

Harassment of the AFL and attempts to prevent establishment of franchise by announcing that the NFL would grant them in the same territories.

Granting franchises in the same territories even though they believed these areas could support only one team.

Threatening players with blacklisting and attempting to get them to break contracts.

Disparaging the AFL by telling coaches and players who had signed contracts or were about to sign contracts that the AFL would never get off the ground or would be driven out of business.

Interference with the AFL's attempts to get TV coverage and a reasonable price for it. As a result of this, the TV contract for the 1960-1965 period had been signed for far less than "actual and reasonable value."

Rozelle reacted to my complaint by declaring that a second team in Dallas was no different from the AFL's placement of a second team in New York. His statement drew fire by sportswriters.

The famed and caustic Dick Young of the New York *Daily News* was particularly hard on Rozelle, calling him the "kiddie commissioner," and "RePete." He remarked that the "kiddie commissioner" had tangled with me for the first time and come off "second best," claiming that "RePete cranked the following statement from the mimeograph where he trained for the job of commissioner."

While Dick Young was on my side, pointing out that Dallas could hardly be compared with New York and Los Angeles as a market, when New York had eight million, L.A. two and a half million, and Dallas a half million, I was not pleased with the column. While the apparent vendetta between two commissioners furnished endless material for the sports rumor mill, few people seemed to notice that Pete and I were the only two people on the planet who could really understand the other's job and the pressures that accompanied it. We were official enemies but private friends, and as time passed my respect and affection for Rozelle grew even stronger as I watched him handle his thorny job.

The Justice Department eventually rejected my request for legal intervention, as I expected they would. In fact, I thought the legal action a waste of time that could be better spent on more pressing problems—like the ones facing our newest team, Oakland. But the owners wanted me to use my familiarity with government to try for a legal advantage. I went along with their wishes at that point, but, as they would find out, there were limits to my compliance.

Another area I ventured into was television. ABC had shown definite interest in broadcast rights to AFL games, and I began discussions with the corporation. Then Harry Wismer came up with an idea that, in my opinion, despite his eccentricities, saved the life of pro football. Wismer proposed that our teams unite to sign one contract together for television rights and share broadcast revenues equally. The relationship

The great bunch of guys who gave birth to the American Football League: Billy Sullivan, Boston Patriots; Cal Kunz, Denver Broncos; Ralph Wilson, Buffalo Bills; Lamar Hunt, Dallas Texans, which later became the Kansas City Chiefs; Harry Wismer, New York Titans, which under new owners became the New York Jets; Wayne "Happy" Valley, Oakland Raiders; Barron Hilton, San Diego Chargers; K. S. "Bud" Adams, Houston Oilers; and old Joe. Missing is Bob Howsam, the original Bronco founder.

between professional football and television was about to change for all time.

Some people charged that this violated antitrust laws. But when I talked to various lawyers and members of Congress, they admitted that we had to share the income to be competitive or the rich teams would take the lion's share and the others would starve to death. The teams with the money to spend on players would beat the brains out of the other ones forever.

That's what was happening in the NFL. Each of the NFL teams signed separate broadcast agreements. In those days the NFL's big guns were the New York, Los Angeles, Chicago, and Washington teams. They got rich from TV revenue and held a terrific advantage, although the wealthy teams wouldn't have had games to play without the other teams. Then along we came with our proposal—share and share alike.

Legal gobbledygook and complex contracts scored near the top of my list of loathings. And you haven't seen anything until you've seen those immense entertainment contracts. So I turned to the experts for help, as I'd done many times in the past. Specifically, I chose Jay Michaels of the Music Corporation of America (MCA) to help handle the television package and the various merchandise licensings. Jay and I dealt primarily with Thomas Moore, vice president of the American Broadcasting Company (ABC). As offers and counteroffers changed hands, it was clear that MCA's assistance would pay real dividends, earning the league far more than the ten percent commission MCA would take.

Months passed before the final version of the agreement saw the light of day. In the meantime, to prove to ABC that coverage of AFL games would turn a profit, I spent much of my time in New York selling the idea of sponsoring the young and untested league to Madison Avenue. I expected and found skepticism. But when I believed in a product I could be a world-class salesman, and potential advertisers began lining up to buy commercial time.

When ABC and MCA finally hammered out a contract and presented it to me, the numbers were more than adequate, but I wasn't satisfied.

"This thing is too complicated," I complained. "Too much legal mumbo jumbo I don't understand. Cut it down."

Two weeks later, they came back with a shortened contract that was still too long. Months passed and the contract was cut further, but not to my satisfaction. Some of the owners really got on my tail because we didn't have an agreement on the table, but I refused to sign some long-winded document nobody could understand. Finally the contract was pared down to an acceptable level, with the exception of one clause.

"It sounds to me like we'll pay you forevermore, even if I negotiate a new contract with someone else," I told the MCA executives. "You'll get a percentage of every contract the AFL ever makes if I sign this. No matter where we go, we'll still have to pay you a commission."

"Well, that's standard," said one of MCA's lawyers.

"Standard?" I asked.

"Standard," several of them chorused.

"Well, it's not standard with me."

They insisted that no one argued about such things—that all agents' contracts contained similar clauses—but I held out.

"Change it to say that if we go back to ABC you'll get a commission then, but if we go somewhere else and you don't negotiate the contract, we won't owe you anything."

The clause was eventually removed. I hadn't played all those poker games for nothing.

When a contract was finally agreed upon, ABC was bound to pay $1,785,000 for television rights in the first season, with gradual increases until yearly fees reached $2,125,000 in the fifth and final year of the agreement. By today's standards those figures seem like chicken feed, but in our first season every one of our teams earned more than the team that won the NFL championship that year.

Pete Rozelle was no idiot. Miffed as he must have been to learn that we'd outplayed him on the poker table of television deals, his league soon followed suit.

This was not the only time the NFL found itself playing catch-up. We also took the lead in transforming the way football was presented on television. The AFL did away with the confusing NFL practice of using two clocks—one clock for the crowd and one for the officials. In the AFL the game clock became the official timepiece, allowing the audience to follow the play accurately and experience the excitement of last-minute drives with the certainty that the time remaining on the clock was the actual time left in the game.

In fact, we began a whole set of traditions, one which the NFL adopted—the practice of printing players' names on their football jerseys. In regard to the latter, the NFL criticized us for labeling players, claiming it was "glamour sports." Actually, I think they were more concerned that certain players might develop too much bargaining power if they were visible to the crowds.

I also allowed ABC to follow the action no matter where it went, even allowing cameras to follow players when action between plays heated up. The NFL limited television coverage to the plays and noncontroversial action between plays; a personal disagreement between players never made it onto the airwaves. On this point I fought some of my own owners to do away with "censorship restriction."

Similarly, the coaches resisted my proposal to let reporters into the locker rooms as soon as the clock ran out, particularly after losing a hot contest. They wanted a cooling-off period of a half hour to an hour before letting the reporters in to ask questions. I tried to put things in perspective for them.

"When I was the age of these football players," I told one coach, "we were playing games of life and death. People were getting killed, and we were knocking off other people. There was never a cooling-off period then. I gave the war correspondents permission to climb up on the airplane wings after we flew back from a mission, because I wanted the news to be hot and just exactly what it was. I always told my boys, 'Don't say anything that you don't want to read. Just tell it like it is and then let it go.' And I expect the same thing from football coverage. There's no reason to hide exactly what the feeling is. What's going on. What happened in the fight. Why'd you win. Why'd you lose. All hot off the griddle. Not some stale baloney. Not some story someone had a chance to concoct while the reporters stood outside the locker room door."

I just laid the pipe to them, and some of the coaches were pretty hot about it at first. But when they thought about it, and they had to be thinking individuals to be coaches of major teams, they realized what a piddling thing a game was when compared to life and death.

Throughout my life, ever since Guadalcanal, I've used that standard for making decisions. When I was a kid I used to hear people ask, "Is that a life-or-death decision?" and it almost never was. A decision may affect life, but it probably doesn't affect the breathing process—which is number one. Because of that I don't get too lathered up about most things.

When I was in the South Dakota legislature, some guys would get all torn apart when it came time to decide on something; some even got the shakes. One legislator complained to me, "I've got a whole bunch of friends that are for this bill and a whole bunch of friends that are against it. I really don't know what to do! I'm just all out of breath!"

I said, " 'Call yourself aside and talk it over,' as a coach from the University of South Dakota used to say"—that was old Rube Hoy.

Sportswriter Charles Burton summed up his enthusiasm for the new AFL style and regulations in a column titled "AFL Rules Made for Man in Stand," saying that, "The American Football League now has the most exciting set of rules in the game—pro, college, or high school. It has free substitutions, of course, and it wisely adopted the optional extra-point rule after touchdown, meaning that the fans will have an opportunity to watch the quarterback call for a kick for one point, or a pass or run for two."

Burton likewise praised the official field clock ruling and criticized the NFL for "stubbornly" resisting the switch. Without doubt, though, I think the most significant football tradition I proposed was my vision for a championship game between the American and National Football Leagues.

From the very first day that I even contemplated taking the job, I envisioned the establishment of a two-league system based on the model of American baseball, where we would stick strictly to ourselves during the regular season and then meet head-on for the championship. To me, accomplishing that would signal the fulfillment of my professional goals as commissioner. My suggestion of a play-off between the leagues, a sort of "super" bowl game, had tremendous appeal for fans and sportswriters alike.

Rozelle and the NFL ridiculed the notion—not based on projections that the public would not respond enthusiastically to a real championship contest, but on the fact that their acceptance of a showdown with the AFL would acknowledge recognition of the league itself. Rozelle regularly dismissed questions about an interleague playoff, implying that the new league couldn't field a team good enough to make it an interesting game.

All this did was create a backlash that worked in our favor. At least one sportswriter predicted that the fans would favor the league that supported a real championship game—if the AFL survived long enough to build teams powerful enough to challenge the NFL. And in March 1960, I publicly predicted that our circuit would be as strong as the NFL in three years.[1]

Another, less obvious, barrier to the realization of my goals stood in my own backyard. Some of my own employers, the team owners, were not fully committed to the goal of a self-ruling league; their agenda supported a separate organization only to the point where it was strong enough to force the NFL to absorb the successful teams. Although I was not certain which of the owners held that view, I knew the sentiment existed.

Complicating internal affairs further were growing signs of Harry Wismer's unpredictability. The AFL bylaws stated that no club owners could own stock in another professional football team, and Wismer held interest in the Washington Redskins. When I forced Wismer to comply with the rules and sell, he took it badly.

By the end of April, I was ready for a break from the pressure cooker. With Peter Barrett, outdoor editor of *True* magazine, and Roger and Gordon Fawcett, owners of Fawcett Publications in New York, I headed north for some hunting and fishing.

The night we left, I had to give a speech at the Waldorf-Astoria in New York. Afterward the Fawcett brothers picked me up in their limousine, and we drove to the airport. Peter Barrett would be meeting us in Kotzebue, Alaska, along with all our hunting gear and clothing.

---

[1] History: August 14, 1959, American Football League organizational meeting: New York, Dallas, Denver, Los Angeles, Minneapolis, Houston. October 28, 1959, Buffalo Bills admitted to AFL; November 22, 1959, Boston Patriots admitted to AFL; January 27, 1960, Minneapolis withdraws from AFL; January 30, 1960, Oakland Raiders admitted to AFL; February 10, 1961, Los Angeles Chargers transferred to San Diego; February 8, 1963, Dallas Texans transferred to Kansas City Chiefs.

The final roster of AFL teams would read: New York Titans, Buffalo Bills, Boston Patriots, Dallas Texans (later Kansas City Chiefs), Houston Oilers, Denver Broncos, Los Angeles Chargers (later San Diego Chargers), and the Oakland Raiders.

We flew nonstop on Northwest Airlines from New York to Seattle, where we hurriedly changed planes for our flight to Anchorage, Alaska. There we climbed into a Beech 18 (C-45) aircraft for our flight into Kotzebue, east of the Bering Strait.

When we landed, the pilot said, "I'll just let you out. I don't want to shut the engine off." Then he pointed to our right. "Go up over that snowbank and on the other side is the radio shack. They can get you into town."

I was still wearing my black silk suit from the banquet, with no overcoat or hat, the brothers Fawcett were in their homburg hats and Prince Albert coats, and it was forty below zero outside. So after we climbed the bank, found the radio shack, and stepped into the hot, tiny room, the Eskimo on duty probably couldn't believe his eyes.

Then Roger Fawcett said, "Would you call us a cab?"

The guy just laughed. "We don't have any cabs here. We do have a couple pickup trucks. One has a broken window and one doesn't. I'll give them a call."

When the pickup truck arrived—the one with the broken window—Peter Barrett was on board, dressed for the weather in his parka and boots and heavy clothing. We crammed ourselves into the drafty pickup and rode into Kotzebue through enormous snowdrifts.

The only place to stay in town was Rottman's Hotel and Grocery Store. The hotel was over the grocery store, and as we went up the stairs to our room, the first sign I saw was *Bathing water—9 cents a gallon*. Our room had four cots, no closets, and Peter had piled all our gear in the middle of the floor.

Gordie Fawcett took one look and said, "Where's my room?"

"This is our room," I said.

"Oh, it can't be," he said.

"Sure it is," I said. "We'll be fine. These are good army cots, and it's warm in here."

Then the four of us sank down on the cots and had a good laugh. And that's the way the trip went from start to finish. It was one of the most fun-laden hunting trips I've ever been on in my life.

A Proud American

We hunted west of Shishmaref in the Bering Strait. When
we landed at Shishmaref we saw only a hole in the snow.
Then we climbed down a ladder and found a whole town
under there. The snow had covered right over the town. While
we were looking around in a little shop there, Peter Barrett
remarked, "South Dakota was never like this, was it, Joe."

"South Dakota?" said the Eskimo behind the counter.
"My son is going to Augustana College in Sioux Falls, South
Dakota."

"Well, I'm from Sioux Falls," I said.

The man told me his name and his son's name, and I said,
"When I get to Sioux Falls I'll look him up and take him out
to dinner." The first time I went back to Sioux Falls I did just
that, and the young man and I had a great time.

At Shishmaref we spent several days fishing and then went
after polar bear. With my .300 Weatherby magnum rifle I
downed the thirteenth largest white bruin in the Boone and
Crockett Club registry at that time. It was a great trip.

Less than a week after leaving for the Arctic Circle I was
back in Dallas refreshed and ready for the first season of play,
complete with a trophy and ample publicity from my successful hunt.

Chapter 24
"He's En Route!"

As the American Football League approached its first season, the bidding war for players intensified. The NFL complained, but college players applauded. More of them were playing pro ball than ever before, and at higher salaries.

We also prevailed in the court battles over all four double signers, including Charlie Flowers and Billy Cannon. A sardonic twist to the story came to light when Pete Rozelle admitted that he, while still the general manager of the Los Angeles Rams, had signed Billy Cannon before the end of the college season. In doing so he violated the National Collegiate Athletics Association's long-standing opposition to the recruitment of players until after their college careers ended. The NFL had always been sensitive to that opposition, scheduling its player draft to follow the collegiate season in compliance with NCAA urgings.

Bill Wallace of the *New York Herald Tribune* wrote of the early signing: "The Rams justified this violation of an informal trust with the colleges on the grounds of keeping Cannon away from the American League. Rozelle was asked if the NFL teams would continue the practice of signing players before their [college] eligibility was over. He replied, 'I don't know,' but later added that he hoped the other league would become agreeable to a reform solution in 1961. 'I hope we can get this straightened out,' he said. So it is a not-very cold war.''

Despite our success in enlisting top college athletes, the AFL was still a league of talented rookies held by unpracticed owners. Only the coaching staffs had real pro ball experience. At the time they were Sid Gillman of the Los Angeles Chargers; Eddie Erdelatz in Oakland; Sammy Baugh with the New York Titans, who himself had been a great quarterback; and Frank Leahy of Notre Dame fame, also with the Chargers; Lou Rymkus with the Houston Oilers; Don Rossi and Hank Stram with the Dallas Texans; Dick Gallagher and Buster Ramsey with the Buffalo Bills; Ed McKeever, Mike Holovak, and Lou Saban with the Patriots; and Dean Griffith and Frank Filchock with the Broncos.

Since we lacked seasoned teams manned by veteran players, spring training was especially critical for the development of our inexperienced clubs. So after deliberating with the team owners, I announced that the league's draftees would not take time away from group practice to play in the college all-star games.

By September, the NFL's preseason ticket sales already indicated that they would break all the league's previous records. The NFL's worst predictions, that the AFL would destroy both organizations by dividing football revenues so that neither would survive, soon proved absolutely false. In retrospect, of course, it is easy to see that the expanding audience and influence of television contributed to the growing popularity of the sport, and the additional attention we brought to the game also propelled football to new heights.

But as regular season play began with our first official game on September 9, 1960, between the Denver Broncos and the Boston Patriots, our meager gate receipts dramatized the challenge before us. At that time Pete Rozelle estimated that an NFL team needed an average attendance of at least 40,000 people per game to survive. By those standards, I had my work cut out for me, since in the beginning our audiences often totaled less than 10,000 fans. So while the NFL enjoyed historic profits, I struggled to limit our losses.

I still maintain that I'm the only commissioner in any sport who ever shook hands with every spectator in the stands during a regular season game. It happened on Thanksgiving Day in New York that first season, when less than a thousand people huddled in the Polo Grounds as the wind howled and the snow whipped around the stands. I was freezing solid, so I decided to warm up by walking around and talking with the fans. As usual I was wearing my cowboy hat—this was before the glamour crowd took up wearing Western gear—and people recognized me immediately as I thanked every one of the spectators for coming to the game.

"At least you all got good seats," I told them.

Some said, "I'm here on a comp ticket."

"I don't care how you're here," I said. "Thanks for coming."

Although the Titans were competing head-on with the NFL's New York Giants, Harry Wismer announced, "There's no question that we're here to stay." Wismer's promise was to be fulfilled, but the greatest obstacle to that achievement would come from the man himself.

The Oakland Raiders, plagued by the problems inherent in management by committee, played that first fall on San Francisco's wet, soggy Kezar Field. All we saw in the stands for the first few games were seagulls. Before the season ended, disappointment over a $400,000 loss and constant media coverage of front office squabbles would precipitate talk among some of the owners about moving the team to another city. Other Oakland owners scorned the talk as the complaints of "crybabies."

The Los Angeles Chargers, in direct competition with the Rams, played their opening season at the Los Angeles Coliseum, with a capacity seating of over 100,000. Understandably, Barron Hilton at times wished for a stadium that did less to emphasize the size of his crowds. Actually, we didn't draw flies in L.A. that year. The city fathers, who were supposedly looking after new business, never seemed to notice that we were in town, and Hilton dropped $1,450,000 before the year's end.

Similarly, the Dallas Texans, who played in the Cotton Bowl, fared badly in the turf battle opposite the NFL's Dallas Cowboys, losing a half-million dollars of Lamar Hunt's money in the process. The oilman took some consolation in the Cowboys' miserable season, both athletically and financially. Losses in Dallas, the home of our league, did not spell the end of the AFL, as some critics hoped. It did, however, prompt discussions about finding a less crowded hometown.

Our second Texas team, the Houston Oilers, failed to win access to the 70,000 seat Rice Stadium, where Bud Adams had hoped to play. Instead, Bud spent $250,000 on improvements for Jeppesen Stadium, a high school field with a maximum capacity of 15,000 fans, and his team's losses were limited to roughly $185,000.

The Denver organization did surprisingly well. Although it spent nearly a million dollars in alterations to the Bears' baseball stadium, dedicated fans helped the club reach a near break-even point in its premier season.

The Boston club spent $300,000 improving the old Braves Field before moving to Fenway Park. Area residents quickly took the Patriots to heart, limiting the team's losses to an estimated $100,000. Club President Billy Sullivan was agreeably surprised by the success of the team and enthusiastic about the future.

Ralph Wilson's Buffalo Bills played in fair conditions at War Memorial Stadium, where Wilson lost close to $200,000 before the season ended. But he was confident that the club would soon be in the profit column. "Twelve months ago the skeptics were calling the AFL a big joke," said Wilson. "Now I wonder what they'll be saying." He inherited his optimism from his father, who always greeted me with, "We'll make it!"

Each club played five preseason games and fourteen regular season matches. The Houston Oilers won the Eastern Division title and went on to beat the Los Angeles Chargers, the Western Division winner, on New Year's Day before a crowd of over 32,000 fans. The opposing quarterbacks were George Blanda of Houston and Jack Kemp of L.A.

Despite a deficit for the first season totaling over $2,000,000, the owners remained confident. I figured if they could absorb the start-up losses until attendance reached profitable levels, and with the support of the excellent television deal, the AFL was on track for success.

Nevertheless, storm clouds still brewed overhead. In December we held our player draft for the upcoming year prior to the end of the regular college football season. Mending important alliances with the NCAA and other outraged college officials tested every diplomatic skill I had. While I tried to sort out the mess, my relations with my employers were strained, and it was months before I was able to extract a promise from the owners that there would be no recurrence of the premature draft. This went in the form of a pledge letter to the American Football Coaches Association.

In the meantime, the ongoing bickering among the eight primary owners of the Oakland Raiders threatened to finish the team before it had a chance. The Oakland ownership had been divided almost from the beginning. Even naming the club had been a major undertaking. From a list of entries gathered in a community "name the team" contest, four of the owners chose the "Señors" as the team title, only to have the Oakland City Council side with the other investors in rejecting the baffling name. Other monikers under consideration had included the Oaks, Jets, Sea Wolves, and Saints.

The troubles in Oakland really bothered me, and I found myself in an unpleasant position. Personally I admired all eight men, but they had settled into two camps, and eventually one of the factions was going to have to take over the club to provide consistent leadership and policy for the team. A local columnist, George Ross, accurately assessed, "The man with the biggest 'crush' on Oakland is the commissioner himself, Joe Foss. He's a one-man superpatriot for Oakland, an invaluable and unpaid Chamber of Commerce."

Finally I had no choice but to involve myself in the situation. Armed with the authority to revoke the city's franchise if the group didn't learn to cooperate and get on with building a football team, I flew to Oakland in January 1961 with two of our league lawyers to deliver the ultimatum: Shape up or ship out. I met with them on Sunday afternoon at a law office downtown, and they were already fighting among themselves when I walked in. I sat at the head of the table with the league's lawyers, Bob Dedman and Sullivan Barnes, on either side of me. Five owners sat to the right and three owners sat to the left.

The faction on the left consisted of City Councilman Bob

Osborne and construction magnates Ed McGah and Wayne (Happy) Valley. The gang on the right was composed of Y. C. Soda, Don Blessing, Wally Marsh, Roger Lapham, Jr., and Charles Harney. The mood in the room was volcanic.

Marsh and Blessing wanted out of their contractual obligations completely; they were tired of the wrangling and reportedly short of money. I recommended that they be freed from their obligations, forfeiting only the money invested thus far, which came to $25,000-plus each. But I couldn't even get the group to agree about that. Don Blessing, a fine man, then left the meeting after telling me, "Commissioner, I just don't have the working capital at this time."

Wayne Valley and Charlie Harney didn't like each other, and Valley responded to a sarcastic comment of Harney's by saying, "You're always trying to sue somebody. I see you have a cast on your foot because your driver stopped too fast. I suppose you're trying to sue somebody over that." Then they called each other names until Charlie hauled back and swung his cane at Valley. It whistled past the left side of old Happy's face, just missing his nose; it could have killed him if it had hit him on the temple.

At that point I yelled, "Sit down! Here you all just came from church and you're acting like jerks! If you don't shape up, I'm going to pick up the franchise and leave town!"

After that they settled down enough so we could proceed with negotiations, but it was evident that the resentful undercurrents would pull them all out to sea if something weren't done. First, I directed both sides to agree on a suitable price; then one side or the other could buy out the club. When they had finally reached a figure, Charlie Harney threw a coin on the table and said, "Somebody flip and we'll call it." The coin was tossed and Harney snarled, "Tails."

Valley, McGah, and Osborne won the toss, and the losers walked out of the meeting. I wanted them to stay, but at that point there was nothing I could do. A few weeks later, Bob Osborne had a heart attack and had to sell out his share the next year.

Within months I was back in Oakland again, this time to lobby the city for permission to build a new facility for the Raiders because the Frank Youell Stadium was too small. A high-powered committee that included Senator William Knowland, young Edgar Kaiser, son of Liberty shipbuilder Henry Kaiser, and Bob Nahas headed the effort to bring the games to the Oakland side of the bay. At the first public meeting to discuss the project, Knowland, Kaiser, Nahas, and I faced several hundred people, many of them opposed to the idea of a stadium in Oakland.

As the moderator introduced me and I walked to the podium, a voice from the crowd rang out, "Go home, you carpetbagger."

I looked out at the woman who had shouted; she was standing defiantly and glaring at me. "I'm glad you called me that," I said with a smile. "It's a good name, but I've come here because I've been invited, and what I want to do is get this sports complex underway."

Another voice yelled, "Why should Oakland want a professional football team? This is just a bedroom community."

"I'm glad you mentioned that bedroom," I responded. "It's time you woke up. You've been sleeping in the shadow of San Francisco long enough. Now these gentlemen here," I said, gesturing to the committee, "starting with Senator Knowland, are going to get things rolling.

"What you do now to attract business and prestige to Oakland is to go around spending money and getting nothing done. If you have a professional football franchise, you broadcast all over the world and you get to put your pitch in about what a great town you live in. The whole thing is done with private capital and the money that comes in, according to the experts, rolls over seven times. This is something that will really get your city going. In my opinion, a local team is the single greatest community catalyst you can have."

The meeting created such enthusiasm that the community raised the funds to build a fine football facility known as the Oakland-Alameda County Stadium.

As hectic as that time was, trying to get the league off the ground, my life was not limited to football. I was elected president of the Air Force Association, an organization of qualified people who work closely with the members of Congress and the Defense Department to see that our air power

is ready to go. It is a grass roots organization made up of
people of all ranks, from private to general, active and in-
active. They're a ready teddy outfit, and I was proud and
honored to be president of the unit and to serve as chairman
of the board.

Also, after serving as national chairman of the Society for
Crippled Children and Adults, I continued on the board of
trustees. I was active in the Confederate Air Force, a group
of patriotic Americans who have spent incredible amounts
of their own money to preserve World War II aircraft. I
assisted in fund-raising for the Boy Scouts of America. I also
continued as chief of staff of the South Dakota Air National
Guard and belonged to the executive board of the U.S. National Guard Association. I was on the Mount Rushmore
Commission and served as president of the organization building the Crazy Horse Monument, the gigantic sculpture in
South Dakota honoring the Native Americans.

And I always found time to hunt and fish. No matter what
the circumstances or situation, nothing could dampen my enthusiasm for hunting. One day when I was back in South
Dakota, I stopped in to see Duke Corning, as I always did,
and while we were talking he said, "Hey, Curly Haisch out
at Mulehead Ranch just called. He says the geese are really
flying."

"Well, let's go," I said. "We'll take the old Supercub and
buzz out there and pick up a limit."

So we flew out to Curly's ranch. When we'd called to let
him know we were coming, Curly said to come in low and
not circle around or we'd scare the geese off his fields. So I
made a low, short approach. As I came in, I spotted what
looked like a good strip of dirt in front of his ranch house.

Just as I was setting down, when it was too late to pull out,
I noticed that what I thought was solid black dirt was snow-
filled Russian thistles. The soil from a plowed field nearby
had blown over into the thistles, making it look like bare
ground, a perfect spot to land. Actually the top surface was
two to three feet above the ground, and as soon as our wheels
got into the thistles the plane nosed up and over.

Duke started yelling from behind me—in the Supercub we
were flying tandem one seat behind the other—as we teetered

back and forth, with shells and guns and hunting equipment flying around our necks.

"Be quiet," I said. "This is no big crash. I doubt if it did much damage." The plane hadn't flipped over, just nosed up. "Let's get our weight out of here before we wreck something and get over there while the geese are flying." We could see them off to our right. "Let's get our limits and then come back and worry about the airplane."

"I don't know if I feel like shooting," Duke said. He owned half of the airplane, and he thought it was damaged worse than it was. As it turned out, all we had to do was get a different prop and fly it off Curly's driveway the next day, along with our limit of geese.

Another favorite event I never missed was the One-Shot Antelope Hunt held every year on the weekend closest to September 20 outside Lander, Wyoming. Celebrities from all over the world participated in the hunt, going after their prey armed with a rifle and one round of ammunition apiece. Those who successfully brought an antelope back to camp knew they had exhibited real sporting skill in every sense of the word.

The Lander One-Shot was started in the 1940s by a guy named Harold Evans, and I had first been invited to participate in 1949. The night before the hunt there was always a ceremony with the Indians, during which they would bless the bullets. Then in the morning each team would go out and bring back meat for the camp with one bullet.

When I became involved, we began to get dignitaries from around the country interested, such as Jimmy Doolittle, Curtis LeMay, Bob Stack, and Roy Rogers, to name just a few. We added teams of U.S. senators and governors, and we even had a team of Russian cosmonauts come and shoot against our astronaut team led by Donald (Deke) Slayton of Apollo 18. Deke's team consisting of Tom Stafford and Vance Brand won, and the Russian team came in second. The general of the Russian team missed his shot, and I've jokingly said that we've never seen him since that day.

The Past Shooters organization of the Lander One-Shot Antelope Hunt is one of the greatest conservationist groups in our country. One of their projects is the Water for Wildlife program. Creatures—feathered, furred, or whatever—must

Jimmy Doolittle and I have shared so many of life's experiences—flying, hunting, fishing, and the Congressional Medal of Honor Society. Here we're attending the One-Shot Antelope Hunt, Lander, Wyoming, in September 1977. (Photo by Donna Wild Foss)

have water to survive. The advance of civilization diverts water to populated areas, causing great areas of land to dry up. Water for Wildlife establishes wells in these arid areas, often by using the wells abandoned by oil prospectors.

While some accused me of spreading myself too thin with all of my interests, I believed that rather than detracting from my duties as commissioner, these activities provided opportunities to spread the AFL message, gaining reams of free press and publicity for the league. There were those, however, who disapproved of my inclination to travel.

Maxine Isenberg's standard reply, "He's en route," now became a perpetual joke. My nearly impossible schedule meant I was constantly on the run; because of this, it was not unusual for me to show up late for an appointment.

Since I was still an active member of the South Dakota Air National Guard, I had to meet my flight requirements of better than 132 hours per year, and I always wanted to have at least 150 hours or more so that I felt confident to fly the equipment, which at that time happened to be jets. To kill two birds with one stone, as I traveled about the country for the league, whenever I could I used a military airplane. It not only got me where I needed to be, but enabled me to work in my flight time and practice letdowns at various places. Then I would fly back to South Dakota and drop off the airplane.

The first thing I knew, columnist Drew Pearson wrote a nasty piece about me. Pearson had gone after me a couple times when I was governor. I think he liked to take his shots at me because I was not afraid to speak up or to disagree with anyone if I thought they were wrong. In this instance he accused me of using military planes and costing taxpayers a lot of money to finance my trips as commissioner for the AFL. This was far from the truth, and I issued a story to state the facts and clear the air.

In the process of getting myself from one place to another, I was meeting my qualifications as an active member of the armed services that defend this country. One way or another, I had to spend that amount of time in the air in those planes. Instead of riding first-class on a commercial airline, which I could have done and which the league allowed, I was beating myself around in a fighter-type aircraft where I had to make the flight plan myself and check the plane over myself, all of which takes a great deal of time. And if the bell ever rang for another war—which was always a possibility—I was qualified and ready to go.

Chapter 25
Wild
About Harry

✯ ✯ ✯

My foremost critic was still Harry Wismer, and as our second season began, he became more and more vocal, charging that I was absent from my desk in Dallas too much. His recommended solution was to bring the AFL to New York, presumably so he could better oversee the commissioner.

While I questioned Wismer's motives, and rightly so, the idea of moving our headquarters to New York was not totally invalid. Working out of Dallas, we did lack convenient access to advertisers and major media outlets. Pete Rozelle had reached the same conclusion for his league and had moved the NFL offices from Philadelphia to New York.

Increasingly, Wismer, who was the play-by-play announcer for Notre Dame, used his contacts with fellow sportscasters and journalists to complicate my life. Before the 1961 season started, someone planted rumors that the AFL would soon merge with the NFL. Los Angeles columnist Bob Oates published the story, citing several well-placed but anonymous sources. I suspected one of them was Wismer, though I could never prove it.

Wismer delighted in putting people on, as I knew firsthand. We'd get on an elevator together in New York, and he'd start talking about having heard a news flash that Castro had just been shot. Some bystander would ask who shot him, and Wismer would say, "His brother Raoul. They haven't been getting along." Then he'd say to me, "Don't you think that's a good thing, Commissioner?"

Not only would the folks on the elevator think I was the police commissioner, they would also start spreading the Castro story because Wismer had made it sound so real. If anyone came back later and confronted him about something like this, Harry would say, "Well, that's what I heard." He'd do this kind of thing all the time.

Wismer was always holding press conferences in New York where he would charge the NFL or the New York Giants with offenses that were often purposely ludicrous. This kind of constant attack on the NFL really aggravated me; it diminished the dignity of the AFL and distracted from the job of building good teams.

I think the major problem between us was that Wismer always tried to crawl under the fence in any situation, while I insisted on enforcing the rules. As far as I was concerned, the rules applied across the board to everyone in the organization.

Wismer's growing animosity toward me finally blossomed publicly in November 1961.

Two weeks before the final college game on December 2, the AFL owners arranged an eight-way conference call to decide among themselves who would have first bidding rights to the year's top college players. I was in Denver at the time and knew nothing of these negotiations.

The press got wind of the owners' secret draft almost immediately, and the first story appeared in *The Dallas Morning News* on November 19.

My initial reaction was bewilderment—I didn't know what in the hell was going on. After talking to the owners and fielding hundreds of questions from the press, I issued a statement that partially attempted to justify the draft. Calling it an "intraleague negotiation rights poll," I conceded that the poll had the appearance of wrongdoing and I confessed great personal embarrassment over the affair. I also announced an immediate investigation of the matter.

As days passed and the true story came to light, I realized that the "negotiation rights poll" had been a secret, premature draft in all but name, and the incident blossomed into a major scandal. Not since the beginning of the league itself had the AFL generated such headlines. Pete Rozelle was among the first to jump on me for allowing my owners to violate pledges to collegiate organizations, and columnists used up a forest of trees thinking of new ways to pose the question, "What sort of commissioner would be unaware of a draft by his own team owners?"

I was madder than hops. To think that grown men would try to pull something like this. They thought they could play games under the blankets—pick the players and sign them early to beat the NFL—and make an ass out of me in the bargain.

As the college backlash grew, so did my anger. Officials from around the country expressed shock and outrage. Among them was Bill Reed, commissioner of the Big Ten and cochairman of the Football Coaches NCAA Committee, who called the draft "a breach of faith."

Stanford's Jack Curtiss, president of the American Football Coaches Association, sent his message to the press: "It is not fair to a college football coach to have his players tampered with until the season is over," and he charged, "I am rather surprised that people of the AFL would disregard their agreement with the coaches. We have had the utmost confidence in them and we are certainly shocked to see this discrepancy in their actions."

My reputation was plummeting along with the league's and my first impulse was to resign in protest to make my own stance clear. If I let the owners get away with it, the league would be finished. I also knew that if I quit at that point, they would really be in trouble. Being on the defense is like backing up with glass in your heels, so I took the only step I could: I publicly canceled the secret draft.

On November 22 the Associated Press reported the statement I had given them over the phone: "After investigating and considering more fully the various ramifications of the negotiation poll conducted secretly by presidents of the American Football League, without the knowledge of myself or my office, I feel such a poll has the aspects of a premature draft and exercise my power as commissioner and hereby declare the draft null and void. Only the draft on December 2 conducted by the commissioner will be the authentic and official one."

The owners were livid. But my philosophy has always been that you go by the rules of the game. When they told me that they didn't see anything wrong with the draft, I said, "Any of you who move on the draft and sign those players will be in trouble. You'll get fined and that's it."

"We didn't hire you to protect the NFL," was their reply. "Maybe we should get a commissioner who will look out for our interests."

"The one thing you did hire me for was to enforce the rules," I said. "And that's what I'm doing. And as for the other, well, if that's the way it is, so be it. I don't give a rat's ass about being out of work."

The newspapers, of course, were already predicting that I was on my way out the door, while Harry Wismer was trying to lock it behind me.

Wismer went to the press again and again, claiming that I had been fully aware of the draft and that I had lied to the media when the infraction I had organized was uncovered. However, Ralph Wilson, owner of the Buffalo Bills, came forward and admitted that he and two other owners had not only planned the early draft but had concealed it from me.

New York Mirror writer Harold Weissman reported: "Never one to hide behind the veil of expedience when the going got sticky, Ralph Wilson identified himself to this bureau as 'one of the three owners' who organized the AFL's controversial 'sneak' draft."

Weissman also recounted that

> while expressing sincere regret for the unintended face-losing consequences to Foss, the forthright Buffalo magnate justified the clandestine pool of 48 players as an act of necessity. "Next year is a year of decision for our league," explained Wilson, "and it is of utmost importance to make a representative showing in the race [with the NFL] for outstanding collegiate talent. I strongly supported the secret telephone poll, along with Lamar Hunt and Bud Adams, as the most practical approach to an early advantage to negotiating with players." The

highly principled man who pays the Bills—the Buffalo
Bills, that is—insisted the AFL had not resorted to any
illegal practices "since we've done nothing to jeopardize
a boy's eligibility." Admitting disappointment in Foss's
subsequent step of voiding the premature draft, Wilson
said he would, nonetheless, fully abide by that decision.
However, what the Buffalo proprietor could not abide
to any degree was the irresponsible and lamentable attack on the Commissioner by his New York colleague.
"I was shocked by Harry Wismer's statements," said
Wilson after absorbing the contents of an interview
which labeled Foss—a figure of dignity, marine hero,
winner of the Congressional Medal of Honor and a
former governor—a liar for denying he had advance
knowledge of the early draft.

Wismer, however, didn't let up. He expanded his charges,
pointing to the fact that I still held stock in Raven Industries,
owned largely by H. P. Skogland, who had left the AFL to
start an NFL team in Minneapolis. Wismer suggested that I
was a mole in the American League and still loyal to Skogland,
who had first pushed for my appointment as commissioner.
Wismer insisted that I had no power to cancel the draft and
that he would go ahead and sign the players he had drawn.
Wismer's plan to carry through on the original plan was
thwarted by the other owners, who finally accepted the wisdom of my judgment. But Wismer's attacks continued, and
he stated publicly that he had the support of enough of the
league's owners to evict the "farm boy from Sioux Falls" from
his post.

I responded with the statement that "The Titans would be
better off if they had a new owner," and the feud was off and
running.

Wismer, in a postgame press conference, countered with,
"I think we need a new commissioner."

"This man [Wismer] can't be allowed to continue to do
what he's been doing to the league," I told reporters. "He's
hurting us with his press battles and constant accusations
against other people. He's diverting interest from his team."
Later I added, "The time has come to decide whether I am

going to be commissioner or whether Wismer is going to be commissioner."

As the AFL prepared for its Dallas meeting in January, the eyes of America's sportswriters were fixed on the two of us.

"The sooner we get this thing settled, the better," I told reporters when asked about the controversy. "You can't ride along down the trail with a burr like this under the saddle."

Though chafing under the press coverage that the quarrel focused on the league, I refused to back down from Wismer's challenge. Sportswriters sometimes irritated me. I thought that, under the guise of getting at the truth, what they often really wanted to do was hit you on top of the head and drive you deeper into the sand. But I had to admit that journalistic support for me was nearly unanimous during the conflict with Wismer.

New York columnist Ed Sullivan, better known to the rest of the country as television's leading impresario, rallied to my defense when he wrote: "My stomach turned when I read Harry Wismer's blast at grid commissioner Joe Foss because Foss issued a ruling that could dent Wismer's bankroll. . . . Guys like Wismer should tip their hats every time they see Foss!"

Even Pete Rozelle was the subject of several editorial censures. Sportswriter Sam Blair wrote:

It's true that American Football League club owners committed a huge blunder with their not-so-secret player draft but we don't believe this entitles everyone in the U.S.A. to blast them with criticism. One guy who certainly should have remained silent is Pete Rozelle.

But the NFL commissioner just couldn't keep his mouth shut. He preached a lengthy sermon in New York on the "discredit to pro football" which the AFL owners had performed, evidently thinking that all was forgiven and/or forgotten about his distasteful role in the Billy Cannon case.

But plenty of folk remember it. Rozelle should have known they would and kept quiet. . . . It beats us how Rozelle could be shocked by anyone's audacity. . . . It

301

was proved that Rozelle saw nothing wrong with working in secrecy when he was general manager of the
Rams. He signed the LSU All-American to a 3-year
contract on Nov. 30, 1959, although Cannon hadn't
completed his college eligibility.

Blair went on to name various other NFL players who had
signed with their teams before the end of the season. The
practice was standard procedure, he said, and most people
knew it. Thirty years later, premature signings are still evident, and the only unusual thing about the entire episode was
probably my renunciation of the practice.

With public opinion against him, Wismer finally backed
down. I speculated at the time that Wismer had started the
whole controversy thinking that any publicity was good publicity but had allowed it to get out of hand. It was something
Harry would do. Instead of demanding my job, he now announced that he would be satisfied if the AFL offices were
moved to New York City.

"If Foss is willing to come," he told the press, "then I'm
willing to let him stay as commissioner."

I refused to compromise, and when high noon arrived, I
asked for and received a vote of confidence from the owners.
Even Wismer, realizing he was not going to get his way, cast
a vote to renew my contract for another five years with a
healthy raise. My authority as commissioner was firmly established, and the league office stayed in Dallas, although I
knew the move to New York was inevitable.

Perversely—in typical Harry fashion—almost immediately
after the well-publicized fight, Wismer asked me to be best
man at his marriage to Mary Zwillman.

Wismer could be a nice guy when he behaved himself, but
he swigged too much, and you get goofy when you do that.
He was drinking heavily at the wedding reception and dinner,
and at one point he said to several of us—Sully Barnes, the
league lawyer, Mims Thomason, the head of UPI, and I—
"What you just witnessed was a merger." Harry thought
Mary, who was the widow of Longy Zwillman, a prominent
figure in the Senator Kefauver hearings, had inherited a bun-
dle and that he was going to get his hands in the cookie jar.

By the time the wedding reception was over, we had to carry him into his flat, undress him, and put him to bed. I felt so sorry for Mary.

Shortly after that, Wismer threw a wet towel on yet another gathering. Sonny Werblin, the head of MCA Television and the first man I'd talked to when seeking help with television contract negotiations, and his lovely wife, Leah Rae, held a birthday party for me at Kriendler's 21 Club. This brought back memories, because the 21 Club had been a favorite of Ben Finney, who had patronized the establishment before, through, and after prohibition, and I'd heard a lot about it from him. Flattered and cheered by the celebration, I enjoyed myself to the hilt—until Harry had at least one too many drinks and took issue with Werblin over some trivial matter. I grew more and more annoyed as Wismer tried to bully the unbulliable Werblin. Finally Wismer blew up and spewed a series of invectives at Sonny that ended with the word "kike."

Sonny, son of an immigrant Jewish family and a man who had started as an errand boy and turned his efforts into millions, was a robust man; having suffered a heart attack earlier in his life, he had pushed himself into excellent physical condition. He was going to punch Wismer's lights out, and he could have. I stepped between the two of them, holding off one man with each hand. Fortunately I was stronger than either of them, since I kept up a strenuous daily exercise regimen of running and military calisthenics, maintaining a weight of 178 and a waistline of thirty-three inches on my six-foot frame.

"Someday I'm going to own your club!" Sonny snarled at Harry.

"Sit down!" I said. "Let's have a good time." They did, but there was bad blood between them from then on.

Wismer's unpredictability affected everyone and everything he touched, including his own organization. Unable to delegate the management of the team to the people he had hired for that purpose, he personally interfered in every aspect of the team's business and quickly developed serious trouble with his own people. During the 1961 season only two of the players who started the season finished with the team, and head coach Sam Baugh, whom Wismer fired, commented that his ex-boss seemed "to be in a fog."

During 1962, however, the rest of the league saw slow but steady growth as gate receipts rose. Hilton's Chargers settled into much friendlier territory in San Diego; the owners of the increasingly popular Oakland Raiders began to draw up plans for construction of the Oakland Coliseum; and Lamar Hunt came to grips with the fact that the Dallas struggle against the Cowboys was counterproductive and began negotiations to move the team to Kansas City as the Kansas City Chiefs. The big question was Harry Wismer and the Titans.

Harry kept most of his wealth in the stock market and frequently passed tips on to me. I never played the market, but I encouraged Harry, unsuccessfully, to sell some of his stock holdings to support the Titans when the team's finances began to suffer. Wismer's response was always, "What do you know about stocks?"

The problem was, Harry liked the high life. Wherever he went, he spent high, wide, and handsome. In a restaurant—always the best, of course—he often bought drinks for everybody—people he had never seen before. He wanted them to know he was Harry Wismer, owner of the New York Titans.

Then in 1962 the stock market took a dive, and his stocks went down, down, down. He sold low, at fifty, then bought at thirty-eight. He told me to buy too, but I said, "Like you said, Harry, what do I know about stocks?" Unfortunately prices didn't go up; they kept falling, and Harry was ruined.

By October it was questionable whether the Titans personnel would ever be paid. Harry knew he would have to sell the club, and agreed to do so. With Harry, however, nothing was that simple. I concentrated on finding a buyer, but every time I got close to a deal with somebody, Harry would scare them off. We met with Mrs. Payson, who was a member of the Whitney family and owned the Mets, and Don Grant, her brother-in-law, who was manager of the Mets. Then Harry came out with some statements in the press that upset Mrs. Payson, and Don Grant called me up to say they were no longer interested.

Several other buyers showed interest. Harry didn't have the money to get the team's jockstraps out of the laundry, but when he got down to dealing, he wanted $3 million. Then he said $2 million. Nobody would buy at those prices.

Finally the other league owners grew desperate. Much more than the New York franchise depended on the sale of the team. The failure of the Titans could destroy all the confidence the AFL had built to that point. The owners asked me to make the sale happen, no matter what, and each one put in over $50,000 to pay Wismer's debts and expenses—that is, players' salaries, advertising, administration, laundry, and other operating costs. At the owners' meeting at the Shamrock Hilton in Houston in early December, Lamar Hunt stated, "You *must* effect a sale of the Titans."

I contacted some of my friends from Sioux Falls—contractors Dick Sweetman and Joe Beckman and banker Tom Riordan—who were going to pool their resources. But, again, when they came up to the line, Wismer backed them off.

Fed up to my Stetson with Wismer's erratic behavior, right after Christmas of 1962 I called Sonny Werblin. "Hey, Sonny, you said one time that you were going to own the Titans."

"I'll talk to you at the end of the month," he said.

"No," I said, "the owners want to move now."

"How about tomorrow?"

I was in South Dakota getting in my flight time for the South Dakota Air National Guard at the time, so I flew all night to get to New York, walked into the 21 Club at noon, and told Sonny what the deal was. Sonny called his lawyer, Bob Schulman, who hotfooted over there. Following lunch, the three of us went to Bob's office, where Sonny made out an earnest check for $100,000. Bob stood over us both, lamenting, "Sonny, this is probably the dumbest business deal you ever made in your life."

Sonny turned to look up at Schulman. "Bob, I've always hired lawyers to handle my legal work, but I've always maintained that they aren't very good businessmen." Then he agreed to pay $1,350,000 for the club and gave me the earnest check with a smile.

The Titans' problem seemed to be solved, until Wismer found out who was buying the team. Apparently he decided that if he could not continue in the AFL, no one could, and he filed for bankruptcy under Chapter 11 to block the sale to Werblin. I shuddered when I thought about the sort of publicity we could get from a legal battle starring Harry Wismer.

Our deliverance came from an odd quarter—the great New York communications strike, which, miraculously, lasted through the entire hearing. There wasn't a single reporter in the courtroom; they wouldn't be caught dead anywhere near the place.

Added to this, the court was down near Greenwich Village, where there were a lot of derelicts. It was cold weather, so these guys packed the courtroom every day to stay warm. Between the dozing drunks and the missing media, nobody even heard about the hearing at which Wismer tried to prove that he was capable of getting the job done if he were given the opportunity of refinancing the Titans.

Despite the fact that Harry had three outstanding lawyers representing him, the court ruled against him, forcing him into a sale. That meant the Titans were up for auction, and there was only one bidder—Sonny Werblin. But by then Sonny had reduced his offer to $1,000,000, which meant Harry lost $350,000 by not going along with the original sale.

You read and hear all the time what bad guys professional club owners are. Well, this is how vicious they were. Harry was flat on his back financially, so they decided to forgive his debt on the money they'd put in to bail him out. The league held approximately $350,000 in private stock holdings (held for security in other companies), which the club owners, unanimously, instructed me to return to Wismer.

Werblin's assumption of leadership over the New York team, which he renamed the Jets after the sale in the spring of 1963, provided tremendous relief to me. Freed from constant worry about New York, I could concentrate on other areas, such as Oakland and Kansas City, the only other teams that weren't yet in the black.

During our third year of play many of the previously critical onlookers began to concede that the AFL would not fail at any moment, and season ticket sales rose thirty-five percent over the previous year. Our antitrust lawsuit against the NFL still pended, but it no longer made headlines. Nothing really depended on its outcome, but the suit did serve to keep the NFL from further direct attacks on our territory.

Sam Blair reflected the growing air of acceptance when he wrote in the *Sporting News:* "This is the year of maturity for the American Football League, and Joe Foss is delighted to see that the crowds are growing along with the players. The greatest champion of equality since Abe Lincoln, the commissioner happily watched the three-year-old pro league reach new peaks in balance and popularity during the first two weeks of its regular season. This, he'll quickly tell you, could be the start of something big."

Chapter 26

Elephants
at Twenty Paces

In truth, 1962 and 1963 were big years for me as well as for the league. Perhaps a better adjective would be eventful. First of all, they brought some endings and beginnings in my personal life.

In the fall of 1962, my mother died at age seventy-nine, and I suddenly became the oldest member of the family. That's a strange feeling. Not only the final cutting of parental ties, but also passing on to the position of being the oldest generation in the family.

Then, just a few months before Mother died, I met someone who would play a major role in the rest of my life.

Back when I was still in the South Dakota legislature, a friend of mine, a senior officer in the reserves, was killed while flying a jet because he forgot to shift tanks and ran out of gas. It was an accident that shouldn't have happened, but I began reading about others dying in similar incidents. So I went to General Charlie Meyers, the four-star general who was head of Training Command for the U.S. Air Force, and recommended that senior officers get thoroughly checked out in jets. But not the kind of checks we got in the old reciprocating engines. The check in the early days, especially during World War II, was just like driving a car. Someone would point you toward an aircraft and say, "There it is. Here are the keys."

The more senior they got, the more hesitant some men became about asking for instructions. They didn't want to be classified as dummies. As a result, some of them got in big trouble and ended up deader than a doornail.

After our discussion, General Meyers set up a six-week jet training program for senior officers, and in July 1951 I had gone to Williams Air Force Base in Chandler, Arizona, to go through it. It wasn't long before I figured that anybody who lives in Arizona in July hasn't got the brains God gave a goose. Somebody checked the temperature one day, and it was 146 degrees on the blacktop runway. Despite the heat, I stayed there for six weeks, and it was during that time that I met Donna.

Donna co-managed the Kiva Club atop the Hotel Westward Ho in Phoenix. The Kiva Club was a private business and professional club operated by the Thunderbirds, a special events group of the Phoenix Chamber of Commerce, where they entertained visiting dignitaries from all over the world. Donna with her children, Coni and Dean, and her parents, Harry and Delia Wild, had originally come to the state temporarily to test the climate because of her father's arthritic condition. Donna loved Arizona and decided to stay, while her father and mother returned to their home in Michigan but continued to come out every winter.

As she tells it, one Saturday Evelyn Vodden (Carroll), a dear friend, called and said, "Donna, I've got the neatest guy I want you to meet."

"Thanks, but no thanks," was her response.

Then Evelyn told Donna that she had never met the guy (me), a visiting pilot, but that she and her friend needed to take him to dinner and would like her to help entertain him. Finally Donna agreed, with the stipulation, "I'll drive my own car so I'll be free to leave when I choose."

The two of us hit it off immediately, and I saw Donna several times during that training stint in Arizona. She had been divorced for many years and was raising her children alone—her daughter, Coni, then twelve, and her son, Dean, ten. In fact, our lighthearted friendship might have developed into something more serious except that I was still married. I was separated from June, but when Donna, a committed

309

Christian, learned that I was married, she declined to see me again.

Over ten years later, in June 1962, I was attending an Air Force Association gathering in Colorado Springs when I spotted Donna in the lobby of the Broadmoor Hotel, where our meetings were being held. I had not seen her since 1951, but I recognized her immediately. Surprised and pleased, I hailed her, and learned that she was in the area visiting Dean, who was now in the Army and assigned to Fort Carson.

I asked Donna to have dinner with me, and that evening we caught up on the events of the past few years. I soon discovered that I was still strongly attracted to this talented, outgoing, positive, and warm woman. The attraction must have been somewhat mutual, because she agreed to spend the next day with me. We went sightseeing, exploring Pikes Peak and other local attractions. By the end of the day, the two of us agreed that we wanted to see each other again.

While I still was not divorced from June, we had been separated for years. Given that situation, this time Donna agreed to continue our friendship. During the next five years we developed what she has described as a "long-distance courtship." She was living in Arizona and Iowa and I was in New York, where we had moved the AFL office—when I wasn't traveling around the country—but we saw each other whenever we could.

However, the changes in my personal life were not the only things that made 1962 and 1963 eventful.

In 1962 I also came very close to getting back into the political arena. The day after Senator Francis Case of South Dakota died, I was walking across the lobby of the Statler Hilton in Buffalo, New York, when they paged me. It was a call from Governor Archie Gubbrud of South Dakota.

"Joe, are you aware that Francis Case died yesterday?" he asked.

"Yes, sir," I said.

"Well, I want to appoint you to take his place as U.S. senator. How about it?"

I said I couldn't give an answer at the moment because I was working under contract, but I would discuss it with my employers and get back to him. I took the rest of that day and the next to think about it and to contact all the owners. All of them said they were willing to release me and thought it was an honor that I'd been asked. So I contacted the governor and said, "Okay, appoint me."

"Well, Joe, I can't do it now. Everyone is after the job. But I know you'll get elected if you put your name in and say you want the job."

Archie was a kindhearted guy who didn't want any ripples in the water. He said he'd turn it over to the Republican State Committee and they'd vote on it. So I put my name in the ring and went to the convention a month later at Pierre. I led the balloting for seventeen ballots, finally lacking only one vote. Someone was holding out, not wanting me to get it. So I said, "Let's teach 'em to quit sucking eggs." I got my people together and said, "On the next ballot we'll give our votes to Joe Bottom from Rapid City and that will push him over the top." That's exactly what happened. Joe Bottom was elected on the next ballot. He went to Washington and did an outstanding job.

So I didn't go back into politics, but another event that year paved the way for a future career change.

Nearly every October since the end of the war I had gathered friends to enjoy an outing of superb pheasant hunting and camaraderie in my home state. As the years passed, the size of the group grew to a hundred, then to two hundred. While I was governor, the shoot took on official status and became known as the Joe Foss Pheasant Hunt.

Though the hunt helped promote South Dakota, it also served as an occasion for me to hunt with friends and people I admired. In the 1963 hunt we had General Jimmy Doolittle, Roy Rogers, General Curtis LeMay, Cy Porthouse, the co-owner of Pyramid Rubber and the Questar conglomerate, General "Doc" Struthers and his brother George, the vice president of Sears Roebuck and Company, along with a number of men from the television side of the football business, such as Tom Moore, the vice president of ABC, and Richard Kotis, owner and president of Arbogast Fishing Baits. Carl Burgess, Speaker of the House, and Joe Floyd, owner of

Whether in tuxedos or blue jeans, General Curtis LeMay
and I always had a good time together. Here I am still
commissioner of the American Football League and president
of the Air Force Association. We are attending the banquet at
the Annual Convention in Colorado Springs, June 1962.

KELO radio and television stations in Sioux Falls, and Mort
Hankin, owner of station KSOO in Sioux Falls, set up the
hunt.

It was the sort of South Dakota day that always lured me
back—a frosty morning warming into a crisp day filled with
sunshine in a bright blue sky. According to the law, we
couldn't begin shooting until noon, when we divided the hunters into groups of sixteen and headed out into the several
hundred acres of hunting grounds. Each group had a local
farmer or rancher as a guide.

As we loaded our shotguns and prepared to start our slow
walk through the rich cornfield, Tom Moore, fresh from the
streets of Manhattan, looked around and said, "Wouldn't it
be great if a guy could put something like this on television?"

"Well, that should be fairly simple," I said. "You're a big
dog with the network. Why don't you?"

Moore turned to Struthers, who spent millions on advertising for Sears, and asked, "Would you be interested?"

"Yeah," Struthers said thoughtfully. "I would."

Cy Porthouse also agreed that he would like to sponsor an outdoor sporting program.

The following morning Tom Moore asked me, "If I got a hunting show started, would you be interested in hosting it?"

"I certainly would," I responded enthusiastically, "provided we can start the show in the southern hemisphere during their winter and spring so it doesn't conflict with our AFL schedule."

Several days later an excited Moore called me from New York. "We're going to do it! We'll go to Africa next year in the off-season so it doesn't interfere with your football." This was the birth of ABC's *The American Sportsman.*

I was thrilled. Somebody was actually going to pay me to go hunting!

That spring of 1963, before Easter, I had another meeting with a U.S. president; this time it was John F. Kennedy. I had first met President Kennedy the year before, when Senator George McGovern and I accepted a torch from him to take back to South Dakota to launch a NAIA (National Association of Intercollegiate Athletics) track meet. This time our meeting came about when I presented the Easter Seals handicapped child to the president. After the ceremony, he told me to sit down and cleared everyone else from the room.

Jack Kennedy was a guy who really liked to talk, and the two of us had quite a lot in common, despite some political differences. For one thing, both of us were lifelong members of the National Rifle Association, and we both enjoyed hunting. Most of our conversation that day, however, centered on football. For nearly an hour, the president surprised me with his exhaustive knowledge of the AFL. He knew about the owners and all the controversies, and he knew how the individual teams were doing.

At one point he surprised me by saying, "Of course, you know that I have a flat right above Harry Wismer's at 277 Park Avenue in New York City?" From what he said, Wismer used to give him a bad time, too.

The press corps was parked outside the door, and after the meeting they wanted to grill me. They asked me what the

President John F. Kennedy entrusting the NAIA (National Association of Intercollegiate Athletics) torch to me to carry to Sioux Falls, South Dakota, to light the flame to set off the national track meet of 1962. Senator George McGovern is on the right. (Photo courtesy of National Archives, President's Press Office)

president and I were talking about. Were we talking football? I wouldn't give them any information. If the president wanted them to know, he would tell them.

Within months, President Kennedy was killed on that grim day in Dallas. Out of respect, I canceled all the AFL's games that weekend. Although I did this out of humanitarian motives, not for any publicity or personal gain, the decision to delay the season schedule was acclaimed.

Chicago columnist Warren Brown wrote: "The American Football League which has been sneered at by the NFL since its inception was in this 'what to do?' period the BIG league of professional football." The NFL schedule had proceeded as planned.

During that season, for the first time, the outcome of our AFL games consistently drew more attention than the owners' meetings. Though Pete Rozelle still refused to entertain the possibility of an interleague world series, many of the NFL owners accepted the allure of such a game and privately discussed the potential of a "super" bowl game. When asked about the matter on several occasions, Rozelle's response was, "We don't play with people who sue us."

By now I had worked out a contract with ABC, and in June of 1964 I left for Africa to begin filming as the host of the new television series *The American Sportsman*.

Compensation for my role in the five television shows we contracted for wasn't going to make me rich, but I had more important reasons for taking the job. As detractors and fans alike began to accept the American Football League's wildly improbable success, the greater part of my "impossible" task was nearing completion. Heading an organization with well over five hundred employees required considerable administrative and diplomatic skill, but I had put an excellent staff and procedures in place. Furthermore, several of the owners were ready to sell their teams and take their profits. The original old-boy camaraderie and dedication that had lured and challenged me was flagging as the league turned into a major money-making enterprise.

In 1964 Barron Hilton was about to sell the Chargers and was dealing with Walt Dickson from New Orleans, who wanted to purchase an AFL team. I called Barron and said, "You aren't going to leave me now. You said you would stay with me till the bitter end." When Hilton decided not to sell, Dickson tried to buy out Oakland. At that point I got hold of old Happy Valley and said, "You aren't going to sell. You told me you'd stay."

So Walt Dickson was out; he was the guy who later came up with the United States Football League. If the USFL had hired a powerful commissioner who would have told Trump or anybody else to shut up the first time they opened their mouths in public, they could have made it. But they were too busy criticizing each other and worrying about whether they could get into the NFL when they should have been concentrating on being a success. Having been through it, I knew they were going to come to a tough day. Chet Simmons, a guy who had been with me when we did the first *American*

Sportsman shows, was their commissioner. Maybe I should have called him and warned him.

On Guadalcanal when the American victory turned from the miraculous to the routine, I became restless and impatient; now the same thing was happening with football. I was losing the keen-edged thrill of piloting the wobbling AFL against seemingly hopeless odds. I suppose a lot of guys would have leaned back to enjoy the ride, but I was on the verge of boredom. The television series came at a good time.

I had been hunting animals and birds since I was a small boy, and had all kinds of hunting experience, so I felt well qualified to do the program. My father had started my brother and my sister and me as soon as we were big enough to carry a gun, teaching us all the safety procedures and good sportsmanship practices. Whether we were in the field hunting or out on a lake fishing, we were to respect property and people the way we should. As the years rolled on, hunting on my own or with others, I always abided by the safety doctrine Pop had drummed into me.

Some of my earliest hunting memories go back to when Cliff and I would go with Dad in the hayrack to get a load of hay. He'd say, "Let's take our guns along and we can get a few ducks." Down at the hayfield, a good four miles from the house, we'd load the hay and then tie the horses so they wouldn't run away when they heard the shooting. Then we'd tramp over to the cattails by the pond and see if there were any ducks. Pop would go one way around the pond, and Cliff and I the other. Once one of us had flushed the ducks off the pond, whoever was in the best shooting position got the first shot.

The longest trips I first made in my life involved hunting and fishing. Like the time we went a hundred and some miles north to Big Stone Lake on the Minnesota/South Dakota border. That time was especially memorable because Cliff and I ran the boat into a rock and deep-sixed all of Pop's fishing gear.

When I was in college, I would often take some of the guys pheasant or duck hunting. Then we'd clean the birds and cook them up for one of the fraternity or sorority houses.

Overseas during World War II, I found that one thing the

great percentage of the men dreamed about was getting back home after the war to do some hunting or fishing or just walking in the great outdoors. During my second tour of duty in the Pacific war zone I carried along various guns that had been awarded to me for giving speeches during the dancing bear act days. With this equipment some of the men and I would go out and shoot pigeons or jungle cocks, which were in plentiful supply. Fresh fowl made a welcome change from Spam, as did the wild goats we found on some of the islands. Our seabee brothers were happy to cook up and share in this feast.

After Duke Corning and I came back from the war, as I've already mentioned, we took a year off to hunt. Each year, from then on, we hunted elk and antelope and deer. Through the years I had met many true sportsmen and conservationists, fine people who were really the forefathers of the present conservationist movements.

With these years of varied hunting experiences behind me, I was confident I could do *The American Sportsman*. And although I had never hunted in Africa, where we began filming, I had read countless books by Robert Ruark and others who had been going to that continent for years, and I had listened to an old deer-hunting pal from the Black Hills, Ken Keller, spin tales about his trips to Africa. So when it came to the hunting, I figured I was in good shape. Filming it, of course, was another matter. But I viewed this strictly as a new chapter and challenge in my hunting career—trying to put the action on film.

Hosting a nationally televised series may sound glamorous, as well as relatively simple and safe, but I was forty-nine years old with no experience in show business. Also, we were experimenting, venturing into unknown territory by attempting to document a big game hunt with sound and film, so those involved on the business end of the production were by no means certain they were backing a winner. With a relative newcomer as a host and an untested format as a show, the sponsors—Liberty Mutual Insurance Company, American Airlines, Remington Arms, and Shakespeare Fishing Tackle —were holding their breath, unable to predict how well it would do in the ratings.

To add spice to the experience, elaborate arrangements were made to hunt dangerous, rogue animals—with additional uncertainty provided by the presence of "show biz." For the sake of drama, the director wanted the game shot at precise angles at very close range in the best possible lighting. Since wild animals don't read scripts too well, just about anything could go wrong.

Former national skeet shooting champion Robert Stack, better known as Elliot Ness of *The Untouchables* television series, was to be my first guest star. The renowned professional hunters, Bill Ryan and Terry Matthews, and the chief warden of Kenya, Ev Lynn Temple Borham, acted as our guides. Other personalities who accompanied the group without appearing on camera included Tom Moore, Vice President of ABC, Dick Griffith, an account executive for a New York advertising agency, and Roone Arledge, who would later head the ABC news department.

When we went out to the Campfire Club in New York to sight in our rifles, Bob Stack discovered that he had never fired the particular firearm we were to be using, a .458, which is a powerful gun used especially for elephant and Cape buffalo. Bob braced himself and fired at the target, and the heavy recoil on that baby just about blew him out of the sandbags. After a few shots he had an aching shoulder, but he figured that by the time he got over to Africa in a few weeks the soreness would be gone.

Actually, the entire safari nearly went wrong before it began. With our entourage of bearers, guides, and cameramen, we were ready to head out for the Kenyan ranch of film star and conservationist William Holden. At the last minute, however, renegade native Shiftas went on the warpath in the area, and we had to relocate our base camp to an area near the jungles of the Narok district and Lake Rudolph, about two hundred miles northwest of Nairobi. If our expedition had gone in a few weeks earlier—before or during the beginning of the uprising—the show might have had quite a different ending!

By the time Bob Stack and I flew out to the village of Ithong on the Mara River, the advance group had set up a beautiful camp on a side hill. It was cool at night, and hyenas, zebra, and all sorts of game roamed the area—including a five-foot-long cobra we found in one of the tents. The lions were so close that when they roared they rolled you over in your bunk.

Our first venture was to have Bob Stack shoot a lion that had been killing cattle in Masai territory and coming closer and closer to a village. The lion was old and had broken teeth, so it found cattle easier to kill and better tasting than the wild game. Old lions could be very dangerous and would sometimes attack and kill the villagers.

Bob shot the lion and we got it on film. Afterward, we rode back to camp, where the game warden informed us that the Masai chief, the head man of the village, wanted to meet Bob. In fact, everyone in the village wanted to see the hero who had shot the lion that was killing their cattle. They wanted to give him a celebration.

When we arrived at the village, the chief honored Bob by asking him to enter his hut. I said I'd wait outside, but both Bob and the chief insisted that I come, too.

When we crawled into the hut, which was shaped like a

Robert Stack sharing a very nice honor with me the evening I received the Los Angeles Philanthropic Outstanding American Award, 1980. (Photo by Donna Wild Foss)

loaf of bread and constructed of sticks and cow dung, we discovered there were no windows. It was darker than a black cat in a coal bin. Besides that, the air was thick and biting with smoke. Trying to get our eyes refocused in the dark and blinking away the burning from the stinging smoke, we couldn't see a blamed thing. Then old Bob went to sit down, and in the dark he ended up in the lap of one of the chief's wives. Bob jumped so high he hit his head on the top of the hut, which showered dirt and dung down on his always-neat hair.

Indicating that he would fix it so Bob could see better, the chief reached up and punched a hole in the roof with his staff. Along with the sun shining through the hole, we were now showered with more dust and dung and just about choked. We couldn't breathe but at least we could see.

We squatted down, and the game warden interpreted what the chief was telling us. The warden also explained that the chief had several wives, who slept on the skins that were lined up on one side of the hut. In the back was a cagelike structure where the chief slept with the wife he had chosen for the night.

All in all it was a great celebration as the villagers gave thanks to Bob and the crew for doing away with the lion that had been killing their cattle. Cattle were like gold to the Masai. They bartered with them, and a man's wealth was gauged by the number of cattle or sheep he owned.

Prior to the hunt, the closest Stack had been to a lion had been the circus. After returning to the States, he told a reporter, "You can take it from me, it's a lot different hearing one roar from behind a bush several feet away. Frankly my heart jumped right out of my skin. I felt like all my adrenaline had run out and I was living through a dream. Suddenly none of it seemed real. It was as though it was happening to someone else. It's similar to the feeling you have when you're playing a role in a movie."

The next stop on the expedition was an elephant hunt about thirty-six miles north, where we went after a big fellow who had been knocking down native huts and chasing villagers. When we finally spotted him, he came within fifty yards of us, but the breeze was in our favor, so he didn't wind us. We kept very still and watched as he and another elephant walked right by us. He had beautiful ivory that would have run about a hundred pounds on each side. That was the elephant I wanted, but at that moment the clouds were wrong and the camera angles weren't right!

About that time a runner came huffing up, wearing shorts and a buttoned-up army coat. He had run over thirty miles with news that an elephant was sitting on the watering hole of another village. "Sitting" meant the elephant was staying in one area and running everybody and everything off that came near. It was a big elephant, we were told, but they didn't mention the condition of the ivory. I wanted one with nice tusks. I figured I'd never get another shot at an elephant, and I wanted a good trophy.

We were up before light the next morning, driving overland—there were no roads—to the village where the elephant was terrorizing everybody. The entire village turned out to welcome us. It was a very poor village, just some huts in a flat area where the jungle was thick. They told us, through the game warden, where the elephant was.

E. B. (Ev Lynn Temple Borham) told us to set up our equipment so the elephant would smell us and come roaring out of the jungle, and the director said to me, "Now, Joe, let him get within twenty paces of the camera before you shoot."

We had just got set, with three cameras running, when suddenly an elephant trumpeted. He was probably 150 yards away, and I never realized an angry elephant could run that fast. There's no sight quite like an African elephant in full charge—his tail in the air, his ears straight out from his head, his trunk up, screaming as he comes. About then I started wondering about this twenty paces stuff!

The disappointing thing was that he had only one tusk. I felt like turning around and telling the guy who had recommended that I go after this elephant to shoot it himself. I wanted an elephant with decent ivory. But when the bull was what I thought was twenty paces, I squeezed one off with my .460 Weatherby.

The shot was perfect. The elephant made a quarter turn to

the left and bounced, dying instantly. And when I marked off the distance, it was exactly twenty-one paces.

The director was astonished that I'd followed directions so accurately, but several of the cameramen had been on the verge of running themselves when that old boy charged. Fortunately it all happened so fast that nobody really had time to do anything but shoot—gun and cameras. ABC used that picture showing the elephant charging full bore at the camera for a long time in the introduction to ABC sports programs.

My disappointment over the ragged trophy diminished considerably when the villagers began to celebrate the death of the animal that had threatened their lives and livelihood. And as they have done since the dawn of history, they made full use of the animal.

As soon as the elephant hit the ground, the villagers started hacking it up. The way they were swinging those machetes, I was afraid they would decapitate someone. Each person would take a square on top and cut right straight through the elephant to the ground. When they got the stomach cavity open on the high side, a pretty girl wearing just a *lava lava,* a piece of cloth around her middle, stepped inside and started cutting off pieces of entrails and handing them out of the hole. Soon another girl crawled inside, and they kept bobbing up with pieces of elephant to hand out to the waiting villagers. Some of my cameramen got a little ill watching this, but these people weren't about to waste anything.

After they had passed all the sections out and created a hole large enough, they took out the entire stomach like a big tub. Then the villagers gathered up ten or fifteen boys and girls and stripped them bare and bathed them in the gastric juices. After that, they covered them with the blood, all over, from head to foot. When the blood dried and shrank, it looked like their eyeballs were going to pop out.

We wanted to know what was going on, and they told us that these kids were sick and that this would cure them, though I don't know how it would cure anything. In just a matter of hours there wasn't a sign of that elephant.

I was particularly impressed by our two native trackers, Wareel and Konduki. If an animal had been in the grass a week before, they could tell you about it. They had eyes!

One day I accompanied the two trackers, along with the famous professional hunter Bill Ryan, to find food for the Moslems in camp. Barred by religious law from eating meat killed by others, they required live game they could kill themselves.

The trackers led us up over a hill to a herd of twenty or thirty impala. Every time I started to shoot, the Moslem who was with us to make the kill would raise his bent arm with a fist over his head and say, "No."

Finally I spotted an impala with one horn that came up about eighteen inches and made a right turn across its forehead. It was a strange-looking critter. When I pointed the animal out, the Moslem nodded and nodded.

When you're just trying to wound an animal, to get it down rather than making a clean, killing shot, it takes a little bit of study. Finally, when it turned sideways I squeezed one off and the bullet broke the impala's back. It fell down and began dragging itself along on its front two legs.

Immediately the Moslem ran with his scimitar and jumped on the animal. When he reached around to cut its throat, the impala threw its head back and hit the man with its horn. The blow threw the Moslem end over appetite, knocked off his fez, and slashed a deep cut in his forehead. But he got right back up, picked up his scimitar, and ran after the impala again. This time he almost cut off its head.

Back at camp the man lay down on the grass and somebody threw a bucket of water on his face to wash off the blood. Then Bill Ryan took out a needle and thread and stitched up his head. I thought the poor man would die of infection, but within a week he was up and around with only a bad scar to show for his mishap.

The African hunt continued, although Bob Stack was plagued with gun problems. On two occasions his safety fell off, and he couldn't get his gun to work. He tracked an eland for a long time and got a big old bull lined up, but couldn't get a shot off. The same thing happened with an elephant. He got up so close he could almost touch the animal, and then his gun wouldn't fire.

I bagged several other trophies for the camera on that hunt, including a renegade Cape buffalo that was threatening another village. The Cape buffalo is even more aggressive and dangerous than the elephant; in fact, it is the most dangerous animal you can go after.

Meanwhile, back in the States other sorts of hunters were taking aim at me, foremost among them Cleveland Amory. I was somewhat mystified by Amory's objections to the safari, since human hunters have always been an important part of the ecology. For example, that old elephant we killed died instantly and painlessly. If he had been left to die of natural causes, his death would have been slow and painful, and while he was dying he would have been threatening the lives of villagers and destroying their livelihood. Predators are predators, animal or human, and they are all vital in the ecological chain.

When bans on elephant hunting were enforced in Africa in 1976, whole herds died from overpopulation and starvation. And, as always happens when proper management and legal hunting are outlawed, only the outlaws had free range. The poachers went to work and shot everything in sight in their greed for ivory. It was disgraceful. Proper herd management requires hunters, but some people don't want hunters to pay for the right. The so-called animal rights people would rather pay a game warden to cull excess animals—and, of course, some of them are so radical they don't even want that. If some people had their way the animals would inherit the earth and the human beings would be extinct. It's peculiar, if not downright sinister and sick. They worship animal life.

Hunters bring economic value to underdeveloped habitat, making it profitable to leave the wild in its natural state. Destruction of habitat and poaching are the real threats to animal life. Real hunters care more for the herds than anybody else. Hunters also contribute millions of dollars to American habitat every year. Bans on hunting destroy much of the economic value of wild habitat, making it far more difficult to justify preservation efforts in a world where people die of starvation every day. In Third World countries, pressures to exploit those lands are often overwhelming.

This conservationist message filled the documentaries we made, calling attention to the need to preserve the world's habitats long before antihunting environmentalists jumped on the bandwagon.

Before closing our filming season, we had fished for tuna off Bimini with Bill Carpenter, one of the owners of the Philadelphia Phillies, and hunted for pheasant in South Dakota with Bob Stack and General Jimmy Doolittle. When we decided to wrap up, we had a lot of film in the can for the editing room.

Chapter 27
Moving On

Cleveland Amory wasn't the only faultfinding voice. Although the AFL was doing far better than many had expected by that spring of 1964, with gate receipts up yet again and my negotiations with NBC for a five-year, $36 million television rights contract being finalized—a deal that bested the NFL's broadcast income significantly and at that time was the largest television contract to date—some of the owners voiced dissatisfaction over my absence from the league offices during filming. They voiced their discontent to sportswriters, who immediately echoed this carping in the sports pages.

At the 1964 owners' meeting, the team owners asked me how much the AFL owed the Music Corporation of America.

"Nothing," I said. "They didn't negotiate the deal with NBC. I did."

The men couldn't believe that MCA had no claim on their contract. It was "standard" that MCA would get a cut of all television contracts.

I smiled and explained that from the very beginning I had gone out of my way to see that the AFL was free of future commission fees of this kind, except in deals with ABC. The owners refused to believe that we owed nothing.

"City slickers" underestimated me more than once, possibly because of my indifference to what other people thought of me. Long before the jogging craze hit the country, I ran to work in a business suit on New York City sidewalks after our AFL office was moved there in June 1963, and my jaunty white cowboy hat was as out of place in Manhattan as an old pickup truck filled with hay bales.

Exasperated over their skepticism toward my assurances that I had out-negotiated the country's foremost negotiators, earning over $3.6 million in bonus revenues for the league, I finally told the assembled group, "I'm going to jump on an airplane and talk to Lew Wasserman. He's an honorable man, and he'll back me up."

That evening I checked into the Beverly Hilton, and the next morning I was having breakfast in the hotel dining room with Lew, president and CEO of MCA.

We talked politics for a bit. Lew was a vocal Democrat, and we had a good time ribbing each other. Finally, as we finished our meal, I asked, "I don't owe you a thing, do I?"

"That's right," Lew agreed.

"Would you do me a favor and put it in writing?" I asked.

Wasserman readily agreed, and the two of us called for a hotel stenographer. Lew signed a letter clarifying and verifying the situation, and I flew back to New York with the proof that I had earned the league over twenty times the amount they had paid me in salaries.

Afterward a hunting buddy of mine commented, "You must have got a big bonus for that little maneuver."

"Yeah," I said. "Two boxes of cigars, the finest available —one from Ralph Wilson and one from Barron Hilton. And an encouraging, thoughtful letter from Lamar Hunt."

The AFL's lucrative television contract brought new prestige to the league, as well as over twenty new requests for franchises and several offers to buy existing teams. That year I estimated that the weakest team in the league would sell for at least $9,000,000.

As the season drew to a close, we prepared for our All-Star game scheduled for January 16, 1965, in New Orleans. It was an important game for several reasons.

New Orleans was one of a number of cities expressing interest in AFL franchises. Contrary to the wishes of a majority of the team owners, who preferred to wait until the league was more profitable, I was urging expansion. They figured

Jack Kemp has remained a good friend since our days together in the American Football League, where, he claims, I sold him for a hundred bucks. (Photo courtesy of National Rifle Association)

additional teams might dilute their earnings. A successful All-Star game in New Orleans would help me make the case that we should expand before the NFL made a move on the South.

Only a week before the game, however, things went seriously sour, and a group of twenty-one black players training for the game in New Orleans contacted me with unsettling news.

My relationship with the players had always been excellent, and I got along particularly well with the head of the players' union, young Jack Kemp, whom I encouraged to take up politics after his football career. Jack, of course, was Secretary of HUD (Housing and Urban Development) during the Bush administration, and he still refers to me as "Joe Foss, my friend who sold me for a hundred dollars."

What happened was that Jack, who was with the Chargers, had broken the middle finger on his right hand and had to be pulled off the squad. Not wanting to lose him, Sid Gillman, the coach, tried to hide him so he was not listed on the official squad. When we found out at the league office, we said they had to put Kemp up for any team that wanted him. The Broncos, the Dallas Texans, and the Buffalo Bills tried to claim him, but I felt the Bills needed a promising young quarterback, so I awarded him to them—for one hundred dollars! And Kemp brought them a championship.

I regularly toured the training camps to be sure the players knew what the league expected of them. We couldn't afford a scandal of any sort, and in those days gambling scandals were the most common. So I made a practice of handing out copies of the rules to all the players and owners personally. I talked turkey to those guys, just like they were my own sons. Ernie Ladd said, "I learned more about living from you, Commissioner, than I did from my own dear mother." In fact, today some of them still say to me, "Boy, you put it plain when you came around."

When I heard rumors that one player in the league was betting on AFL games, I went directly to the young man and confronted him. I caught him off guard, and he just stuttered.

"It would be best if you just wander off the scene," I told the man. "You can fight it, but then it will all come out."

The player retired, and a day later two tough guys approached me in the lobby of the hotel where I was staying. The one doing the talking sidled up, and after some discussion about this same player, the guy said, "He owes us money and he's not going to leave the game. If he does, you're going to be in more trouble than you've ever been in before."

I leaned back and glared at the hood. "You're probably the one who talked him into betting," I said.

"I'm going to cause a scene that will really hurt the AFL," the man threatened.

"You'll get the hard time," I countered, leaning in threateningly. "And you better not come crawling around me again. I ought to just mash you now."

The extortionist began to back up, and I walked after him. He was backing up, and I was mad. Then he threw out a lot of comments you wouldn't want to put in print and left in a run.

Even when I talk about this today, two and a half decades later, I never name the city where the episode took place. I told the player if he would resign he would be forgiven forever, so I've never wanted to leave a track that would lead to him.

Anyway, because of my straight shooting with the team members, the black players knew they could trust me when they called me from New Orleans. They were hurt and out-raged.

Taxi drivers and café owners were giving them a bad time. Cabbies would drive them out to the boondocks, take their money, and speed off leaving them stranded. Or they'd go into some café in the French Quarter, hang their coats up, and somebody would take them off the hook and throw them on the floor.

After they described what was happening, I said, "Handle it like gentlemen and don't hit anybody. I don't want you causing any trouble."

That's just what they did, but it didn't make any difference. The harassment continued. Finally I sent word, "We're moving." It was less than a week before the game, but there was no way I was going to have my players subjected to that kind of crap. I just said, "Adios," and moved the All-Star game to Houston.

The sportswriters were outraged and predicted that the AFL would soon have a new commissioner. "When you walk in there [the French Quarter] you're asking for trouble," wrote New York columnist Dick Young. "Bill McIntyre wrote that the long wanted playoff game between the two leagues would never happen because Joe's action proved that the AFL was 'not in the same league' as the NFL."

But my hometown paper, the *Daily Argus-Leader,* head-lined an editorial with the encouraging words, "Old Joe Comes Through."

That same month I clashed with college coaches over "redshirting," the practice of taking a college football player out of play for a year to extend his college career into a fifth season. This was particularly effective when a coach antici-pated a weak team in the coming season and wanted to assure that he'd have some proven players available.

Specifically, I had it out with Darrel Royal at the University of Texas when he held back George Sauer, who wanted to play pro ball. But other coaches were doing the same thing. I worked overtime to make sure my people didn't approach college players until after their last games, but the college coaches weren't living up to their side of the deal. I told them they were sticking it to the taxpayers by supporting these players for a fifth year; college wasn't a place to roost.

Actually, the timing of all this was significant. They didn't know it, but I was, in effect, cleaning out my desk. Four of the AFL club owners were in a sweat to join the NFL. Our relationship had been good, and I didn't want to destroy that. Also, I didn't want to battle with them. So I figured it was time for me to move on.

Less than a month later, after testifying in Washington about the ongoing antitrust question, I spoke at the Lynchburg Sports Club in Virginia and surprised the audience by announcing that I expected the two leagues to merge under one commissioner in the near future. Furthermore, I said, I was in favor of such a unification based on the baseball model, although I certainly did not expect to head up the combined leagues myself.

The next day one headline declared: "Foss Campaigns for Loss of His Lucrative Job." Ben Garlikov of the *Daily News* wrote: "Did you ever know of a man whose pay was about $50,000 per year, not including a virtually unlimited expense account, who publicly was campaigning to lose that job?"

I had said, "All the club owners in both leagues are practical businessmen, and they'll force a championship play-off, no matter what any commissioner thinks."

I stepped out on the limb even further when I predicted that an AFL-NFL play-off game would be played by 1967. "I've said for years that the two leagues would play someday, and it now appears the play-off will take place in 1967 or at the end of the 1966 season."[1]

The first segment of *The American Sportsman* aired a few days after the New Orleans cancellation hit the fan. Our ratings were excellent, and the network began planning for a second series for the following year. The attention I focused on the league through these groundbreaking sporting documentaries with the growing "sports network"—ABC—was

---

[1] Quoted by Newton Spencer, sportswriter, *The News*, Lynchburg, Virginia, 2/17/65.

worth more than anything I could have done sitting behind a desk in New York. Yet my visibility only fueled the complaints of those who thought I should dedicate myself exclusively to the AFL. I could even make the case that I deserved overtime pay for the public relations duties I performed during these "vacations." It never ever occurred to me to ask for such, but I certainly didn't appreciate the carping critics. As the nitpicking grew, so did my frustration.

We filmed the second season of *The American Sportsman* in early 1965 in India. The highlight that year was a hunt for tiger and Sambar stag, with Craig Stevens, television's Peter Gunn, as our guest hunter.

We were northwest of New Delhi, about eight hours by train, at a place called Kota near the Pakistani border. The heat was horrendous, 115 to 132 degrees every day. It was so hot that when we hooked a fish in deep water, it died when it came to the surface water because of the extreme temperature change.

Our filming took a month, and while we were there we got the royal treatment as guests of the Maharajah of Bundi, who

A hot day in the hills of India, near Kota, with the Maharaja of Bundi and actor and sportsman Craig Stevens, filming ABC's *American Sportsman*, 1962. (Photo by Robert Halmi)

had won the Victoria Cross in World War II with the Bengal Lancers. While the Maharajah's son was studying for a job with the Hilton Hotels, the appearance of the Maharajah himself still inspired instant obeisance within his 70,000-plus square mile domain—the size of South Dakota. When his sacred gold turban and the flags on his homemade jeep came into sight, the people would stop whatever they were doing, kneel, and touch their foreheads to the ground.

Back home, on March 2, Joe Robbie, whom I'd known since my college days but hadn't seen for several years, appeared with Sullivan Barnes, who had retired from his role as AFL legal counsel and gone into land development in Denver, Colorado. They had heard there was going to be an AFL expansion and wanted to apply for a franchise in Philadelphia.

"You might as well forget Philadelphia." I laughed. "Philadelphia already has an NFL franchise, and that one isn't doing too good. And right now the stadium is tied up in litigation because of the exclusive NFL lease for the Philadelphia Eagles. It will be several years before that area will open up as far as the AFL is concerned."

Knowing that the combined wealth of Robbie and Barnes at that time was a negative, I asked, "Who's putting up the money for this deal?"

"A friend and some people in Miami who have other interests in Philadelphia." Then they asked, "Where would you go if you wanted a new franchise? What about New Orleans?"

I knew that the NFL was dealing to get into New Orleans, and I didn't want a repeat of the experience we'd had in Atlanta. There we were used as a pry bar in negotiations between the city of Atlanta and the NFL, so they could get a better deal—and where, of course, we got the stub end of the stick.

"Why don't you put a franchise in Miami. That's the best open territory in America for another professional franchise." This was before Atlanta and New Orleans had franchises, and the common wisdom across the country was that those two cities were better prospects for a new franchise than Miami. I thought otherwise.

Years later, Robbie would say, "Joe, you told me what

nobody else had ever said prior to that, and you were absolutely right. You were the most instrumental man in America in bringing pro football to Miami and in steering me there. In fact, you were the one who really got me into pro football."

"How would we go about setting this up?" Barnes and Robbie asked.

"First, you go down there and look up the mayor," I said. "His name is Robert King High, and he's a very capable individual who would be happy to get some publicity at this time—I just saw in *Time* magazine where he's gonna run for governor. Go down and see what he thinks about it and check about getting a facility. Maybe the Orange Bowl. That's the best one there. See what you can do."

Within a few days I received a call from Barnes and Robbie, indicating that they had seen the mayor of Miami and that he would be calling me shortly. They'd hardly hung up when the mayor was on the line, asking, "Commissioner, do you know these two gents who are down here? Are they for real?"

"Oh, yeah, they're for real," I said. "I've known them since college days."

A few days later Robbie and Barnes let me know that they had things cooking as far as the Orange Bowl was concerned.

About that time we had a league meeting coming up in New Jersey, and there were a lot of comments in the newspapers about the fact that we were holding a football meeting at Monmouth racetrack, where they had betting. The sportswriters had fun knocking home runs off our heads for that. The truth was, we were having our meeting there because Sonny Werblin and Phil Islan, two of the owners of the New York Jets, were involved with that track and had invited us to have our meeting there on the house.

With all this coverage in the press, of course, our meeting was no secret, and the next thing I knew I got a call from Robert King High wanting to know if he could attend.

"I want to bring the director of the Orange Bowl with me," he said. "We'd like to get a franchise here in Miami."

"Sure, come on up," I said.

The night before the meeting we had a reception and dinner to which I invited the two gentlemen from Miami, and during the course of the evening they had a great time with all the owners. The next day we had meetings in the morning, and when I recessed for the noon luncheon I said, "The first thing we're going to do after lunch is have a presentation by the mayor of Miami and the director of the Orange Bowl."

Some of the owners immediately piped up, "Why? We're not thinking of moving to Miami right now."

"Well, since the day we started we've been talking about expansion," I said, "and this is a good chance."

"Miami's a retirement area," someone said. "People down there won't be interested in pro football."

"Well, they've got a presentation," I said, "and we'll have it at two o'clock."

The men from Miami gave such an enthusiastic presentation that after they left I said, "Do you want to vote on this thing now?"

Someone moved that we vote on it, and it was decided right then and there that we were going to have an expansion franchise in Miami.

Legally we had to give notice that we would hold a meeting to award a franchise in the allocated city, so I immediately announced the date of that meeting at the Waldorf-Astoria in New York City. About seven different groups wanted the franchise, including Robbie and Barnes.

When the day came to award the franchise, the groups drew numbers to establish their order of presentation. We started at noon and went to six o'clock, then I recessed until eight o'clock that evening.

Robbie and Barnes had drawn one of the last slots, and just before the opening of the eight o'clock meeting they came up to me and asked, "Do you have any last-minute advice for us?"

"Yes, I do," I said. "You guys are both lawyers, and you have a tendency to talk too long and explain too much. Why don't you just make a fast presentation on this and say, 'Are there any questions?' Short and to the point."

When their turn came, that's exactly what they did, and of course Sonny Werblin's first question was, "Where's the money coming from that's going to handle this franchise?"

"From Danny Thomas," said Robbie.

Sonny exclaimed, "Danny Thomas! You mean the actor?

The comedian? I've known him since I put him to work. Hired him out of a nightclub in Indiana. He's a good friend of mine, a real capable man." Sonny couldn't say enough good things about his friend Danny. Then he wanted to know how Robbie knew Thomas.

"I've worked with him at St. Jude's," Robbie said. "I'm counsel for St. Jude's and a member of the board and have worked very closely with Danny. We're good friends."

Later Robbie told me how Thomas's interest had come about. Shortly after his initial meeting with me about a franchise, Robbie happened to be talking to Danny about St. Jude's Hospital affairs—Robbie had been on the board of governors of the hospital since a year or two before they even dug the first spade of dirt to build it. He remembered that a couple years earlier Danny had arranged a shake-hands deal over the telephone to buy the Chicago White Sox. In fact, Robbie had been in Thomas's dressing room in the Sands Hotel in Las Vegas when Danny got word that the club had been bought out from under him. So Robbie told Thomas about the Miami deal, and Danny said, "Put my name on the franchise application."

Well, after Thomas's connection and interest were established, the owners asked a few more questions, and then another group made their franchise pitch. When all the presentations were finished, I asked the owners, "Are you ready to vote?"

"Sure," they said. And I believe it was Sonny Werblin who moved that we give the franchise to Danny Thomas, Robbie, and Barnes, and that was it.

The next day Robbie and Barnes showed up in my office.

"Commissioner," they said, "would you make a trip with us out to Los Angeles?"

"What for?" I asked.

"Well, we want to stop and visit with Danny Thomas."

"You mean you don't have this thing set up yet?" No, they didn't.

So we went to L.A., where we met with Danny and his manager in his downtown office. The first thing Danny did was pass out cigars for everyone, so the room was soon filled with smoke. It was evident that Danny was anxious to be involved with the franchise, but his manager did not want any part of it. "It's a bad business deal," he warned, complaining that the league was too new.

But Danny said, "I'll get my money in within thirty days." His initial investment was $100,000.

On August 16, 1965, the Miami Dolphins were awarded an AFL franchise. And the rest is history.

Joe Robbie deserves a lot of credit for making Miami what it is today. He had to fight all the way with finances. It was so close one time that the AFL owners figured they were going to be able to take the team over the next day. However, I had introduced Robbie to a Chicago banker who, as he attested over and over to my friends later, had a lot of faith in me and my vision for the league. He worked with Robbie to get the financing to buy out the other partners. Robbie was also fortunate in getting a great coach like Don Shula and forming a partnership that was a winner.

Looking back at the old clippings reminds me of how many of the well-known sportswriters carped about how we'd lost out getting a franchise in Atlanta and had to settle for a second-rate place like Miami and that it was my fault. How wrong those guys were! Miami turned out to be one of the top spots in the entire pro football circuit.

My contract with the AFL would have expired in 1967, but on April 17, 1966, I resigned, and Ralph Wilson, owner of the Buffalo Bills and league president, took over as acting commissioner.

In my letter of resignation I suggested to the executive committee that pro football should have a single commissioner.

"Professional football should be operated with one commissioner and two league presidents as is major league baseball," I said. "Those in pro football owe it to the general public to present it with an annual world series and an all-star classic."

I also cautioned against expansion of more than one team a year. "Taking in two cities at a time would drain the depths of the existing franchises and create an unnecessary player problem," I wrote, and I advised the committee to give my

successor constant assurance of public support and to keep
all internal league differences within the privacy of the conference room.

"I advise my successor to wear a thick skin," I added, "a
soft smile, and carry a sense of humor and determination to
do the job as you see best after you have weighed all sides
of each problem."

During my tenure the commissioner's office had often come
under fire from league owners, even though they publicly
denied it. I was no whiner, but I knew that a leader needed
support. Despite the constant rumors that I was merely a
figurehead and that the owners ran roughshod over me, I ran
the commissioner's office with an iron hand. If any owner got
out of line, he got fined. At times I wasn't very popular, but
I enforced the constitution and bylaws with coaches, owners,
players, and anybody else concerned.

When you're commissioner you either run the show or you
don't. If the owners had been running things, we'd have been
run out of business. Every once in a while they wanted to go
off on some rabbit trail that would have hurt the organization.
I always said that the important thing was to discuss the various ideas in our meetings and keep things behind closed
doors, disputes and otherwise, until we were ready to go
public.

Occasionally someone would talk out of turn to the press
"in confidence" or "off the record." Well, there is no such
thing with the press. Whatever you say, you're going to read
later.

At the time I announced my resignation, I told the press
that I was considering several offers—the press always made
it sound like I'd starve to death if I lost the job—but rumors
flew hot and heavy that I was resigning to return to politics.
"I may be interested in politics when I'm a little older," I
told them. "Of course that could be tomorrow!"

On June 8, 1966, the NFL and AFL agreed to form a
combined league of twenty-four teams under the title the
National Football League, and Pete Rozelle was named
league commissioner. The first Super Bowl was played in
January 1967, between the Green Bay Packers and the Kansas
City Chiefs.

I had always maintained that if the league would stick together, through good times and bad, even when they were
losing money, we could build something great, and we did.
As far as some of the troubled times we'd been through—
well, dwelling on that would be like barking at a truck that
went by yesterday. As a result, I built some friendships that
have lasted a lifetime with people like Pete Rozelle, NFL
coach Tom Landry, owners such as the Rooneys, George
Halas, the Mara family, Tex Schram, Rankin Smith, Clint
Murchison—and various network people.

One thing I did want to do before I left was see that everybody would be taken care of, so I worked on a retirement
plan and had my people working on it—a plan that would
include the players, the coaches and assistant coaches, and
the rest of the crew. The only person who got left out of the
retirement plan was me, which was fine. I wasn't interested
in setting up anything for myself because I didn't want to be
accused of feathering my own nest. When I resigned, they
gave me a few bucks and that was it. In fact, after I left the
league I even bought my own Super Bowl tickets, with the
exception of those we received from Joe Robbie for the Miami
Dolphins' games. Also, Pete Rozelle did let me buy my tickets
through the commissioner's office.

I truly enjoyed every day that I was commissioner. The
occasional nitpicking never worried me. I always put things
in a life-or-death perspective, and when you do that, the little
arguments don't amount to much. I never stayed awake nights
about anything. People said I was an optimistic nut because
I was always saying, from the beginning, that we could make
it. We did.

Chapter 28
Arsenic
and Cornstalks

I stayed with *The American Sportsman* for three years. The last show I participated in was a trophy elk hunt, and my guest was my old sidekick and business partner, Major General Duke Corning. When we got to our filming location in the wild and beautiful backcountry of the majestic, awesome Tetons in Wyoming, the crew and the director decided they wanted the creature comforts and nightlife of Jackson Hole. So they drove the twenty miles into town every night, while Duke and the guide and I camped at the filming site. Then they'd roll back into camp about nine o'clock in the morning.

The October weather was picture-postcard beautiful. The trees a riot of oranges and reds, with some shades of green still clinging on, set against the snow-covered Grand Teton and the Teton mountain range. The temperature warmed to the fifties during the day and dropped to thirty at night. The setting was perfect, but after about ten days all we had were some great shots of the countryside, miscellaneous wildlife, and smaller elk and deer, which we weren't hunting.

The camera and sound crew had set up in low brush in a semiclearing adjacent to a forested area where, hopefully, the elk would come out to the clearing to graze. Finally, Duke managed to rally some action with his expert calling.

Before he began calling the elk, Duke cautioned the camera crew, "If something's going to happen, it will happen quick.

My dear friend and business partner, General Duke Corning.
We are at the United States Air National Guard Camp,
Oscoda, Michigan, 1963. (Photo by Gordon Edman)

You want to get everything set and be ready because they'll
be here in a flash and then they'll be gone."

Well, two good-size bulls came out of the woods, and Duke
shot one of them, a big six-pointer. But the cameramen
weren't ready. We did get the sequence in the can, but it
didn't show to advantage. When you photograph wildlife you
don't have all day to get ready. It's just like shooting your
gun; if you aren't ready, you've just missed.

Freddy Gaudet, the director, said, "What are we going to
do now? You haven't got your elk yet, Joe, and it doesn't
look like you're going to get one."

"No, I don't think I will."

"We're running out of time," he said. "In fact, we're out
of time. We have another show coming up."

"Don't worry, we've got plenty," I said. "We've got everything we need. Our guest did get a trophy elk and a dandy.
And we've got all the other little things that go into a hunt."

"Well, you tell me how you think we can end this thing so it will amount to something," Freddy said.

"It's real simple," I said. "I'll go down there on the point by Jackson Lake and I'll be cooking coffee. You have the packtrain come by with Duke and the guides, and Duke can say, 'Hey, Joe, what are you doing there?' and I'll say, 'I'm fixing coffee. I figure we need a little before we finish our trip down the trail. It's a long ride out of here.' And Duke will say, 'I'm sure sorry you didn't get your trophy elk,' and I'll say, 'Well, that can happen to anyone when they're hunting. You don't always just go out there and get game. You go out and get all of the side things and have a good time. Just the scenery alone is worth the trip. Look up there at that snow blowing off the ridge. I think it's time to get out of here.' And Duke can say, 'Well, if you're happy with that, so am I.' And I'll say, 'Yep, this is a typical hunting trip. And it gives us an excuse to put in for a permit next year, and maybe then it will be my turn.' "

"What makes you think the boss will buy that?" asked Freddy, referring to Tom Moore, who was now president of ABC.

"Because he's a hunter!" I said.

Interestingly enough, we got better ratings with that show than just about any other because it was so true to life. But that was the last one I did with the ABC crew.

Basically, I left *The American Sportsman* because the writers were scripting things I didn't agree with about the hunting scene; they wanted me to imply that hunters were bad guys. Well, I'm a born hunter, and I believe that game management has to be carried out responsibly and that that is done by sportsmen. So that's the first place we didn't mesh too well. The second was that the writers really knew nothing about the great outdoors and hunting; they were more familiar with dog tracks and horse races and professional sports.

Win Mergott, vice president of Liberty Mutual Insurance Company, and his peers realized my feelings and contacted me to ask if I would be interested in forming a production company to film a weekly syndicated television show, to be called *The Outdoorsman: Joe Foss*.

In August 1966 Bob Halmi, Donna Hall, and I formed Foss-Halmi, Inc., with offices in New York City.

Donna, whom I had nicknamed Didi, and I had been dating for several years. Since I was now divorced, we had talked about marriage, but hadn't gotten around to doing anything about it. However, with her excellent management skills, Didi had begun helping me schedule my time and served as the administrative brains behind Foss-Halmi, Inc. She was also a talented photographer in her own right and worked as the still photographer on location.

Mark Dichter was our primary sound man. Mark, who was a young professor of sound at Columbia University when we hired him, had never been out of New York City.

Bob Halmi, a fiery Hungarian, had taken game pictures all over the world. Bob was one of the pioneers in action photography, and his pictorial coverage of the outdoors in *True* magazine had long been outstanding. As Roger Fawcett, the publisher, said, "Bob is the sort of guy who'd drive a burning car into a lake and take pictures inside as the water rushed in."

We all loved our jobs and shared many wonderful experiences during the nine years that *The Outdoorsman* ran. During that time we went after elk in the Gros Ventre River country of northwestern Wyoming and went waterfowling at Remington Farms on Maryland's eastern shore; we fished for tarpon in the Florida Keys, stalked mountain lions in the Green River country of east-central Utah, and tracked Rocky Mountain goats in British Columbia, Northwest Territories of Canada; we trekked out on exotic safaris for aoudad, eland, and Indian blackbuck in the middle of Texas at Charles Schreiner III's Y O Ranch, traveled to Alaska and the Bering Strait for brown bear and walrus, and hunted Scotland for grouse and red stag. We also went to places like Amwell, New Jersey, for the Duck Shooting Championship of America, started by big band leader Paul Whiteman, who was a great shooter; and we went goat hunting and quail shooting on Catalina Island with my guest Willie Mays, the great Giants baseball player and a wonderful gentleman.

One of the first shows we did was on the American bison, and we shot it at Custer State Park in South Dakota. We had

This is the day Willie Mays's gun blew up while we were quail hunting on Catalina Island, 1968. (Photo by Robert Halmi)

an excellent guide, Ben Black Elk, a Sioux. Ben and I had been friends for years. He had traveled with me when I was governor and we would go to sports shows around the country, advertising tourism in South Dakota. In the summer months, Ben often spent time at Mount Rushmore, letting visitors photograph him in his full regalia as he told them tales of the Sioux. Ben's lovely wife, Alice, always traveled with him.

For our *Outdoorsman* show, Ben told stories about the buffalo and how important they were to the Indian nations. While we were filming, a lot of folks would come up and call him "Chief." Ben was a very humble man, and he would always say, "I'm no chief. It was my father who was chief. I'm just a brave trying to help my people."

The great bison story made a good show. Not long after that, however, in the fall of 1966, after we had begun filming for the first season, I nearly went down for the count.

When the grim reaper finally caught up with me, it wasn't a Zero, or a plane crash, or even a charging elephant. It was a cornstalk, like the kind I used to plant and cultivate and harvest back in South Dakota.

We were filming a segment of the *Outdoorsman* series on upland game birds, and between takes during our usual seven-to nine-day-shoot I was chewing cornstalks in the Nebraska cornfield, a habit from my old farm days. When the camera started rolling, I'd spit out the stalk and swallow the juice. What I didn't know was that the farmer had recently sprayed for corn borer with an arsenic-based poison. It hadn't rained, so I got the full benefit of the poison collected in the joints of the cornstalk.

By the time we finished filming, I felt like I had a bad case of the flu. I ached all over. When I got to Arizona, I went to see Dr. Josef Gerster, who gave me a complete physical and declared, "There's nothing wrong with you, Joe. You've got the constitution of a twenty-one-year-old." The second opinion, from Dr. Richard McMillan, was, "You've got the constitution of a seventeen-year-old." Either I was getting younger, or someone didn't have their marble collection in order. The docs were reaching in both ends and shaking hands in the middle and were still not able to determine what was wrong with me. Later we would learn that with arsenic poisoning you usually find it out by accident, if you find it at all.

One of the doctors said, "I think the problem is you're thinking too much about yourself." Well, I guarantee you I was. I was down to 150 pounds and was ready to die. But we had more shows coming up, so I headed off to do a segment on mountain lions. They had to tie me on my horse because I'd lost the strength in my legs. By the time that show was over I could not even undress myself, and I was losing the use of my arms and my legs as well as my sense of taste.

When we discussed where I should go next for medical treatment, Didi wanted to take me to the Mayo Clinic in Rochester, Minnesota. I wanted to go to a chiropractic clinic near Pittsburgh. So we compromised and went where I wanted to go!

I spent a couple weeks in the Pittsburgh clinic, but they couldn't figure out what was wrong with me either. Didi and I spent our first Thanksgiving together that year at the clinic, sharing the day with the medical staff.

Then I made Didi carry me off to do another show so we wouldn't get canceled. This time we were filming migratory waterfowl in Maryland, and I could barely get my arms up to shoot the old 12 gauge. When I did shoot, it blew me over backward. The crew finally rigged up a cable covered with cornstalks. This blended into the habitat, and I could hang onto it for support while I shot. I ached all over, but we got some great film.

After we completed that segment, I headed west to the Mayo Clinic, with Didi pushing me in a wheelchair, to spend another holiday with medical technicians. I was there for two weeks, over Christmas, and another committee of doctors still couldn't find out what was wrong with me, other than that they thought I'd gotten a heavy dose of poison of some kind.

Then the film crew viewing the dailies of our Nebraska shoot noticed I was chewing on the cornstalks, and with that information we figured out what had happened.

So poor Didi towed me out of there and back to Arizona to recover. The doctors at Mayo had said, "We think you're going to live," but I figured maybe I was down to the one-yard line and the Grim Reaper was going to score.

All this time Didi had been praying for me—not only for my body, but for my soul. And with the end of the game in sight, she finally got me to go with her to a little church in Scottsdale. During the sermon Pastor James Borrer told us that we must be "born again" and have a "personal relationship with Jesus Christ," all of which meant nothing to me. I always thought Christians were nuts. I believed in God and figured Jesus was the Son of God and that was about as far as it went. My mother had taught me the Lord's Prayer, which had seen me through Guadalcanal and which I prayed every night. But I'd get hot under the collar when church folks preached about social and political topics and I'd challenge them on everything, making me about as popular as a flea collar at a pest circus.

Then Pastor Borrer started talking about some guy named Nicodemus in the New Testament who came to Jesus and asked how he could be "born again," and the reverend asked all of us to consider doing the same thing. Well, I didn't know whether I wanted to get involved in this or not, but I figured, "Foss, you don't have much to trade in."

Considering the shape I was in, I realized I wasn't immortal and could cash in at any time. So I quickly prayed, "Lord Jesus, forgive me of my sins. Come into my life and have me say and do what you want me to."

I didn't do much to follow up on my prayer, although I began going to church with Didi, and I listened. But I really didn't want to discuss religion myself. While I was recuperating, I stayed at the Casa Verde Lodge, a resort hotel that happened to be directly across the street from the Presbyterian Church and Scottsdale Bible Church—which seemed like some kind of omen to me. Didi and her granddaughter Shelly were living in a casita at the same resort. They lived in Scottsdale during the school year so Shelly could be near her father, Dean, who was a student at Northern Arizona University.

I recovered from the effects of the poisoning, although it took about a year before I was completely back to normal. Early in 1967, however, we were back filming, and Didi and I finally decided to make time in our schedule to tie the knot. She has her own perspective on this:

Joe was beginning to feel better, and we were scheduled to film in Hawaii on the big island. We decided that would be a wonderful place for our wedding, so we began making plans. As always, we were under deadlines for the program. Getting the film in the can ruled our lives.

We had one afternoon left after the final shot, so we engaged Mokuaikaua Church and Pastor Henry Boshard for four o'clock, January 12, 1967.

Mokuaikaua Church in Kailua-Kona on the big island of Hawaii is the oldest Christian church in the islands, built in 1823. It is a charming stone and mortar edifice, with a white New England–style steeple. The surrounding grounds are beautifully landscaped with palms and flowering bushes.

Our precious friend Maggie Woods orchestrated the whole event for us. She even had the church decorated with hibiscus and orchids and fragrant mylie leaves,

Didi and I on our wedding day in Kailua-Kona, Hawaii, January 12, 1967. (Photo by Robert Halmi)

gathered from high in the mountains. It looked like paradise.

Everything about that day was perfect. I was confident that God was in control of my life, and I was so grateful that Joe was recovering and would be well again. I loved him and felt so blessed to become his wife.

My only regret was that our children couldn't be with us for this very special time in our lives. My daughter, Coni, was teaching in Des Moines, Iowa. My son, Dean, a veteran of the Korean conflict, was currently in his senior year at NAU. At that time I had not met Joe's children, but I knew that Cheryl June lived in Rockford, Illinois; Mary Joe was in Boston, Massachusetts; and Frank was in his senior year of high school in Sioux Falls, South Dakota.

Our friend Woodson K. Woods, who was Joe's guest on that particular *Outdoorsman* segment, owned the airline that serviced Kailua-Kona and had a ranch in the northern part of the island. There, Woody and Maggie graciously hosted a festive luau wedding reception, complete with roasted pig. Woody ferried all of the guests from Kailua-Kona to the magnificent setting high in the mountains of Mauna Kea in one of his planes.

Again, we felt like we had been set down in paradise. There were gorgeous flowers everywhere, birds of paradise, orchids, hibiscus, and the house itself was buried beneath blooming bougainvillea. When Joe and I arrived, a Hawaiian combo greeted us with "The Hawaiian Wedding Song." I knew that God was in his heaven—all was right with the world.

After we were married, Didi and I tried to involve our children and grandchildren in our lives whenever we could, even though we were spread all over the country. While we were filming, this meant taking them on location when possible.

Dean and Frank accompanied us on the expedition to the British Northwest Territories. Didi and the crew and I went on ahead to begin filming, while Frank and Dean flew in later with a bush pilot to join us. En route they ran into a front of severe snow squalls, forcing the pilot to land on a small, uncharted lake. While they waited for the weather to clear, the boys went fishing.

The area where they had landed was so isolated that not even the Eskimos had fished the lake. As a result, the waters had become overpopulated with fish, and the scarcity of food through the years had inbred some strange specimens. When the boys turned up late that night, after much anxiety on our part regarding their safety, they proudly displayed their trophies of lake trout, featuring the head of a twenty-pound fish on an eight-pound body.

Eight-year-old Shelly, Dean's daughter, was also with us on this trip, and that same day while she was running between our cabins and the community building, she encountered a Canadian black bear rummaging the area for food. Shelly and the bear went their separate ways, one probably as scared as the other. In the evening we all had lots of stories to tell about our day's experiences.

Charlie Schreiner's YO Ranch in the Texas hills north of San Antonio offered an ideal setting for another show. It was a beautiful place, well kept, and well stocked with wild game.

The YO, situated in a broad valley filled with scrub live oak, scattered cedar and cactus, rocky draws, and lots of good grass, could have been a scene from India or certain parts of Africa.

Hunting preserves like this have zoomed in popularity in recent years because civilization has moved in and taken over what was once wilderness. If it were not for such preserves, many animals would have no place to go—not only game animals, but our feathered friends such as pheasants and chukar partridge and quail. The owners and their guides do an outstanding job preserving the game and giving people who cannot travel long distances an opportunity to enjoy good shooting in the natural habitat.

It was during our show at the YO that Didi had her first instruction in shooting with a rifle. I often say that if someone in your family wants to learn to shoot, it's better to have someone else give the lesson—it's sort of like not teaching someone you love to drive. When people remark on how well Didi shoots, they often say, "You must have done a great job in teaching her, Joe." And I say, "No, I didn't have a thing to do with it."

A chap on the YO Ranch named Bobby Snow was the one who took Didi down to the range and showed her how to shoot the target. He started her with a low caliber rifle, a .22. Didi put her first shot and every one thereafter in the bull's-eye. Then Bobby moved her to a bigger caliber, a 6 mm rifle. This made more noise and kicked with more recoil, but once again Didi put every shot dead center.

After several rounds of that, Bobby said, "Now let's go out in the field and see how you do."

The first thing Didi spotted was a running target, an armadillo. No one figured she'd hit it; it was off at a range of a hundred and some yards. But she pulled up and, pow, no more armadillo.

That was the beginning of Didi's excellent marksmanship, proven time and time again. On a trip to Africa she made sixteen one-shot kills with a Remington 7 mm magnum, which earned her the Africa First Shotters trophy for that year (a Gary Swanson three-dimensional bronze of a charging elephant). Her game included a leopard and two Cape buffalo, the latter taken with a Remington caliber .375 rifle.

My sharpshooting Didi hunting doves in Arizona, 1991.
(Photo by H. Dean Hall)

Another trip took us to the Scottish Lowlands near Balmoral Castle, where Great Britain's royal family has its summer home. Balmoral is about fifty miles inland from Aberdeen, on the east coast of Scotland. Prince Albert originally bought the estate in 1852 and built a grand, white granite Victorian country home in the baronial Scottish style. Although technically in the Lowlands, the area offers spectacular Highland scenery.

We were guests of the Laird of Invercauld at Invercauld Castle, and while we were there the laird invited us and our crew to attend the church located on the estate. We were fortunate to be there at a time when the royal family was in residence, so we sat across from Queen Elizabeth, the Queen Mother, and the rest of the family, including little Andrew, who had to be removed because he was causing a disturbance.

Invercauld Castle was big and cold, with drafty fireplaces in every room for heat, and featherbeds to keep you warm at night. You really had to learn your way around or you'd easily get lost. Shelly, who was with us, was the first one to learn her way around, as kids always do. She ran up and down the hallways examining the suits of armor they had standing around the place. We also got our practice in coming to dinner in formal dress, which was the order of the household.

Out in the field, Didi hunted with one group and I hunted with another. One day I was watching her group, across the valley from where we were working. It was a wet day, so Didi had on a blue rain suit, which stood out against the dark heather on the hills. Watching through the field glasses, I could see the group moving up on a herd of red stag. In the herd I spotted an enormous stag with a big bouquet at the end of his horns, making him a royal stag. I was positive that was the one Didi was going to get.

She crept up on the herd, then hesitated. When she did shoot, with her usual precision, a stag dropped, but it wasn't the royal.

When we got back to the castle, I asked her why she hadn't taken the big one. She explained that the ghillie had told her, "Don't shoot that big stag. That's reserved for royalty."

Boy, that put me up in the air. Here we were paying a royal price for this hunt, and that trophy should have been hers. But Didi was a good sportsman, and all in all we had a great time.

The grouse shooting was terrific, too. The crop that year was tremendous, and the beaters who flushed the birds did an outstanding job, climbing along the steep ridges. And when the action started, it was fast. I was using two Browning over-and-under 20 gauges, and it really tested my skill. The ghillies knew how to pass the guns to you, too. You'd fire your two rounds, then pass the gun back for reloading and take the second gun.

The laird was also a great fisherman and took me fly-fishing on the River Dee. Fly-fishing is my favorite, but this was a little different type, using a longer pole. The laird and his lady were great people, and we had an outstanding trip that produced a good film.

In the course of our years of hunting for the television series we had much fine shooting, but three shots stand out in my memory as those I consider the best. The first was with a flintlock, made in 1778 at Lancaster, Pennsylvania, a gun given to me by the New York Campfire Club. We hadn't planned on using that particular gun, but we decided to put in a segment about shooting with a flintlock. While we were filming, a bobcat came running by at a range of about seventy-five yards. I fired, and when the flash of fire and smoke cleared, I had killed the bobcat.

The second occurred while we were hunting dahl sheep up in Alaska. I was using a Remington 7 mm magnum, a firearm with good velocity, a heavy bullet, and flat trajectory. It was a 400-yard shot and went right through the heart. The animal dropped on my first shot, but the guide told me to shoot again to make sure the animal was dead. I shot twice more, and when we retrieved the sheep, all three shots were grouped in an area the size of a baseball.

The third shot is the one I've already described, when we were filming *The American Sportsman* in Africa and I dropped the elephant with the .460 Weatherby, a shell slightly smaller than the .50 calibers I had used in the Wildcat on Guadalcanal.

Often during those years of filming I felt like I'd died and gone to heaven. Not only was I getting paid for doing something I truly loved, but I was learning what went on behind the scenes in the fascinating world of television. When you mix the film business with hunting and fishing, you have a unique combination. If directors think they have difficulty with actors and scriptwriters, they should try working with wildlife!

Elephants don't read scripts, walrus don't take direction, and fish don't know whose lure they're swallowing. For a half-hour show, where we needed to end up with twenty-four to twenty-six minutes of film, depending on the advertising time, we usually put about six to seven hours of film in the can; this meant seven to nine days of shooting. After that, you spent hours in the cutting room to get what you wanted.

When we went on location, we'd always try to get the climax of the show filmed right off the bat; then we'd go after the lead-in and work through to the end. That was the ideal. Reality more often resembled the time we wanted to do a show on the walrus.

We made two different trips to Alaska to get the story on the walrus. The first time we spent nearly a month in the hotel in Nome waiting for the fog to move out and the walrus to move in. We waited and watched and waited. Finally we traveled over to St. Lawrence Island to the village of Gambell to go out with the Eskimos in their walrus-hide boats called umiaks. Each umiak held, at the most, six people and their gear. In rough seas the homemade vessels twisted and groaned, but they were very practical because the ice didn't hang on to them. Every day we'd load up all our filming gear and head out among the icebergs in the Bering Strait looking for the walrus.

One day we encountered a Russian fishing ship out there shooting and skinning seals. The Russians wanted to trade with the Eskimos. The Eskimos happened to have some cigarettes our crew had given them, so they traded cigarettes for watches—one pack of cigarettes for one watch.

Since we all looked like Eskimos in our fur-lined parkas, we just kept our mouths shut and observed the whole thing. In those days, running into Russians off the coast of Siberia wasn't any American's idea of a good time. Russian planes flew over every day we were there, at high altitude; they'd come over the Strait, make a turn, and go back.

Besides Eskimos and Russians, the only other people we saw were Bible translators from Wycliffe, who lived a lonely life there, devotedly translating the Bible into the local Eskimo dialect. But no walrus.

The following year we returned to the Bering Strait for a second attempt, staying south of Gambell at a place called Nunivak, where you find the musk ox. We were going to film the musk ox and their peculiarities and also try to do the story on the walrus. Ed Shavings, our guide, showed us around the island, and we filmed reindeer and musk ox. Meanwhile, we were getting reports as to when the walrus would be coming north. Every day for nine days the Eskimos would say, "the walruses are coming." We waited and waited and filmed everything under the midnight sun. Except walrus.

While we were there I paraded around the island in my Stetson, and the Eskimo children would fall in behind me chanting, "Roy Rogers. Roy Rogers." They had seen his films, and no matter how much I told them my name was Joe Foss, they insisted that my "cowboy hat" made me the King of the Cowboys. Later I told Roy about this and we had a good chuckle.

Finally our time was up and we had to leave the area. We had great footage of Eskimos and the surrounding habitat, but very few walrus.

We took off from Nome on a bright, sunshiny day and swung out over the ocean. We hadn't gone more than fifteen or twenty miles south down the coast when we ran into the walrus. Just as the Eskimos had predicted, they were coming. The experts estimated there were probably 80,000 walrus moving north at that time; the sea was brown with them as far as we could see from the airplane.

We spent two years and a lot of money working on it, and we still missed filming that great migration. But we did manage to produce a good program by putting together the Eskimos, sea lions, the seals, the little auklets, the eider ducks, and everything that makes up an Alaskan summer, which lasts, as some say, "almost one whole day."

Another thing that amazed me about the television show was the number of people it took to make it happen. Behind the scenes were wranglers chasing horses on frosty mornings, guides who worked overlong and carried big loads, and the crew who patiently dealt with the eccentricities and technical demands of camera and sound equipment. Then there was American Airlines, that got us places without losing our gear; Remington Arms, who gave us both technical advice and the use of its products; and the Shakespeare Company, who donated the latest fishing tackle and valuable suggestions. I tipped my Stetson to all of them.

Eventually, however, "environmentalists" and animal-rights groups destroyed the hunting and fishing programs by intimidating both the sponsors and the networks. The U.S. Humane Society, Friends of the Animals, and other outside pressures wielding powerful influence created major headaches for everyone concerned. *The Outdoorsman*, which ran from 1966 to 1974, was one of their victims.

If you stay up late, though, you can sometimes catch one of the programs. It's still on television in some places at two or three in the morning. Every once in a while someone says to me, "I saw you last night on television."

Chapter 29
God and Didi

After we finished filming *The Outdoorsman,* Liberty Mutual Insurance Company retained me to do seventy-two personal appearances. Along with those, I took many other speaking engagements. Didi kept my schedule and negotiated the contracts for my freelance personal appearances, acting as my business manager.

While we were still filming *The Outdoorsman,* I had received a letter from Scandinavian Airlines, asking whether I would consider endorsing their company. I didn't do anything about this, but Didi—who can carry on more jobs at once than a ten-armed paperhanger and who had been hired as an outside public relations agent by Fritz Kielman for KLM Royal Dutch Airlines—got the idea of contacting Fritz about me. She had learned that Les Stroud Brown, who was running the Washington office for Governmental Affairs, was going to retire.

"Joe would be a natural for the job," she told Fritz.

I'd gotten to know Fritz Kielman myself in 1962 when he first came to work for KLM in New York City. At that time we were setting up our AFL office on the seventh floor of the KLM building on the corner of 49th and Madison. Fritz was rather unhappy about being in the U.S., especially since he didn't have any of his hunting buddies over here and didn't know anything about hunting in this country.

Once we got acquainted and I found out he was a hunter, I said, "I'll line you up to go with me." The two of us became fast friends, and to the best of my knowledge, Fritz still holds the record for being the only non-U.S. citizen who ever became president of the Past Shooters Club, whose membership is made up of those who have shot on a competition team at the Lander One Shot Antelope Hunt.

KLM hired me in 1972, and we moved to Washington, D.C. This gave me a different perspective on the political arena. Now I sat through hearings and called on the House and the Senate and the White House and the State Department and the Federal Aeronautics Authority and the Civil Aeronautics Board so I could brief the KLM people. As part of the job I also traveled to Europe at least once a month to meet with Henri Wassenbergh and Koos DeVries and the other executives of KLM at their headquarters in Amstelveen, just outside of Amsterdam.

After one of those European jaunts, Didi and I had to go directly to a meeting in Los Angeles and our flight was routed through Minneapolis. That happened to be the weekend of a preseason game between the Miami Dolphins and the Minnesota Vikings, so we called Joe Robbie and let him know we were in town.

"Come on over and stay with us at the hotel," he said. "We've got plenty of rooms and you can take in the game." We had enough time, so we did.

Didi had been a bit unhappy with me that week because I'd bought two used Cadillacs within a few weeks of each other. "Are you collecting those things?" she had asked.

"No," I said, "I'll keep the best one and trade or sell the other."

While we were hanging around the hotel, talking with the players and others we knew, Didi ran into Howard Cosell in the lobby and they visited for a while.

"How's the commissioner doing these days?" Howard asked.

"He's doing great," she said. "He's buying old Cadillacs."

The next day I ran into Howard at the stadium, and he said, "Would you come on at the half for a couple minutes?"

"Sure," I said. "I'd be happy to."

So I went up to the broadcast booth, and as I walked in, Howard said to Frank Gifford, over live television, "You know the commissioner, don't you?"

"Sure," Frank said and held out his hand. We'd known each other for years, from back when he was playing for the New York Giants.

"You know what the commissioner's doing these days?" Howard said. "He's buying old Cadillacs."

I didn't have time to explain, because Cosell and Gifford immediately switched to the topic of football. But as a result of that brief comment, I started getting letters and calls from people all over the country who were looking for Cadillac parts—a certain model, a doorknob, a fender, a radiator cap, you name it. I had to tell them all that I wasn't in the Cadillac business.

It just shows you, though, why the sponsors pay so much for television time.

In 1973, not long after I began working for KLM, Didi and I were in San Antonio, where I was to speak to the Game Conservation International, a conservation group that gives a great deal of time and money to the preservation of wildlife worldwide. While I was there, I followed my daily morning regimen of calisthenics and running.

After I gave my talk at the noon luncheon, I felt a twinge in my chest, but thought it was some minor strain from my workout. That night there was a reception at the home of James and Norma Midcap for five or six hundred people from around the world. I was having a great time, when suddenly a sharp pain shot through my chest. I slipped away and sat down in a big chair inside and prayed, "Lord, help me. I'm in trouble." I figured it was probably the end of the waltz.

While I was sitting there, Didi came through the door, looking for me, and asked, "What are you doing here?"

"I don't feel good."

"You don't look good."

She ran out and got my old friend and hunting buddy Dr. Bob Speegle. When he took my pulse, he said, "Joe, your heart's skipping beats."

"I hope it doesn't skip two in a row," I quipped.

He informed me that this was no joking matter and told me to take off my shirt and lie down. Just then Mrs. Midcap came in and let out a screech when she saw me flat out there on her white sofa. She hurried to get a doctor she had on duty, and he came in with his black bag of tools. He put on his stethoscope and listened and gave the same verdict as Dr. Speegle.

"Are you allergic to any drugs?" he asked.

"No," I said. "Never take any."

So he shot me with something that felt like a rattlesnake bite, and I began feeling a little less pain.

"I'll be okay," I said.

"You'll be okay in the hospital," he said.

By this time the green gremlins (paramedics) had arrived with a stretcher. They plugged me into a bottle of something in a hurry and carted me to the meat wagon. Didi climbed aboard and we were off to the hospital.

The next thing I knew, I was in a receiving room and everybody was dithering around. I was laying there thinking, *Maybe this is it,* when in walked our friends Chuck Connors and Tom Bass, who had been out at the GCI meeting. I guess they wanted to know if I was dead yet. Well, when old Chuck walked in, it stopped the whole clock. Nobody knew me from a load of hay; they just wanted Chuck's autograph.

After that melee was over, they shoved me off to the heart ward, which already had five people ahead of me. *Well, at least everyone in here has television over their bunk,* I thought.

But when I got in bed I saw this was a different kind of program, with a straight line that jerked up and down. They informed me that was my heart, and I saw right away that this was a program I wanted to keep on the air.

I entered the hospital on Thursday night and was still there on Sunday. When I woke up on Sunday morning, the sun was shining in the window, and I thought, *Wouldn't it be great to be in church today.* Then about midmorning the man on my left got a straight line on his set, and the doctors and nurses flew in with the battery charger and pulled the curtain.

I prayed that the man would make it, and he did. But that afternoon when the curtains were open once more, I looked over at the guy with hoses up his nose and in his mouth and thought, *Boy, if he's dying, I'd like to talk to him about where he's going*. That was the first time I realized I wanted to tell somebody about what I believed—and I didn't know how! And I thought, *If I ever get out of here, Lord, I'm going to get involved*.

It took another week or so before they found that I had pericarditis, a viral infection in the outer lining of the heart, and it was six months or so before I was supposed to get back full speed ahead again.

Not long after I was released from the hospital, Didi discovered a little yellow book called *The Four Spiritual Laws,* which turned out to be just the ticket I needed. The author was Dr. Bill Bright, founder and president of Campus Crusade for Christ International, and in the booklet he explained simply, step by step, how to talk to people about God, beginning with the statement, "God loves you and has a wonderful plan for your life."

When we learned that this Campus Crusade outfit offered seminars at their headquarters at Arrowhead Springs, California, Didi decided we should see what they were about. The first time she took me there I wasn't sure I wanted to go. Fortunately I had laryngitis, so I couldn't argue with anyone. I had to just listen. And I was amazed to discover how many wonderful people from industry and the military and every walk of life were involved in this ministry—Roy Rogers and Dale Evans, Caroline and Bunker Hunt, and other people I'd known for years. It was one of the greatest sessions I'd ever had in my life, and it got me excited about Bible study and interested in the organization itself. We got to know Dr. Bill and Vonette Bright, and later I served as chairman of Here's Life World, along with vice chairmen Roy Rogers and Bunker Hunt. We have had some great times together there at Arrowhead Springs.[1]

Didi and I have worked with Here's Life, World for several years, and now we're working on New Life 2000, which includes setting up distribution of the film called *Jesus,* produced by Warner Brothers. The film has been translated into 212 languages and used in 183 countries, making it the most trans-

---

[1] The primary operation has moved to Orlando, Florida.

Bunker Hunt and I being installed as vice chairman and chairman of Here's Life, World (Adult Ministry of Campus Crusade for Christ International) in 1980. (Photo by Donna Wild Foss)

Dr. Bill Bright introducing Didi and me at an executive seminar at Campus Crusade for Christ International Headquarters in Arrowhead Springs, California, 1984. (Photo by John Galvin)

lated film in the world. The next is *Gone With the Wind*, translated into thirty-three languages. Currently Campus Crusade for Christ has 230 teams showing the film around the world, and to date 461 million have seen the film.

When I got on my feet again after the pericarditis, I plunged back into my work for the airlines. I worked for KLM from 1972 until 1978. At that time KLM was flying into seventy-

four different countries, so we met countless interesting people from many nations. Didi and I were frequently invited to
various embassy receptions in D.C., where we met diplomats
from around the world. As glamorous as it sounds, this part
of the job was never my favorite. Didi has her own theories
about why this is true:

> During our tenure with KLM, Joe was very secure
> in his business negotiations and always acted with great
> confidence. But when it came to social engagements,
> particularly the embassy affairs, he expected me to take
> the lead. I was the one who had to introduce myself to
> strangers and in turn initiate Joe's involvement in
> conversations.
>   Joe was a very handsome man, and during what I call
> his "dashing, handsome, dancing days," he was forever
> plagued by beautiful women demanding his attention.
> He assured me there was never a problem. Whenever
> he felt overwhelmed by a woman's attention, he would
> merely puff on his big, fat cigar and blow smoke in the
> lovely lady's face!
>   When I met Joe, I noticed that despite all his achieve-
> ments and experience, there was something very naive
> and innocent and shy about him. As handsome and
> gregarious as he was, he was never a ladies' man.

So Didi kept me out of social hot water, and I kept KLM
on track with government regulations. Occasionally I had to
deal with the crew at the White House. One piece of business
I remember particularly occurred when Jerry Ford was president. At the time there was a big discussion as to whether
or not the NATO nations were going to buy fighter planes
from the U.S. or from France and Sweden. This involved a
$16-billion contract. In the early days of aviation, the United
States was the world leader. For example, we sold most of
the transport aircraft in the world. But now the NATO nations
were thinking of buying fighters from Europe.

Coinciding with this, the U.S. had decided that the foreign
airlines were hurting our domestic airlines. They figured the
best measure was to reduce the number of flights in and out

of the country by foreign airlines, particularly the European airlines. In our case, they cut KLM from twenty-six flights per week to eleven.

This cutback led to lengthy discussions involving almost everyone, it seemed, including Henry Kissinger, who initially said, "Don't vorry, ve'll get it straightened out after Christmas."

Well, Christmas came and went and it didn't get straightened out. So I went to the White House and visited with some of President Ford's assistants, stressing the seriousness of this matter. The next thing I knew, the State Department was on the line, and I gave it to them straight.

"If you guys are going to substantially reduce the flights of the British, Scandinavian, and Dutch airlines into the U.S., you won't have a leg to stand on when it comes to aviation sales." Why should the NATO nations worry about patronizing us and buying our fighters, I said, if we were going to cut their business?

One thing led to another, and I ended up being the runner between the White House and the State Department and the foreign airlines.

As a result of these discussions, the U.S. government finally decided to leave the foreign airlines alone, and President Ford traveled to Belgium and did a great job of selling the NATO people on purchasing $16 billion worth of U.S. fighters.

I also had some dealings with President Jimmy Carter during my last year at KLM. At that time someone contacted our headquarters about a group of World War II veterans from the Netherlands who were coming to visit America. These folks had all served in the Dutch underground and had been responsible for saving the lives of many of our airmen during the war. While they were in the U.S., this veterans' organization wanted to meet the president.

Considering what they had done for the fighting men of our country, I didn't think this was too much to ask. I contacted the White House staff and put in the request. They turned it down in a hurry, saying, "The president is too busy."

About then I happened to remember that Senator Howard Cannon of Nevada had once told me about his World War

II experiences and how he had been rescued by some people in the Netherlands. I got on the phone and told the senator my problem. "These were the people who saved your hide and made it possible for you to be breathing regularly today," I reminded him. "Why don't you call the president and see what you can do."

In a matter of minutes Senator Cannon called back and said, "President Carter will see your group in the Rose Garden on such and such a date."

On the appointed day it was pouring rain. When we arrived at the White House we were ushered into the cabinet room in the Oval Office area. There President Carter shook hands with everyone in the group and allowed them to take pictures. Last of all he came over to shake hands with Didi and me.

"I wish I had time to sit and visit with you folks," he said. "But I'm so busy I've got to get right back to work."

Our seven years in Washington were filled with interesting work and fascinating people. It was a very different world from South Dakota, Dallas, or even New York. I think those folks along the Potomac were shocked the first few times I walked in wearing my Justin boots, Stetson hat, and Western-cut clothes, but I got the job done in the halls of Washington. Working for KLM was a treat. They told me what they wanted ahead of time, so I never had to listen to a lot of chatter. I knew what they expected, and I accomplished it. No one ever bothered me, and I was my own boss. I enjoyed every moment of the association until I retired in 1978.

During the late sixties and the seventies, in the midst of learning some new things about my spiritual life and experiencing new challenges in my professional life, I was also learning some lessons in my personal life. Heart-to-heart relationships had never been my greatest strength. While I had many friends and acquaintances, when it came to family, I had faltered a number of times. Because of my problems with their mother, I had long had a strained relationship with my own children. They especially resented the fact that I had divorced their mother and remarried.

To Didi, however, family was very important, and being

Didi and I enjoyed a great day with Governor and Nancy Reagan when they were in Scottsdale for a speaking engagement in 1978. (Photo by Troy Murray)

married to her gradually brought about some significant changes in my own attitude toward home and family. Some of this initially began simply because Didi and I shared so many interests. From the beginning we worked together and played together—as husband and wife and as best friends. While Didi is an elegant, sophisticated, and well-educated lady, she learned to hunt and fish with me. She soon loved it as much as I did, and she could hold her own on any range or hunt. So while some of my attitude can be accounted for by my own maturing and mellowing, Didi has to take a lot of credit for it.

For example, holidays never meant anything to me. Christmas and Thanksgiving were just two more free days to go hunting. Didi couldn't believe that. For her those were special times when the family gathered and enjoyed each other, and she wasn't about to let me off the hook. Also, my heart was warmed by the loving, caring bond that existed between Didi and her son and daughter and her granddaughters. It was always fun to be with them; they all had positive attitudes and personalities, and they willingly drew me into their family circle. Didi also wanted to help me draw in Frank and Mary Joe and Cheryl. The atmosphere was still strained sometimes, but all in all we were family.

Didi, as usual, has her own analysis of the situation:

Visiting with Vice President George Bush and Peter
Brennan, Secretary of Labor, at a reception in
Washington, D.C., in 1981.

I think Joe has always lived in a different kind of
world than most of us mortals. He lives in the present
tense. Whatever is happening right now is the most
important thing. Because of this it sometimes seems as
though he does not have deep feelings for those around
him who love him the most.

Yet I sometimes wonder if that sense of the present
isn't the ingredient that caused him to be so fearless in
everything he did, that made him a loyal patriot and
an outstanding fighter pilot. Joe is what heroes are made
of, and there is something in heroes that makes them
go on regardless of who they hurt. Consequently they
sometimes end up hurting those they love.

The interesting and puzzling and sometimes frustrating thing about Joe is that while he would never
fear or run away from any battle or from standing up
for what he believes is right, he will tend to run away
from anything that's unpleasant in a personal relationship, especially a family relationship. It's just part of
his nature. For example, he cannot deal with sickness.
He would stare death down on the battlefield, but he
hates to visit someone in the hospital. In the past, when

there was something he couldn't cope with, he just left—he went hunting or fishing.

But through the years Joe's relationship with God has changed all that, and as far as I'm concerned, it's nothing short of a miracle.

Didi's right, no doubt about it. God made all the difference. The biggest changes in my life came about through her prayers and the wonderful life we have made together. She has always brought out the best in me. It didn't happen overnight, but gradually my life-style, my language, and even my attitude toward family and friends has changed. My language used to be salty, to put it mildly, and for years I was a pretty heavy Scotch drinker, although few except my cronies knew it—not even Didi. She rarely saw me drink when we were dating or even after we were married. I tried to be on my best behavior with her.

Then in 1971, on St. Patrick's Day, we were at the Arizona Biltmore, where we celebrated Pat Magruder's birthday each year. Pat was part owner of the Buffalo Bills, and we were celebrating with Frank Kush, the ASU football coach and his wife, and George Halas, who owned the Chicago Bears—I always called him Papa Bear. We had a wonderful dinner and evening, during which I consumed a number of whiskeys. When we were leaving, I lost my balance and ended up sitting in a flowerbed.

Didi was very unhappy, to say the least. George reached down to help me up, and Didi politely suggested that maybe she should drive home.

"Okay," I said meekly, handing her the car keys.

That night I took a hard look at myself. If the hard stuff made me that unsteady, I'd better quit. And I've never had hard booze since. I quit smoking just as abruptly.

We were at a family gathering when I noticed that my daughter-in-law was coughing badly.

"If I had a habit that bothered me that much, I'd quit," I told her, jumping in with both feet.

"Well, Pop, you've got the habit and so do I," she said.

"No," I said, "I can quit any time I want." I'd been smoking

A great aggregation of friends from all over the world attend the prestigious Weatherby Arms annual Big Game Hunters international awards dinner in Beverly Hills. I served on the selection committee for over 25 years. From left: General Robert L. Scott (World War II ace, author of *God Is My Co-pilot*), Admiral Robert Garrick, Didi, I, and Roy Rogers. (Photo by Rothschild Photo)

or chewing cigars for thirty-three years. I rationalized by never inhaling and always beating the fire to the middle.

"How many have you smoked today?" she asked.

"I'm on number eighteen," I said after checking my pockets.

"I know I don't have anything to worry about," she said.

Well, she'd thrown down the gauntlet, and I never passed up a challenge.

"I just quit," I said. And I did.

As I've often remarked, I've been smart enough to surround myself all my life with people smarter than I am. I've always said, you can be a great leader when you have great people pushing you ahead. Whatever I have accomplished I owe to the great people who assisted me. After I retired from KLM I kept going full bore, speaking and serving on various committees and organizations, including the President's Council on Physical Fitness, the White House Conference on Handicapped Individuals, the selection committee for Weatherby

Arms Big Game Hunters Trophy Award and Here's Life,
World for Campus Crusade for Christ. Didi keeps my sched-
ule; I just follow orders and try to make the flight on time.
Ellie Martin also keeps things in line. Ellie has worked with
Didi and me for years, long enough to have had a pretty good
firsthand look at our life:

> I've worked with Joe and Didi since 1969 as a book-
> keeper, secretary, and all-around factotum. We have a
> relationship that's evolved from professional to per-
> sonal. The amazing thing about it is that we are at
> opposite poles in our beliefs about almost everything
> —gun ownership, hunting, religion, politics—and it
> hasn't eroded the affection we all have for one another.
> I can only describe Joe as a character. He can be
> totally exasperating one minute and as lovable as a
> teddy bear the next. On one or two occasions during
> the twenty-three years, he "fired" Didi and me in a fit
> of pique. I always ignored these "firings," and the next
> time I reported for work there was "ol' Joe," making

President-elect Ronald Reagan, Chuck Lein, and I
discussing campaign strategy—serious business,
1979.

sure he had coffee ready for me the minute I came in and serving up toast just the way I like it—burnt.

What Joe and I do have in common are humble roots in the farmland of the Midwest and the values that seem to go with those beginnings. We frequently reminisce about our early days on the farm, and I believe it is this commonality that draws us together despite our divergent beliefs.

Knowing Joe has been an experience—an experience I wouldn't want to have missed.

Another perspective on our activities and our marriage comes from John D. Colbrunn, a good friend who is Assistant Director of Special Events for the United States Olympic Committee:

I met Joe in 1980 at the beginning of our pursuit of an NFL expansion franchise in Arizona. It wasn't long before all the partners felt they should have called it the NFFL—the first "F" for Foss.

Several years into our franchise odyssey, the doctors at Mayo's decided Joe could use a pacemaker. In Joe's case the pacemaker could never keep pace with the patient. A few days after the operation Joe showed up in Colorado carrying three large bags and bleeding from the shoulder incision. He was accompanied by his true-life pacemaker, his wife, Donna (Didi). For the past twenty-five years Donna has used her exceptional talents, energies, and career opportunities in a supporting role to those of her husband, and by his own admission and with his praise has become the team's MVP.

If it was possible to harness the power and toughness of a Mack truck with the style and sophistication of a Rolls-Royce, then remove the reverse gears, you would have Joe and Donna with wheels.

Chapter 30

Lessons from
a Fortunate Life

⭐ ⭐ ⭐

I remember one time telling Bart Starr, the great quarterback who led the Green Bay Packers to five NFL titles and two Super Bowl victories, about the first time I met Vince Lombardi, the football legend who coached the Packers to those victories. It was during my AFL days in New York and I was attending an NFL game between Green Bay and the New York Giants. The Packers had just arrived at the stadium. They were coming in the side door with their duffel bags and I was going out, and who should I run into but Coach Lombardi.

"How are you, Coach?" I said. "I'm Joe Foss."

"Joe Foss," he said. "I've been wanting to talk to you. Did you say that I was the most impossible man in the National Football League to work with?"

"Yes, sir, I did," I replied.

He steamed up right away. "What are you talking about?"

"Well, you're busy right now," I said. "Why don't we meet tomorrow or whenever you can over at Toots Shors."

The famous restaurant and bar on 52nd Street south of Madison Avenue was a gathering place for sports personalities, entertainers, and the press. Toots was a crusty, forthright character—generous to a fault. He either loved you or would literally throw you out of his joint. His favorite name for me was "creepy bum." So the coach and I set a time after the game and met there. Toots gave us the corner booth, which was Number One and always reserved for special friends.

Lombardi and I got right at it, and I told him why I thought he was impossible to work with. He had said that it would take years for the AFL to catch up with the NFL. He said if we were to score 100 to 0 in the first half of a game, it would still take us years to be where the NFL was.

"I disagree with you," I said. "Whether it's sports or anything else, if people are dedicated enough, they can make it. If you have the desire to do it—which is something you preach on yourself, Coach—you can take anybody that is dedicated and they can knock your block off in four years."

Despite this somewhat rough beginning, Lombardi and I ended up as friends. I always said he coached the way I would have wanted to if I had been a football coach—with the fundamentals.

There are good coaches and bad coaches in life. The good ones focus on the fundamentals. It's like building a house. The Bible says if you build the house of life on the sand, it will wash away. If you build on the rock, it will stand against everything. With the right attitude and the right foundation, a little guy can do miraculous things. The fundamentals are worth fighting for as far as I'm concerned.

Bart Starr had some good things to say himself about attitude and foundations:

> All success stories come back to a foundation or a basis or a common denominator, and that is why I start with attitude. If the person with a good attitude has worthwhile goals for himself or his family, his business or profession, for the government, for a league . . . whatever, he establishes goals for himself and all these things he is involved in. In Joe I see the practice and preparation and desire, the self-motivation that is a part of all this, the willingness to discipline yourself, the genuine quest for excellence. He is a man that has succeeded in every single thing he has done.

I don't know if I've always succeeded, but I have always tried. And as diverse as my various careers may seem, I have

To climb into the F-16 and take the controls was an exciting moment in my life. My dream was to fly an airplane that I could take straight up and do slow rolls with all the way to 40,000 feet (1983).

developed lifelong interests in each that seem eventually to overlap. And, in some way, I have kept up my interest in all of them.

Didi and I are still very active with the adult ministry of Campus Crusade for Christ International, which includes working with the business, professional, and governmental people of the world. Another interest in our lives is the Endowment for Community Leadership, which is committed to confronting the devastating effects of crime, drugs, and the destruction of the family, particularly in the urban centers of this nation. We are working to bring purpose and hope to individuals, restore families, and strengthen the local community. The Endowment sustains ethnic men and women who are re-establishing traditional Christian moral and ethical values.

When it comes to flying, I'm working with a group hoping to get a jet port in the Phoenix area by 2005. We're known as the Arizona Partnership for Air Transportation, and we

A Proud American

are preparing for the economic imperatives of the next century. Don Meyers serves as chairman, Mike Ingram as executive vice president, and I serve as a director.

I haven't done any flying since I turned sixty-five, and the last airplane I flew in the military was an F-16. I don't own a plane because of all the headaches involved in storage and insurance. It's so easy just to climb on a plane, work while I'm traveling, and have no worries when I arrive. I carry my own luggage on and off, so I'm downtown while most folks are still waiting at the baggage pickup.

Although I retired from the Air National Guard in 1980, I've continued to follow the actions of our military troops around the world. The purpose of the Guards and Reserves is to maintain proficiency at the highest degree so that you are ready to go at a moment's notice. That's the way I always conducted myself. I felt that way during Vietnam, and today I am still ready to do my part whenever my country wants me. I get many requests from the branches of the military to address the troops at all levels. To the young men and women in our armed forces, I'm a part of history; I can tell them firsthand about things they've only read in books. I talk to military groups all the time and am pleased and proud to do it.

During Desert Storm, Commandant Al Gray of the Marine Corps asked if I would be willing to go to Saudi Arabia to address the troops. "Yes, sir," I said. "You bet." I was standing by, ready to go. But with the action so short—which is what happens when you let the professionals do their job and keep the politicians out of it—I was never called. In September 1990, however, they established Landing Zone Foss in Saudi.

When I think back to my own wartime experience, I hold no grudges against the Japanese. I spoke at the Confederate Air Force facility in Midland, Texas, on Pearl Harbor Day, 1991, and there were ten Japanese pilots there. The night before, they took me out to dinner, and I had a hunch at least one of them fought me once or twice.

Some people are still mad at the Japanese, but bashing is a waste of time. It doesn't help to call one another names. If you sit across the table and talk it out, you may not end up

374

Suburo Sakai, the leading living ace of the Imperial Japanese Navy, I, and Shiro Ishikawa, another fighter pilot, reminiscing about World War II, Kerrville, Texas, 1990. We were at one time shooting at each other; today we're the best of friends. (Photo by Donna Wild Foss)

loving one another, but at least you can settle some differences.

When it comes to politics, from 1987 to 1990 my close association with the National Rifle Association required every bit of experience and knowledge I'd acquired through the years.

I had been a member of the National Rifle Association, off and on, since World War II and in the spring of 1966 I became a life member. To my way of thinking there are few things more important than what I have termed "The War that Won't Go Away"—that is, the fight to save the Constitution's Second Amendment, the one that protects our right to keep and bear arms. It's a tricky battle because there are no rules, and the combatants change names and faces faster than a weasel in a woodpile after a chipmunk.

Finally, about nine years ago, with the antigun people and the antihunting characters coming out of the woodwork, I decided I'd better get active, so I ran for the board of directors of the NRA. At the first meeting I sat and listened to what was going on—that's always my style, to get the lay of the land first—and toward the close of the meeting the president called on me. "As a new member, what do you think of the meeting so far?"

"Well," I said, "I can't imagine how seventy-five men and women can sit here and listen to a small group that worries about dotting the i's and crossing the t's more than they do about getting the hay hauled as far as the membership is concerned." They were stewing about some inconsequential nonsense unrelated to legislation. "There's just a small group in here that's been causing confusion, so when they come up for election why don't you forget about them and get them out of here. I cannot see sitting here and wasting that much time." So from day one I became known as a battler around NRA headquarters.

During my time there I appreciated working with the NRA staff, all the way from the doorman and the mailman and the chauffeur, William Drumming, to the former executive vice president, Warren Cassidy. We worked as a team, with everyone dedicated to promoting the goals of the organization.

Through the years the leadership of the NRA has included outstanding men and women from all walks of life: former governors, attorney generals, judges, farmers, ranchers, lawyers, teachers, actors, doctors, college professors, police officers and chiefs, senior military officers, legislators, congressmen, senators, and presidents. The board and the committees that make up the organization insure that all of the objectives and purposes come to pass, whether it's gun collecting, gun safety, hunter safety, or the Olympic team, for which the NRA is responsible. At our Olympic training center in Colorado Springs, young men and women prepare for world competitions, where we've won our share of gold, silver, and bronze medals.

From 1988 to 1990 I had the honor of serving as president of the NRA, and during that time I faced off in some confrontations that were far more devious and mean-spirited than most of the things I've encountered in my life, and I've met up with a few. Whether it's the antigun organizations, the

JANUARY 29, 1990 $2.50

SOVIET REPUBLICS: "Almost Civil War"

TIME

WHO
IS
THE
NRA?
A look at
America's
embattled
gun lobby

National Rifle Association
President Joe Foss

Serving as president of the National Rifle Association
was an exciting challenge to me, defending a cause in
which I believe—a part of the constitution of the United
States of America.
(Photo by Neil Leifer, *Time* magazine)

media, or a small but growing force of rogue politicians who
have nothing but their own personal interests at heart, there
is little honor among those who are conspiring to rob us of
our individual rights. We've been inundated with malicious
media reports, misleading and erroneous information, and
scare tactics that make the kamikazes look like Tiny Tim.

When it comes to the Second Amendment, there are all
kinds of interpretations—especially those who believe there's

no need for it anymore. They maintain that it was put in there by our founding fathers as a protection at that time, but since times have changed, we don't need it now. Well, that's just not true. We need people to be armed today, just as much as we ever did. This was borne out recently in the Los Angeles rampage where innocent people's homes and businesses were ransacked and set afire. The only properties that survived had armed owners who could keep the rioters at bay. The world situation could change at any time, as it does frequently. Sweeping changes have occurred around the globe, plunging countries and citizens into turmoil making it necessary for them to defend their homes and their lives. And it could happen here. But I believe in the government established by our founding fathers, which includes the right to keep and bear arms, and I'll fight for that all the way.

The war to abolish our Second Amendment rights is happening right now, and the fighting is fierce. So the NRA has been a good place for an old general who's grown used to this kind of action and is still in fighting form.

After our romantic Hawaiian wedding, Didi and I lived in Scottsdale for several months. Didi still had a home in Des Moines, Iowa, so we spent our summer there while we were deliberating where to establish our permanent home.

Then, since our office was still in New York City, we experimented by staying one week in Darien, Connecticut, and another in Greenwich, commuting into the city. We quickly realized that we are country folk and really like the West.

Phoenix provided excellent air service, and because of the nature of our business this was important. So Scottsdale became our home, and we enjoy living in this beautiful part of the world. However, we are fortunate enough to be able to escape the extreme summer temperature by migrating to the splendid Black Hills of northeastern Wyoming that spill over from South Dakota.

There, Didi designed and built our dream cabin in the pines sitting on a great trout stream. We both enjoy digging in the dirt and working with the flowers, and I have a fine vegetable garden. We also have plenty of apples in the fall to share with friends, as well as plums and raspberries. At Sand Creek we

The Patriot's Fund Event—Endowment for Community Leadership (helping the homeless) honoring me for fifty years of military service. From left: Lamar Hunt, Didi, I, the Honorable Sam Skinner and Mrs. Skinner, 1990. (Photo by Spencer Brand)

With Senator Barry Goldwater at the Endowment for Community Leadership event (helping the homeless), Scottsdale, 1991. He is a true statesman, and we feel privileged to call him our neighbor and friend. (Photo courtesy of Endowment for Community Leadership)

retreat from the busy life we still lead to savor the country life we both love. In this unhurried atmosphere we can also enjoy our families and many good friends.

My favorite pastimes are still hunting and fishing. Wading the stream, you're out there alone with the birds and the animals and the sky and the land; climbing over the rocky ridges, you somehow feel real close to God.

Our Sand Creek home is a woodsy house that blends in with Mother Nature, situated beside a crystal clear trout stream. We call it "Paradise," and Didi calls it our "happy-time home."

When we built it, we designed it with guests in mind. We wanted it to be a warm, welcoming kind of place where our family and friends could come to relax and enjoy themselves and exchange ideas and share our souls. It's a wonderful retreat where you can fill your lungs with fresh mountain air and find release from pressures and demands of time.

Birds have always fascinated Joe, and Sand Creek affords him a bird-watcher's paradise. Its main claim to fame, as far as he is concerned, is "one of the best trout streams in the world."

Life has not always been a coming-up-roses event. We have experienced many valleys. Some Joe and I have weathered together; at other times I've felt very much alone. We've learned to accept each other with our weaknesses and our strengths. And today marriage to Joe is wonderful. Every day I thank the Lord for giving him to me.

Together we work very well. One of my favorite lines is, "Joe does the things I can't do; I do the things he won't do—and together we make a good team." We are twenty-four-hour people—working together, playing together, and just being together. We are both absolute in our commitment to the Lord and to each other.

Our eldest daughter, Coni, who has been teaching in Cottonwood for the past four years, recently moved to

(Above) Another part of the Foss family in Arizona. From left: I; Didi; daughter, Coni; her daughter, Misty; son, Dean, and his daughter Dona Michelle and her husband, Jim. Krystal Lyn is sitting in her mother's lap. Scottsdale, 1985. (Photo by B.J.)

(Below) Part of our Foss clan at our cabin in the woods in Wyoming. From left: son, Frank; daughter, Mary Joe; I; granddaughter, Nicole, and Frank's wife, Pam. Insert: Cheryl and her husband, Bob; grandsons Jon and David and granddaughter Kim, 1989. (Photo by Donna Wild Foss)

(Above left) In 1987, our son Dean married Elizabeth.
(Above right) A wonderful day at the duck pond, sharing life with my buddy—our great-granddaughter, Shelby. (Photo by Donna Wild Foss)

Jackson, Wyoming, to be near her daughter, Misty Ostby, and granddaughter, Shelby Lee. Shelby was three years old in June 1992, and she's the delight of her great-grandfather's heart. Our eldest son, Dean, and his family live near us in Scottsdale. Cheryl June lives with her husband in Holdenville, Oklahoma, and Mary Joe with her family are in Billings, Montana. Our youngest son, Frank, and his family are in Mankato, Minnesota. Our granddaughter Dona Michelle (Shelly) is married and lives the farthest from us. She and her family are in Danbury, Connecticut. We love our family and regret it is not possible to have them together more often.

I still get letters every week from people wanting my autograph or information about my life. I even get letters from schoolchildren, like the following:

Dear Mr. Foss,
I am in the fifth grade. Our class had the choice of writing about any famous man or woman that is from South Dakota. I chose to do my report on you. I was wondering if you had any pictures or specific things you would like me to put in my report, also if there is any advice you would like to give to the young people of today?

I have lots of things I like to say to young people today. I tell them what my dad always told me, "It's not where you come from that matters; it's where you're going that counts." And I tell them that my father taught me to shoot straight and to shoot honest, and that's what I've always tried to do.

When I was young, I learned to stay within the guidelines my father set or suffer the consequences. When I went to college I learned that if I forgot to study, I flunked. In the Marine Corps I learned that attention to duty was number one. In aerial combat I learned that if you didn't have teamwork, you died. As a football commissioner I learned that everyone had to play by the same rules. As a television host I learned that I had to check the words the writers wanted to put in my mouth; someone else might have written it, but I was responsible if I said it. And when I thought I was dying of arsenic poisoning, I learned that without Jesus Christ as my Savior, none of the rest mattered.

So I guess if I had to give just one piece of advice, I would have to say that all the medals in the world wouldn't solve my dilemma with God. That only happened when I stepped out of the cockpit and turned the controls over to Him.

For years when the press interviewed me, they would ask, "Joe, out of all the things that have happened to you, what do you rate number one?" And I would always say, "It hasn't happened yet."

Today when reporters or interviewers ask me, "Joe, out of all the great things you've had happen to you, what do you rate number one?"—and they still ask me that—I shock a lot of them when I say, "The greatest thing that's ever happened to me was the day I accepted Jesus Christ as my Lord and Savior."

After all these years, I guess I still have some of that little boy in me, the one who loved to climb up and sit high on the windmill surveying his world; the one who loved tromping out across the woods and fields and streams of South Dakota. Just an ordinary kid from a typical rural family who happened to have a fascination with the mail plane as it passed overhead. From the moment I climbed that windmill as a toddler, the thought of being lighter than air, of having a bird's-eye view of life just nudged me along.

Through the years, a lot of people have applauded me for the courage I demonstrated in the skies over Guadalcanal. I've got to admit that what some people call courage was really self-preservation. Once I was in the middle of a swarm of Zeros, I was mainly trying to get myself back to Henderson Field before I got blown to bits after exterminating as many Zeros as I possibly could. But I appreciate all the honors that have been given me.

In 1984 it was my honor to be inducted into the National Aviation Hall of Fame, which their statement says is "dedicated to honoring the outstanding pioneers of aviation and space who . . . represent the history of flight—and include some who dreamed of its possibilities, some who gave their lives in its cause, some who make it a practical reality, and some who have shown the way to the limitless universe."

Wally and Jo Schirra joined us to share this exciting event. Wally acted as Master of Ceremonies and did his share of razing me. Hugh Downs honored us by coming out from New York City to present me for the prestigious Hall of Fame. Even our buddy John Galvin flew from California to surprise us.

That year the other "enshrinees" were John Leland Atwood, the "dean of aerospace"; Major General Albert Boyd, USAF, "the father of modern flight testing" and "the test pilot's test pilot"; and Henry Ford, "builder of more than automobiles," the Ford Trimotor, bridge to reliable modern air transportation. What august company! It was a wonderful evening.

As I sat there looking at the roll of those who had been inducted through the years, the great men and women of aviation, I spotted "Charles Augustus Lindbergh, 1967." Good old Charlie. I remembered the first time I'd seen him, that bigger-than-life hero, out on that little airfield in South Dakota where it all began for me. And all I could say was, *Thank you, Lord.*

Joe Foss is available for personal
appearances by contacting:

Rodney Smith, President
Dynamic Sports International
7031 E. Camelback Road, Suite 102
Scottsdale, AZ 85251

(602) 990-7580 or (800) 745-7580

Chronology

1915—born near Sioux Falls, South Dakota
1933—father, Frank Foss, killed
1937—first flying lesson
1939—enlisted in South Dakota National Guard
1940—soloed
　　—graduated from University of South Dakota, Vermillion
1942—married June Shakstad
　　—arrived at Guadalcanal
　　—awarded Distinguished Flying Cross, presented by Admiral William F. Halsey
　　—recorded 23 air victories in first 6 weeks of combat
1943—awarded Congressional Medal of Honor
　　—one of ten Outstanding American Award Jaycees
1944—promoted to Major
1946—resigned from Marine Corp Reserve to accept appointment as Lieutenant Colonel in South Dakota Air National Guard
1948—elected to South Dakota House of Representatives
1950—promoted to Colonel, South Dakota Air National Guard
1951—activated for Korean conflict
1954—promoted to Brigadier General, South Dakota Air National Guard
1955—took office as Governor of South Dakota
　　—Joe Foss Field named in Sioux Falls, dedicated by Admiral Halsey
1956 1961   President of National Society of Crippled Children and Adults

Chronology

1956—honored on Ralph Edwards's television program, *This Is Your Life*
—reelected to second term as governor

1959—separated from June Shakstad Foss

1959–1966—served as Commissioner of the American Football League

1961—elected President of Air Force Association (later Chairman of the Board)

1962—began 3-year run as host of ABC-TV's *American Sportsman*

1966–1974—starred in weekly syndicated television series, *The Outdoorsman: Joe Foss*

1967—married Donna Wild Hall

1968—named chairman of Veterans for Nixon

1972–1978—served as Director of Public Affairs, KLM Royal Dutch Airlines

1975—separated from Air Force

1978—named member of President's Council on Physical Fitness

1979—named member of White House Conference on Handicapped Individuals

1980—awarded Outstanding American Award by the Los Angeles Philanthropic Foundation

1983—named International Chairman of Here's Life World
—received National Veteran award for 1983

1984—inducted into Aviation Hall of Fame

1988–1990—served as President, National Rifle Association

1990—named Founding Chairman of the American Patriot Fund
—Landing Zone Foss established in Saudi Arabia [during Desert Storm campaign]

1991—inducted into South Dakota Aviation Hall of Fame

1992—inducted into Scandanavian-American Hall of Fame

Selected Bibliography

Finney, Ben. *Feet First*. New York: Crown Publishers, Inc., 1971.

Foss, Joe, with Byron Dalrymple. *The Outdoorsman: Joe Foss*. New York: Robert Halmi in association with the editors of *True*, 1968.

Hubler, Richard G., and John A. DeChant. *Flying Leathernecks: The Complete Record of Marine Corps Aviation in Action 1941–1944*. Garden City, N.Y.: Doubleday, Doran & Co., Inc., 1944.

Miller, Thomas G., Jr. *The Cactus Air Force*. New York: Harper & Row, Publishers, Inc., 1969.

Morison, Samuel Eliot. *The Struggle for Guadalcanal: August 1942–February 1943*. Vol. V. History of United States Naval Operations in World War II. Boston: Little, Brown & Company, 1950.

Sherrod, Robert. *History of Marine Corps Aviation in World War II*. Washington: Combat Forces Press, 1952.

Thomas, Lowell. *These Men Shall Never Die*. Philadelphia: The John C. Winston Company, 1943.

Index

Index

Index

Index

Index

Index

About the Author
DONNA WILD FOSS

Donna Wild Foss, a native of Michigan, began her business career during World War II as a department head for the Federal Public Housing Authority. For the next several years, as a matter of necessity, she pursued a varied business career to support herself and her two children. During her tenure as co-manager of the Kiva Club, a special-events arm of the Phoenix Chamber of Commerce, she met the well-known World War II hero and sportsman, Joe Foss.

In 1966 they formed a filming company, traveling to locations in many parts of the world, producing segments for the weekly syndicated national television show, *The Outdoorsman—Joe Foss*. Donna worked in administration and did the still photography used by sponsors in their advertising.

In 1967 Donna and Joe were married. They currently live in Paradise Valley, Arizona, where she acts as his business manager. She also works as a freelance photographer and manages their commercial rental properties.

Donna and her husband travel the world, speaking on their Christian faith. She also hosts evangelistic events at home and away from home in connection with activities such as hunts, business conventions, and air shows. She currently serves on the board of Generation Ministries.

Donna is an avid reader, stream fly-fisher, and international big game hunter. She holds the Hunter of the Year award presented by the Conservation Hall of Fame for the highest number of one-shot kills in Africa in 1975. She also holds the record, at 639 yards, for the longest single-shot kill during the One-Shot Antelope Hunt held annually in Lander, Wyoming.

Private Lives of Very Public People